GROUCHO

GROUCHO

THE LIFE AND TIMES OF
Julius Henry Marx

STEFAN KANFER

ALLEN LANE
THE PENGUIN PRESS

ALLEN LANE
THE PENGUIN PRESS

Published by the Penguin Group
Penguin Books Ltd, 27 Wrights Lane, London w8 5tz, England
Penguin Putnam Inc., 375 Hudson Street, New York, New York 10014, USA
Penguin Books Australia Ltd, Ringwood, Victoria, Australia
Penguin Books Canada Ltd, 10 Alcorn Avenue, Toronto, Ontario, Canada m4v 3b2
Penguin Books India (P) Ltd, 11, Community Centre, Panchsheel Park, New Delhi – 110 017, India
Penguin Books (NZ) Ltd, Private Bag 102902, NSMC, Auckland, New Zealand
Penguin Books (South Africa) (Pty) Ltd, 5 Watkins Street, Denver Ext 4, Johannesburg 2094, South Africa

Penguin Books Ltd, Registered Offices: Harmondsworth, Middlesex, England

First published in the USA by Alfred A. Knopf 2000
First published in Great Britain by Allen Lane The Penguin Press 2000
1 3 5 7 9 10 8 6 4 2

Copyright © Stefan Kanfer, 2000

Grateful acknowledgement is made to the following for
permission to reprint previously published material:

Miriam Marx Allen: Excerpts from *Love, Groucho: Letters from Groucho Marx to His Daughter Miriam*,
edited by Miriam Marx Allen (1992). Reprinted by permission of Miriam Marx Allen

Simon & Schuster: Letters by Groucho Marx from *The Groucho Letters* by Groucho Marx.
Copyright © Groucho Marx, 1967, copyright renewed 1995 by Miriam Marx, Arthur Marx and
Melinda Marx. Reprinted by permission of Simon & Schuster

Warner Bros.: Dialogue excerpts from the films *A Day at the Races* and *A Night at the Opera*.
Reprinted by permission of Warner Bros.

Printed and bound in Great Britain by The Bath Press, Bath
Cover repro and printing by Concise Cover Printers

A CIP catalogue record for this book is available from the British Library

ISBN 0–713–99469–X

For Lili and Andy Castle

Contents

Acknowledgments

I MET GROUCHO MARX, along with his brother Zeppo, in the late 1960s and early 1970s when I was *Time*'s cinema critic. He had retired from performing, but was still responsive and amusing. I took copious notes with the intention of writing a biography someday. He died several years later, other books intervened, and by the time I got around to Groucho's life many of his friends had also passed away. Those who remained had faulty memories—the anecdotes tended to vary with the teller. I decided to rely more heavily on printed material contemporary with the decades of Groucho Marx's long and varied career—a career that eventually diverged from the collective history of the Marx Brothers.

As it turned out, almost all of the books about Groucho were out of print, and much of the periodical literature was so obscure that even major libraries lacked copies. The biography then became a matter of intensive research, going back to the newspapers, magazines, and volumes covering the periods and venues in which Groucho flourished. The detective story began at Yale University's Sterling Library. With the aid of John Bennett, a unique amalgam of sleuth, literary researcher, and librarian, I was able to get my hands on obscure articles written by or about Groucho dating back to the early part of the century. This research led to other libraries, notably the Billy Rose Theatre Collection of the New York Public Library, whose scrapbooks are readable but in parlous shape; the library of the Players Club; the Library of Congress and the Smithsonian Institution; and the resources of New York University and Columbia University. Of vital import was the guidance and generosity of two authorities on the Marx Brothers in general and Groucho in particular. Robert S. Bader, the editor of *Groucho Marx and Other Short Stories and Tall Tales*, allowed me to copy such ephemera as Groucho's letters to the Marxes' family physician, Dr. Samuel Salinger, and to borrow books and records, view Groucho in forgotten TV performances, and eavesdrop on such rarities as a tape of Harpo speaking about the old days. Bader's impressive collection of Marxiana was entirely at my disposal, and his patience and generosity never flagged. There is no way I can properly express my gratitude for the many hours he spent going over small points and large ones, and for his pointing me in directions I might have easily overlooked. Paul Wesolowski's business card reads, "The Most Complete Marx Bros. Research Facility on This Planet," and it is an example of truth in advertising. Wesolowski, the editor of *The Freedonia Gazette,* a publication entirely devoted to the lives and times of the Marxes, generously granted permission to copy pieces from his vast archives and to use his unparalleled collection of photographs. His patience and forbearance were remarkable as I went back again and again to clear up various details of chronology and performance.

In the *Time* days Woody Allen spoke to me about Groucho in affectionate terms; more recently his friend Dick Cavett went into considerable and insightful detail about the Marx style and psychology. Two of Groucho's family members were immensely helpful: Maxine Marx, Chico's daughter, reminisced about her uncle Groucho at length and with wit; and Miriam Marx, Groucho's daughter, had many perceptive things to say about her father and about herself. Steve Stoliar, who was a member of Groucho's household in the final years, not only shared his memories and perceptions, he also did the most accurate imitation of the master to date. The late S. J. Perelman and Sidney Zelinka spoke to me about their former employer some years back, and the late Stanley Prager had many recollections of the troubled production of *Minnie's Boys.* More recently, I have been aided by the encouragement and advice of Scott Moyers, who provided the initial push; Chuck Jones; Al Hirschfeld; Jules Feiffer; Harry and Joseph Stein; Bernard Seligman; Matthew Ringel; Josh Greenfeld; Kenneth Turan; Ned Chase; Christopher Porterfield; Myron Kolatch; Susan Dryfoos; Dick Miles; Marianne Sussman; Barbara McManus; and, as Groucho would (and did) say, others too humorous to mention. My gratitude for Kathy Robbins's counsel grows with each work, and speaking of work, Peter Gethers's stringent editorial demands were, once the dust had cleared, on the money every time. I am also grateful to Janet Fletcher for close and invaluable copy reading. As always, my family remained stalwarts during the composition of two books written or compiled simultaneously and intensely, the biography and the accompanying collection of pieces by and about Groucho. Yet another book testifies to the omnipatient May, Lili, Andy, Nate, Sari, and, once again, Lea and Aly, who know that Papa, no matter how preoccupied, will always find time for a smackerel.

GROUCHO

Introduction

ON THE NIGHT of May 6, 1972, a frail, bald, eighty-one-year-old trouper enters from the wings of Carnegie Hall and takes center stage. He has not performed in New York for some fifty years, and in that time he has risen to the status of pantheon figure. He has been on the cover of *Time* twice. Scholars have written Ph.D. theses about his humor; his remarks have appeared in H. L. Mencken's *The American Language,* as well as in *Bartlett's Familiar Quotations* and *The Oxford Dictionary of Quotations.* Whatever awards broadcasting has to offer he has won. He has been impersonated by George Gershwin, made the subject of a Broadway musical, feted in London and Paris. The French government has just invited him to Cannes, where he is to be made Commandeur de l'Ordre des Arts et des Lettres.

Ticket holders have become used to him as an ageless two-dimensional black-and-white figure. They have to get used to him as a man—especially this man. For arthritis and small strokes have made his missteps a parody of the old choreography, and his rheumy eyes can barely decipher the cue cards. All the same, he seems to occupy the entire hall, and 2,800 onlookers, some of them sporting clawhammer coats, greasepaint moustaches, and oversize cigars in homage to the speaker's signature costume, rise to their feet and applaud for nearly five minutes. Groucho Marx is no longer in full control of his body or his memory, but his fans have decided that these infirmities are irrelevant and unworthy of comment. As he sings and reminisces in a broken voice, senior members of the audience look past old age to see the springy vaudevillian of their youth, playing straight man to his brother in a schoolroom routine:

What is the shape of the world?
I don't know.

Well, what shape are my cufflinks?
Square.
Not my weekday cufflinks. The ones I wear on Sundays.
Oh. Round.
All right, what is the shape of the world?
Square on weekdays, round on Sundays.

What are the principal parts of a cat?
Eyes, ears, neck, feet.
You forgot the most important. What does a cat have that you don't have?
Kittens.

Middle-aged fans are more familiar with his celebrated stage lines, supposedly launched when one of his brothers tried to throw him off stride:

The garbage man is outside!
Tell him we don't want any.

I'd like-a to say goom-bye to your wife.
Who wouldn't?

In their minds the past fuses with the present, and they recall the outrageous comedian of some forty years before capering in films, walking on half-bent knees and waggling his expressive eyebrows as he insults plutocrats, pursuing or insulting Mrs. Upjohn, Mrs. Rittenhouse, Mrs. Teasdale (all played by the same woman), without missing a diphthong:

As chairwoman of the reception committee, I welcome you with open arms.
Is that so? How late do you stay open?
I've sponsored your appointment because I feel you are the most able statesman in all Freedonia.
Well, that covers a lot of ground. Say, you cover a lot of ground yourself. You'd better beat it. I hear they're going to tear you down and put up an office building where you're standing. You can leave in a taxi. If you can't leave in a taxi, you can leave in a huff. If that's too soon, you can leave in a minute and a huff. You know you haven't stopped talking since I came here? You must have been vaccinated with a phonograph needle.

They recall his annihilations of high society ("*The strains of Verdi will come back to you tonight, and Mrs. Claypool's check will come back to you in the morning*"), the campus ("But Professor Wagstaff, if we tear down the dormitories where will the students sleep?" "*Where they always slept. In the classroom*"), the medical profession ("*Either this man is dead or my watch has stopped*"), statecraft ("*We have to have a war. I've already paid a month's rent on the battlefield*").

They quote anew the offscreen anecdotes, recalling, for example, how Groucho had approached Greta Garbo from behind, lifted her hat, and then apologized: "*Sorry, I thought you were a guy I knew from Pittsburgh.*" How he rejected the offer of a Hollywood group: "*I don't want to join any organization that would have me as a member.*" How he responded when the members of an anti-Semitic swimming club refused admission to his daughter: "*She's only half Jewish. How about if she only goes in up to her waist?*"

The youngest fans—and there are many in attendance—know another Groucho: the master of ceremonies of their favorite quiz show, *You Bet Your Life*, equipped with a real moustache, operating sans props or supporting cast, fluently putting down guests like the housewife who proudly declared that she had ten children because she loved her husband (Groucho: "*I love my cigar, but I take it out of my mouth once in a while*") or the heavily accented linguist who boasted that he could speak eleven languages (Groucho: "*Which one are you speaking now?*").

The performer's well-known grenades detonate onstage and off, as audience members remind each other of richer times:

Time flies like an arrow. Fruit flies like a banana.

One morning I shot an elephant in my pajamas. How he got in my pajamas I don't know.

I never forget a face, but in your case I'll make an exception.

Outside of a dog, a book is man's best friend. Inside of a dog, it's too dark to read.

Even now this frail figure, this embodiment of Yeats's image of old age as a coat upon a coat hanger, throws a long shadow. He was, after all, the centerpiece of *Duck Soup*. In that film Groucho plays the dictator of a mythic country, Freedonia, and his extravagant satire so threatened Benito Mussolini that the fascist leader barred it from Italy. Groucho was also the star of *Horse Feathers*. Winston Churchill was watching *that* movie when the top Nazi official, Rudolf Hess, parachuted onto the Duke of Hamilton's estate carrying a peace offer. If the Prime Minister would allow Germany to go to war against Russia unopposed, Germany would declare a ceasefire with Britain. To underline his point, that night twelve hundred Luftwaffe planes flew over London in the heaviest blitz of the two-year-old war. At the time Churchill was at Ditchley Park. His memoirs record that, after dinner, "News arrived of the heavy air raid. There was nothing that I could do about it so I watched the Marx Brothers in a comic film which my hosts had arranged. I went out twice to inquire about the air raid and heard it was bad. The merry film clicked on, and I was glad of the diversion."

It was Groucho whose jaunty attitude compelled the Missouri-born T. S. Eliot, the most prominent poet of the age, to write a fan letter meekly requesting an autographed portrait. The anti-Semitic bard and the Jewish comedian struck up an odd friendship, now recalled by the speaker on the Carnegie Hall stage: "I read up on *Murder in the Cathedral* and a few other things, and I thought I'd impress him. And all he wanted to talk about was the Marx Brothers. That's what happens when you come from St. Louis." This leads to a reminiscence of the poet's funeral, attended by most of the leading intellectuals of the time. Groucho could not erase the feeling that he was as out of place as a bagel at high tea. Laurence Olivier, seated nearby, calmed his fears and urged him to say a little something, if only for the widow's sake. "It was a tough audience for an old vaudeville actor. And this came to me while I was standing on the stage: It was a story about a man who was condemned to be hanged. And the priest said to him, 'Have you any last words to say before we spring the trap?' And the man says, 'Yes, I don't think this damn thing is safe.'"

Warmed by remembered laughter and current applause, Groucho seems for a moment to be his younger self as he reaches back for more anecdotes. He remembers the night he went to the Winter Garden when Harry Houdini headlined the show. "I was sans moustache. That means 'without.' I'm sitting in the second row and Houdini is doing a trick. He would take some needles and put them in his mouth. And then a spool of thread. And then he would thread the needles with his tongue. He asked for a volunteer out in the audience. And who do you think went up on the stage? And he opened his mouth wide: 'I want to prove that there's no trickery. What do you see in there?' And I said, 'Pyorrhea.'"

As he goes on, the energy and affection of the audience are reflected in his invigorated movements and sturdier voice. He nods to an accompanist, Marvin Hamlisch, and with surprising fervor summons up a song from the distant past—a 1914 number disowned by his friend Irving Berlin, but which Groucho has always loved because it spoke out against war. In these last fading days of the Vietnam conflict, he wants everyone to know how he feels. (They already know; Groucho is on record as suggesting that the only way to get rid of President Nixon is assassination.) Taking the part of the devil addressing his son, Groucho croons Irving Berlin's forgotten tune:

> You stay down here where you belong.
> The folks above you, they don't know right from wrong.
> To please their kings they've all gone out to war,
> But not a one of them knows what they're fighting for.
>
> Way up above they say that I'm a devil and I'm bad;
> But the kings up there are bigger devils than your dad;
> They're breaking the hearts of mothers,
> Making butchers out of brothers;
> You'll find more hell up there than there is down below!

The house booms its approval. Heartened, the speaker delightedly rambles on, scattering anecdotes like coins before the crowd. He recalls an old acquaintance, Otto Kahn, who walked down Fifth Avenue with a deformed friend. "You know," said Kahn, "I used to be a Jew." His friend responded, "Really? I used to be a hunchback." Groucho drops the name of his old friend W. C. Fields. "One day he allowed me in his house. And he had a ladder leading to an attic. And in this attic he had fifty thousand dollars' worth of whiskey. And I say to him, 'Bill, what have [you] got that booze there for? We haven't had prohibition in twenty-five years.' He says: 'It may come back.' "

And yet when Groucho takes his final curtain calls and the house lights are turned up, there remains a melancholy undertow to this unprecedented evening of laughter and memories. The star's complicated and irrepressible siblings have gone, Chico in 1961, Harpo three years later. Groucho will be next, and the general feeling is that the event is not far away. So the audience lingers in the aisles, reluctant to leave the theater, as if staying a bit longer might give the star a few more ergs of vitality, a few more months of life.

Most New Yorkers get from their apartments to the concert in about twenty minutes. It has taken Groucho more than six decades to get to Carnegie Hall. Tales of that trek have been related from the first days of his celebrity. They change with the venue, the journalist, and sometimes the mood of the teller. Yet the hard facts of his life and art are as unique, as beguiling—and, in a funny way, as American—as anything he has ever invented for public consumption.

CHAPTER ONE

A Severed Head

THE BIG MAGICIAN had only three assets: energy, audacity, and speed. But these were enough to feed and clothe a large family. Energy attracted audiences. Audacity brought them closer. And speed allowed him to make an exit when they found him out. Somewhere in his routine Levy "Lafe" Schoenberg would begin by flashing a large knife and making his customary offer: "Do I have a volunteer for a beheading? If all of you pay with a coin, I promise to restore the head to the neck, just as good as before." Dependably, the onlookers would exchange glances, giggle, and shrink back. Having intimidated them, the Dutchman would pass on to other tricks. Astonishing the yokels, he produced coins from empty hands and flourished an egg from his beard. In the background his plump little wife Fanny accompanied his antics, playing folk songs on a small portable harp. It had all gone well until one epochal morning. Confidently daring the crowd, Lafe was dismayed to see an onlooker raise his hand. Perhaps encouraged by drink, nodding and smiling to his friends, the rube said he would allow his head to be cut off—and then put back where it belonged. Lafe looked to Fanny; she returned his helpless stare. The event was unprecedented and neither of them knew what to do. Certainly his children had no idea. The magician stammered a vague reply and tried to move on to a few sleight-of-hand feats. The audience grew loud and derisive. A few of them heaved rocks at the entertainer.

As the Schoenberg family clambered aboard the wagon the stones fell in a hail. Lafe snapped the horses' reins, and the wheels revolved until their spokes turned into a blur. It was time for the family to move on again. But to where? The newspapers kept proclaiming a new and better Germany; Lafe preferred to believe his own eyes and ears. They informed him that little had really changed since 1785, when the philosopher Moses Mendelssohn wrote to a confidant about his own son, Joseph: "He has no inclination for medicine, and as a Jew he must become a physician, a merchant, or a beggar." Well, Lafe was no physician, and shopkeeping and money changing were not for him—there was a shortage of action, no applause, not enough new people to meet and amuse. He preferred combining the skills of the schnorrer and the *badkhn*. And why not? he demanded. The Christians had their traditions, the Jews had theirs.

Technically, the schnorrer was a beggar, moving from community to community in search of funds. But he was neither as foolish nor as indolent as the big-city layabouts. Outrageous, funny, daring, he worked for baksheesh by circulating stories, jokes, gossip. At times he made himself the butt of the jokes, pretending to be shocked by his own chutzpah: "A schnorrer knocked on the door of a rich man at 6 a.m. The rich man shouted, 'How dare you wake me this early?' 'Listen,' the schnorrer replied, 'I don't tell you how to run your business. Don't tell me how to run mine.' "

As for the jester—*badkhn* in Yiddish—he, too, was a favorite of the Jewish communities. *Badkhns* first appeared in the Middle Ages, irritating the rabbis with their impudence and boisterous humor. A scholar of the Jewish past notes certain modern parallels: "The merry maker did not occupy a prominent social position. He was feared on account of the rhymes which he freely utilized to his own purposes and frequently caused embarrassment. People exploited his friendship for their personal advantage, they were amused by his apt parables, paraphrases and merry songs and then proceeded to censure him as a sinner."

By the 1870s in Germany these Jewish sinners enjoyed some delightful compensations for the risks they took: their hours were their own and they answered to no boss except the public. On the other hand, that public was growing increasingly fickle. Anti-Semitism was bad enough; the post-Napoleon enlightenment made matters worse. Jews, rubbing their eyes at the world outside the ghetto, discovered the delights of the concert hall, the theater, and, for that matter, the gaming table. "Once, early in the morning on a summer day," recalled a nineteenth-century stager, "I met a jester coming from a wedding. He complained to me, 'Brother, things are bad. If the best people, the cream of the public, leave me on the platform and retire to play cards, there is no longer any room for me here.' Six months later he left for America."

Lafe was not far behind him. With the help of his older daughters, who worked as domestics, and his sons, who earned deutsche marks as handymen, the fifty-year-old performer amassed $300 plus—more than enough for ten steerage tickets to America. Like so many others that year, Lafe, Fanny, and the eight Schoenberg children boarded a liner in Bremen and tried not to look back.

•

IN 1871 a defeated France ceded Alsace-Lorraine to Germany, and in the process lost the nation's largest group of Jews. Yet those Jews continued to identify themselves as French, still spoke the language, still praised Napoleon for making them free citizens. Simon Marrix was nine at the time the war ended, an alert, frightened child, aware that in a few more years he could be conscripted for another conflict; with the Germans in charge, there would never be a shortage of battles. Five years later his worst terrors were confirmed when the Berlin *Post* ran an editorial, "Is War in Sight?" At nineteen he apprenticed himself to a tailor, determined to save his wages for a one-way passage to America. He wanted no part of the German army—or indeed of any army—and when he saw that his parents had no intention of leaving the Old Country, wrote to his cousins in New York pleading for sponsorship. He could not have picked a better time. Max Marrix, a gentlemen's tailor, was flourishing in his trade. Sam Marrix, working with the Jewish voters of Lower Manhattan, had become a Tammany Hall politician. These men wrote to the immigration authorities, certifying that an eager twenty-year-old Alsatian would shortly be landing on Ellis Island, that he was a young man of good character, free of disease and anxious to work. A grateful Simon arrived in the Promised City in 1881 with only a few words of English, a new moustache, several dollars, and the clothes on his back. The people back in Alsace had already become ciphers in his mind. The only relatives he ever spoke about with affection were two great-aunts, Fratschie and Frietschie, and this was because they were the oldest twins in Alsace-Lorraine, dying on the same day at the age of 102. Simon's children would never even learn the names of their paternal grandparents because Simon refused to talk about them. As far as he was concerned, uniforms and orders and gunsmoke were over there, on the other side of the Atlantic. Life was over here.

Among the first things Simon discovered in America was that Max and Sam had altered the family surname to Marx. Lettered on a store window, Simon noticed, the x really stood out. Anxious to get on in the New World, he copied their example. The immigrant had never completed his apprenticeship, never truly mastered the art of scissors and needle—but what did that matter? Here a man could do anything if he had the will. Simon opened a shop and waited for customers.

They came in waves. Assuming that all tailors named Marx possessed similar skills, the men brought him their trousers and jackets. They returned, a few crumpled dollar bills in hand, expecting the finest work. It was not to be. To begin with, Simon had no use for a tape measure. With an assured air he would walk around the prospective customer muttering "Ja, ja, dot's it," assuring them—and himself—that he knew to the thread just how much to tuck in and let out. His ex-customers knew each other on sight: they suffered from jackets that bagged and trousers with one leg shorter than the other. Still, New York was a large place, and downtown was overrun with men who needed their jackets and trousers fitted. The tailor spoke fluent French, German, and Yiddish, and his countrymen kept coming, even if they seldom came twice. Simon did well enough, and on free evenings he taught dancing to attractive Jewish women.

One of them was a bright nineteen-year-old blond. Minnie (Minna) Schoenberg had been forced to grow up fast. The census of 1880 reported that the Schoenberg family living at 376 East Tenth Street was composed of Louis, fifty, Fanny, forty-nine, and three children: Minnie, fifteen, Adolph, twelve, and the seven-year-old baby, Henry. The five older children may have been married, living elsewhere, or just hiding from the official-looking man from the Census Bureau. Lafe and Fanny had found no foothold in the New World; that year, the duet earned a total of $12.50 for their efforts. Vaudeville agents thought them too old, and their act outré; audiences wanted the flash and swirl of Harry Blackstone in a cape and top hat, not the cornball gestures of a street magician. They hankered for the new sound of ragtime, not the grinding notes of oompah. Decades later Groucho was to note wryly, "For some curious reason, there seemed to be practically no demand for a German ventriloquist and a woman harpist who yodeled in a foreign language." Lafe met disappointment with equanimity: he told neighbors and friends that he was sixty-three instead of his actual fifty-one, and announced his retirement. He had raised and succored eight children long enough. It was time for them to support him. His statement was not negotiable; the children went to work. Minna and her sisters took sweatshop jobs in the garment industry, increasing their meager paychecks by taking piecework home. Determined to lose all traces of the greenhorn, Minna covered her forehead with bangs and wore fashionable long skirts and cinched-in waists to show off her zaftig figure. In a further step toward assimilation she changed her first name to Minnie. This was in homage to Minnie Mad-dern, the Broadway star who possessed, according to one contemporary critic, "a peculiar gift of emotion, imitating tears and smiles in the same breath, which was more pathetic than undiluted grief and more diverting than undiluted laughter." At night, Minnie and her sister Hannah, then between husbands, learned new steps in the dance halls of the Lower East Side. And there, one evening, they took a few lessons from a handsome Alsatian tailor. As Simon and Minnie whirled around the floor they found many things in common besides their religion. Both worked long hours in the garment industry; both had an easy, flirtatious charm; both were Western European immigrants who tended to keep their distance from the Ostjuden. The two differed in only a few respects, but these were pro-found. Minnie was smart and ambitious; Simon was . . . amiable, content to play cards and ogle the ladies. Still, he cut a dashing figure among the first-generation Americans, and seemed to have prospects. Had Minnie examined those prospects a little more closely, had she taken a closer look at Simon's handiwork, she might not have responded to his overtures so swiftly. But she was nineteen and smitten. Following the custom of the time, she withheld the sweets, he entreated, she hesitated, he promised marriage, she succumbed.

In the late 1880s, the newlyweds left the clamorous, disease-ridden Lower East Side, settling in on East Eighty-second Street and then moving to the East 100s. Along with Minnie came Lafe and Fanny, and, on occa-sion, a few more Schoenbergs would drop by. Hector Arce, Groucho's offi-cial biographer, noted that Simon had fled German dominance but "let down his guard" and was "subjugated, by [another] German horde." Like many immigrants of the period, the young couple planned to have a large family; like many immigrants they were almost immediately thwarted. The Marxes could run from the ghetto, but they could not outrace the bacilli of the "worker's disease." Their firstborn, Manfred, perished of tuberculosis before his first birthday.

Minnie and Simon (his name now Americanized to Sam) went through a mourning period, but refused to succumb to that other plague of the ghetto, melancholia. They trusted in their American future, and that faith was vindicated in August 1887, when Minnie gave birth to the first of five sons who would survive. Leonard greeted the world with loud and lusty cries; he had no health problems at all. Fifteen months later he was joined by an equally robust brother, Adolph. Both boys were chunky and blond, like Minnie. In October 1890 yet another son, Julius Henry, was born. He was not as vigorous, and his coloring was nothing like his mother's or his brothers' fair skin; nor did he possess his father's small, distinguished features. Julius had dark and somewhat kinky hair, a prominent nose, and eyes that seemed out of focus, one peering straight ahead while the other looked off to the side. Minnie regarded the strabismus as a kind of insult, and did her best to ignore it.

Julius Henry was named for two uncles: Henry, the youngest of Minnie's brothers, and, more important, Julius Schickler, her sister Hannah's second husband, a grocer who seemed well-to-do and might be favorably disposed toward mentioning the boy in his will. Yet it was a third uncle who made the difference in Julius's life and art. Minnie's favorite brother, Adolph Schoenberg, had a knack for close harmony. He abandoned the pants-pressing business the year of Julius's birth, joined a singing quartet, and thereafter identified himself as Al Shean. Although the new moniker had an Irish lilt, he had not abandoned Judaism. He had entered show business. From here on he would be Uncle Al to the three Marx boys—and in time to their two younger brothers, Milton, born in 1892, and Herbert, born in 1901.

After a series of rent battles with various landlords, the Marxes finally moved to a residence they found financially and physically comfortable: 179 East Ninety-third Street. In this modest three-room apartment they were to stay for fifteen years. Here Sam set up shop and Minnie provided a place for her aging parents as well as other relatives who needed occasional shelter. Here the boys came of age. And here the couple discovered more differences than similarities between them. Sam's idea of contentment, for example, was a day of tailoring and a night of pinochle. His wife sensed there was more to life than needlework and cards—a feeling that intensified as she watched her brother make his way up the vaudeville bill. Uncle Al often came by when he was in town, and as he approached the Marxes' apartment house he distributed pennies to every child on every stoop. Leading them, Pied Piper–style, he would march up to the front door and knock vigorously. The desired effect was always spectacular: Uncle Al walked in to the accompaniment of cheers from the outside and envious comment inside. As he made himself comfortable on the sofa, his nephews would gather at his feet to receive their own coins and listen to stories of the singers, jugglers, comedians, and chorines who traveled the circuit with their philanthropic relative. A member of the Manhattan Comedy Four, Uncle Al earned $250 a week at a time when the salary of a pants presser was $25 for sixty hours of work. Shean further dazzled his admirers with a wardrobe that advertised prosperity:

loud flannel suit, matching fedora and spats, ten-dollar shoes, and a maximum of diamond rings and stickpins. The Marxes came to understand that these jewels were more than mere accessories: they made a statement. "To the smalltimer," recalled headliner Fred Allen, "a diamond represented security. It impressed the booker, the manager, and the audience, but more important, the diamond was collateral."

Watching the faces glisten, Al's sister wondered if any of her children had inherited the Schoenberg talent to amuse. Adolph, always a watcher of women, could find no human equivalent of his mother, and so resorted to comparisons with members of the animal kingdom. He was to remember Minnie as someone whose "doe-like looks were deceiving. She had the stamina of a brewery horse, the drive of a salmon fighting his way up a waterfall, the cunning of a fox, and a devotion to her brood as fierce as any she-lion's." Minnie, he went on, "even in her gayest moments was working—plotting and scheming all the time she was telling jokes and whooping it up." She made much the same impression on the next generation. Leonard's daughter Maxine recalled a grandmother who "loved to be the center of attention.... Placing her one good ear against a pillow to shut out the noises of tenement life, Minnie would catnap most of the day in order to be fresh for the evening's songs, skits and wicked impersonations."

One of Minnie's most persistent schemes consisted of disguising ambition as entertainment, taking the boys to watch Uncle Al caper onstage in such immigrant-pleasing numbers as "It Isn't What You Used to Be, It's What You Are Today." Her little experiment had the desired effect. The Marx brothers were enchanted from the first notes of the overture. Individually and collectively, they came to regard vaudeville as America with its shirt unbuttoned and its shoes kicked off, a place where applause led to a paycheck, and energy was eternal delight.

•

BECAUSE THE WOMAN was so seldom at rest it will pay us to examine her as she sits with her boys in the darkened vaudeville theater. To appraise Minnie Schoenberg Marx is to discard a century's worth of comic bromides. Certainly she is a Jewish mother, but not (or not only) the possessive guilt-producing Mama of the stand-up jokes: of "Eat, eat, look how skinny," "Have I got for you a nice Jewish girl," and "How come you're wearing that tie, you didn't like the other one?" Certainly she is a stage mother, but not (or not only) the kind of hard-driving figure featured in *Gypsy*, goading her young charges to sing so that the people in the last row can hear.

Minnie has become the central force in the family because her husband has ceded the role. He calls each of his sons "darling," and there is no question of his affection for them all. But he hardly stands as a model of industry or discipline; indeed, when one of his "poys" misbehaves he pulls him into a room, holds a whisk broom aloft, makes a great show of furious imprecations, dispenses a few whacks—and then lets him go. As a cook Minnie is hopeless; she has never learned how to prepare appetizing meals. As a result, Sam has taken over the task and become the true homemaker, displaying such a flair for Gallic cuisine that the boys now address him as Frenchy.

Minnie's flat is run as a Yorkville version of the German wayside inn. The door is left unlatched. An aroma of coffee pervades the place, the pot kept simmering on the stove for visitors who pop in unannounced and vanish without notice. In winter comes a reek familiar to the poor: kerosene fumes from an overworked heater. Voices are seldom modulated; Sam conducts business in a little room off the kitchen, where his customers can be heard negotiating prices and hollering about style and fit. At other times—and recently they have become more frequent—Sam puts away the cloth and shears and picks up a pinochle deck. Long after dinner the men palaver and play pinochle while, in an adjoining room, peals of laughter can be heard as Minnie and her favorite sister Hannah Schickler smoke cigarettes and discuss the day's events. Sam's ineptitude as a tailor is often the source of their humor: Minnie has become adept at the verbal put-down. Even so, as a husband Frenchy remains beyond reproach. In Minnie's eyes he is still the elegant bantam she met at the dance hall, as attractive as the day they married. When she catches him in bed with one of the young and comely Schoenberg cousins, her fury is directed exclusively toward the girl. She explains to Hannah that Frenchy was a victim of this temptress, this Jezebel. Minnie's boys overhear her words, and the lesson is not lost on them.

When Grandma Schoenberg dies at the age of sixty-six, Minnie is released from the last few bonds of orthodoxy. Throughout all her wanderings "Omie," as Minnie and the boys called her, had been a pious soul, familiar with all the candlelighting ceremonies and prayers. To please her the family had observed the major holidays and learned some Hebrew. After Omie's death, the widower, "Opie," assumes her place as religious leader, taking his grandsons to synagogue and making plans for their bar mitzvahs. But he has never been much of a believer and his heart is not in his supervisory role. The household becomes less overtly Jewish and the European influence recedes.

Downtown, the Russian and Polish immigrants, having fled from violent oppression and pogroms, thirst for social justice. They form labor unions, agitate in the streets, crowd the meeting halls, electioneer for progressive candidates. These Marxes stay apolitical; they want no part of the picket lines and the stridency of these Litvak-Galitzianers who had re-created their shtetls right here in Manhattan. There are other ways out of poverty and obscurity. Minnie has before her the example of Rose Pastor Stokes, who enlivens the new century by marrying a goy—and not just any goy, but an heir to railroad money. The *New York Times* itself acknowledges the importance of the event with an unprecedented headline: J. G. PHELPS TO WED YOUNG JEWESS.

And there is another Schoenberg, once a German Jew like his namesakes, now a Christian with another identity: August Belmont. Banker, socialite, millionaire, he began his career in Europe, as an agent for the great Jewish banking house of the Rothschilds. But once in New York he discarded his background like an old bowler, became a Christian, and bought his way into society. And now look at him, with his mansion and his shiksa wife, the daughter of Commodore Perry, no less.

Au fond, however, Minnie is a realist. She has no wish to discard the traditions into which she and her husband and their children were born. And she is well aware that if their names were changed tomorrow to O'Brien they would deceive no one. The boys are too young for her to think about morganatic alliances, but when she imagines them as young men she doubts that any female of means would be attracted to nobodies. Therefore they must become *somebodies*. After due consideration, Minnie decides to aid God in His work. She will sculpt something significant from the rawest of materials. The clay will be Leonard, Adolph, Julius, Milton, and Herbert. Exactly what she will make of them she is not sure. Minnie Schoenberg Marx is only positive that when she finishes her work, the whole world will sit up and take notice.

•

WHILE THE FAMILY waits for the curtain to go up, we might also take a closer look at the brotherly quintet. The first two boys and the last two break off into natural pairs. Leonard and Adolph have their own jokes and secrets; in early adolescence they could pass as twins except for an intellectual disparity. Leonard, the natural charmer, the adored eldest son, is the one Marx child with mathematical ability. He can recall strings of numbers and solve complicated arithmetic problems in his head. But Leonard applies this talent only to street-corner gambling. Public School 86 bores him and he keeps begging his parents to let him quit. Adolph also is unhappy at school, but for different reasons. He can barely assimilate the elements of reading and writing. Eventually he will be expelled— not by the principal, but by a couple of classmates.

For Adolph has been facing a regular and humiliating ritual. Several times a week two tough Irish classmates take him by the shoulders and belt and heave him bodily from a first-floor window onto the sidewalk. He is too frightened to resist and too closemouthed to complain to authorities. After each incident he stoically mounts the school steps, silently reenters the room, and takes his seat. On an autumn afternoon he is ejected once too often. On that occasion he dusts himself off, reconsiders the steps, and then walks away. Adolph will never again enter a school for purpose of instruction.

Together, the two elder Marx brothers taunt boys from other blocks, indulge in petty thievery, test the limits of drivers by dodging in and out of traffic and mugging at anyone who dares to stare at them. Adolph's favorite moue is an imitation of a cigar maker. The man works in the window of a local tobacconist, and as he twists the tobacco leaves he unconsciously grimaces, making his eyes bulge, his tongue contort, and his cheeks swell. His name is Gehrke, and Adolph calls the faces he makes "gookies." They are to serve him well in the coming years.

The two youngest children, Herbert and Milton, have formed their own alliance. Herbert is too small to be anything but tractable. Milton has failed to thrive; when Minnie takes him to a clinic, she is informed that the child has a rheumatic heart. Long past his infancy she pampers the child, refuses to let him play rough games, awards him the best of dinner treats. He shares favored status with Leonard, partly because of his delicate health, but also because he has turned out to be as blond as Minnie is—or was a decade and six births ago. (Light hair and skin signify a great deal to her; blondness separates the German Jews from those swarthy black-haired ones downtown. It means so much to her, in fact, that when she gives the infants a shampoo she likes to mix in a little peroxide.)

Only once in these early years do Julius and Leonard draw close, and then because of circumstances rather than choice. After the death of her mother, Minnie decides to make a sentimental visit to Europe. Somehow she scrapes up enough money to take two children along with her. The boys are given two choices: a trip or a toy. Only Julius and Leonard elect to cross the Atlantic instead of playing with a miniature truck. Julius is to remember only one incident from the trip. En route, a young cattle trader finds Minnie irresistible. She wants no part of a shipboard romance, and continually puts him off. Wounded by rejection, the spurned lover plots his revenge. The night before the boat is to land, he gives each of the Marx boys a bar of chocolate, tells them about a masquerade party on the top deck, and informs them that Minnie wants them to appear naked. They cause a sensation upon their entrance. The embarrassment, while intense, is short-lived; the sound of laughter lingers.

Save for this brief adventure with Leonard, Julius, the classic middle child, prefers to go his own way. He does well enough in school, fascinated by the lessons in history and science, alternately intrigued and terrified by a teacher who separates keys from a large ring and throws them at recalcitrant children. At home he seeks refuge in the cheapest entertainment of his era: pulp magazines. Intelligent, withdrawn, he receives no special favors from either parent or from his siblings. Julius's envy of the oldest and youngest Marx brothers is so obvious that Minnie refers to him as *der Eifersüchtige:* "the jealous one." Literature compensates. The power and consolation of reading can scarcely be understood in our own time, when a child's attention may be beguiled by video games, CDs, films, radio, the Internet. But in the early years of the century, dime novels and true-life adventures take hold of young imaginations and often seem more real than life itself. Julius's contemporary, comedian Bert Lahr, once found a pulp novel so involving that during the account of a fight he shouted, "Hit him! Knock him down!" to the page. And S. J. Perelman, the humorist whose career is to intersect with Julius's, will one day look back at the days when dime novels and pulp magazines gripped him so closely that Edgar Rice Burroughs's Tarzan exerted a "hypnotic effect": "I flung spears at the neighbors' laundry, exacerbated their watchdogs, swung around their piazzas gibbering and thumping my chest, made reply only in half-human grunts interspersed with unearthly howls, and took great pains generally to qualify as a stench in the civic nostril."

Julius begins with Horatio Alger's stories of city boys rising to riches through hard work and honest dealings. Then come the military accounts and lion-shooting safaris of Teddy Roosevelt in Africa. Ultimately Julius arrives at Burt L. Standish's influential tales of Frank Merriwell, a youth created on the assembly line of Street and Smith's publishing house. Early on, Smith informed Standish that he wanted a series about a young man who studied well and played hard, came into money, and then traveled the globe in order to broaden himself. It would be an advantage, the author was advised, "to have introduced the Dutchman, the Negro, the Irishman, and any other dialect you are familiar with." In addition, "a little love element would not be amiss, but this is not particularly important." Above all, the youth had to be an All-American type, and to that end, Standish remembered, he chose a name "symbolic of the chief characteristics I desired my hero to have—*Frank* for frankness, *merry* for a happy disposition, *well* for health and abounding vitality." This icon would give him "an opportunity to preach—by example—the doctrine of a clean mind and healthy body."

Reading independently, Julius conceives an image of himself as a contemporary hero. Jewish boys of the period are not the varsity type, nor can he expect to explore the Dark Continent or charge up San Juan Hill. He is neither good-looking nor charming—Minnie has reminded him of that more than once. But perhaps he can be another kind of leader, a doctor—the kind his family could rarely afford—healing the sick and the needy. If he cannot please the most important woman in his life by being handsome or blond, surely this will be the way to court a disappointed Minnie and win her heart.

CHAPTER TWO

They Grow So Fast

IN SCHOOL, what Julius thought difficult and Adolph found totally out of reach Leonard accomplished with ease. Teachers praised his extraordinary affinity for mathematics; with that kind of talent the boy could be an accountant or a bookkeeper someday. But for Leonard, arithmetic had one primary function: to calculate the odds on long shots. Scarcely into his teens, the wiry urchin had become a habitual gambler, playing cards and craps for money, running with a bad crowd based several blocks uptown, fighting in the streets. Delinquency continued at home. If one of his brothers acquired something of value, Leonard was liable to lift the item, take it to the pawnbroker, and pocket the proceeds. Nothing was safe: on one occasion Adolph protected a gold watch by removing the hands, rendering the timepiece unhockable. It was then that Leonard turned to soft goods. The tailored suits he delivered to Frenchy's clients began arriving without the promised pants. There would be a great *tochu-bochu* at the East Ninety-third Street apartment—clients would yell and threaten, Sam would protest: there must be some mistake. But he knew there was no mistake. The trousers were always to be found at the same place: the closest pawnshop, where Leonard had hocked them for $2.50— money he then squandered on illegal street-corner games. These rarely began until dark, and they went on past midnight. The eldest Marx child was generally among the last to leave. The route to prison lay straight ahead, and Leonard probably avoided it because weapons frightened him. His friends carried pistols, and few of them lived past their twenties.

Sam threatened his eldest with violent consequences. These amounted to the standard lecture "Pad poy! No-goodnick, stay out late!" accompanied by a few perfunctory blows with the whisk broom. Such reproofs only encouraged smirks, followed by more bad behavior. Rankled by the behavior of both, Minnie sought another way to handle her favorite. He would be enticed from a career of gambling, and God knew what else, by acquiring a marketable skill. He would learn to play an instrument. Omie had once made a living with music, why not her grandson?

This was just before the Victrola changed entertainment forever, a period when song pluggers hawked their wares in department stores and sheet music sat on pianos in more than a million American parlors. When Minnie heard about a Viennese lady who gave lessons for twenty-five cents she made up her mind then and there to acquire an upright. For five dollars down and the promise of a dollar a week, an owner was persuaded to part with his battered instrument. Hoisted by crane, it was brought in through a window and placed at the center of the living room, dominating the furniture and the conversation. To placate his mother Leonard briefly submitted to the discipline of instruction, and after a few weeks it was evident that he had indeed inherited some of the family talent. The amount of that legacy would never be known. For one thing, he had no *sitzfleisch;* not for Leonard the hours of practice and concentration. For another, the instructor was no better than her salary. Although in the Old Country she had been taught the art of the treble clef, she had never absorbed the lessons concerning the bass. As her right hand confidently picked out melodies, her left faked the tune with a measured oom-pah. Leonard aped as much of this technique as he needed, told his mother to save her money, and scrambled around town seeking work as a house pianist, just as his mother had hoped. Minnie did not know—and did not want to know—the kind of house Leonard played in.

Along with cheap beer, willing ladies, and a heavy aura of tobacco smoke, a pianist was considered indispensable for atmosphere in the New York honky-tonks. Leonard auditioned with his tricky interpretations of "Love Me and the World Is Mine" and "Waltz Me around Again, Willie." Impressed, the bosses usually hired him without hearing any more—just as well, since those were the only tunes he had mastered. After several weeks he felt assured enough to try out for other jobs. Leonard soon found himself in such demand that, unknown to his employers, he subcontracted several assignments. The surrogate was his lookalike Adolph, who had picked up what little keyboard technique he knew from his elder brother. So it was that Leonard Marx solved the mystery of how to appear in two places at the same time. Each honky-tonk owner thought he had hired Leonard; half the time he had hired Adolph. Under one name the brothers played over a hundred different renditions of "Love

Me and the World Is Mine" before the patrons and the owners caught on to the deception, at which time the pair moved on to other fields of endeavor. Adolph apprenticed to a butcher; his older brother bounced from place to place, forever looking for an office with available women and a crap game in the basement.

There came a time when Leonard went too far. Weary of visiting the pawnshop for yet another pair of pants, Sam finally exploded with authentic rage, threatening to kill his son if he ever stole from clients again. For the first time Leonard understood how much he had injured his father, and vowed to reform. The promise lasted one week, after which his wages were lost once more. There was no way he could face his father and tell him the truth. Then an idea came to Leonard. He had been working at the offices of a wholesale paper distributor, and after everyone had gone he grabbed a huge bag of samples, displaced a few riders on the elevated train, and came home with his unwieldy prize, intending to persuade Sam that he had been paid in goods instead of money. For the first time in any Marx bathroom, toilet paper took the place of the *Morning World*.

All the while Julius remained far behind Leonard in his pursuit of money and females. Only once did he summon the courage to invite Lucy, a pretty neighbor, to attend the vaudeville at Hammerstein's Victoria. What happened next was to foreshadow many of his misadventures with women. The suitor calculated the exact sum he needed for the date. Seventy cents would cover it all: fifty cents for two tickets in the balcony, twenty cents for two round trips on the streetcar. On the appointed day the young couple chatted amiably all the way to Forty-second Street, disembarked, and passed a vendor hawking coconut candy for a nickel a bag. Lucy informed her escort that coconut was her favorite confection. Julius recalled: "I did what every sucker has done all his life when beauty demands something. What this beauty didn't know was that her casual request for candy had knocked my carefully budgeted bankroll sky high and ruined the afternoon before it had begun."

Up in the second balcony, Julius alternated between watching the performers and sneaking a glance at Lucy as she consumed the candy without offering him a single bite. When the curtain came down they walked out into a gathering snowstorm. Julius steeled himself and informed Lucy that he had left the house with seventy cents. He had not planned on buying candy. Now there was only enough for one carfare home. Still, he wanted to be fair. He would toss a coin. If it came up heads, Lucy would get to ride and Julius would walk. Tails, and the reverse would happen.

It was tails. Lucy never spoke to him again. Julius tried to console himself with Leonard's philosophy: girls are like streetcars; another one will be along any minute. Somehow this schedule failed to operate for him, and he stopped listening to his brother altogether—except during the music lessons. During the rare times when Leonard had actually practiced, Julius stood at the side of the piano, humming and singing along. Minnie suddenly took more notice of the vocalist than the pianist. Her middle son not only stayed on key, he articulated the lyrics in a clear, appealing boy soprano, a much-desired sound in the early 1900s. Had she wasted money on lessons for the wrong one? Hardly. Leonard was good-looking, talented, a charmer; everyone said so. Julie was . . . presentable. Perhaps something could be done with him someday. Meantime, he had to earn a living. Sam's tailoring business was beginning to falter; prices were going up. If the Marxes were to survive in the city, the boys needed to contribute—especially since Leonard's salary was being leached away in gambling losses.

Shortly before Julius's bar mitzvah, Minnie presented the news: they needed a delivery boy at Heppner's wig factory on Forty-fourth Street. For the whole summer? Julius wanted to know. He hoped not; there was a good deal of reading to do before classes began in September. No, his mother informed him, he would not be working just for July and August. He would be leaving school for good. Julius knew that his weekly salary of three dollars might make the difference between solvency and poverty. What was it Dickens had written? "Annual income twenty pounds, annual expenditure nineteen nineteen six, result happiness. Annual income twenty pounds, annual expenditure twenty pounds ought and six, result misery." Julius played the dutiful child and went uncomplaining to his new assignment. But he would not forget the sound of the school's metal door clanging behind him for the last time, as if Minnie had personally closed it. Nor would he forgive the irresponsibility of a sibling whose recklessness had pushed him from the house and into the world before he was truly ready. The notion of Julius H. Marx, M.D., was something he would joke about later, speaking of the patients he saved by *not* becoming a doctor, and boasting about all he had achieved without formal schooling. All the same, his humor on the subject was never to lose its resentful edge.

•

ONCE HE WAS out of school, Julius attacked work the way he went at his schoolbooks. Of all the temporary jobs he took, one made very few demands. For $3.50 a week all he had to do was answer the telephone in a one-man real estate office. Eager to please, he came in early and settled down to business. He discovered that the phone hardly ever rang, and that his employer arrived late, left early, and often did not come in at all. With these lax conditions, Julius saw no reason to hang around when he could be at the ball game. En route to the park he saw a man's hat blow off. The eager youth retrieved the fedora and handed it back, expecting a return for his effort. He received one. The man was his employer, and the reward was a pink slip. Julius sought other employment. At this point Minnie intervened. Her son would keep whatever day job he could find, but he would supplement it with something quite different. She had found a profitable use for Julius's soprano.

Outside of the family, the first people to hear Julius sing were members of an Episcopal church on Madison Avenue. With Minnie's encouragement he had tried out for, and won, a place in the boys' choir. Eyes cast skyward, white surplice gleaming in the stained-glass light, Julius sang Christian hymns at the handsome rate of a dollar per service. One Sunday morning in midsong an unlikely possibility struck him. Leonard was turning out to be unmanageable, and the label "promising" manifestly did not adhere to Adolph. Herbert and Milton had yet to exhibit any exploitable abilities. Could it be that lonely, jealous, walleyed Julius was the one Marx son capable of following Al Shean into show business? It was as if Minnie had learned the trick of ventriloquism from her father: the boy put the question, the mother supplied the resonance. Minnie's nudging and urging permitted no self-doubt. Julius had to make the rounds of the booking offices, had to persuade the indifferent world of booking agents that he was a young man on his way.

No one evinced any interest in a slight fifteen-year-old with worn clothes, an abundance of curly black hair, and an inability to dance, play an instrument, or read music. Never mind, Minnie badgered him, there were plenty of jobs out there, too small for an agent but just right for a youth. Keep looking. Something will turn up. And so it did in the summer of 1905, when Julius's eyes lit on the enchanting words "Boy Singer Wanted for Touring Vaudeville Act. Apply Leroy, 816 Third Avenue, between 2 and 4." Fearful that every kid in New York had already seen it, he jogged the sixty blocks from his house to the address at Thirty-third Street, took the five flights of stairs two at a time, and knocked on the door. A willowy gentleman in a kimono answered. Julius noticed that he was wearing makeup and lipstick in broad daylight, but thought little of it. Show people tended to be outlandish; look at Uncle Al.

"Just go up there with the other boys," said Mr. Leroy, appraising him. "I'll be right along."

Julius caught his breath, climbed the last flight of metal stairs—and joined forty other boys, equally ambitious, equally nervous, crowded onto a steaming tin roof. It might have been the lively hopping he did in order to cool his feet; it might have been his clarion soprano: in any case, Julius beat out all the other singers. Mr. Leroy also hired a tough-looking young "buck dancer" who called himself Johnny Morris and sent the losers packing. The Leroy Trio, he told his new charges, would open in Grand Rapids and then move on to Denver. No mention was made of other cities en route. That made no difference to Julius. He was in bigtime show business now.

Julius quit his job at the wigmaker's; the assignment had been a grind and a bore anyway, except for one memorable occasion when he brought a box home for delivery the next morning. Adolph tried on one of the blond wigs, and mischief lit up his eyes. He talked Julius into helping him get into one of their mother's dresses; then he put rouge on his cheeks and sashayed in on some neighbors engaged in a game of pinochle. Adolph flirted outrageously, piquing the men's interest until three women, one of them Minnie, entered the room. Shocked, they demanded that this hussy be thrown out on the street where she belonged. At the right moment, Adolph removed the wig, first to general relief and then to laughter and applause. He was dubbed "the family character" for this prank, a great feat in a clan that included Opie, Leonard, and Minnie herself. Even so, it was one thing to star in a living room, and quite another to get paid for entertaining strangers, like Julius. That boy was turning professional, like Uncle Al. No higher praise could be found in the Marx lexicon.

Yet there was a subtext to the foolery. Their contemporary Elbert Hubbard spoke about the "street Arabs" of his time, boys like the Marxes who moved easily around New York, dipping in and out of street crime, fleet enough to run from trouble or to talk their way out of it. "What boy well raised can compare with our street gamin who has the knowledge and the shrewdness of a grown-up broker?" asked the writer. "But the Arab never becomes a man." Such was the case with these youths. They would enjoy great success as family clowns, and soon enough as professional ones. But recognition would come at a cost for all of them. Julius led the way. Pushed out of the nest before he was ready, he would forever be immature in matters of women, money, and power. The other four siblings would follow the lead that began on Leroy's overheated roof.

After two weeks of rehearsal the young singer joined the Trio at Grand Central Station. "For the first time in my life," he would remark significantly, "I felt like I wasn't a nonentity." Once aboard the westbound train Julius put his luggage in the overhead rack. It consisted of a new straw suitcase bought for the occasion by a gratifyingly teary Minnie, and a box of sandwiches and hard-boiled eggs prepared by a worried Sam. No performer could have been greener. Save for that dimly remembered trip to Germany at the age of five, Julius had never been out of New York City. His notion of travel came directly from novels where young gentlemen like Frank Merriwell ate in walnut-paneled dining cars and spent their evenings stretched out in comfortable Pullmans.

Two days and two nights on a hard-backed seat, plus a diet of cold sandwiches and hard-boiled eggs, left Julius stiff, dyspeptic, and disoriented. But he had no time to adjust. No sooner had he left the train when Leroy barked his orders: the entertainers were to proceed posthaste to the Ramona Amusement Park on the outskirts of Grand Rapids. They arrived with just enough time to struggle into their costumes as they watched the bombing of the opening act. It featured the Whangdoodle Four, a quartet of black men dressed as Chinese. The Leroy Trio was next, its cast in female regalia singing the lamentable tale of Liza and her lover, who expect a check that never arrives:

> I wonder what's the matter with the mail;
> It was never so late before;
> I've been up since seven bells,
> And nothing's slipped under my door.

At the closing chords, Julius ducked into the wings; slipped off the skirt, high heels, and floppy hat; assumed his old choirboy's outfit; and reentered for a spiritual solo, "Jerusalem, Lift Up Your Gates and Sing." This was met with silence, except for one audience member who shouted "Hallelujah!" and was vigorously ejected by the manager. Johnny Morris followed with his specialty, an explosive dance. As he hit his stride, one of his tap shoes accidentally slipped off, striking a woman in the audience. When Johnny subsided, Leroy glided onstage in an elaborate evening gown to sing Victor Herbert's "Kiss Me Again." All three members joined in the patriotic finale, a tableau starring Leroy as the Statue of Liberty, with his supporting players dressed as an honor guard of Continental Army soldiers.

Although only scattered applause greeted the players, Leroy considered the reaction "bully" and his Trio's performance nothing short of "a lallapalooza." The manager was the first to disagree with him. At the end of the engagement he deducted one-third of the group's $60 fee. The lady struck by Johnny's shoe had threatened a lawsuit, he claimed, and the $20 had served to mollify her. Other reviews came in; they were equally ungenerous. The rest of the tour consisted of a split week—three days in Victor and three days in Cripple Creek, Colorado.

Even the unworldly Julius knew that his employer was a homosexual. What he did not know was that during the tour, the aggressively masculine, street-smart Morris had become Leroy's lover. The awakening occurred shortly after the Trio's last performance in Cripple Creek. Julius wandered around town, then returned to the boardinghouse where they had stayed for the last couple of nights. He discovered that Leroy had run off with Morris, taking everything he could put in his satchel, including all the money Julius had secreted under his mattress. Minutes later the fifteen-year-old was hit by an aftershock: the landlady wanted her rent money.

"Boy," she warned him, "I'll give you forty-eight hours to come up with a dollar and a half, or out you go on your ear! I never met an actor yet who wasn't a crook!"

Instead of intimidating Julius the warning gave him courage: she had referred to him as an *actor*. His spirits brightened a bit more when, rummaging through Leroy's abandoned room, he discovered one of the costumes from the act. In their haste to leave town the thieves had overlooked it. Julius peddled the garment for $3.50—enough to quiet the landlady.

The next day another harbinger appeared. A hand-lettered sign had been put up: EXPERIENCED BOY WANTED TO DRIVE GROCERY WAGON BETWEEN CRIPPLE CREEK AND VICTOR. MUST KNOW HOW TO HANDLE HORSES. The only horses Julius had seen in New York were the roans under policemen and the drays pulling coal and ice wagons. No matter; he told the grocer he had appeared in rodeos and knew all about nags. Seated on the buckboard, he snapped the reins authoritatively and set off across town and down a narrow mountain road. On one side was a natural wall of stone, on the other a gorge four thousand feet deep. The horses, perhaps aware that an ignoramus sat in back of them, hysterically picked up speed. But Julius's luck held: in the middle of the journey one of the animals ran out of wind and collapsed. Several hours later a new and competent rider came by with a fresh horse, hitched it to the wagon, and took Julius to his destination. From Victor, the ex-driver wired Minnie the bad news and she sent him money for the fare home. Decades afterward Julius swore that he had no idea where his mother found the necessary cash: "Probably hocked one of my brothers," he quipped.

Julius came home crestfallen. He had gone out a youth, become a man on the road, and returned as a boy rescued by his mama. Now he would have to prove himself to Minnie all over again. Without any lectures about show business predators, she took over his professional as well as his private life. As his self-appointed representative, she went around midtown, knocking on the doors of booking agents, importuning them to hire her client, an experienced performer who had starred in vaudeville way out west. The initial response was tepid, and for a while only Uncle Al and another uncle, Henry, could claim to be professional entertainers. The envious Henry had worked up a ventriloquist turn with young Milton cast as the dummy. The man would pretend to throw his voice. The boy, sitting on his lap and moving jerkily, would actually do the talking from behind a papier-mâché mask. Two problems surfaced during their performances: Henry had no stage presence, and Milton stuttered. No one, least of all Minnie, was surprised when the misbegotten act died in a matter of days.

Minnie went back to pushing Julius at the bookers. A few beer gardens hired him to sing "illustrated songs"—numbers whose plots were illustrated by lantern slides—but these engagements led to nothing grander until the day that mother and son encountered an attractive English performer. Lily Seville was in the market for a juvenile to entertain the customers while she changed costumes. The salary: $15 a week, a 300 percent improvement over Julius's last vaudeville job. Better still, Lily was already booked for seven full weeks on the Interstate Circuit, a string of theaters in Texas and Arkansas. A fortnight later, fully rehearsed, completely smitten with his employer, armed with suitcase and food, Julius was westbound once more. This time he carried a "grouch bag"—a small chamois sack in which treasures and bills could be hidden. To guard against pilferage he let no one except his employer know about it.

"Lady Seville and Master Marx" showed off the Lady in an elaborate white gown, and Julius in yellow silk hat, white trousers, purple blazer, and matching boots. The oddly matched pair bounced from Hot Springs to Waco, with stops at such big towns as Houston, Dallas, and Fort

Worth. To Julius's disappointment, their relationship was purely professional. *Variety* caught up with the pair in Texas and reported, "Lily Seville
and Julius Marx, singers, were fair." Not a rave, but not a pan, either.
Quite possibly they could have gone on to better notices and bigger
venues, save for the Lady's weakness. All along she had been nourishing a
passion for a married man on the same bill, and just as Leroy had eloped
with young Morris, Lily took off unannounced with Professor Renaldo,
the Animal Trainer. Sorry as Julius was, he consoled himself with
thoughts of his newly acquired riches. He patted his grouch bag, an item
he had removed only a few times during the whole journey. It was gratifyingly full, noisy with the sound of crisp bills. A bit too noisy, perhaps? To
reassure himself he peered inside. In place of the $65 that had been there
only yesterday, he now found scraps of newspaper. Minnie mailed him
some money and a bag of food. Julius returned to Manhattan, chopfallen
once more.

A fifteen-year-old with two credits as a singer and two as a dupe: this
was not an encouraging tally in Frenchy's eyes. His advice to Julius had
nothing to do with show business, probably because he was convinced
the boy had no future there: "You won't be a man until you learn to play
pinochle." Minnie must have had her doubts as well, particularly when
she failed to land any more assignments for her middle son.

But by now Julius was hooked on applause and travel, and he went
out on his own to audition for the Gus Edwards troupe. In his day
(c. 1900–1920) the swarthy composer/impresario was referred to publicly
as a genius and privately as "the Dago"—even though he had been born
in Poland of German and Polish parents. Edwards (né Gus Simon) had a
gift for melody (his songs included "By the Light of the Silvery Moon,"
"In My Merry Oldsmobile," and "School Days") as well as an almost infallible eye for young comers. The children who graduated from his troupe
included scores of subsequent headliners, among them comedians
George Jessel and Eddie Cantor, dancers Ray Bolger and Eleanor Powell,
actors Mae Murray and Ricardo Cortez, producer Mervyn LeRoy, and
columnist Walter Winchell. He hired Julius on the spot for a group called
the Messenger Boys. A few months later, the youth was granted the ultimate accolade: his portrait (actually a snapshot from the family album
showing a younger and more winsome Julius Marx) adorned the sheet
music of Edwards's own "Farewell Killarney." The other highlight of
Julius's brief sojourn with Edwards & Co. occurred in May 1907, when he
shared the stage of the Metropolitan Opera House with Enrico Caruso
and Ignace Paderewski. The soloists and chorales on the program all per-

formed for the same charitable purpose: to raise money for "The San Francisco Sufferers" of the recent earthquake. The Messenger Boys went on to theaters in upstate New York and Massachusetts, but now that Julius had sung "Somebody's Sweetheart I Want to Be" accompanied by a seventy-piece orchestra at the Met, the role of boy soprano seemed anti-climactic. He was only too glad to try out for the part of Jimmy Arm-strong, an impudent office boy in a legitimate melodrama entitled *The Man of Her Choice*. After he won the part he had second thoughts; the weekly salary would be $10, a considerable markdown from the Lily Seville days.

On the other hand, he would be given the opportunity to brandish a pistol and articulate the act 1 curtain line: "Stop, or I'll blow you to smithereens." The chance was irresistible. He threw himself into the part so vigorously that the papers took notice; the *New York Dramatic Mirror* stated that the slender young Julius H. Marx was making "quite a hit as a juvenile." In various memoirs, Julius liked to claim that he never learned the meaning of "smithereens," although he did admit that other lessons had been absorbed during the tour of *The Man of Her Choice* in New York and on the road. One was that if he stacked his bureau up against his door, no one could steal his savings. The second was that even on his mea-ger salary he could afford a prostitute. One evening a young streetwalker offered herself and a price was negotiated.

In a few minutes he had lost his virginity and acquired a case of gonor-rhea. Julius's childhood was effectively over—over, but not finished. If, as Graham Greene has suggested, a writer's capital is his childhood, a come-dian draws even more fervently on the same source: the memories of humiliation and resentment, of local bullies and tyrannical schoolmas-ters, of neighborhood characters and family members. An unhappy child-hood seems a requisite for humorists, and virtually all who depend on public laughter have drawn on early psychic wounds and deprivations. But there was a central difference between Julius and his contemporaries. Those comedians constructed their routines around the child buried deep within. Julius was about to make a very different statement. No ripening process was possible for a youth thrust onstage and kept there through his adolescence. His way of coping was to inter the adult and present a child persona to the public. His brothers followed suit; soon they would all be boys dressed up as men in funny faces and outlandish costumes, like cele-brants en route to a costume party.

•

A CANADIAN DOCTOR treated the sixteen-year-old and the symptoms of venereal disease disappeared, only to resurface years later. But for the time being Julius's health returned, and his bruised ego recovered when he opened a copy of *Variety*. His mother had placed an advertisement telling the world about "A Very Big Hit. Master Julius Marx." There was the proof in the public print: Minnie did care for her middle son. Julius worked hard to keep her affection as the other boys jostled for her attention and love. She was the epicenter of the family now, and she continually reminded her sons that she was all that stood between the warmth and safety that money could bring and the chaos that waited right outside the front door. Did they want to end their days in some factory, worn out by meaningless work? Worse still, did they want to be hounded by policemen? Get locked in jail? End as beggars on the Bowery, only a couple of miles downtown? The boys gave her no backtalk. They waited and they watched. For unlike them, she made few mistakes. During the period when Julius sang with the Gus Edwards troupe, for example, she sensed that Edwards's codirector, Edward C. Wayburn, was really the man to cultivate. (And, indeed, was right on the money. Long after Edwards had become passé, Ned Wayburn was producing and directing the Ziegfeld Follies.) Now she buttonholed him, pointing out that "kid acts" were the hottest thing on vaudeville nowadays, and that she had a houseful of talent. In addition to Julius, there was Leonard the piano player, as well as Milton who trilled like a nightingale. She neglected to mention that Milton stuttered *except* when he sang, or that Leonard was currently in Pittsburgh, plugging songs for the publishers Shapiro & Bernstein.

Minnie pushed an open door. If anyone knew that children were box office it was Wayburn. He agreed to hire Julius and to take a chance on the untried Milton. They would be paired with the producer's own discovery, sixteen-year-old Mabel O'Donnell, a little girl with a soprano capable of reaching any theater's upper balcony. The title of the new thirteen-minute act came from two sources. The producer supplied the famous name, Minnie added the avian image. Wayburn's Nightingales starred the two Marxes in straw boaters, white duck suits ornamented with paper lapel roses, and clip-on bow ties. For her part Mabel wore a bright dress and a peek-a-boo hairstyle. The Nightingales made a smashing debut in Wilmington, Delaware, before moving on to Tony Pastor's in New York. The *Dramatic Mirror* somewhat disdainfully praised their "neat little turn of songs and dances" that "pleased those who like to encourage precocious children." A more enthusiastic *Variety* found the Nightingales "surprisingly good," but added that "a 'plant' used in the box does not help the act any." The plant was Frenchy, employed to generate laughter and applause on cue.

Once the act was booked to travel, Minnie gave her husband another assignment. Frenchy became the Marxes' advance man, buying tickets for their complicated railroad schedules and negotiating prices for rooms at boardinghouses in dozens of towns and cities. Occasionally he would call home with the desperate query, "Where am I?" He meant, "Where am I going next?" But his sons, who depended on his ability to negotiate fares and accommodations, used these grammatical confusions to mock him, and to the ends of their lives they spoke about Frenchy as if he were a cartoon character. They were amused by Frenchy, and most of the time they loved him, but none of the five boys ever granted him respect. That was reserved for Minnie.

The trio, each member pulling down a weekly salary of $25, moved through the big cities and small towns of the East until November 1907, when a monumental change occurred. Wayburn stepped aside for more remunerative projects, and Minnie Marx took over, advertising herself as the manager of the newly dubbed Three Nightingales. Her first move was to dismiss Mabel O'Donnell, not only because the female lead wasn't a relative, but also because she was cockeyed and sang off-key, frequently leading the brothers from G to A-flat without warning. Mabel had developed a crush on Julius—one of the few times when he found himself the pursued instead of the pursuer—and the parting went very hard. But the Nightingales' new manager had no time for the ingenue's entreaties; she was too busy reinventing the act, replacing Mabel with Lou Levy, a talented singer about Julius's age. Presently Minnie heard that Henderson's Coney Island needed a kid act to entertain its summer customers, and she sold the management on her group. Not until opening night did she learn that the theater had promised its customers a quartet, not a trio. Rather than lose the booking she conscripted Adolph, then accompanying silent films in a Thirty-fourth Street movie house. He was nineteen at the time.

Years afterward he could still summon up the image of his mother entering the theater, charging down the aisle, and ordering him to follow her. Not a word of explanation was given to the bewildered spectators. On the elevated train to Coney Island, Minnie screened Adolph with newspapers as he hysterically changed into a white sailor suit. While he jammed legs into trousers and arms into sleeves, she recited the words of "Darling Nelly Gray," praying that her son would turn out to be a quick study. Minnie urged him to fake the bass part, mouthing the "boom-boom" while the others carried the melody and articulated the lyrics. The more she entreated, the more apprehensive Adolph became. It was one thing to perform in a movie house, hunched over a piano and protected by the dark. But the idea of a spotlight trained on him while an audience stared . . . Minnie brought him to the wings as the band struck up the Nightingales' cue, and shoved him onstage before he could change his mind. Adolph's rueful memoir concludes: "As I caught my balance, the thought sizzled in my mind. *You're not a boy anymore. You're a man. Don't let them know you're scared.* I came to a halt beside Lou Levy. And there They were. A sea of mocking, hostile faces across the footlights. And here I was, with nothing to hold onto, absolutely nothing. With my first look at my first audience, I reverted to being a boy again. I wet my pants. It was probably the most wretched debut in show business."

Like most performers, Adolph labored under the delusion that all eyes were upon him and him alone. As it happened, an appreciative audience greeted the act with loud and continuous applause, and the *Variety* reviewer went out of his way to praise the act's "high degree of excellence." The reviewer did point out one flaw: from time to time the players attempted to deliver some comic lines; these were "ineffectual" and should be dropped. "The precious moments thus saved could be devoted to more singing." His words were regarded as law by Minnie and all humor was deleted. This made the Nightingales yet another musical kid act. The trouble was, they were not really kids anymore. While the act meandered around the country Julius turned eighteen; Adolph, twenty; Milton, sixteen. Although they looked younger, they displayed the characteristics and felt the spermy irrepressible urges of young men. This was to cause difficulties. Because the Nightingales were all supposed to be minors they traveled at half fare, something conductors accepted until one scrutinized the boys as their train traversed the Midwest. One was in the dining room smoking a cigar. Another was in the washroom shaving. Maintaining the straightest of faces, Minnie sighed philosophically: "They grow so fast." As usual, the response was mixed with truth.

Separated from the family, Leonard provided a brightly hued illustration of Freud's observation "A man who has been the indisputable favorite of his mother keeps for life the feeling of a conqueror, that confidence of success that often induces real success." Leonard was barely five feet six in shoes, and not markedly handsome or expensively dressed. Yet his palpable self-assurance, his air of irresistibility to women, made him a prime seducer, totally impervious to rejection. In show business, too, he never doubted himself, and he conveyed that feeling upward to theater managers, sideways to his brothers, and downward to disbelievers. The trouble was that he carried that feeling over to his other habit, gambling, and here the adrenal rush, and the belief that victory could be only a couple of aces away, was to bring trouble time and again. Adolph, persuaded by teachers that his blond-topped head had nothing in it, was becoming a Jewish Huckleberry Finn. After his sorry start he made up his mind that all careers (and all women) were the same, and he went along with whatever skit or scheme the others concocted. Adolph boasted that he knew of "no such thing as a bad meal or a bad show," and this lack of critical faculties would make him one of the least demanding, and ultimately one of the happiest, entertainers who ever lived. In late adolescence Julius was already fully formed as the antithesis of his older brothers: a bit taller, thin with the worried energy of youth, swarthy, fearful, pessimistic, forever carping about working conditions, audiences, the opposite sex. As for the younger ones, the chunky Milton was a serious boy, already less interested in show than in business, and Herbert, virtually unsupervised these days, was developing into a wiry street kid and premature skirt chaser.

Since the boys were no longer boys, when her sons ogled girls on the train and backstage Minnie did more than look the other way. One of her granddaughters, Maxine Marx, was later to note that the lady actually "encouraged her sons to chase after fast women, perhaps because she didn't want the boys to be trapped into marriage. Minnie didn't want to share her boys with another woman." But something else operated here, something a bit less Freudian. Minnie had labored long and hard to make something of her brood, and the early results were promising. The Marx brothers would not, *must* not, leap the rails on which she had so carefully placed them. Dalliances were all right, but along with marriage came children and mortgages and emotional commitments. As she saw it, you had obligations or you had a career in show business. But not both.

Onward the Marx brothers went, pursuing careers and females with equal vigor, but achieving far better results with the latter. One evening in Nacogdoches, Texas, a hint of their future stared them in the face, but they were too angry to understand it. Just as they hit their stride, the audience began to file out of the theater to follow the adventures of a runaway mule. Seething, the Marxes waited until the ticket holders returned to their seats. The clowning that had always been supported at home, and discouraged onstage, erupted from all of the brothers. Here Julius began his first assault on propriety, however brief, leading the way with extemporaneous rhymes: "Nacogdoches / is full of roaches" and "The jackass / is the finest flower of Tex-ass." There was a moment when the words "lynching party" crossed the brothers' minds—and then the audience dissolved into laughter. The relief was palpable, and the Marxes responded with one of their wildest and most appreciated shows. Brimming with a new bravado, the Nightingales returned to New York and informed Minnie about the reception in the Southwest. Might there be room to shoehorn a little humor into the act? There might not, she told them firmly. Indeed, there might not be room for the act at all.

The facts could no longer be hidden from the boys: major bookers had stopped listening to Minnie's sales pitch. Without euphemisms or subtleties they let her know that while some kid acts remained hot, this particular one was strictly small-time. Out-of-the-way venues might still accept her boys, but the Nightingales were not ready for New York, and probably never would be. Minnie knew better than to bang her head, much less her sons' heads, against the metal theater doors of midtown. The bookers were right: the act needed changes and seasoning and the freedom to experiment. It needed to get out of town for a while. While they were on tour a thought had occurred to her. What if the Marxes were to relocate? Three vaudeville circuits—Gus Sun, Pantages, and Considine & Sullivan—used Chicago as their hub city, sending acts throughout the Midwest and South. Why not go there? What did the Marxes have to lose except the apartment on Ninety-third Street and a lot of discouraging words?

It was an audacious move in the shaky year of 1910. Overseas, Russia was expelling thousands of Jews, causing concern and fears among the Jews of the still overcrowded Lower East Side that Frenchy and Minnie had been so anxious to leave. Child labor was still the subject of political agitation, along with women's right to vote. Minnie, who could run the lives and fortunes of her family, could not enter a ballot—a situation that was quite all right with many journals, including *Life*. "Woman's suffrage," the magazine predicted, "would vastly increase the ignorant and the purchasable vote, and in the mixed population of American cities would prove the strongest enemy of civic reform." Meantime, the wealthy extended their power, causing ex-President Teddy Roosevelt to advocate "a policy of far more active governmental interference." Theatrical producers, threatened on one side by increased taxes and on the other by the new medium of silent movies, which were already attended by more than 40 percent of the nation, pulled their purse strings tighter.

It would take a combination of bravado, faith, and lunacy to trade New York for Chicago at this time, and those were precisely the words to describe Minnie. Not only did she insist on taking Julius, Adolph, Herbert, and Milton, she also brought the aging Opie Schoenberg along in her slipstream—"Lock, stock, and grandpa," was the way Adolph remembered it. The house Minnie wanted was a comfortable three-story brownstone at 4512 Grand Boulevard, then a Jewish section of the city. The owner, a dour banker named Mr. Greenbaum, accepted the $1,000 down payment (borrowed from Al Shean), but not before expressing doubts about whether he would see the rest of the $21,000 asking price. Miss one monthly payment, and out they went, he warned. The boys overheard Minnie lying to him, heartily assuring Greenbaum that her family was on the cusp of prosperity. As proof of their financial solidity she went out and hired a black maid, pushing the family closer to the edge of financial catastrophe. Never mind, she told her sons, appearance was the key to success. This, too, was a lesson they would absorb at great cost.

Within weeks Opie had made himself completely at home, lazing on the front porch or lasciviously attempting to get his hands on the housekeeper. Frenchy went on the road, peddling textiles and boxes. Herbert was too young to go anywhere on his own, but Julius, Adolph, and Milton spent a lot of time exploring the city and taking in baseball games—the Chicago White Sox played nearby, and they could watch Ty Cobb and Shoeless Joe Jackson before the World Series "Black Sox" scandal did him in. The rest of the time, Julius let his brothers go their various ways while he explored bookstores. With awe, the nearly illiterate Adolph recalled his brother borrowing "a stack of books from the public library and curling up to read his way through the summer." None of the boys were to remain idle for long, however. Minnie had brought them out here for a purpose. She started to repackage Julius, Adolph, and Milton, buffering them with three nonfamily members: a bass, Freddie Hutchison, who replaced Lou Levy, and two female dancers. Almost every vaudeville show had at least one family act, for economic reasons. From the production side it made sense: child actors earned less than adults. Performers also liked the setup: the more family members in the show, the fewer salaries had to be paid to outsiders. The Four Cohans were the ideal to which every other family aspired; there were also the Three Keatons, featuring Buster Keaton, whose father used him as a broom; the Gumm Sisters, with Judy Garland; and the Ponselle Sisters, one of whom, Rosa, graduated to the Metropolitan Opera Company. And then there were the Ritz Brothers; the Allen Sisters, starring Gracie Allen, later of George Burns and Gracie Allen; Willie and Eugene Howard, who became major theater stars; the Dolly Sisters, later played by Betty Grable and June Haver in a film biography; and many others.

This particular family act, the Six Mascots, consisted of a few undemanding solos from the girls, some music played by Julius on the guitar and by Adolph and Milton on mandolins they had only recently learned to play. It was not a hit, and both dancers gave notice as soon as they found better roles. Reluctant to revise the act yet again, Minnie put on her tightest corset and dragooned her sister Hannah. They took the female roles themselves, grateful for a lark, as well as for the opportunity to save on salaries. By now, both ladies had gained too much weight to do much prancing around; they got winded easily and were only too happy to sit whenever the act permitted. One evening they both settled down on one flimsy chair. It collapsed under them. The incident served to put them all on notice: soon enough, the boys would have to carry on by themselves. But not as Mascots. In their next incarnation they were simply the Three Marx Brothers & Co. Julius had stumbled upon a central insight: he and his brothers were dependably, explosively funny onstage, not just at home. He worked up a kid comedy, much of it plagiarized from other acts, called "Fun in Hi Skool." He played the teacher, with a "scratch wig" to make him look bald and a Plattdeutsch accent not very different from Opie's. Milton was a young "Hebrew Boy" with Yiddish intonations, and Adolph took the part of a half-Irish village idiot stereotype named Patsy Brannigan, complete with violent red wig sewed and glued by Aunt Hannah. A new outsider, Paul Yale, played the "Sissy," with standard limp wrists and lisping diction. Every time Julius turned away the boys would misbehave, or join in choruses of "Peasie Weasie." This was the Marxes' first special material from the outside, bought from a comedy writer who charged them $27 for ten stanzas of rhyming puns and elemental gags:

> My mother called Sister downstairs the other day.
> "I'm taking a bath," my sister did say.
> "Well, slip on something quick, here comes Mr. Brown."
> She slipped on the top step and then came down.

> CHORUS

> Peasie Weasie, that's his name.
> Peasie Weasie, Peasie Weasie, what's his game?
> He will catch you if he can,
> Peasie Weasie is a bold, bad man.

A humpback went to see a football game,
The game was called on account of the rain.
The humpback asked the halfback for his quarter back,
And the fullback kicked the hump off the humpback's back.

(CHORUS)

Went fishing last Sunday and caught a smelt.
Put him in the fire and the fire he felt.
Of all the smelts I ever smelt,
I never smelt a smelt like that smelt smelt. (Etc.)

Other musical interludes featured parodies of songs. "Waiting at the Church" turned into "Waiting in My Shirt," and the same garment was used in a send-up of an operatic aria—the Habanera of *Carmen* became "I want my shirt. I want my shirt. I won't be happy without my shirt."

This time the act flourished. Good notices came in, and word of mouth attracted new and enthusiastic crowds. Julius dared to see himself as a writer—not a prose writer, the kind he admired most, but still a person who could face a blank page and produce something worthwhile. This should have been a moment to treasure. But by now Julius had learned to distrust good signs: smiling employers and coworkers had turned out to be thieves; a minor bout of lovemaking had led to venereal disease. He slept badly, doubted loudly, and kept goading his brothers to do better. And so they did, slowly building a reputation for unfettered comedy and unpredictable ad-libs, a reputation that caused Minnie to suffer anxiety attacks. Traveling with the trio through Alabama, she once watched horrified as all three of her sons interrupted their own number to follow the progress of a large bug crossing the stage. They hunkered down and speculated aloud about the insect. Was it a beetle? A cockroach? Maybe an oversize bedbug? To their mother this was just the sort of wild behavior that made theater managers tear up contracts. It showed indifference to the paying guests who had paid to see performers stick to the script, not fool around on the ticket holders' time, on the ticket holders' money. When Julius, Adolph, and Milton started to crawl after the bug, Minnie hissed to get their attention. She wanted to remind them that applause and laughter meant nothing without the accompanying paycheck. With all advance bookings they remained perilously close to the poverty line, and missing even one mortgage payment would land them in the street. A tirade was out of the question. She uttered only one word, but it served to throw cold water on the manic ad-libs: "Greenbaum!" The boys straightened up and returned to their roles. From time to time she would need to hiss, "Greenbaum, you crazy kids"—always in the same urgent tone, and always with the same restraining effect.

By 1911 the boys were each pulling down $35 a week. Minnie felt successful and powerful enough to rework her own image, managing under the nom de vaudeville of Minnie Palmer, a genuflection to the Palmer House, a first-class Chicago hotel. In addition, Julius was to write, "there was another Minnie Palmer, a vaudeville star who was as petite as Mother was ample. Perhaps Mother saw herself in the same blonde and lovely light. At any rate, any confusion about the two couldn't hurt. Mother thought borrowing the name would give her own enterprise added prestige." Now, in addition to representing Julius, Adolph, and Milton, the plumper of the Minnie Palmers took on another client: the double act of Marx and Gordoni. These were her eldest son Leonard and his colleague Arthur Gordon. They had left Shapiro & Bernstein the previous year to strike out on their own as a comedy duet, with Leonard playing eccentric piano—shooting the keys, playing the treble with an orange, and spreading a sheet across the keyboard and then banging out a tune while Arthur sang popular airs. Adding the i to Gordon's name had been Minnie's idea; Neapolitan tenors were all the rage. She also had an idea about Julius, Adolph, and Milton. They were ready for a vaudeville revue, with a larger cast and a better school routine. Al Shean wrote it, in between his own busy and profitable vaudeville bookings. He had recently entered a partnership with Ed Gallagher, another comedian/singer, and, using patter songs and genial exchanges, the two had scored a series of triumphs. Clearly this was a man worth listening to. Better still, his services were free.

The new Marx Brothers show did well enough, but it lacked something, some panache, a component no one could quite identify. In 1912, the missing ingredient acquired a name. The boys were still doing a variation on the school act, and one night in Waukegan, Illinois, Julius looked out over the footlights to see an unexpectedly familiar face. Adolph, in his new Patsy Brannigan costume topped with a fruit-covered hat, followed his brother's astonished gaze. There was Leonard, unannounced, playing along with the orchestra. By way of greeting, Adolph hurled an orange and an apple at the pianist. Leonard picked up the pieces of fruit and threw them at Julius. He tossed them at Milton. More objects followed. The food fight ended when someone wisely lowered the curtain. In the next few days the printers were notified: the Three Marx Brothers were now the Four Marx Brothers. Leonard the gambler had decided to play with the house money.

Once the senior Marx brother clambered aboard, the act took on a more accelerated pace and displayed a wider range of eccentricities. Leonard's approach to the ivories, coupled with a metronomic sense of timing and an outrageous Italian accent copied from a favorite barber, won him acclaim before the footlights. Backstage his confident charm made new conquests of all chorus girls within reach. Afterward he treated the chorines like hand-me-down clothes, passing them on to his brothers. For Julius this was an unexpected benefit. Persuaded from childhood that he was unattractive to women, he had been paying hotel chambermaids two or three dollars for an hour's entertainment. Leonard's largesse gave him a wider world to exploit. *Au fond,* however, he remained convinced that he was "an ardent lover but an ineffectual one," and for all the eyebrow-waggling and double entendres, Julius, now twenty-two, regarded himself, correctly, as the most straitened and least sexually aggressive male in the family.

Leonard helped the act evolve from "Fun in Hi Skool" to "Mr. Green's Reception," an elaboration of the schoolmaster, now portrayed as a retired old fool, and his misbehaving pupils who have grown up without having matured. The Four Marx Brothers—Julius, Leonard, Adolph, and Milton—began the most arduous trek of their lives. In a typical week they might play three days in Burlington, Iowa, catch the overnight train and play the following four days in Waterloo—four-a-day vaudeville for five days, five-a-day for two days, for a total of thirty shows per week. The process went on unvaryingly, in the cities around the Great Lakes, in Ohio, Illinois, Texas, Alabama. Unlike many of their contemporaries, neither Adolph nor Julius was inclined to glamorize their vaudeville period. In his memoirs, what the older man mainly recalled was a montage of railroad waiting rooms, boardinghouses, and small-town theaters with confused or unresponsive audiences. Quite often during those years he had asked himself why the team persisted in the face of continual failure. No one ever supplied a satisfactory answer until Julius gathered his own recollections. The Marx Brothers, he concluded, were a contradiction in terms—ignorant perfectionists. They had absolutely no marketable skill outside of comedy, and they instinctively rode that skill as far as it would take them. This meant working longer hours than any company executive, and earning lower wages than any factory employee. But there was no other way to learn their trade; nobody could show them the route. They had to fail firsthand.

And fail they did. "Mr. Green's Reception" opened for a week's run in Chicago, at the important Thalia theater. The reception was nowhere near as warm as the brothers had hoped; they got only one review, and it was not indulgent: "The so-called Marx Brothers do well, but in the worst kind of vaudeville. In other words, they are so good they stink." The Marx Brothers' early biographer, Kyle Crichton, says that after the review was read and assimilated Julius thought of returning to school to study medicine. This seems highly unlikely; it would have been too long a climb for a man in his twenties who had never received a high school diploma. Besides, by then he had taken too many bows and seen too many mediocre vaudevillians with larger salaries than his. There is no question, though, that the review and reception had depressed an already dour nature and that his attitude had infected his brothers' outlook. They all acknowledged that the past week was an omen: another such reception and they could very well be one of those groups they kept running into on the road, entertainers who always seemed to fall just short of the big time. It took very little imagination for the boys to see Leonard back at the profession of song-plugging, Adolph behind the butcher's counter, and Julius at loose ends, a good mind without a single professional skill outside of show business.

Minnie sought advice from the only authority she could trust, her brother Al. The timing was exquisite: ordinarily, the popular Gallagher and Shean would have been on the road, booked solid for the season. But it so happened that Shean had recently and acrimoniously split with his partner. Suddenly at liberty, he responded to his sister's telegram by showing up on her doorstep. That evening he watched the final performance of "Mr. Green's Reception." An hour later, sitting on a kitchen chair at 4512 Grand Boulevard, Uncle Al filed his own review: the boys were indeed funny, and their material did indeed stink; it had grown stale and obvious. He cast himself as play doctor, scrawling ideas and lines on scrap paper. By morning he had concocted "Home Again," mixing elements of the old characters but placing them in a fresh context. Shean briefly considered joining the boys, but concluded that his nephews could provide enough comedy to break up "ninety-nine percent of the audience." Adding Uncle Al to the mix would be "too much talent for one act."

Shrewdly assaying his nephews' strengths and liabilities, he assigned the long speeches and setups to Julius, whom he rightly regarded as a reader, a quick study, and an "eccentric" monologist. Leonard was again to be the Italian rascal, with an increase in lines to provide more "boob" comedy. As Patsy Brannigan, Adolph would be the "nut," with more motion and fewer lines—only three, in fact. Milton, as before, would be the bland and smiling juvenile. Of the four, only Adolph objected to his new role. Al pointed out that pantomime would make an effective contrast to all the frenetic dialogue, but Adolph was in no mood for explanations. If he had no lines, he warned the others, he would ad-lib his way around the stage. This time it was Uncle Al who played pantomime. He nodded sagely and made no objections.

"Home Again" took to the road, revising lines and characters en route. For one night in Flint, Michigan, Minnie shoehorned her youngest into the show. An alert critic gave the boy his first review: "There is a fifth Marx brother in the company. Master Herbert Marx, a lad of about 14, who gives promise of becoming as much of a favorite as the rest of the family. Master Herbert added some four or five songs to the rest of the program last night in a manner which left no doubt as to his future." No doubt in the reviewer's mind, perhaps; the other Marxes were not so sure. Herbert did not make another professional appearance for three years.

As a boy S. J. Perelman had encountered the first four Marx Brothers in performance at a Providence, Rhode Island, theater. Out of the haze of memory, he later picked out the other acts on the program: "Fink's Trained Mules, Willie West & McGinty in their deathless housebuilding routine, Lieutenant Gitz-Rice declaiming 'Mandalay' through a pharynx swollen with emotion and coryza, and that liveliest of nightingales, Grace Larue." By this time, Perelman adds, the other acts were mere appetizers for the roast.

The mise-en-scène was the Cunard docks in New York, an illusion conveyed by four battered satchels plus a sleazy backdrop purportedly representing the gangway of the liner *Britannic*. Julius entered in a clawhammer coat, "his eyes shifting lickerishly behind his specs and an unlit perfecto jutting from his teeth." Behind him came his termagant wife (played by Minnie), his son (Milton), and two shipboard cronies (Adolph and Leonard).

Julius's initial speech set the flavor of the proceedings. "Well, friends," he observed, stifling a belch, "next time I cross the ocean, I'll take a train. I'm certainly glad to set my feet on terra firma. Now I know that when I eat something, I won't see it again." Heckled at every turn by Milton, he remarked waspishly, "Nowadays, you don't know how much you know until your children grow up and tell you how much you don't know."

According to Julius, no pundit had been able to explain exactly what the foregoing meant or why it always elicited cheers and applause; "apparently the customers sensed some deep undercurrent of folk wisdom."

There was then "considerable horseplay" involving Adolph and the ship's cutlery. This was a piece of business originally suggested by Julius. An outrageous theft of cutlery occurred midway through the first scene, and a policeman clomped on to investigate. Adolph was his prime suspect. But Patsy Brannigan's tearful response moved the onlookers, and they protested that he was completely innocent. After a fruitless search, the lawman agreed. He and Adolph shook hands, at which time a piece of silverware fell from the thief's capacious sleeve. Then another. And another. Originally twenty pieces were scheduled to tumble out, but because the laughter increased with every item, the number kept rising until during some performances it hit one hundred. When the last knife crashed to the ground, Julius commented, "I can't understand what's delaying the coffee pot"—and on cue the pot crashed to the ground.

"The plot structure," concludes Perelman, "was sheerest gossamer; vague reference was made to a stolen chafing dish, necessitating a vigorous search by Adolph of the corsages of two showgirls drifting unaccountably about the premises, but on the whole there were few nuances. Following a rather soupy rendition of 'The World Is Waiting for the Sunrise' by Adolph, Leonard played 'Chopsticks' with gruelling archness, and the pair exited rear stage left in a papier-mâché boat on wheels, knocking down three members of the troupe. Those who remained thereupon joined in a stylish chorale entitled 'Over the Alpine Mountains E'er So Far Away' [and] the orchestra segued into von Suppé's Light Cavalry Overture to herald the acrobats." Few would disagree with Adolph's satisfied summary: "It was a far car cry from 'Peasie Weasie.' "

Three important events happened during the tour.

First, Adolph discarded his handful of lines, goaded by the critic in the Champaign-Urbana, Illinois, paper. That reviewer had interrupted his rave to note, "The Marx Brother who plays 'Patsy Brannigan' is made up and costumed to a fare-thee-well and he takes off an Irish immigrant most amusingly in pantomime. Unfortunately the effect is spoiled when he speaks." Adolph grudgingly acknowledged that Uncle Al might have something after all. He acquired a raincoat to stow his props, and an old automobile horn to honk his replies, and never spoke in performance again.

Second, the Marx Brothers were reborn, this time as nonpareil comedians. Whatever the shortcomings of structure and motivation, "Home

Again" had shoved the Marx Brothers in the right direction. Audiences flocked to see this new look at a seasoned team, and *Variety* praised the "merry little musical short" that gave all four brothers "an opportunity to do some very effective work in their several lines. They all have talent and shine in this piece which allows them to display their own brand of rollicking humor in which they excel." They excelled to such an extent that pretty soon no one wanted to follow them—especially other comedians. No less a star than the juggler/comedian W. C. Fields refused to appear on the same bill with the Brothers when they were booked together in Columbus, Ohio. Recollecting the occasion in his memoirs, Fields wrote: "They sang, danced, played the harp and kidded in zany style, were vaudeville entertainers. Never saw so much nepotism or such hilarious laughter in one act in my life. The only act I could never follow." Accordingly, he confronted the manager: "You see this hand? I can't juggle anymore because I've got noxsis on the conoxis and I have to see a specialist right away." He was nowhere to be found that week. Jack Benny suffered from a similar reaction: "My God, they did thirty-five minutes of their stuff and when my quiet act followed, it was disaster!" Yet in some ways the Marx Brothers helped him. "I just can't describe their act but after a while I used to stand in the wings before I went on and laugh like hell; which meant I stopped worrying about *my* act."

The third event had less to do with material than with image. During a break between shows at a theater in Galesburg, Illinois, all four Marxes set up a poker game with Art Fisher, a traveling monologist. The subject of nicknames arose. Wherever they appeared the air seemed to be saturated with "kiddos" and "boyos" and "Henpeckos" and "Tightwados." The custom of tacking an *o* onto words and names had been triggered by the popular comic strip "Sherlocko the Monk." To Fisher, the boys seemed like so many comic strip characters themselves, and with good reason. Across the country, readers were following the syndicated pranks and pratfalls of German immigrants in "The Katzenjammer Kids" (the literal translation of *Katzenjammer* is "cats' yowling," German slang for hangover). The French were represented by Alphonse and Gaston, two pathologically courteous greenhorns spouting phrases that outlived them ("After you, my dear Alphonse." "No, after you, my dear Gaston"). Maggie and Jiggs satirized the arriviste Irish—Maggie wanted to join society, while her husband Jiggs pursued his fondest dream, a plate of corned beef and cabbage. These and a score of similarly inclined strips developed an intellectual following. Social historian Gilbert Seldes praised the "hardness" of the American comic strip: "It is male and ugly, whereas all the other magazine features of our newspapers are 'sweet femininity' for the delectation of washerwomen. . . . The draughtsmanship itself is hard and angular; the faces and figures are of an intense ugliness, and the strip rejoices in a brutality of color." He might have been describing the Marx Brothers onstage.

Around the table Fisher went, singling out each brother. Julius, the dour one with the grouch bag, he dubbed Groucho. Leonard, pursuer of ladies—"chicks" in vaudeville parlance—ought to be Chicko. Since Adolph and his instrument were inseparable, he would be Harpo. Milton, the sickly child who had become a career hypochondriac, wore rubbers or "gumshoes" at the first sight of rain. Gummo seemed appropriate for him. At the time the brothers thought very little about the sobriquets. As Julius told it, they were preoccupied in playing an insignificant poker game in an insignificant town on an insignificant evening. Lines, timing, and energy level were what people remembered. Who cared about nicknames?

CHAPTER THREE

"Humorisk"

IN OLD AGE Groucho told his friend and biographer Hector Arce that he hated the nickname he had carried for some sixty years. It made him sound, he said, "like I'm the kind of guy who goes around whipping children." That was not the case when Art Fisher dispensed it. Julius had never been comfortable with his forename—fellow performers called him "Julie," which he felt was no improvement—nor did he look up to the uncle for whom he had been named. In 1914 he and his brothers gleefully addressed each other by their new handles. Before long, fellow performers also began to call them Groucho, Chicko, Harpo, and Gummo, and there was no turning back. (The eldest later became Chico when a typesetter accidentally dropped the *k,* and Leonard liked the result; Adolph changed his own unlikable name to Arthur but found Harpo more congenial.)

Among their favorite colleagues now were men and women en route to worldwide celebrity. Groucho first saw Charlie Chaplin's act in Winnipeg. He entered out of curiosity when he heard explosions of laughter from outside the theater. Charlie's pantomime so impressed Groucho that he returned with his brothers. This little guy, he told them, just might be "the greatest comedian in the world." At the time Chaplin was still an unformed personality onstage and backstage. Groucho remembered how shabby the little man appeared; he seemed "a little like a pale priest who had been excommunicated but was reluctant to relinquish his vestments." The Marxes and the tramp hit it off, and one night they invited him to watch their capers. Hungry as Chaplin was for adulation, he loved a gag even more. As the Brothers kept peering over the footlights to see how their guest liked the show, Charlie elaborately opened a newspaper and affected to read it throughout their entire routine. The Marxes said nothing about this, and told him they would come by to see his act one more time. They bought a box and filled it with four Orthodox rabbis in gabardine, with the customary beards and forelocks. Assuming that this quartet was the Marx Brothers in disguise, Charlie outdid himself with comic improvisations and movements. In the middle of his act the clergymen, offended by some joke or other, rose from their seats and exited the theater. Round two went to the Brothers.

The entertainers ran into each other again in Salt Lake City, where the Marxes invited Chaplin to visit a well-appointed whorehouse with them. The quartet made selections and retired to rooms upstairs. Too shy to participate, Charlie stayed below, chatting with the madam and playing with her lapdog. Afterward, he and the Brothers lined up garbage cans and played an impromptu game of leapfrog—boys away from home and on the loose, attempting to recall an innocence that was never really theirs, since they had all been working full-time since childhood.

Chaplin spoke about an offer from Hollywood to appear in some one- and two-reel comedies. The brothers congratulated him, and Groucho asked, "When do you start?"

"I'm not going to take it."

Groucho spoke for all of them. "You're only getting fifty dollars a week now. Don't you like money?"

"Of course I do. But look, boys, I can make good for fifty dollars a week, but *no* comedian is worth five hundred a week. If I sign up with them and don't make good, they'll fire me. Then where will I be? I'll *tell* you where I'll be. Flat on my back!"

The Brothers assured Chaplin that he was indeed worth the money, and wished him well. Five years were to go by before they met the comedian again. Then it was as dinner guests at his home. A butler stood behind each brother. By then Chaplin's name had been linked with more than a dozen young women, some of them very young indeed. Whatever his inhibitions about the female sex, Charlie had managed to overcome them.

Groucho also befriended Carl Sandburg, poet of Chicago, the City of Broad Shoulders; comedienne Fanny Brice, who, he noticed, had three sets of false teeth ("One for show, one to eat with, and a spare"); and Will Rogers, who enjoyed playing sandlot ball with the Brothers. Groucho treasured a valuable bit of philosophy handed down by the Oklahoman during a game. After popping a short single to right field, Groucho noticed the second baseman playing out of position. In the process of stretching his single into a double, he looked up to see Rogers catching the relay, spinning around and exulting, "You're out!"

The runner protested, "How can that be? You have to touch the base and you're standing twenty feet away!" Rogers replied amiably, "Groucho, when you're my age, wherever you stand is second base."

Games provided one way to relieve the pressure of performance; sex offered another. For female companionship Groucho usually relied on houses of pleasure, or on Chico's uncanny ability to attract women by sitting at a piano and shooting the keys until he gathered a group of admirers. But on occasion Groucho went out on his own, all too often with disappointing or disastrous results. There was, for example, a deceptively pleasant afternoon in Muncie, Indiana. Strolling in his up-to-date outfit of checked cap, Norfolk jacket, cane, and spats, Groucho was the glass of fashion and, since he had carefully left a bit of makeup on his chin, manifestly in show business. He caught the eye of a comely young woman pushing a baby carriage, and opened the conversation by talking about himself and his career. Then it was her turn. She explained that she was nineteen and single, baby-sitting her sister's child for the afternoon. Would the actor like to come back to her house? "The boys in Muncie," she confided, "have nothing on you." Groucho's blood jumped. They had just put the baby in its bed and begun the afternoon's entertainment when a harsh voice sounded. Like a temptress in a melodrama she shouted, "Oh, my God! My husband!"

This was not a stage play, however, and Groucho was in no mood or condition for a confrontation. He ducked into a closet and listened to the outraged male booming about the smell of cigar smoke: "There's some son of a bitch in this house and I'm going to find him and kill him!" The husband opened the closet and felt around inside, but failed to make contact; Groucho had covered himself with coats and was now cowering in the corner. The moment the threat stomped into the next room, Groucho leaped out of the second-story window, crashed into some bushes, and ran for the boardinghouse. He arrived ahead of his brothers and feigned sleep rather than provide any humiliating details.

Happily, there were alternate methods of deflecting tension. Groucho's favorite was the practical joke. On one occasion the Marxes found themselves in a college town where undergraduates booed the Brothers—and awarded a standing ovation to an act starring two beautiful sisters. After a particularly disastrous matinee Groucho and Gummo glumly passed by the sisters' empty dressing room. On the wall were four "symmetricals" used to round out stockings, and two pairs of overstuffed brassieres. The Marxes exchanged looks and without another word purloined the devices and took them back to their room. They knew,

Groucho admitted, that if the sisters went on with thin legs and flat chests, their act would bomb, and bomb it did.

The brothers sneaked into the sisters' dressing room and returned the symmetricals. That night the sisters were a hit again. The brothers bombed. But they felt better.

For spur-of-the-moment madness, Harpo was a nonpareil accomplice. Chico was mischievous enough, but he preferred to venture out by himself. Alone of all the Brothers he would hang on to his immigrant persona onstage and in life, uncomfortable in all but the lowest social settings. And besides, he disliked Groucho's censorious attitude toward wenching and gambling. Who the hell was he to look down on his older brother? With Chico keeping himself at a distance, Groucho and Harpo went out on the town during a Manhattan sojourn. Harpo knew a couple of girls and the boys made a house call, bringing with them four dozen oranges as an alternative to flowers. As a lark, they started to bowl the fruit from one end of the room to the other. Harpo impulsively pitched a piece of fruit at Groucho, in a style reminiscent of the evening Chico had made his surprise appearance in the orchestra pit. Groucho answered in kind, and the battle was under way. Within half an hour the place was carpeted with peel and juice, and neighbors were pounding at the door. As the firing ceased, the landlord irately entered. Without bidding good-bye to their dates, the brothers scooted out. The landlord's foot missed Groucho; Harpo was not fast enough to escape injury.

In the same city, another stunt had more spectacular results. Invited to a bachelor dinner at a fancy restaurant with many private rooms, Groucho and Harpo brought along two suitcases. In a scene recalling that long-ago event when two little Marxes entered a shipboard party stripped to the skin, they planned to make a spirited and unique entrance. The two men entered the elevator, held the door, stuffed every garment in the suitcases, and pushed the up button. The elevator arrived at their floor. They stood grinning widely as the doors swung open but not on the stag party. It had stopped at another party—for friends of the bride. A headwaiter eventually came to their rescue, snatching up two large tablecloths and enveloping the Marxes. A busboy led them down a flight of unused stairs. Neither brother was invited to the wedding.

Victims of the Marx Brothers learned that practical jokery was a one-way street. In Decatur, Illinois, while his brothers were sleeping or playing pool, Groucho took it upon himself to rehearse the band and the rest of the cast. As he entered the local vaudeville house, the manager, a burly and unpleasant figure called Jack Root, confronted him. "That'll cost you five bucks," Root growled. He pointed to Groucho's cigar, and then to a sign on the back wall: FINE FOR SMOKING IN THIS THEATER $5.

When his brothers arrived Groucho gave them the news. There was no point in a face-to-face with the boss; at one time Root had been the middleweight boxing champion of New Orleans. They closed ranks and went on a sitdown strike. It was nearly Christmas, and a restive audience stamped and hooted when the Brothers failed to appear. Root went around to the Marxes' room, but they refused to get into costume until the fine was rescinded. Neither side budged until Chico came up with a solution. If Root was willing to give Groucho's five-dollar fine to the Salvation Army, the Marx Brothers would match the fine and do the show. Rather than return the ticket holders' money, Root agreed. But there was something about his peaceable smile that made the Brothers uneasy. When payday came around an assistant manager appeared, dragging three heavy bags. They contained $900 worth of pennies, nickels, and dimes. The Marxes had no time to count the cash—they had to catch a train in half an hour. As it pulled out of the station, Harpo raised his fist and yelled into the night, "You son of a bitch, I hope your theater burns to the ground!" The next morning they read that Harpo's fondest wish had been answered. Groucho, as usual, turned the incident into a punch line. The conflagration in Decatur was the reason why his brother never talked. Harpo's voice, Groucho maintained, was like the ax that hung on every backstage wall, to be used only in case of emergency.

•

SHENANIGANS WENT ON HOLD in the spring of 1915. The morning of May 7, German submarines, attempting to cut off supplies to England, torpedoed the *Lusitania* in the Irish Sea. Some 1,200 men, women, and children drowned, 139 of them Americans. Literally overnight, traditional German products and people received new identities. Sauerkraut metamorphosed into "liberty cabbage," ballplayers whose names sounded Teutonic were suddenly called "Dutch," and German accents were all but outlawed onstage. On the seventh, the Brothers happened to be playing Shea's Toronto Theatre. That afternoon Groucho did his character, Mr. Schneider, in the usual way, singing *"Alle shafft aber nicht Vater"* (Everybody works but Father). News about the *Lusitania* made the afternoon papers, and that night he metamorphosed into a Jew, singing a tune in English with marked Yiddish intonation: "It's better to be in Toronto / Than to live in a place you don't want to."

Now that the Hun was loose in Europe, Washington lawmakers made plans to conscript men between the ages of eighteen and thirty. All the brothers except Herbert, who was still underage, would be subject to the draft. The elder Marxes knew all about conscription; that was why Frenchy had come here in the first place. Minnie checked the various avenues of escape. The papers reported that anyone involved in agriculture would be exempt from the draft. That was all Minnie needed to know; she made immediate plans to acquire a farm. Something else was operating here as well: in addition to protecting her boys, Minnie had little taste for a war with Germany, her home country. Despite its anti-Semitism the place held warm memories and a language she never forsook. It would not do to have the Marx Brothers engage in a pitched battle with the past.

The family moved to a twenty-seven-acre homestead in La Grange, Illinois, a couple of whistle-stops from the city on the Chicago, Burlington & Quincy railroad. Since no one knew the first thing about truck farming, the Marxes decided to raise poultry. They ordered two hundred chickens and arranged to have coops constructed. With everything finally in place the family sat back, waiting for the eggs. Very few ova saw the light of day. Every night rats entered the coops and made off with them—plus a hen or two. In the beginning the boys attempted to keep farmer's hours, getting up dutifully for chores at five in the morning. The rats' behavior depressed them and they allowed themselves to sleep until six, then seven, then eight and even later. Within a month Chico made an interesting discovery. If you left the place by noon you could catch the CBQ train to Chicago in time to see the Cubs' home games at Wrigley Field. That was the end of early rising. The sojourn on the farm became notable principally because during that time Herbert received his nickname, Zeppo. It might have come from the newfangled zeppelins then making the headlines, from the fact that hick farmers were sometimes called Zeb, or from Mr. Zippo, a vaudeville performer whom Herbert resembled. No one—including Zeppo—was ever quite sure.

Following the poultry failure, the Marxes tried to raise guinea pigs in the cellar. This was Zeppo's idea; he had heard that the rodents were in big demand at medical laboratories. These creatures remained intact and bred enthusiastically. But Zeppo had been misinformed; the labs sent out word that their mammal of choice was the white rabbit. Hundreds of guinea pigs were released into the Illinois night, and not long afterward the family agreed to resume their show business careers. So much for animal husbandry.

At about this time Chico may have decided he needed another barrier to the draft; in any case, in 1916 he astonished his brothers and his parents by taking a bride. She was Betty Karp, an attractive, outspoken, nineteen-year-old Jewish girl from Pittsburgh. When the act returned from the road, Betty encountered the entire Marx family in situ. Thereafter, Chico and Betty were allowed a room of their own. The other brothers still lived at home like teenagers, doubled up in adjoining rooms. Cousins occupied other rooms, and Al Shean and his wife were in yet another room. Opie still took up space, exhibiting signs of senility but maintaining his interest in a pretty ankle and, when the weather permitted, in ice-skating round and round at the nearest pond.

Betty made the mistake of speaking her mind. That was a privilege only accorded to the brothers, as she discovered the day Minnie swept into the dining room, wig piled high, corsets laced tight, gesturing imperially to the little audience of relatives. It was all too much for her new daughter-in-law. Betty turned to Chico and, sotto voce, compared her hostess to the Queen of Sheba. Minnie took it in good grace but her boys expressed their disapproval. Betty learned to mute her criticism and edit her wisecracks. It was not easy. She joined the cast of "Home Again" to keep an eye on her errant husband, but found it impossible to put the brakes on his womanizing. At one rehearsal she caught Chico kissing a chorus girl and remonstrated. Chico protested his innocence: he was not kissing the young lady; he was merely whispering in her mouth. Offstage, some of the boys made a move on Betty—they reasoned that a wife, no less than a girlfriend, was fair game. Onstage, matters were no better; during a performance Harpo tripped her to get a laugh, and Chico publicly appraised her dancing: "Baby, with your looks and your legs, if you had any talent you'd be worth a million bucks." Only Groucho had respect for Betty's candor, as she did for his. He instructed his sister-in-law not to sing so loud lest she throw everybody off-key, and she muted her voice. She informed him that his thin moustache covered a sensitive mouth; he shaved his upper lip and went back to gluing on theatrical whiskers before each show.

During this time Groucho made the sports pages as well as the entertainment section. He had been trying to learn golf, and between shows in San Francisco went out to Lincoln Park. There he shot his first and only hole-in-one. As Groucho told it: "The next day, my name was in the newspaper. It was stuck between the pictures of Walter Hagen and Bobby Jones. The headline read, MARX JOINS THE IMMORTALS." That afternoon he went out on the course again, trailed by photographers. Determined to prove that his achievement was not merely beginner's luck, he aimed carefully and let fly. He shot a 12 on the hole. "The following day there was another headline: MARX LEAVES THE IMMORTALS."

"Home Again" was still on the road in the winter of 1918, when Minnie and Frenchy's first grandchild was born. Betty took her new daughter, Maxine, to meet Chico in Oakland, and the event provides a glimpse of their married life. The couple chatted in Chico's hotel room until a series of knocks sounded at the door. Chico opened it. The gruff house detective ordered him to get the woman out of his room. Chico, putting on a show of moral outrage, identified the female as his wife, and, on cue, the baby began to wail. The detective backed out, apologizing all the way. The next morning Betty overheard Chico in an adjoining room, whispering about the incident to his brothers. The one time a house dick nails him, he's with his own wife! Betty walked out of the suite, the laughter echoing in her ears. It would not be the last such affront.

Slowly Groucho jettisoned the Yiddish accent, experimented with the cigar as a way of punctuating gags, and worked on his comic lope. "I was just kidding around one day and started to walk funny," he recalled. "The audience liked it, so I kept it in. I would try a line and leave it in too if it got a laugh. If it didn't, I'd take it out and put in another. Pretty soon I had a character." That character went on evolving until 1917, when the Selective Service Board finally caught up with the Marxes. One by one the brothers were rejected. Groucho suffered from bad eyesight; Harpo had a malfunctioning kidney; Chico was overage; Zeppo was underage. "You should see the fifth Marx brother," Groucho told the recruiting sergeant. "Two heads." Actually, the other Marx brother was Gummo, and even though he was the weakest and sickliest child, the medical examiner considered him hale enough to serve. The irony was not lost on his mother, but she was the frankest of them all. Gummo had been cute as a child; now he was merely a dead weight on the act. Besides, he had the trace of a stutter—the result, perhaps, of the inconstant attitude she displayed toward her fourth son. She wished the draftee well and added the words he did not need to hear: "We can do without you."

Off he went—to spend the war in Illinois, finding dates and borrowing his brothers' cars for officers. For Gummo the draft was a godsend; he had secretly detested performing since the Sunday matinee he found himself unable to speak before a waiting audience. He later recalled: "I was standing in the spotlight with Groucho so I could give him a feed line. Nothing came out! Groucho sensed this and he started to ad-lib until I regained my composure enough to give him the line. That was when

I decided I had to get out. I couldn't live the rest of my life with a thing like that."

On Minnie's insistence, her youngest boy stepped in for Gummo. "A good thing I did," Zeppo was to recall. "Else I'd have gone to jail. I was working as a mechanic for the Ford company and I was a real bad boy. I was a kid, but I carried a gun and I stole automobiles." The day his mother telephoned, Zeppo was preparing to go out on a double date with his friend Louis Bass. Minnie said, "Quit your job and come home immediately." Such was her power over all the boys that Zeppo, the budding delinquent, obeyed without question. He would not have done the same if Frenchy had given the order. Once the boy arrived home, Minnie clarified the situation: "Gummo just joined the army and that leaves three Marx Brothers. You go and get packed and get on the train, here's the fare, go to Rockford, Illinois, and join your brothers. I want the name of the Marx Brothers intact. We started that way and we're getting along pretty good." Zeppo protested that he had a date. Minnie snapped, "Well, you'll have to cancel your date because this is important to me and to our whole family." Zeppo sighed like a lover and obeyed like a son. That night, Louis Bass took both girls out by himself. He was set upon by two toughs, and he pulled out his pistol and shot one to death. Relating this incident, Zeppo concluded: "Now, I would have been there too and because this was my buddy I'd have done the same thing and I'd have gotten in the same trouble—he went to prison for twenty years. I don't know what would have happened to me if my mother hadn't called me, sent me to Rockford, Illinois, and Gummo hadn't been patriotic and joined the army."

While the Great War continued in Europe, the new and improved Marx Brothers quartet (unlike Gummo, Zeppo never suffered from stage fright) attempted to boost morale at home. They starred in a new musical farce commissioned by Minnie, who had been suffering symptoms of withdrawal since her last appearance onstage. This time, however, her sister would not be alongside. Hannah had discovered Christian Science, and currently spent her days studying Mary Baker Eddy's writings and attempting to convert the family. In this she had no success at all. Frenchy mispronounced her belief "Christian Shine" and wanted nothing to do with it—or, for that matter, with Hannah. Minnie and the boys were far too busy to attend her living room sermons.

Gag writer Jo Swerling, who had been contributing gags to Groucho, confected the book for "The Street Cinderella"; Gus Kahn and Egbert Van Alstyne composed the score. Groucho belittled the show in a memoir: "Chico hired six dancers out of a five-and-dime store, and gave them each ten dollars. They were overpaid." He had a point. Inept as the show was, though, the Brothers might have been able to save it except for a virus. Just at that time an epidemic of Spanish influenza swept through the country, affecting every aspect of American life. Author Mary McCarthy, who lost both parents to the plague, would later write about those fatal weeks in the fall of 1918 "when no hospital beds were to be had and people went about with masks or stayed shut up in their houses, and the awful fear of contagion paralyzed all services and made each man an enemy to his neighbor." Vaudeville theaters were only allowed to be half full—members of the audience had to leave the seat on either side empty so that they would not breathe on one another. To further protect themselves many wore surgical masks, so that even when they laughed the sound was muffled. "The Street Cinderella" could be chalked up as another victim of flu, succumbing in Michigan to bad reviews and empty houses.

The Marxes retreated en bloc to the farm. In the time allotted between this show and the next, Groucho explored Chicago music stores in search of scores written by two men whose work he had discovered on the road. A comic actor, Ed Metcalf, had been vocalizing backstage when Groucho remarked, "That's a goddamned good lyric. Did you write that?" No, Metcalf told him, the words were by William Schwenck Gilbert. That exchange at once revealed Groucho's ignorance and his innate and unselfconscious good taste. From then on he was a Gilbert and Sullivan devotee, reading, listening to, and memorizing as many of their works as he could find.

After the Armistice in November 1918, Gummo headed for New York, where he set up as a manufacturer of cardboard boxes. His brothers went back on the road with "'N' Everything," a thinly disguised rewrite of their one dependable vehicle, "Home Again," this time with an accent-free Groucho. It was good for two more years of full houses, and a scrapbook of rave notices. The *San Francisco Chronicle* led the cheering section: "There has not been anything like it, and there probably will not be anything like it again, at least until the Marx four are around once more." Having perfected his gookie and polished his musical technique, Harpo was singled out as "quite the funniest comedian that has stirred the mirth of Orpheum audiences for some time." Leonard received praise as "a piano-teasing character comedian with gifted fingers," and Groucho for being "a clever eccentric dancer, comedian and general utility man."

"Home Again" had "a finish and care for detail that suggests some of the French clown acts."

After two years on the road the Brothers returned to the farm and pondered their next move. Did they dare to rewrite "Home Again" once more? Should they attempt something entirely new? Chico reread the notices. In his opinion they were in the wrong town. It was time for them to head for the East, where the major circuits were centered and the most influential critics were quartered. "Why don't we all move to New York?" he asked them. "Why are we wasting the whole summer here?" "Wasting" was the operative word. In the days before air conditioning, troupers took an enforced vacation every summer. They earned nothing and did nothing but play cards and go to the races, an amusing way to kill time for a few weeks. After that, most of them went stir-crazy and were anxious for the autumn winds and the crackle of money.

For once Groucho went along with Chico's logic. Who needed any more split weeks and one-night stands? Who wanted the tyranny of managers, of provincial audiences, of landlords who wanted two days' rent in advance and gave you tiny rooms and ghastly meals after you paid through the nose? If the Marx Brothers had any chance to crack the big time, to earn long engagements and long green, this was the moment. The others went along, and before the winter solstice of 1920 all five were back in the place of their birth. Chico the irrepressible, the one Marx brother who had been out on his own, quietly displaced Minnie as de facto manager, crapshooting for the Marx Brothers' careers. In the city for a second round, the siblings took up residence in separate apartments. Chico was thirty-two; Harpo, thirty-one; Groucho, twenty-nine; Gummo, twenty-six; Zeppo, eighteen. Their long collective adolescence was over.

•

IN HIS THIRTIETH YEAR Groucho took two significant steps. He married, and he starred in a silent movie. The first project took twenty years to fall apart; the second bombed immediately.

In the past, Groucho had dated Chico's hand-me-downs. Ruth Johnson was Zeppo's hand-me-up, a blond actress and dancer who had been casually dating the youngest Marx when she caught Groucho's eye. Ruth was a Christian, which upset no one; Opie had died at the beginning of 1920, and he represented the last connection with Jewish orthodoxy.

Neither Minnie nor anyone else in the family expressed surprise that Groucho was marrying out of the faith. He had always gone for shiksas. Only one Jewish woman—his mother—ever got close to him, and Minnie's demands were all Groucho could handle. Let Chico have a forthright wife like Betty; he could get around any female. For romance the unconfident Groucho needed someone with Ruth's credentials: raised outside New York City, unsophisticated, deferential, easy to please.

The wedding took place in February, in the Chicago home of Ruth's parents. As Groucho said later, it was not a union made in heaven. He put down Ruth's mother as "a small-town bigot," displeased with the idea of a Jew as son-in-law. "She never failed, when visiting us," he remembered, "to declare that she was as busy as a skunk in a hen house. I don't know about the hen house, but the first part was certainly accurate." On the other side of the aisle, Minnie looked upon her new daughter-in-law as an interloper without dowry, humor, or style. By attitude and speech she saw to it that Ruth remained an outsider.

Photographs of the couple during their courtship show Ruth to be attractive in the mode of the time, with bobbed hair and a placid demeanor. Groucho, underweight and restless under the lens, sits uncomfortably, his surprisingly refined face softened by spectacles and by thick black hair parted in the middle. With the groom-to-be there is a sense of the antic waiting to be released; in contrast, Ruth projects a placid, contented demeanor, growing a bit rounder in each succeeding set of prints. Neither a rabbi nor a minister could be found to sanction their interfaith union. Eventually someone found a justice of the peace with impeccable credentials: he was a Jew and an ex-vaudevillian. The JP would have performed the ceremony without incident except for the use of the phrase "holy matrimony." Unable to leave a straight line alone, Groucho replied, "It may be holy to you, judge, but we have other ideas." The justice noted that Jo Swerling, author of "The Street Cinderella," rather than any of the siblings, had the role of best man. He also noted that Chico was missing, presumably on some show business errand. That was not the case. Groucho had not been invited to his brother's wedding and this was his cold reply.

Whatever their temporary feelings for each other, however, the Brothers knew that they were professionally joined at the hip. Harpo never thought much of Ruth's talents as a singer or dancer, and once tried to get her fired. Chico looked upon her with disfavor; he didn't even find her attractive. But Groucho wanted her along as chorine and wife and he got his way with them. He also got his way with Minnie—a far more significant event. Groucho could do nothing about his mother's derisive view of his wife. But he was willing to stand up to her on financial matters. He reminded her that he and Chico were both married men now, and that it would no longer do to have her handle money and dole out allowances to her sons. Minnie backed off, surprised, and perhaps gratified, by her son's strength, and from that point Groucho assumed a leadership role equal to his mother's.

But what were they to lead? It was clear that the Marx Brothers were stars of a dying medium. "Home Again" never failed to get its laughs and pull in its grosses, but as *Variety* reported every week of 1920, motion pictures were rapidly replacing vaudeville as the epicenter of show business. Mack Sennett had already enticed Charlie Chaplin and Buster Keaton from the stage to the screen, with spectacular results. The Marxes wanted in on the movie business. Groucho expressed the strongest desire to get off the road; in his twenties, he had become the most socially sensitive of the brothers. The others had grown a kind of psychological carapace, but the middle son had yet to develop an adequate defense against insults and snobbery. He deeply resented the public's attitude toward showfolk, particularly in the small towns of America. Performers were unwelcome at first- or even second-class hotels, and no one of good reputation would be caught strolling with a player in public. Generally, he and his fellow entertainers were relegated to boardinghouses, two to a room, six dollars each. Every night he spent in such a place was an affront. "The bedrooms contained an iron bed, a lumpy mattress, a thin rug and a bowl and pitcher. Draped over the pitcher would be two sleazy face towels and two threadbare bath towels. These were yours for the entire week. By the end of the week the towels would be so dirty you would usually bypass them and fan yourself dry."

On the few occasions when some small-town girl looked upon an actor with favor, his life took on more risks than pleasures. During a tour of Louisiana, Groucho said, Gummo met a girl. The young people took an instant liking to each other. "The following day her father came to our dressing room and said, 'You've been seeing my daughter, haven't you?' And Gummo told him he had. At which point the father said, 'If you see her again I'll send you back to New York in a box.' He would have killed Gummo just because his daughter was going out with an actor."

That threat alone would have kept Groucho on the straight and narrow. But he was never much for sexual adventures. "I used to try to behave myself. I wasn't wild like Chico. He was always getting chased from town to town by some father with a gun." The odd thing was that of all the brothers, Groucho had become the best-looking, with a winning smile and an affable, if guarded, manner. No less a judge of men than the actress Maureen O'Sullivan described him in his salad days as "very sexy. He had physical presence and a good build." But Groucho had already been formed in the family crucible, dominated by a mother who thought him unattractive and let him know it; intimidated by Chico, Minnie's favorite, and by the devil-may-care Harpo, who had always paired off with his older sibling. The two younger boys, Gummo and Zeppo, had been buddies from their toddler days. This situation left Groucho isolated and unsure of himself as a child, and he could not overcome such feelings even as a young husband and father. Only when he put on makeup did he convey the sense of a lascivious and authoritative male. Inevitably the artifices of show business became more fulfilling, and in a sense more real, than the life he led offstage.

The trouble was that show business did not seem eager to sustain Groucho—or his brothers—now that vaudeville was on its way out. Since no movie studio seemed interested in what they had to offer, they decided to produce their own screen test and show it to Hollywood executives. "Humorisk," a parody of silent films, cost more than $7,000 to make. The Brothers invested $1,000 each; the rest of the money came from Jo Swerling and a couple of other financiers who knew even less about film production than he did. The feature was shot near Fort Lee, New Jersey, then a center of film production, located half an hour from Manhattan via the George Washington Bridge. Since the Marx Brothers were appearing at a nearby theater, this eliminated travel and kept them within their narrow budget.

Not a single frame of the movie remains—a mixed blessing, according to Groucho: "We made two reels that didn't make any sense at all. But it wasn't trying to make sense, it was trying to be funny." In this it did not succeed. According to various accounts, "Humorisk" opened with Harpo, the love interest, wearing a top hat as he slid down a coal chute. The final scene showed Groucho, playing the heavy, being led off in chains. Between these incidents came a thin story line, punctuated with meager and uncoordinated gags. One of Swerling's relatives owned a theater in the Bronx; he agreed to run a sneak preview. "Catastrophic" does not begin to describe the reception. Boos and catcalls accompanied every scene, affirming what the Brothers suspected but did not dare to acknowledge: they had produced a totally unusable product. Should anyone from Hollywood get a peek at it they were finished. The master reel was quietly consigned to the flames. One of the producers kept a copy in his closet for years. By the time historians learned of its existence the last remaining evidence of "Humorisk" had deteriorated into celluloid fragments.

Once more Chico bucked up his brothers, convincing them that vaudeville still had life. In that medium, at least, they were big names. With luck they could play a year without ever leaving the precincts of New York City. No travel, no schedules, no boardinghouses. The Marxes put on their costumes, rehearsed their lines, and went back to work, doing sixty straight weeks in the New York area, including the vaunted Palace Theatre. In the definitive reference book *Show Biz, from Vaude to Video,* Abel Green and Joe Laurie Jr. point out: "What the White House represents to a political hopeful, a Palace booking signified to an actor. It was honor, recognition and a springboard to fame. But it was also a severe test, before the most critical vaudeville audience in the nation." The Marxes passed that test with such high marks that they felt ready to field a major production with first-class script, scenery, and personnel. Written by Herman Timberg, a veteran of the Gus Edwards troupe, "On the Mezzanine" featured original songs, a strong story line, and a sizable cast, edging the Brothers closer to the lineaments of Broadway musical comedy. The curtain rose on the office of a theatrical agent, Mr. Lee. One by one, the Brothers entered and proceeded to audition, mimicking Gallagher and Shean. This was more than a salute to Uncle Al. By 1921, the reunited team was considered the most popular two-act in the country. Almost every vaudeville bill featured an impression of the pair, and an elaboration of their song, interpolating current events with established patter:

> "Why Mr. Shean, why Mr. Shean,
> On the day they took your old canteen,
> Cost of living went so high
> That it's cheaper now to die."
> "Positively, Mr. Gallagher?"
> "Absolutely, Mr. Shean!"

Before matters got out of hand the Keith Circuit put out a notice forbidding theaters to offer more than one imitation of the team per night.

In act 1, the Brothers (except for the totally pantomime Harpo) spoke in rhymed couplets. Zeppo, the first one onstage, introduced himself by chanting:

> My name is Sammy Brown
> And I just came into town
> Saw your ad—you're Mr. Lee?
> Say, you can make a mint on me.

LEE: What do you do—dance, sing?
ZEPPO: I play a role, do anything.
LEE: What do you call your specialty?
ZEPPO: You mean my big sensation? I knock 'em cold when I do
my imitation. . . .

As his brothers went through their own auditions Zeppo attempted to sell Mr. Lee a theater piece he had just written. Act 2 consisted of that piece, enacted by the Marx Brothers and their supporting players. It was set in a hotel lobby, with a balcony overlooking the place—hence the play's title. Although Herman Timberg received sole billing, the lines and interludes were not always his. Harpo tended to place solos and gookies wherever he liked, and Chico and Groucho included parodies of whatever songs were popular at the moment: "Tiptoe through the Tulips" became "Slipshod through the Cowslips"; "I'm a Dreamer, Aren't We All" turned into "I'm a Dreamer, Montreal."

Timberg's sister, who billed herself as Hattie Darling, not only performed in the chorus line, she also served as manager for "On the Mezzanine." Hattie was assigned that double role for good reasons, not all of them nepotistic. She had stage presence, knew how to read a balance sheet as well as a line, and, most important, was the girlfriend of lightweight champion Benny Leonard. The great Jewish boxer liked the Brothers so much he not only put money in the show, he often appeared in it, giving the Marxes boxing lessons with oversize gloves until Zeppo, who knew a thing or two about street fighting, unintentionally bopped the champion too hard. Leonard retaliated by "accidentally" giving Groucho a black eye. Hattie and Leonard eventually broke up, but they both retained their affection for the comedians. In her nineties the veteran chorine could still summon up memories of Chico gambling away his earnings and Groucho resenting his brother's profligacy, the team's nonstop pranks that made her so angry she sought revenge by wiping the floor with Harpo's red wig, and, in the end, the Marxes' generosity once they realized that she was a one-man woman and that none of them had the slightest chance of seducing her: "They took me out for dinner. They took me all over. The best notice I ever received was with the Marx Brothers in 'On the Mezzanine.' They were wonderful to me. And Groucho had a sense of humor I have never seen in anybody else."

Her brother did not grin so widely when he spoke of the Brothers. On a slow day they had secretively passed Timberg the address of a very willing and inventive prostitute. At the appointed hour he knocked on the door of a private house. A large frowning gentleman asked his business. As instructed, Timberg spoke seven words: "I came here to lay the girl." Outraged, the man roared, "Do *what* with my wife?" Terrified, Timberg ran off without so much as a backward glance, as gunfire sounded in the background. The explosions came from lightbulbs dropped on the pavement by the Brothers, and by the actor who took the role of Outraged Husband.

Groucho offered a more amiable humor to the capacity house in a Flushing, New York, theater. The first year of his marriage had not been an easy one. He learned too late that Ruth was what she appeared to be— and very little else. She liked the after-hours life, clubs, parties, celebrities, drinking, chatter. Groucho went for privacy, quietude, the chance to wipe off the greasepaint, read Somerset Maugham, and listen to Gilbert and Sullivan. In a letter to a friend he confided, "You know me well enough by this time to know that I dislike nightlife and clubs, and only go out when there is no way out." What he wanted most was to get "away from the hooey and hoopla that the night club thrives on." With this background, a collision was inevitable. But the couple had actually spent very little time together thus far, and when he addressed the crowd on a hot July night, hope and merriment were in his voice. He spoke in what was to become his trademark style—a statement, followed by a line deflating it. "I have been informed that Ruth, my wife, has made me the father of a six-pound bouncing baby. (*Pause*) When the baby stops bouncing I'll let you know whether it's a boy or a girl."

It was a boy, and the delighted Groucho spent most of the next week shuttling between Ruth and the infant Arthur at Lenox Hill Hospital, and the theater in Queens several miles distant. The bulk of his off-hours were spent in the maternity ward, cracking jokes with the nurses and blowing cigar smoke around the corridors. One evening he completely lost track of time. Dashing into an empty dressing room, Groucho heard the final notes of the overture. The glue for his customary stick-on moustache would take precious minutes to dry. Impulsively he grabbed a stick of greasepaint, smeared a broad black streak on his upper lip, and entered just as the curtain lifted.

The evening went on without incident, the laughter, if anything, more explosive than usual. When Groucho got back to his dressing room, however, he found the theater manager lying in wait. The grease moustache would have to go. The patrons had paid for hair.

Failure to comply, he warned, would mean a report to E. F. Albee, owner of theaters, maker and destroyer of stars, and quite the most powerful name in vaudeville.

The threat left Groucho unmoved. E. F. knew what he could do with the hairy moustache; the greasepaint would stay. Albee heard about the confrontation in Flushing but decided to hold his fire until the insolent, profitable Marx Brothers gave him a reason to discipline them. He did not have long to wait.

•

PROHIBITION CAME IN during the Brothers' return to New York in 1920, and like most adults they patronized a speakeasy now and then. But it was to flout the law rather than to down the booze. None of the Marxes ever cared much for liquor. Chico would rather gamble than drink, any time of the night or day; Harpo could not drink at all because of his kidney trouble; and Groucho had never downed a Scotch until booze became illegal. The same could not be said for his wife. On several occasions Groucho took Ruth along when he did the speakeasy tour. She enjoyed the nights out, and the alcohol even more. Perhaps a little too much. Then again, she had her reasons, for domestically Ruth continually found herself displaced by her husband, who dashed home between performances to bathe Arthur, change his diapers, play with him, excluding Ruth all the while as if he were making up for the years of neglect he had felt in his own childhood.

At the same time Ruth was being forced to the margins of the show. During their dance number together Zeppo would force her backward into uncomfortable contortions, and one memorable evening he lost his grip—or so he claimed—in the middle of a tight whirl. Ruth landed in the orchestra pit, right on top of a kettledrum. Uninjured but mortified, she rushed backstage to Groucho. He was waiting with a wisecrack. "What are you bellyaching about? That's the first time you two ever had a decent finish to your act."

Ruth challenged her husband to do something. The something would have been to fire Zeppo, and to Groucho that was unthinkable. Very well, Ruth told him. If Zep stayed she would go.

Those were the words her husband had been longing to hear. More than once he and the other Brothers observed that wives caused more friction around the theater than they were worth. Betty had already announced plans to quit because of the general family feeling, and Groucho encouraged Ruth to join her. Weighing the odds, Ruth agreed to become a full-time housewife and mother. But she neither forgot nor forgave the events of the night she landed on the kettledrum, and in the absence of support she began to seek solace in the bottle.

During this period the Marxes signed with the William Morris agency. Minnie knew that she had taken the boys as far as she could; they would need big-time representation from now on. All the same, she was not happy about relinquishing power, and fretted about losing them in other ways. Her worries were confirmed when Abe Lastfogel, the Marxes' new agent, brought them their latest *Variety* review. It stated that "On the Mezzanine" "should lift the Marx family right onto Broadway." He thought he had found the route. First, the act would go to England. If the boys clicked in London they could be billed as International Stars. Next stop: the Main Stem. To an invigorated Groucho, the remaining Brothers chose this moment to make a new declaration of independence. All of them agreed that this was one trip Minnie would not make. They needed to go out on their own for a change, to test themselves without Mama. Minnie got wind of their plans and fired off a letter that would have done credit to Napoleon: "I am a maker of men, and everything you are you owe to me." When the *Mauretania* sailed out of New York on June 6, 1922, the manifest listed two baby Marxes, Chico's daughter Maxine and Groucho's son Arthur, plus five of the original Marxes: Leonard, Arthur, Julius, Herbert—and Mrs. Samuel. The maker of men had nurtured her brood in the hick towns of Illinois and Alabama; damned if she would miss their London debut. Along with the family came eight other members of the cast, including Ed Metcalf, the Gilbert and Sullivan enthusiast, and Helen Schroeder, an undersized singer with a squeaky voice. She would soon be better known as Helen Kane, the Boop-boop-a-doop Girl.

En route, the script underwent certain changes. To accommodate British audiences "Balcony" replaced the seldom-used "Mezzanine." The auditioners gave imitations of the Englishman Charlie Chaplin rather than the American team of Gallagher and Shean. Several jokes were

Anglicized, and weakened in the process. The celebrated garbage man exchange, for example, became "The dustman's outside." "Tell him we don't want any—who needs dust?"

Advertised as a "Musical Revuette," "On the Balcony" opened at the Coliseum in St. Martin's Lane on the afternoon of June 19, 1922. Despite a collective show of bravado for the cast, the Brothers were edgy. This was a strange crowd in a strange city; who knew how they would respond to the Marxes' free-for-all style? The answer came at about 2:20 p.m. In the words of Harry Stanley, a British musician, "I was at the first matinee performance and it was disastrous. Most of the audience were balletomanes, and they were there to see a fantastic company of Russian dancers—all-time greats of ballet—zany comedy was hardly their cup of tea. 'On the Balcony' was way over their heads." Moreover, "the audience were not tuned in to the American patter. The Brothers' comedy was unsuited for that type of audience at that period."

What George Bernard Shaw said in jest—that England and America were separated by a common tongue—held true in the early 1920s. Before the advent of sound film, the British music hall and American vaudeville represented entirely different forms of entertainment, with idioms, slang, and gestures peculiar to their country of origin. Reliable old songs, lampoons of regional accents from Scots to Yorkshire and back again, toilet humor, alcoholism, and cross-dressing—these were the ingredients of the music hall, given fresh turns and new interpretations by entertainers of genius like Harry Lauder, who traveled well, and Dan Leno, who did not. American vaudeville was composed of individual talents and a cacophony of musical styles and comic approaches. The mimes and buck dancers had a chance overseas, and so did entertainers with a gimmick, such as W. C. Fields, who mixed juggling with his japes. Those, like Groucho, who spoke urban American with the rapidity of a Gatling gun bewildered the ticket holders. Chico's accent provided no help. Alone, Harpo's silent comedy might have worked; in a quartet, it was drowned out.

Fifteen minutes into act 1, patrons in the balcony gave derisive whistles. As Groucho made his first exit he muttered to no one in particular, "They must know *some* language, but what the hell is it?" Upon his next entrance he tried to slow down his delivery and enunciate each sentence clearly. That seemed to aggravate the situation. Whistling was bad enough; now some of the coarser patrons threw pennies onto the stage as if the Marx Brothers were street buskers. At the time English one-cent pieces were the largest coins in circulation, and they clanged loudly and dangerously onstage. Groucho stopped the action and stepped to the apron of the stage. "Friends," he said mildly, "it's been an expensive trip over. Would you mind throwing a little silver?" That line received the one genuine laugh of the day, but it could not save the situation. Word spread throughout the States when *Variety* headlined a story MARX BROS. NOT SO GOOD. The story began, "Why the Marx Brothers were imported as the Coliseum headliners June 19 is a mystery. We caught the act Friday night, June 23, and their curtain was icey. . . . Rumor has it they are asking $2,000 but they'll never get it."

Frantically, the Brothers shortened the narrative by twelve minutes, Anglicized the gags, and toned down their approach. Nothing seemed to work. After a mirthless, frustrating week they took "On the Balcony" off the boards, replacing it with the surefire "Home Again." The London *Times* took note: "The Four Marx Brothers have a new entertainment at the Coliseum this week which is considerably better than that which they introduced at their first appearance there a week ago." The members of the quartet "so obviously enjoy their own performance that it cannot be long before they persuade their audiences to do the same."

For the third week the company moved to the Alhambra, a smaller London theater, then moved on to Bristol and Manchester. There they received favorable press without igniting the general public. Sandy Powell, a young Yorkshire comedian on the same bill, recorded his memories of "Home Again" many years later. He still smiled at the way Groucho ended every evening by surveying the house and shouting, "Minnie, they've gone, get the supper ready." The truth was, though, that in Manchester the Marxes "did not do very well. The audience simply did not understand their style of humor. I suppose they were really ahead of their time. . . . Of course they were all very worried, and tried to alter the act as the week went on, but they couldn't alter their style."

By this time copies of *Variety* had reached the team, and as the most literate member of the family Groucho was elected to speak for the defense. His letter to the paper read in part: "We opened at the Coliseum, London, in fifth position, and were such a big hit we were switched that night to closing the show, switching positions with the Russian dancers.

"Ardent admirers of the Russian dancers, sometimes known as a claque, took exception to the switching of their favorites, and were responsible for the pennies that were thrown. After they were ejected, the act ran smoothly and we finished to a terrific hail of applause. . . . Why your correspondent here gave such prominence to the penny throwing and none to the reasons thereof, I do not understand." He added with special pique, "Why he quoted our salary at $1,000 a week, when as an actual fact we received 400 pounds a week [then $1,768], is also a mystery to me."

In his haste to repair the Marx Brothers' reputation Groucho omitted a few details. The reason he knew a claque when he heard one is because Frenchy had led so many on his sons' behalf. Hand-clapping did sound at the end of that humiliating evening, but most of those who applauded evidently felt embarrassed rather than amused. Their response was by way of apologizing for the rudeness of their countrymen. No mention was made of the substitution of "Home Again" for "On the Balcony"—a clear indication that all had not gone well for the Marx Brothers. The letter represented Groucho's last attempt to cosmeticize the unhappy trip abroad. All agreed to regard this past summer as no more than a pebble in their shoe; the Marxes would shake it out and move on. The morning of July 29, they boarded the *Cedric* in Liverpool, turned their backs on Britain, and faced home, expecting to resume their profitable careers in New York. Calamity waited for them on the dock.

For the most powerful man in vaudeville was also the most vindictive. In E. F. Albee's view the Marx Brothers had done wrong in England not by failing to please the audience, but by going there in the first place. They had violated their contract with Albee by crossing the Atlantic. His lawyers pointed to the fine print: none who worked for E. F. could accept employment elsewhere without his express written permission—even if he had no work for them in his own circuit.

The Marxes protested that they knew nothing of this arrangement; Albee countered that ignorance of the law was no excuse, and levied a large fine. The Brothers not only refused to pay it, they set fire to his wastebasket. In reply Albee tore up their contract and assured the Marx Brothers that they had meddled with the wrong man. From this point on the team was effectively blocked from performing at any major theater on the Albee Circuit, and therefore condemned to ride on what Fanny Brice called "the death trail." Essentially this meant going on the road the way they did in the old days, carrying their show from small town to small town, subject once again to roadhouse food, shoddy accommodations, autocratic managers, and all the other small-time evils they had left behind them years before.

But the Brothers thought they saw a way out of their fix. A rival syndicate had just set up operations. Headed by Lee Shubert, it was challenging Albee's virtual monopoly on talent and theaters. The Marxes looked upon the Shubert Advanced Vaudeville Circuit as the equivalent of a deus ex machina, rescuing them just before the villain foreclosed on the mortgage. Not only would they perform at their old salaries, they could blithely thumb their noses at old E. F. What they could not know was that Shubert planned to run his syndicate just long enough to threaten the Albee operation—at which time he expected E. F. to buy him out at a huge profit. To that end Shubert was willing to run his vaudeville shows at a loss, intending to cover debts in the near future. But as he overextended himself, no call came from Albee. Rumors circulated wherever showfolk met: Lee was in financial straits; Lee was cutting back; Lee was about to fold his circuit. The Shubert office got wind of the gossip and issued statements assuring everyone of its solvency and willingness to stay the course.

The Marxes had no choice but to push on, appearing in *The Twentieth-Century Revue,* a show that had trouble paying its performers. Along with another headline act, Kranz and White, the Marx Brothers took over the show, bankrolling part of it with funds from the Betty Amusement Company, named after Chico's wife. When funds grew short they found a new investor, Charles Moy, a Chinese restaurateur, who invested $10,000. But they never had a chance to regain their momentum. In the late spring of 1923, less than a year after it had begun with so much fanfare and optimism, the Schubert Advanced Vaudeville Circuit suddenly went out of business. *Variety* read the funeral oration in an acrimonious Open Letter: "They are asking us, Lee, where Shubert Vaudeville is, and Lee, we don't know. . . . You said there would be Shubert vaudeville while you had a dollar left. It's a horrible thought, Lee, that you might be broke, but don't you remember, Lee, you have your word of honor on it. So you either haven't any money or any honor left. . . ." Many of the acts could crawl back under the Albee marquee, if they showed sufficient contrition. The blacklisted Marxes were not among that number. Moy forfeited his investment and the Brothers lost their places. They let it be known among the bookers that they would work for anyone, anywhere. The asking price: $400 per week, a sum more appropriate for entry-level acrobats. And still they had no takers worth the name.

Months of idleness went by. Groucho, yet again, talked of getting out of the business altogether, and this time his brothers could not summon up the energy to disagree—except for Chico. "Despair" was not in his lexicon, and wherever he went—bookers' offices, poker games, parties, street corners—he continued to talk up the Marx Brothers as the best out-of-work act in New York. Somehow, he kept saying, somewhere, some way, he and his brothers would get back on track. In later years Chico took to embroidering the next event, but it seems likely to have occurred on an ordinary summer day as he strolled before the Palace Theatre. An old acquaintance happened by and watched Chico looking wistfully at the scene of his past triumphs.

Will Johnstone asked what he was doing.

Nothing, replied Chico truthfully, and that was the trouble.

Johnstone, newspaper cartoonist and aspiring comedy writer, pressed him for details. Chico recited the descent of the Marx Brothers from the London flop to their present state of near bankruptcy. Johnstone stood openmouthed as the litany went on. Why, at this very theater he had seen the Brothers bring down the house night after night. There was no way their kind of talent would remain idle—not if he had anything to do with it. Ten minutes later Johnstone and Chico stood in the office of Joseph M. Gaites. Many an actor said the M stood for "Minimum," because that was all the shoestring producer ever paid them. Gaites's most recent failures, *Love for Sale* and *Gimme a Thrill*, had featured librettos by Johnstone and music by his brother Tom. Both shows had shuttered rapidly at the Walnut Street Theatre in Philadelphia, and the elaborate scenery (recycled from previous flops) remained there gathering dust. Johnstone suggested a new musical built around the Marx Brothers and the leftover furniture—written, of course, by himself and his brother.

Gaites knew about the Marxes' track record at the Palace—and nothing about their current straits. He found the idea of a show built around the quartet so compelling he made ready to sit down and negotiate then and there. But Gaites caught himself in mid-assent, unwilling to make the first move. Suppose he were to insult the headliners with too low an offer? And yet so little money remained in his bank account. Meanwhile, Chico feared that asking too large a sum might frighten away this last chance at a comeback. In the suffocating silence he heard himself blurt, "We don't want any salary. Just give us ten percent of the gross." The two men shook hands, Johnstone went off to collaborate on the new show with his brother, and Chico went off to discuss the new show with *his* brothers.

When Groucho heard the conditions he exploded. Here was the latest of his brother's gambles: no salary, no written guarantees, just a promise of 10 percent of maybe, and there were probably conditions that hadn't been mentioned. Well, Chico admitted, there was one. The Walnut Street Theatre had recently been purchased by Joseph Beury, a prosperous family man and owner of several coal mines. Beury would be happy, nay, flattered to have the Marx Brothers in his theater. He would back his words with the long green, investing heavily in the show. There was just one thing. He had a friend, a young woman who danced and sang professionally. Now, if a place could be found for her in the chorus. . . . This was hardly a unique situation; it happened just about every time a musical went into rehearsal. With minimal changes in choreography, a place could always be found for a modestly gifted young lady with good connections. But the Brothers lived by their unwritten motto—Why have it simple when you can have it complicated?—and the Beury situation presented a delicate problem in diplomacy. For while the infatuated coal man had been carrying on with the actress she had been two-timing him with a New York entertainer, a fellow with a peculiar stage name. They called him Harpo.

CHAPTER FOUR

Charged with Electricity

LIKE THE THREADBARE SCENERY, the title for the Johnstones' show derived from their two previous musicals, *Love for Sale* and *Gimme a Thrill*. They called the new grab bag *The Thrill Girl*. When that failed to strike sparks they tried something more current: *I'll Say She Is!* (appropriating the last half of a popular expression, "Isn't she a beauty?"). Chico, Harpo, and Zeppo warmed to the title and the plot, which centered on an ingenue in search of amorous attention and exotic experience. But the cocksure Groucho vied with the insecure Julius. It was one thing, he told his brothers, to crack the big time in vaudeville. Going legit was another matter entirely. "A theater audience demands class," he reminded them, "and that's something we haven't got." It would have been handy to have Minnie here, to intervene and resolve the conflict. But she was no longer around. Her sons had pushed her into a restive retirement with Frenchy, and she was no longer privy to backstage negotiations. For more than a year the Brothers had been happy on their own, allowing her to bask in their increasing fame. After all, they reasoned uncomfortably, she had overstayed her welcome, playing Mama long after most mothers would have been happy to see their children out of the nest and on their own. How could they ever rise to man's estate if they remained tied to her whims and obedient to her blueprints? But today the troubled group missed her indomitable drive, her ability to pump them up, to coach them to the next goal. And at this juncture the legend of Minnie was born, out of the Marx Brothers' need for autonomy coupled with their feelings of guilt. They started to sentimentalize her in an exaggerated manner. Their attitude was very much in the style of 1920s show business. Mothers were still objects of worship and surefire box office. Entertainers frequently gave interviews praising the mothers they had discarded on the way to the top. Singers donned blackface and changed a single vowel, allowing them to gush about Mommy in the name of Mammy. Even so ruthless a producer as Louis B. Mayer refused to allow any denigration of mother-hood at MGM, and he once sounded off about those who portrayed mothers as anything but saints. Referring to the products of another studio, he griped sarcastically, "Throw the mother's good, homemade chicken soup in the mother's face! *Step* on the mother! *Kick* her! That is *art,* they say! Art!" In the Brothers' eyes Minnie was no longer a controlling stage mother; today she was a woman who had taken her streetwise, world-dumb sons and made them into a four-pointed star. They felt sure that Minnie would have known what to do about vaudeville and the theater; she would have rallied them, harangued the managers, and then taken hold of circumstances and turned them her way. But she was out of the picture, elbowed to the margins of their professional lives. At this juncture Chico was all that stood between the Marxes and the kind of irresolution that guarantees failure.

The eldest Marx Brother took over Minnie's part, arguing for a Broadway debut. If Ed Wynn, Willie Howard, Eddie Cantor, Al Jolson could make the jump from vaudeville to the legitimate stage, why not the Brothers? To him they were "the same audiences we've been killing for years in big-time vaudeville. The only difference is, when they go to a legitimate show they put on their best clothes and arrive late." Speaking with the confidence of a crapshooter on a roll, Chico convinced Zeppo to go along. Then Harpo fell in. It took days of threats and cajoling before Groucho allowed himself to be persuaded. Once he was safely aboard, the problem of Ginny, Beury's girlfriend, had to be faced. Not only was she entangled with Harpo, but, as Groucho put it, the chorine "danced as though she had borrowed her legs from her grandfather."

The Brothers tried a three-step approach. They encouraged Beury to open the show at the Lyric Theatre in his hometown of Allentown, Pennsylvania, far from the major critics. At the same time Harpo agreed to withdraw his amorous advances, suggesting to Ginny that it was inappropriate to carry on in the middle of intense rehearsals. Finally, somebody slipped the problem a Mickey Finn on opening night, and she failed to make the curtain. Local papers praised the show, and on the second night the Marx Brothers allowed Ginny to go on. It was a mistake. "Although we were considered pretty good comedians," Groucho acknowledged, "we couldn't compete with her. Her dance got more laughs than any sketch in the show. She had absolutely no sense of rhythm. She was always either one step ahead or one step behind the other girls. Actually she wasn't a bad kid and we felt sorry for her, but every time she danced we lost ten yards. Columnists began to write gags about her." In the next few weeks their dilemma grew acute. *I'll Say She Is!* overran its budget by 40 percent. To keep the musical running, the Brothers had to ask Beury to supply an additional $10,000—something he would only do if the object of his affections kept her job.

Any number of illegal scenarios suggested themselves, including kidnapping. But before the details could be worked out, sex, which had been responsible for so much mischief, provided an unforeseen ending. Several weeks into rehearsal Ginny developed a monumental crush on one of the chorus boys. One night when the producer entered her dressing room she impulsively declared that she no longer loved him—that, in fact, she had been using him as a stepping-stone to advance her career. The results were gratifyingly explosive. The aggrieved Beury let it be known that unless his former girlfriend left the chorus he would *withhold* the necessary $10,000. Assuming long faces, the Brothers broke the news to Ginny. She took it with blithe unconcern. There were plenty of other jobs on Broadway. That there were, but not the kind she expected. Some time later, Ginny waited on Groucho at a short-order restaurant. Embarrassed and grateful, he overtipped her.

The road to New York began in Philadelphia, where Groucho and Tom and Will Johnstone reworked the book. *I'll Say She Is!* had never been long on coherence; by the time they got through with it, the show was completely schizoid. One part concerned the longings of an ingenue in search of romance. The other was a revue, allowing the Brothers to display their wares: Groucho as the nonstop talker, Harpo as the wild mime, Chico as the immigrant/pianist/clown, and Zeppo as the juvenile and straight man. The "she" of *I'll Say She Is!* opened the show by auditioning candidates for her love. Among the applicants were the Brothers, restating the old Gallagher and Shean imitations of "On the Mezzanine." During act 1, these players turned up in a series of related blackouts, playlets, and dances, ranging from serious ballets to an interlude in a Chinese opium den to a courtroom scene with Groucho as the District Attorney ("You are charged with murder, and if you are convicted you will be charged with electricity"). The black-robed judge in this case was Harpo, whose large sleeves allowed him to perform the knife-dropping routine with clamorous effect. Other sight gags followed; in one, Harpo was seen pulling a rope across the rear of the stage. At the other end of the rope was . . . Harpo, an illusion brought off with the use of a double.

In act 2, the heroine fell into the hands of a hypnotist. He projected her back to the court of Napoleon, with Groucho as the Emperor, dressed in a uniform whose epaulets were rigged to rise and fall in rhythm with his eyebrows. This extended sketch, overloaded with harp and piano solos, pratfalls and puns ("Beyond the Alps lies more Alps and the Lord 'alps those who 'alp themselves"), seized the popular fancy. As Groucho noted, "The girls, like all chorus girls, looked pretty good. The rest of the cast was strictly amateur night in Dixie. What we *did* have, however, was something money couldn't buy. We had fifteen years of sure-fire comedy material, tried-and-true scenes that had been certified by vaudeville audiences from coast to coast."

Word of mouth kept the musical running all summer long, even though Philadelphia sweltered through repeated heat waves. At one point, the parsimonious Groucho felt flush enough to buy a new Studebaker. He had been persuaded by a salesman who spoke with an odd accent, calling the vehicle a Stoo-duh-bay-kaire and reminding his sentimental customer of Frenchy. Between acts Groucho took his shiny new purchase out for a spin. Traffic became snarled, and suddenly it was time for act 2. Groucho leaped from the car with a policeman in hot pursuit. The two men met at the stage door, the cop in uniform, Groucho in his Napoleon outfit. "I'm an actor," he pleaded. "That doesn't give you the freedom to leave your car deserted on the street," the cop replied. Groucho avoided a ticket by giving his doubtful listener two free passes for the evening show. "He came backstage to look me up," Groucho informed his brothers. "And you know what? He still didn't believe I was an actor." Meantime the car had been lifted by thieves who took it for a monthlong joyride.

•

FOR MORE THAN four decades the Napoleon scene from *I'll Say She Is!* was thought to be lost, only to turn up in one of Groucho's overcrowded desk drawers. He included its text in *The Groucho Phile,* a 1977 omnium-gatherum of memories and photographs. Shorn of physical business and outlandish costumes, "Napoleon's First Waterloo" can provide only hints of the comedy. Still, several exchanges indicate the Marxes' emerging style of non sequiturs and irrepressible farce.

For example: Two-timed by the lecherous Gaston (Harpo), François (Chico), and Alphonse (Zeppo), Napoleon grills the Empress, praising her eyes that "shine like the pants of a blue serge suit," then turning on Josephine because he suspects she is "as true as a three-dollar cornet."

NAPOLEON: My Queen . . . when I look into your big blue eyes, I know that you are true to the Army. I only hope it remains a standing Army. Fortunately France has no Navy, but then every man has qualms, even if they are only steamed qualms. Even an Emperor. (*Business with hat*) Where are my rubbers?

EMPRESS: Here they are. (*Harpo puts feet out from under EMPRESS's dress*)

NAPOLEON: Are those your feet? Maybe you better go to war and I'll stay here. You're getting an awful pair of gondolas, Josephine. They must have crossed you with an elephant. . . . Who's been here?

EMPRESS: I have.

NAPOLEON: Alone?

EMPRESS: Alone.

NAPOLEON: Remember, you can feel some of the people all of the time, and some of the people all of the time, all of the—oh, the hell with that. I just made that up. Lincoln copped it from me. . . . Someone has been here. I'm going to investigate. (*NAPOLEON throws snuff*)

EMPRESS: I love but you. (*Business of sneezing by the hidden GASTON, FRANÇOIS, and ALPHONSE*)

NAPOLEON: They say a man's home is his castle. Mine must be the Pennsylvania Station. Come out, come out, wherever you are.

EMPRESS: Napoleon, no one has been here.

NAPOLEON: Why, if I thought there was I'd—(*More sneezing*) What was that—static?

EMPRESS: No, my hay fever. (*More sneezing*)

NAPOLEON: How many statics have you got? Officer of the Guard, remove the swine. (*Business of soldiers pulling Groucho*) Hey! You've got the wrong swine!

Up to now, the Brothers had been keeping pace with the tempo and tone of show business. They were as funny as anyone in vaudeville, but they broke no new ground—indeed, much of their material reached back to the conventions of nineteenth-century entertainment. For all its odd appearance, the Marx Brothers' variety act was actually a conservative mix of the verbal and the physical, hanging new jokes on time-honored structures like the school act. But as they headed to Broadway with *I'll*

Say She Is! they suddenly edged ahead of their colleagues. They could not have chosen a more propitious moment.

In the early 1920s New York played host to new and radical notions. One was that government was the biggest joke of all. The criticism of authority picked up speed when Warren Harding, whose administration had been disfigured by corruption, suddenly died in office. (Groucho was chosen to make the announcement on the evening of August 2, 1923, and he would well remember the audible gasps in the audience.) Harding was replaced by Calvin Coolidge, a closemouthed mediocrity ("I have never been hurt by what I didn't say"), and comedians raced each other for the honor of making the most impudent statements about Washington in particular, and the country in general. H. L. Mencken led the pack. Humorist, journalist, critic, and lexicographer, he delighted in the grotesque, and affected to see it everywhere. To his eye the entire United States was a vast and incomparable circus, containing "ribald combats of demagogues, the exquisitely ingenious operations of master rogues, the pursuits of witches and heretics, the desperate struggles of inferior men to claw their way into Heaven." Nor was the public immune from his scouring. The press, obsessed as always with the violent and the trivial; the clergy; the military; the ordinary citizenry—all were paid-up members in the "booboisie," at once witnesses and collaborators in the great American freak show. The bluenoses officially frowned upon extramarital dalliance; they also forbade liquor—and what of that? To the fast crowd, and those who aspired to join it, the speakeasy was invented to flout the rule makers. So was the next stop after the drinks: the bedroom. The names Sigmund Freud and Havelock Ellis figured in everyday conversation. Sexual iconography appeared on the aggressive canvases and constructions of surrealists, in whose eyes the aesthetically pleasing was no longer paramount in art; "primitive" objects seemed closer to the soul than the refined products on exhibit in the uptown galleries. The mask was becoming more important than the face, the gargoyle more significant than the building.

On their best nights, the Brothers seemed to be swept up in this modern gust. Their defiance of logic and authority, coupled with outlandish costumes and a unique combination of Gatling-gun delivery and mime, seemed to fuse commedia dell'arte and the new American style. On lesser occasions, and there were many, they were just another disorderly team, harassing women and policemen. This was something Mack Sennett's silent clowns did better as a matter of course. Philadelphians saw the high Marx Brothers and thought them comic artists of high degree.

When *I'll Say She Is!* moved north in late summer, Bostonians caught the low Marx Brothers and judged the show second-rate. By now, however, the Marxes were used to reverses and simply moved on, vaudeville-style, doctoring lines and timing as they went. Following a week in Detroit the show entered the friendly and familiar confines of Chicago, and there they stayed for ten weeks. During that time the Brothers met Ben Hecht, a journalist who was soon to become Hollywood's highest-paid screenwriter. In one of his memoirs Hecht recalls that particular summer of card playing and pub-crawling, haunted "by a perpetual Halloween called the Marx Brothers." The encounter was one of very few highlights on a journey that took the Marx Brothers from Chicago to St. Louis, Kansas City, Cincinnati, Cleveland, Buffalo, Baltimore, and Washington, D.C. Harpo recalled: "The road was the road, grueling and tiresome. A hotel was a hotel and a train was a train. When you've been in one you've been in them all, and we had been in them all for fourteen years too many." Tempers frayed, wallets strained, the Brothers announced their intentions to quit. Whether this was just a feint or the real thing, Gaites, Breury & Co. were not willing to take any chances. They had been making handsome profits from *I'll Say She Is!* and raised the team's salary. The concession kept all four Marxes quiet—but only for a few months. Eventually the show returned to the Walnut Street Theatre in Philadelphia, and there the Marxes reached another impasse. Informed that they were still in need of more polishing and revising, and, worst of all, more time on the road, the Brothers walked out.

The management capitulated a little too readily. A week later they leased the Casino, advertising the opening night as March 19, 1924. Harpo predicted that the show would open at the Casino on Thirty-ninth Street, promptly get savaged by the critics—*I'll Say She Is!* was not up to Broadway standards—and then go back on tour. The management evidently felt the same way; cast members were warned not to put their trunks in storage. Still, the producers took Broadway seriously enough to replace the ingenue, Muriel Hudson, with a beautiful, appropriately eccentric actress, Lotta Miles. Her stage name was a nod to the Kelly Tire Company, which had used her in a long-running ad campaign.

Throughout all the rehearsal days, the Brothers kept a standard routine. Groucho would spend his off-hours playing with his son Arthur, indulging the three-year-old's every whim. Ruth believed in corporal punishment; Groucho forbade it, and always met examples of misbehavior with a gag. One afternoon, after Ruth had carefully dressed her son in an immaculate sailor suit, the family went for a walk. Ignoring Groucho's advice to stay away from half-frozen mud puddles, Arthur walked over one and fell down and through the ice. He was uninjured but filthy. "My sailor suit and face were the color of chocolate," the son recalled decades afterward, "when I sheepishly presented myself to my father on the sidewalk. I expected him to be angry, but instead he doubled over, laughing. When his laughter subsided, all he said was, 'I never thought the day would come when a son of mine would be imitating Jolson.' " Similarly, when the family went out to a restaurant, the child occupied himself between courses by mopping up the floor with a piece of toast. Before his parents could stop him, Arthur threw the toast over his shoulder. It landed on a dowager's plate of ham and eggs. Ruth prevailed on Groucho to apologize. He rose, bowed deeply to the offended party, and promised that if his son ever threw a piece of toast at her again, he would make sure it contained a generous portion of strawberry jam.

The day of the opening was no different; Groucho tried to keep his nerves quiet by indulging Arthur at home. Chico went off to gamble, Zeppo to work out and limber up, Harpo to dine out at a celebrated show business hangout, Lindy's restaurant. Rather than suffering from the jitters, Harpo found himself depressed. "It was sad," he reflected, "to think that a month from now I'd be in Albany or Columbus or Baltimore." But at least for that month he would move back to his parents' place. It would be like the old days, with certain changes. There would be no threats of "Greenbaum" from the wings, no insistence on Minnie's playing a part. She and Frenchy had leased a house on Long Island. There, as if to show her brood that she had better things to do with her time than manage the Marx Brothers, she had turned her attention to a new arena, the distribution of soft drinks. Harpo mulled the happy possibilities of dining on Frenchy's cooking for breakfast and dinner. Afternoons he would spend shuttling between Lindy's and Ruben's, "back with my own people, who spoke my own language, with my accent—cardplayers, horseplayers, bookies, song pluggers, agents, actors out of work and actors playing the Palace, Al Jolson with his mob of fans, and Arnold Rothstein with his mob of runners and flunkies."

The clock reminded Harpo it was time to get into costume. He rose with no enthusiasm and instructed his tablemates to save a seat. As he approached the Casino he saw marquee lights aglow, advertising THE FOUR MARX BROTHERS IN I'LL SAY SHE IS! He was unimpressed. Those lightbulbs would soon be extinguished.

The season of 1923–1924 featured some impressive Broadway productions. Those who wished to see serious drama could buy tickets to

Eugene O'Neill's epic tragedy of avarice and incest, *Desire under the Elms;* and Maxwell Anderson and Laurence Stallings's bitter tale of the Great War, *What Price Glory?* But for the most part, this season ushered in what John Updike labeled the "lighthearted era" in which a great premium was placed on cleverness. A vigorous young team, George and Ira Gershwin, composed the score for *Lady, Be Good!* and audiences went out of the theater singing the title song as well as "Fascinating Rhythm," a number introduced by another new team, Fred and Adele Astaire. Gertrude Lawrence and Beatrice Lillie made their American debuts in *Andre Charlot's Revue.* The operetta, still a viable art form, was represented by Sigmund Romberg's *The Student Prince* and Rudolf Friml's *Rose-Marie.* Straight comedies included George Kelly's *The Show Off,* and *Beggar on Horseback,* written by Marc Connelly and George S. Kaufman, a drama critic for the *New York Times.*

So the Marxes would be in good company—perhaps too good. The Shuberts, owners of the Casino, did what they could for the Brothers. On the night of March 19, two shows were scheduled to open, *I'll Say She Is!* and *Innocent Eyes,* starring Mistinguette, a legendary French chanteuse whose career dated back to the days of Toulouse-Lautrec. Her venue was the Winter Garden, another Shubert theater. She needed no introduction and no newspaper or magazine reviews; loyalists would follow her anywhere. The Shuberts persuaded the singer that one opening night was like another, and put her first show off by twenty-four hours. First-string critics were now free to attend *I'll Say She Is!* They would be treated to a show before the show. Minnie had commissioned her dressmaker to create a new outfit for the occasion. Many things scattered her attention on the afternoon of her visit, and when she stood on a chair so that the seamstress could mark the hem, she lost her footing, fell, and fractured her leg. Other women might have been desolated by such an occurrence; to the mother of the Marx Brothers it simply provided a new opportunity for attention. Doing his part to resurrect Saint Minnie, Groucho later wrote, "I doubt if anyone ever entered the theater more triumphantly than she did. Smiling and waving gaily to the audience, she was carried in on a stretcher and deposited in a front row box seat. This was her personal victory. This was the culmination of twenty years of scheming, starving, cajoling and scrambling. . . . Never in the history of the theater had four brothers appeared on Broadway as the stars of their own show, and a little thing like a broken leg was not going to rob her of that supreme moment."

Minnie was in for a few surprises. After touring vaudeville under their sobriquets, the boys were listed in the program under the names she had given them, Leonard, Arthur, Julius, and Herbert; after all, this was Broadway. In the show, rather than auditioning as Gallagher and Shean in the opening scene, the Brothers imitated Joe Frisco, an established song-and-dance man. Their humor and timing was essentially the same, however, and the audience responded vigorously. A few moments later Groucho informed his straight man, "I played a part in *Ben-Hur* once." He replied, "What part did you play, sir?" Groucho's answer: "A girl. She played Ben, and I played her." The line got a surprisingly big laugh, and from that point on the mirth built to a series of crescendos. By the time the Brothers reached the end of the Napoleon sketch the audience was limp with laughter, and at the curtain calls Groucho conceded that *I'll Say She Is!* just might have a chance to run for a month, even if the critics panned it—as they were sure to do.

Harpo was so certain of negative reviews that he went straight to Great Neck and piled into bed. He was alone in the house; Minnie and Frenchy had booked a hotel room in Manhattan. At 8 a.m. the telephone rang. Groucho impatiently yelled, "Hey Harp, wake up! Have you read the reviews?"

"What reviews? *Variety* doesn't come out until tomorrow."

"No, the *newspaper* critics. The *Sun*, the *Times*, the *Trib*, the *World*—the big critics."

"They liked us?"

"They *loved* us. We're a hit. Listen—"

But the unworldly Harpo was unwilling to let his brother go on. He read nothing but a few columnists and the show business publications. Newspapers meant nothing to him. Groucho overrode his brother's objections and quoted Alexander Woollcott in the *Sun*:

"As one of the many who laughed immoderately throughout the greater part of the first New York performance given by a new musical show, entitled, if memory serves, *I'll Say She Is!*, it behooves your correspondent to report at once that that harlequinade has some of the most comical moments vouchsafed to the first-nighter in a month of Mondays. It is a bright-colored and vehement setting for the goings on of those talented cutups, the Four Marx Brothers. In particular, it is a splendacious and reasonably tuneful excuse for going to see that silent brother, that sly, unexpected, magnificent comic among the Marxes. . . . Surely there should be dancing in the streets when a great clown comes to town, and this man is a great clown." Woollcott, incorrectly assuming that Groucho was the oldest of the group, found him "a crafty comedian with a rather fresher and more whimsical group of quips than is the lot of most refugees from vaudeville."

Woollcott's rave was followed by others less self-conscious and fussy. An unsigned review in the *Times* called the Marxes "gorgeous clowns and uproariously funny," with Julius Marx wisely entrusted with the main witticisms. The *Herald Tribune* critic, Percy Hammond, was known as a hard sell. Newspapermen loved to tell about the day Hammond's editors turned him down as a candidate for battlefield correspondent in 1917. "We can't do it in good conscience," one of them was supposed to have said. "What if Percy doesn't like the war?" Moreover, the *Trib* critic had seen— and put down—the Marxes in their Chicago days. This time he thought the Brothers "a comic carnival" and Julius in particular "a nifty composition of all the humorous clowns." Hammond's most discerning line pointed out that "it is not so much what Julius says as how he says it." Endorsement followed endorsement, and superlatives decorated every column. All these were quoted in a large ad for the show. The final endorsement was from their old friend Charlie Chaplin, who had yet to attend a performance: "The Best Musical Comedy Revue I've Ever Seen." Chico's gamble had paid off, big time.

Nothing changed for Chico: he went on gambling and wenching as before. But for Harpo, a whole new life began. Several nights after the smash debut, a knock sounded at his dressing room door. It swung open to reveal a man who resembled a moustachioed owl dressed in an opera cape and slouch hat. "You're the funniest man I have ever seen upon the stage," Alexander Woollcott told him. After a shower of compliments the critic made ready to exit, extending his hand. Harpo offered a leg instead, "the old switch gag I had used since *On the Mezzanine*." Woollcott pushed the limb away in disgust. "Kindly confine your baboonery to the stage. Off it, you are a most unfunny fellow." That exit line marked the beginning of a long and peculiar friendship.

Harpo was taken up not only by Woollcott but by the columnist's associates at the Round Table, an informal group that met for lunch at the Algonquin Hotel. Here ambitious artists, actors, and journalists vied to deliver the most quotable aside and the bitchiest remark. Harpo could hardly compete with the likes of Robert Benchley, Dorothy Parker, George S. Kaufman, Marc Connelly, or Franklin P. Adams, whose *New York World* column, "The Conning Tower," printed doggerel from various contributors—including, eventually, a quatrain or two from one Julius H.

Marx. Nevertheless, the circle accepted Harpo because he related hilarious tales of vaudeville, and because he was an exotic—a semiliterate mime who posed no threat to their verbal competitions, and who laughed generously at their jibes.

When it became obvious that *I'll Say She Is!* was going to be a popular as well as critical smash, Chico entered what his brothers called "Pinochle Paradise" and Groucho moved into a spacious apartment on Riverside Drive and 161st Street. The Brothers agreed to send their parents a generous stipend every month, and Minnie and Frenchy were only too glad to accept. They bought a house in Great Neck, where Minnie founded a ladies' poker club. Now and then she came to the City to see her boys cavort onstage, or to attend a dinner in their honor. At one of these affairs she sat next to Woollcott, who fortified himself with liquor, expecting braggadocio. To his astonishment she made no mention of Groucho, Harpo, Chico, or Zeppo, concentrating instead on plans for her new business. Enchanted, Woollcott saw to it that *Vanity Fair* nominated Minnie for its Hall of Fame—"Because," the magazine said, "as the daughter of a German magician, she felt inner promptings which bade her snatch her five sons from their boyhood occupations (bellhops and the like) and drive them onto the stage. She was not content until the Marx Brothers shone in electric lights on Broadway. Then, feeling suddenly idle, she went into the ginger ale business."

For his part, Frenchy began to sport the kind of elegant made-to-measure clothes he had always dreamed of creating back in Chicago. It hardly mattered that he frequently wore mismatched socks, or that his natty clothes were spotted with food stains. He had always aspired to be a dandy in the European style, and now he enjoyed the stares when he went on long walks with Minnie. After many shopping sprees to distant emporiums the senior Marxes finally tired of their promenades, bought a new Chevrolet, and hired a chauffeur to drive them around. For Frenchy, however, the new lifestyle did nothing to alter his Marxian eccentricities.

The very first day the chauffeur reported for duty, Frenchy asked to be taken to a local grocery store. He emerged with many paper bags, climbed into the car, made two more stops, and ordered the driver to take him home. The driver sat behind the wheel until he was asked to help take in the packages. He was asked if he wanted lunch. The offer was refused. Well then, Frenchy suggested, perhaps he could go outside and clean the car.

"Look, Mac," came the reply. "I don't want no lunch and I'll clean my car when I damn well feel like it. All I want is my money."

Frenchy summoned Minnie. She would know how to negotiate with this tough bird. That she did. The man in the kitchen, she discovered, was not the chauffeur. When Frenchy had stepped from the grocery he had entered the wrong Chevrolet operated by the wrong driver. He had taken a taxi.

Frenchy's progress was not all downhill; he enjoyed some memorable triumphs during this period. At an intermission of *I'll Say She Is!* he listened to a couple arguing about his sons. The husband insisted that the stars had no blood relationship. They were fakes, he confided knowledgeably; it was all a publicity gimmick. Consulting the program, the wife argued that the Marxes really were brothers. Frenchy insinuated himself into the conversation. He insisted that the performers were related.

The man looked down with an amused sneer. Here was a chance to fleece a greenhorn. Did the little man with the funny accent care to make a wager about the so-called Marx Brothers?

Frenchy made a show of irresolution. At last he spoke: "Vot odds vill you giff me?"

•

DURING THE LONG RUN of *I'll Say She Is!* Alexander Woollcott asked Harpo why the Marxes were billed by their real names. Because, came the reply, even though Chico, Groucho, et al. called themselves by their sobriquets, the *os* would look "undignified" in print. Woollcott stiffened. "Dignified? You?" The Brothers thought it over. Marquees and playbills would never again carry the names of Leonard, Arthur, Julius, and Herbert.

Settled in for a long run, the Brothers seldom socialized with one another. When they did, they seemed to act out Woollcott's derisive remark. They gave waiters impossible orders, made faces at wealthy clubmen peering out from their Fifth Avenue windows, horsed around on the street, gave policemen a hard time before identifying themselves. When Gummo left box making to go into the dress business they stopped by to try on the merchandise and chased customers out of the showroom. At the theater they ad-libbed different lines almost every night, driving their understudies to distraction. But there was nothing to worry about; in 304 performances, not one person missed a show. After *I'll Say She Is!* closed in June 1925, the show went on a highly profitable tour, with the brothers traveling first class. The itinerary covered Boston, Hartford, Chicago, and Detroit. In the last city, for the first time someone in the cast missed a performance. It was Chico. He had exited in the Napoleon scene, complaining of an unspecified illness—and vanished. Harpo was of course speechless in the show, and Zeppo played the juvenile. That left Groucho to fill in as best he could, often feeding himself Chico's straight lines. Resentments dating back to early childhood now detonated. Groucho could hardly wait to get his hands on the absentee. The assumption was that Chico had found a new girl. But when he failed to appear the next morning, derision turned to concern, especially when Betty informed Groucho that her husband had run up a large debt to Nick the Greek, a New York bookie. She was certain that the mob was after Chico, and that they might possibly have caught up with him. Maxine, Chico's daughter, remembered that "the whole show broke down: the chorus girls were crying and the remaining brothers could only nervously wait for Chico's death to be announced over the wires." By now Betty Marx was frantic, but Groucho made no attempt to reassure her; nor did any of his brothers. Several days later Chico suddenly surfaced and rejoined the company without a word of explanation. Groucho never quite forgave him and wondered how anyone else could. Especially Chico's emotionally battered wife.

Still, Betty ignored Chico's foibles or pretended not to see them, and their marriage continued. Groucho loathed his brother's unreliability, and their relationship continued as well. He had no choice in the matter; the Marx Brothers were not four soloists, they were an act. Dismissing Chico would be like removing a leg. Still, no one had much appetite for more performances, and the troupe broke up after the incident. The Brothers scattered to various destinations. Harpo journeyed out to Hollywood to play a part in a silent film, *Too Many Kisses,* starring Richard Dix. His work was not particularly distinctive, and no other job offers came his way, so he returned to New York and his new pals at the Algonquin Round Table. Chico went on roistering, although for the time being he took fewer chances with shady characters. "My brother," Groucho dryly observed, "stopped going to poolrooms and started to patronize the more prosperous race tracks. When he got through with them they were even more prosperous." Zeppo bought a forty-foot cabin cruiser and raced it up and down Long Island Sound. Groucho invested in twenty-four beach bungalows in Far Rockaway and became an absentee landlord. He had saved an extraordinary sum from his $1,000-a-week salary, and now concentrated on acquiring more. This meant putting every possible dollar into investments and cutting back at home. Although Ruth basked in her husband's fame, she shared little of his fortune. Her expressions of jealousy only served to get Groucho's back up. Ruth would covetously mention items like Betty's new mink coat or diamond ring, and Groucho would loudly wish for a wife who was thrifty and envy-free.

Once the Marx Brothers' energy came from Minnie's drive and their own memories of deprivation. Now it derived from the collision of public personae and private selves. Onstage, Harpo was a naïf, a faun in a rain-coat. In real life he was an intimate of the most sophisticated group in New York. Chico portrayed himself as a bumbling Italian who could barely count on his fingers. When he was not at the track, he played bridge with masters—and acquitted himself with honor. Zeppo, always cast as the juvenile, was a weight lifter and a great teller of jokes. But the contrast was most vivid in the personalities of Groucho. On one hand he acted the dissenter, mocking the vagaries and excesses of Wall Street; on the other hand he haunted his broker's office, anxious to assure material success.

Groucho also yearned for the company of intellectuals and writers, and he did his best to search them out. With his new fame, he found easy access to the newspaper columns. A quatrain made it into "The Conning Tower."

> My wife takes the breast of the chicken;
> The leg is for Junior, she sings.
> But listen: I feel just like Eugene O'Neill—
> All God's chicken has nothing but wings.

Encouraged to contribute more pieces, he mocked his own accent in a new piece of doggerel:

> For twenty-five cents in old Boston Town,
> One can purchase baked beans that are done nice and brown,
> Or a New England Dinner that's beautifully boiled,
> Or five copies of The New York Morning Woild.

Once he had seen his name in print there was no stopping him. A more literary humorist, James Thurber, observed that "when The New Yorker was six weeks old, in 1925, it printed the first of four casuals that year, signed Julius H. Marx." Later, the magazine's editor and founder, Harold Ross, "insisted that Groucho come out from behind his real name and admit, you might say, who he wasn't." Finally, Groucho received what he considered the ultimate accolade: H. L. Mencken quoted him lengthily in *The American Language.*

That piece, originally printed in the *World,* offered specimens of show business jargon spoken by two vaudevillians:

FIRST: Gettin' much jack?

SECOND: Well, the storm and me is cuttin' up two and a half yards, but when the feed bill and gas for the boiler is marked off, they ain't much sugar left.

FIRST: Why don't you air her and do a single?

SECOND: Well, ta-ta, I gotta go now and make comical for the bozos. If you get a chance come over and get a load of me, but remember, Capt. Kidd, lay off my wow gags.

When he saw his name in Mencken's immense and widely praised work, Groucho burbled, "Nothing I ever did as an actor thrilled me more." His literary ambitions should have made Groucho a regular at the Algonquin Round Table. Yet for many reasons, whenever he visited the hotel restaurant he felt ill at ease and unwelcome. Kaufman and Harpo and many of the other members were expert bridge players. Groucho, partly as a commentary on his father's obsession with pinochle, spoke of card games as a waste of human intelligence. Also, Woollcott was the uncrowned leader of the group, and he seemed intent on discomfiting Groucho. Once, when the two were dining, a waiter served the comedian first. The columnist was made to wait for his order. Woollcott seethed until the waiter came by and inquired, "What was it that Mr. Woollcott ordered?" "Muffins," came the answer. "Filled with pus." Groucho got up and left. He would not return to the Algonquin for several weeks. The Round Tablers noted his absence and ascribed it to a difficult personality. Some members put him down as "suspicious and hostile," with a voice that had "a sneering quality to it." Others thought "Harpo's Bad Brother" to be "arrogant and superior." A letter Groucho wrote to Percy Hammond did not burnish his image. In a column, Hammond had remarked on a certain superficial resemblance between Marx and Kaufman. Groucho fired off a sardonic response:

"I have never seen Mr. Kaufman in the flesh, or the rough, or whatever you call it. I have seen a number of his plays, and I am not sure whether he has a moustache or not, although some authors find it advisable to wear something on the opening night.

"My makeup is sort of a hit-and-miss proposition, and when I start putting it on I am never sure who or what I will look like when I get through. Some nights I resemble one author, some nights I look like another, and it is purely a coincidence that basically I happen to look like Mr. Kaufman.

"If you can suggest any humorous get-up that wouldn't look like the aforementioned gentleman I would be only too glad to adopt it. . . ."

After that, Chico said later, anyone betting on a collaboration between the prickly, free-form Groucho Marx and the disciplined play constructor George S. Kaufman would have received odds of 40 to 1. Yet that long shot would pay off early in 1925. First, several Broadway producers, including the great Florenz Ziegfeld, approached the Brothers with ideas for their next show. Some were attracted by the Marxian humor, but most had simply taken a look at the ledger. *I'll Say She Is!* had paid back its investors tenfold. However, the shrewdest and most scrupulous producer on Broadway, Sam H. Harris, failed to make an offer.

He knew too much about the Marxes and their undisciplined approach to their craft. That was all very well for vaudeville, or for some ramshackle one-shot like *I'll Say She Is!* It would not do for real theater, a subject Harris knew all about; he had been producing shows for thirty-six years. At the age of fifty-three, he could look back on some fifty projects, beginning with *Little Johnny Jones,* a musical written by, and starring, the young George M. Cohan. When Harris failed to contact the Marx Brothers, Harpo asked one of his new friends, Irving Berlin, to plead their case. Berlin was the ideal emissary. He and Harris were both spare, dark-haired men from the Jewish slums; they had hit it off years before, when they joined forces to build the Music Box Theatre. At first Harris expressed no interest in the Brothers, but after a few days Berlin wore him down. The producer made no promises, but he did agree to meet the Marxes in his office. The instant the quartet laid eyes on Harris, they realized, like Berlin, that they had encountered a kindred soul. They learned that the producer was also the son of an impoverished tailor. He too had climbed out of the ghetto with a combination of chutzpah and instinct; he too had stories of out-of-town adventures, of flops and triumphs and chorines. As the conversation went on, the Marxes went into higher and higher gear, chasing each other up and down corridors, making a mess of in-boxes and blotters, and generally reducing the office to a shambles. Harris and his associates tried to keep straight faces, but it was impossible. Several days later the Harris organization signed papers agreeing to produce the Marx Brothers' next show.

But what was that project to be, and who would write it? All along, the team had used the same technique. A sketch was written—by Groucho, Al Shean, the Johnstones—and on that flimsy premise a series of gags would be hung. These would be tried out over the course of many performances. The participants had time and room to sculpt their material until it righted itself. Sometimes a word change would rectify a slow passage, sometimes an ad-lib would be incorporated into the script, as when Groucho found more than the expected gun in a drawer and shouted, "This gat has had gittens!" Sometimes Chico would experiment with a hesitation, or Harpo with the speed at which he chased a chorus girl across the stage. Their parts rarely left the tracks on which they had been placed years before. Zeppo handled the romantic interludes and Harpo pursued maidens and dropped articles from his coat. Verbal machinations were left to Chico and Groucho as the conveyors of puns, one-liners, and more elaborate routines. For the most part, Groucho had his way in story and gag conferences, because Zeppo and Harpo were content with their roles, and because Chico had no ambitions beyond the paycheck and a chance to indulge his passions. But Broadway was not Tuscaloosa, and the team was well aware that they had gotten away lucky the first time. It would not do to deliver another ramshackle work of sketches and slam-bang humor. Groucho appraised the current fare and informed his brothers that their next production ought to be like the others on the Main Stem—a "book" show, with plot, songs, and comedy that was funny in the writing as well as in the playing.

They appealed to Harris for playwrights who could fill the bill. Having seen the Marx Brothers only in *I'll Say She Is!* he sent them a craftsman experienced in the composition of sketches and blackouts. The Brothers handled the problem in their inimitable style. Zeppo, who had been working out with weights, rolled up his sleeves and approached the man with a hostile expression. "I'll wrestle you to a fall," he offered. "You write two shows for us or none." The comedy writer looked to Groucho, Chico, and Harpo for some signal that it was all a joke. Their expressions remained dour. He grabbed his hat and coat and ran. Harris learned about the encounter and it was then that he approached Kaufman with the casual inquiry, "How would you like to write a show for the Marx Brothers?" Kaufman made sure his reply was widely quoted: "I'd rather write for the Barbary apes." But this was strictly for the columns. He knew very well that the Brothers had become the darlings of Broadway— and more important, of Broadway critics. To be sure, Kaufman griped: "How can you write for Harpo? What do you put down on paper? All you can say is, 'Harpo enters,' and then he's on his own." He lodged similar complaints about writing straight lines for Zeppo, Italian dialect for Chico, and puns and non sequiturs for Groucho. But Harris never had a doubt that Kaufman would write for the Brothers, and that he would write well. The man had no shortage of talent or self-confidence; lock him in a room with the Barbary apes and he *would* write for them, and make a hit out of it.

Poring through the newspapers Kaufman was struck by the absurdity of the land boom fifteen hundred miles to the south. By 1925, as historian Frederick Lewis Allen noted, "investors were buying anything, anywhere, as long as it was in Florida. One had only to announce a new development, be it honest or fraudulent, be it on the Atlantic or deep in the wasteland of the interior, to set people scrambling for house lots. 'Manhattan Estates' was advertised as being 'not more than three-fourths of a mile from the prosperous and fast-growing city of Nettie'; there was no such city as Nettie, the name being that of an abandoned turpentine camp, yet people bought." Here was a situation ripe for comic exploitation; it took little imagination to see Groucho as the spieling con artist and his brothers as aides and abettors. Kaufman, who disliked writing alone, brought in a bright young reporter and publicist, Morrie Ryskind, to help out with ideas and dialogue. Ryskind later remembered: "If anybody walked in while George and I were writing they would have wondered about things. I'd be mimicking Harpo, let's say trying to climb a ladder to show what he'd be doing, and George would be crawling around." Kaufman was at his best imitating Groucho's delivery, supplying speeches that only the two of them could deliver without stumbling:

You are now in Cocoanut Manor. One of the finest cities in Florida. Of course, we still need a few finishing touches, but who doesn't. Every lot is a stone's throw from the station. The only reason we haven't got any station is because we haven't got any stones. Eight hundred beautiful residences will be built right here. They are as good as up. Better. You can have any kind of house you want to. You can even get stucco. Oh, how you can get stucco. Now is the time to buy while the new boom is on. Remember a new boom sweeps clean, and don't forget the guarantee. If these lots don't double themselves in a year, I don't know what you can do about it. Now then, take that beautiful lot behind you, lot number 20, right at the corner of De Sota Avenue. Of course, you all know who De Sota was? He discovered a body of water; you all heard of the water they've named after him: De Sota water. This lot has a 20-foot frontage, a 14-foot backage and a nice garbage.

Berlin knew and admired the work of the Marx Brothers. But he knew better than to offer melodies and lyrics that would be drowned out by a chaos of straight lines, punch lines, and physical gags. Instead he came up with his least memorable score, with the exception of one outstanding number, "Always." Years later Kaufman wrote: "I do not know the difference between Handel's 'Largo' and, well, Largo's 'Handel.' But I have always felt that I knew a little something about lyrics, and I was presumptuous enough then to question Irving's first line, 'I'll be loving you, always.' 'Always,' I pointed out, was a long time for romance. There were almost daily stories to that effect in the newspapers—stories about middle-aged husbands who had bricked their wives up in the cellar well and left for Toledo with the maid. I suggested, therefore, that the opening line be just a little more in accord with reality—something like, 'I'll be loving you Thursday.' But Irving would have none of it." Kaufman also feared that the song was so sweet it might cause the comedy to lose momentum. "Always" was excised—to Berlin's secret delight.

Once Kaufman started work he radiated confidence. He and Ryskind wrote the script with no interference from Harris or the Marxes. Even so, some still, small voice told the playwright that all would not be well with this production, that the Marxes, despite Groucho's assurance that they would hew to the lines as written, were an uncontainable force. But he and Ryskind and Berlin plugged away until the last gag was put in place, the final song written. No more delays were possible; it was time to summon the cast and read them the script. Kaufman's dry voice began: "Act one, scene one. The lobby of the Cocoanut Hotel, Cocoanut Beach, Florida."

About midway through the first act Kaufman looked up as he read. Listening with eager expressions were the young female lead, Mabel Withee, and her romantic interest, Jack Barker. The character actors, Henry Whittemore and Janet Velie, concentrated on their villainous scenes. The actress who would play the dowager smiled benignly. She was new to Kaufman; he had admired her work in the recent comedy *The Fourflusher*. Margaret Dumont would be ideal, he thought, as a Floridian grande dame. She sat with great dignity, concentrating on his every word. So did Zeppo. So did Groucho, obviously delighted to be in the presence of a master showman. Perhaps the playwright had misjudged the team; perhaps the Marxes' reputation had created unreasonable fears. That must be it. Kaufman stole a look at the other brothers. They sat still and meek as lambs. He made a closer examination and realized that his instincts had not failed him. Harpo and Chico were asleep.

CHAPTER FIVE

You Can Call Me Schnorrer

OUT OF *The Cocoanuts* came one of George S. Kaufman's classic japes. The phrase was not said by any of the Marxes; it was spoken by the playwright himself. Pacing at the back of the theater, he suddenly paused and cupped his hand around his ear. "I may be wrong," Kaufman muttered, "but I think I just heard one of the original lines."

The Brothers' attitude had come as something of a surprise. Despite the unfortunate naps taken by Chico and Harpo during the first reading, rehearsals had gone better than expected. Groucho settled into his role as the Florida hotelier Henry W. Schlemmer, and his brothers seemed pleased with their roles as written: Zeppo as Jamison, the hotel clerk; Harpo as Silent Sam; and Chico, reflecting the sunset of onstage ethnic jokes, as Willie the Wop. (There would also be a joke about Jews playing Hispanics, referring to them as "Span-yids.")

Then came opening night in Boston. For the first time since *I'll Say She Is!* the Brothers heard laughter and applause and realized how much they had missed public adulation. "Groucho," remembered coauthor Morrie Ryskind, had been getting "sick of saying the same lines. After he said a line three times he would try something," and tonight was the night to try anything. "Whenever a new bit occurred to Chico and me, we did it," Harpo was to confess triumphantly. "Whenever a gag popped into Groucho's mind, he delivered it. The first performance ran forty minutes too long. All the critics and most of the audience had left long before the curtain finally came down." That night, Kaufman and the director, Oscar Eagle, ruthlessly pruned speeches and excised songs. Irving Berlin protested that if things went on this way *The Cocoanuts* would be a musical without music. Kaufman retorted: "I tell you what. You waive the songs and I'll waive the story."

But the Marxes were not to be discouraged by editing of any kind. With renewed perversity they piled on ad-libs and physical business until the second night ran longer than the first. The next few weeks saw even more unplanned additions. As far as Kaufman was concerned, the nadir came when he discovered a sheet of paper headed SEEN 2. This yielded two points of information: a) that an alternate scene 1 had apparently been composed, and b) the identity of the author. This grade school dropout had given himself away once before, during a Round Table parlor game. It involved notes, a murderer, victims, and a detective. One of the cards had read, YOU ARE DED. The writer was, of course, Harpo.

Kaufman confidently pitched the paper in a wastebasket. He knew that none of the quartet—not even Groucho—was capable of creating an entirely new scene, much less a complete rewrite of The Cocoanuts. But he also knew that Harpo's scribble indicated the Brothers' pathological need to add, and that it was unstoppable. Kaufman could only roll his eyes, make sardonic cracks, and watch as the laughs mounted and the curtain fell late, night after night. In Philadelphia as in Boston, some patrons saw the show five times. With good reason: every performance was different. One evening Harpo would stick to the script. The next he would seek to unnerve his brother, waiting until Groucho was deep in dialogue and then pursuing a hysterical chorine across the stage. It was no use. As Harpo honked the horn atop his walking stick, Groucho calmly looked up and told the audience, "First time I ever saw a taxi hail a passenger." Challenged, Harpo reversed direction and chased his quarry back the way she came. As the duet disappeared, stage left, Groucho topped himself. Without missing a beat he consulted his watch and remarked, "The nine-twenty's right on time. You can always set your clocks by the Lehigh Valley."

The cast and management got caught up in the free-for-all. First Margaret Dumont, a thoroughgoing professional who knew her lines and hit her marks, became a nightly victim. In early performances her dress featured a long train. Groucho amused himself by leaping back and forth across it as she walked. One night he landed directly on the train, severing it from the main fabric. Dumont exited in her underwear. On another night she listened vainly for her entrance cue. When no one spoke it she walked onstage, forcing the Brothers to acknowledge her presence. "Ah, Mrs. Rittenhouse," exclaimed Groucho. "Won't you—lie down?" In time she abandoned her customary frilly undergarments in favor of a whalebone corset, not only to reduce embarrassment but to protect her own skin against the "cue" routine. Groucho would pretend to lose his place in the script and whisper, "My cue! My cue!" to an imaginary prompter. At this point the arm of Harpo or Chico would appear from the wings, flourishing a billiard stick. Wherever the dowager stood, she always managed to be in the way. The whalebone helped to deflect the blows and minimize the goosing. Dumont also had the costumer make a few more wardrobe changes after Harpo stuck his foot up her sleeve and had trouble extricating it.

The time of *The Cocoanuts* was the period in which Groucho's comic persona and technique came into sharp focus. Of all the variegated roles he had played in the past, a confidence man was the one that fit without any alterations. In that part he could charm and insult in the same breath. Imagining wedded bliss: "I can see you bending over the stove. Only I can't see the stove." He could also play with words, a favorite pastime of immigrants' children who heard one tongue at home and another in school and on the streets. Familiarizing himself with Groucho's emerging stage self, Kaufman wrote puns to emphasize ethnicity and immigration:

GROUCHO

Now, right here is the residential section . . . now, all along the river, those are all levees.

CHICO

That's-a the Jewish neighborhood.

GROUCHO

Well, we'll pass over that.

But not even the resourceful Kaufman could give Groucho his most salient characteristic—not the painted moustache or ramshackle formality, but the tone. In a pioneering work, *American Laughter*, film scholar Mark Winokur points out that "the irony and disaffection in Groucho's voice, so comic to audiences, is aggressive and hostile. This quality characterizes Groucho as a vaudeville comic accustomed to audience hostility." *The Cocoanuts* took advantage of his attitude, formed by decades on the circuit, making him the aggressor even in a supposedly amiable conversation:

CHANDLER

Captain Spaulding, I think that is a wonderful idea.

GROUCHO

You do, eh?

CHANDLER

Yes.

GROUCHO

Well, then there can't be too much to it. Forget about it.

Groucho took delight in this kind of unpredictable dialogue. Coupled with his ad-libs, it gave the character-in-progress a new dimension—even though it became evident that no understudy could ever adequately replace him. The man who tried, an actor named Liebowitz, went half-mad, Groucho claimed, "trying to keep up with the switches I made with the jokes. They had to come and take him away." The exhilarating *mishe-gaas* came at great cost. For Groucho, like many another star clown, was starting to experience difficulty separating the performer and the man beneath the makeup. One part of him yearned to be the sole grownup Marx Brother, a gentleman apart from the irresponsible Chico, the child-like Harpo, the immature Zeppo. That well-read, stable family figure wished to treat show business like any other kind of business—as a place for acquiring and honing skills, bringing home a substantial paycheck, and making one's place in society. But another part had been hurt too many times to trust the world outside the curtain, relied on no one except the siblings who had been with him from the start (and sometimes not even on them), and tended to get defensive in the company of women. Although Groucho could be polite and well-mannered, the ladies—chorines, agents, mothers, and, most of all, Ruth—were generally kept at arm's length, except when used as the butts of jokes or the losers in a power struggle. All the same, he was not insensitive to their wounded reactions, or unaware of his own incivility. He was uncomfortable with himself every time he went over the line in the theater, or when he and his wife had a loud confrontation. But the engines of resentment and sus-picion, churning since childhood, were impossible to turn off. Every time he considered an apology, or a change of manner, some old memory sur-faced, or some new theatrical crisis came up. He postponed the revisions of Groucho the man; Groucho the character came first.

•

As the show moved closer to its New York debut Kaufman and his colleagues tried one last time to bring the Brothers into line. It was one thing to fool around in the sticks, they argued; it was quite another to give Broadway audiences—and worse still, Broadway critics—a disorderly and undisciplined show. Sam Harris sided with the creative team. The producer led Kaufman and Berlin to the Marxes' dressing room, preparing to lay down the law. But as they approached, Harris expressed guilt about ganging up on the Brothers. "Let me talk to the boys myself," he said authoritatively. "I think I can settle this problem once and for all."

Kaufman and Berlin stepped aside. Harris strode into the room and closed the door. After several minutes of silence, sounds were discernible. None of them suggested that negotiations were under way. A moment later the door opened, and several garments migrated into the corridor. They had a familiar look; Harris had been wearing them only a little while ago. The clothes were followed by their owner, now stark naked. Even then he remained unruffled. Gathering up his wardrobe he conceded mildly, "I guess you two better handle it." Then he turned the corner and disappeared for the rest of the day.

Berlin and Kaufman edged into the dressing room, expecting a fresh assault. But the Marxes, having made their statement, now proceeded to act as if they were in the principal's office. As various scenes and lines were parsed, Kaufman found the comedians willing to jettison favorite jokes and even routines that had failed to benefit the show as a whole. Indeed, during the final countdown to opening night the Brothers became harsher than the writers, ruthlessly taking out or revamping sections that failed to earn the desired response.

Even so, old habits kept reasserting themselves. Groucho would recall: "the first New York audience came in laughing before we even appeared. They were laughing at the seats, the curtain, anything. And so when the action began we went on a tear, not adding scenes and lines exactly, just expanding on what was already written. The laughter built into waves, and the waves built into a flood." At 11:25, Chico was just beginning to shoot the keys as Alexander Woollcott departed to make a deadline. Five minutes later Percy Hammond went up the aisle. In his review he commented: "It seemed that the show was just getting under way. As it is now 12:05, I may be able to get back and see how it ends." For the *World*, William Bolitho wrote an overheated genealogy: "Dead lame on two of its legs, a crib biter, windsucker and roarer, this Marxian quadruped is authentically one of the sacred breed. Its sire is

New York, its dam the Jewish race; but one of its ancestors is Pegasus."
The Brothers never quite decided whether Bolitho's compliment was
genuine or left-handed. Chico spoke for the family when he said, "I
understand this much about it. He means I'm some part of a horse," and
dropped the subject. A more rational appraisal came from Brooks Atkinson, then beginning a long and distinguished career at the *New York Times*.
He singled out Groucho for operating "with the seriousness of the
instinctive man of business, bent on doing his job well, and with such
baffling twists in allusion that the audience is frequently three steps
behind him."

It is worth examining those twists, because in later years so many
authors claimed credit for creating the Brothers' antiestablishmentarian
approach. Unquestionably, the bedrock of their style was formed by the
Marxes and only the Marxes in their vaudeville years. But it was Kaufman
who furnished the polish and professionalism they lacked until *The
Cocoanuts*. The playwright was also the only one who could negotiate
with the team. When Groucho defended his comic inventions with the
question, "Well, they laughed at Edison, didn't they?" Kaufman replied,
"Not at the Wednesday matinee, they didn't," and silenced Groucho for a
while. On the other hand, when the playwright thought the comedian
had contributed something organic to the play's humor, his was the loudest applause. He particularly enjoyed Groucho's Whatever Has Become
of Our Plot Contest. Lamenting that the plot of *The Cocoanuts* had gone
missing, the Brothers offered a reward for its recovery. "Remember,"
Groucho reminded the public, "it is not necessary to see the show to win
the prize. In fact, it is better if you don't see the show."

In later years Groucho became incensed when a Kaufman biographer
credited his bent-kneed amble and staccato chatter to the playwright. "I
was in show business for twenty years when *The Cocoanuts* opened," he
pointed out, "and I'd been walking and talking for at least thirty-three
years, so the evolution had gone on for quite some time before I met
Kaufman." Then he relented: "There is so much more to credit him with.
He was the wittiest man I ever knew, and perhaps some of that quality
rubbed off on me."

The quality could be discerned in act 1, when Groucho confronts the
first of many rich widows:

GROUCHO

Are you sure your husband's dead?

MRS. POTTER

Quite sure.

GROUCHO

I feel better. I guess he does too. What I was going to say was, here I am and you're going to be here all winter, and I'm stuck with the hotel anyhow. Why don't you grab me until you could do better?

MRS. POTTER

My dear Mr. Schlemmer, I would never get married *before my daughter.*

GROUCHO

You did once. Don't forget, I love you. I'm mad about you.

MRS. POTTER

I don't think you'd love me if I were poor.

GROUCHO

I might, but I'd keep my mouth shut.

MRS. POTTER

Really, I'm afraid I must be going.

GROUCHO

Don't go away and leave me here alone. You stay here and I'll go away.

MRS. POTTER

I don't know what to say.

GROUCHO

Well, say that you'll be truly mine, or truly yours, or yours truly, and that tonight when the moon is sneaking around the clouds, I'll be sneaking around you. I'll meet you tonight by the bungalow, under the moon. You and the moon. I hope I can tell you apart. You wear a red necktie so I'll know you. I'll meet you tonight by the bungalow under the moon.

MRS. POTTER

But suppose the moon is not out.

GROUCHO

Then I'll meet you under the bungalow.

Kaufman was right when he said no one could write for Harpo. The parenthetical word "(*Business*)" in the script served as the cue for mime. Chasing a blond from stage left to stage right was infallible; that much Harpo and everyone else knew from vaudeville. The dropping of objects from his sleeve also had the same explosive result in a major theater as it did in the sticks, and if all else failed there was always the gookie, the full-cheeked, cross-eyed stare that he had been beaming effectively at onlookers since childhood. But Chico's deadpan Italian confidence man—the only figure who was ever allowed to fleece Groucho—was refined and clarified in *The Cocoanuts*:

GROUCHO

(*At the reception desk, checking in CHICO and HARPO*): What do you boys want? Garage and bath?

CHICO

We go together him.

GROUCHO

You go together him?

CHICO

Sure me.

GROUCHO

Would you mind coming in again and starting all over?

CHICO

We want a room and no bath.

GROUCHO

Oh I see. You're just here for the winter. Step this way. Now if you'll just sign the register.

CHICO

No, no. We no sign nothing without our lawyer.

GROUCHO

No, don't you understand, you'll have to sign the book. If you don't register, you can't vote.

CHICO

You're crazy. Last year I no register and I vote six times.

•

F. SCOTT FITZGERALD caught the sense of place in *The Great Gatsby.* He called it "that slender riotous island which extends itself due east of New York" bordering on "the great wet barnyard of Long Island Sound." The dappled tree-lined streets of Great Neck, the wheeling of gulls and the glint of sunlight off the Sound, the long shadows on manicured lawns, the green quiet might have risen full-formed from the novels Groucho had read in childhood. Looked at subjectively, they could be seen as the rewards of the Horatio Alger hero who had done hard work for poor wages until he was recognized for his skills and virtue. By 1926, Groucho's salary and investments allowed the purchase of a ten-room house for $27,000 cash—this at a time when the average suburban home in America went for less than $5,000. The burbling owner dropped by the offices of the Great Neck *News* to grant an interview. "We're glad we're here, and we're here for ever and always, in all likelihood," he told the staff. Groucho had only one complaint: "How about electric light? Gee, but they're slow in installing it. My house was like the house of a thousand candles last night." The next day the power lines came in, and that was the last complaint from 21 Lincoln Road. Groucho and Ruth had an acre of garden and grass to cultivate, and enough rooms to accommodate live-in help: a German couple who looked after the cooking, cleaning, and laundry. Groucho commuted to and from the city, reading books and magazines on the Long Island Railroad. "Without the makeup," he said, "I could have been any successful businessman going to attend the theater rather than being in it and of it." With Minnie and Frenchy, Chico and Harpo nearby, Groucho settled uneasily into the upper middle class. Like many new arrivals, he discovered that no matter how much he accumulated, there would always be those with more. Eddie Cantor reminded him sharply of that fact during an afternoon softball game, played by various show business personalities. Morrie Ryskind pitched, George S. Kaufman caught, and Cantor played center field. He had brought his butler along for the occasion, and outfitted him with a glove. Whenever a fly ball was hit in Cantor's direction, he gave it his patented pop-eyed stare and stepped aside for the servant to catch it.

Still, Groucho had come a long way from the slums of Manhattan and the backwaters of vaudeville; he appreciated the material benefits of his comfortable life. Great Neck was pronounced "a happy environment in which to raise kids"—the plural noun covered Miriam, the daughter born the following year. What Groucho could not do was find the same kind of comfort within his marriage. He declined to chase after women in the manner of Chico and Harpo (Zeppo had acquired a fiancée, whom he would marry in 1928). Nor did Groucho hang around speakeasies. "My idea of a good time," he told his son, "is to lock myself in my room with a big Havana and read *The New Yorker.*" But when he emerged from that room he acted like a man with sand under his skin. In a reference to Ruth's Nordic heritage, he called her Svensk, and she called him Grouch, a label that referred not only to his stage name but to his disposition. Ruth relished her husband's new celebrity, and so did he—except in her presence.

Mostly to irritate his wife, Groucho enjoyed playing the part of a nobody, meekly standing in line with all the other patrons at restaurants until Ruth insisted that Groucho tell the management who he was. Obediently, he would tap the maître d' on the shoulder and identify himself—as "Mr. Jackson." If that announcement failed to move the man, and it usually did, Groucho would try again. This time he would state his real name—Julius H. Marx. The wait would continue. With Ruth near tears they would finally leave the restaurant and try a new place. Again Groucho would start the Jackson–Julius Marx routine until a table happened to be free.

Household expenses presented another problem. The years of hand-me-down clothes had gone, along with the ratty costumes and dime store greasepaint. Groucho's shirts and suits were made to measure now; Earl Benham, clothier to Cohan, Cantor, and Jolson, charged $200 for his cheapest suit—this at a time when $50 a week was considered a handsome salary in New York. Yet when Ruth bought an outfit for herself, or a piece of furniture that struck her fancy, her husband had to grant permission beforehand. Otherwise, Groucho would launch into a tirade about extravagance and irresponsibility. In giving these unwanted lectures he tried to rewrite the years when Minnie changed the family's locale from

New York to Chicago, parceled out the boys' salaries, and made the career decisions until they were in their thirties. Groucho's angry lectures usually ended with an ultimatum: the items must be returned to the store posthaste. On the occasions that Ruth refused, or burst into tears—her customary response—he would order her from the table to eat by herself in the kitchen.

It came as no surprise—especially to her children—when Ruth began to seek consolation in alcohol and overeating. At long last Groucho had found a way to dominate any situation: if people were uncertain about his responses, he had them at a disadvantage, and he became the authority figure. The more uncertain they were, the more dominant he became. Groucho's attitude toward his wife and children was the obverse of his old one, in which he was the most insecure boy in the family, and everyone seemed to have the advantage over the bookish and walleyed Julius.

At times (and these occasions would increase with the years) Groucho's quirks and demands caused resentments that smoldered for decades. In her sixties, Chico's daughter Maxine could remember minute details of the day she attended her cousin Arthur's seventh birthday party. Neighborhood children had begun to filter in, and Ruth was visibly tense and worried, anticipating Groucho's imminent arrival. Had she ordered enough food? Did the house look elegant enough?

When Ruth found that there were not enough place settings for all the guests, she asked her niece to go home.

At the age of ten, Maxine was bewildered rather than distressed, and when she ran into Minnie at the front door, she related the incident, hoping that her grandmother might offer an explanation.

Minnie's reaction was simple. Here was Groucho's shiksa attempting to bar Chico's child—in favor of *who*? A bunch of strangers' kids? Indignantly she took Maxine's hand and stormed out. Only when they were out of sight did Minnie slow down to catch her breath. Grandmother and child took a cab the rest of the way home.

The contretemps put Groucho in a difficult situation. The aggressive attitude he could never bring himself to use on Minnie could always be directed at Margaret Dumont onstage, and when Maggie was not around, Ruth made a splendid stand-in. Increasingly he made her the butt of his jokes and the victim of his tirades about expenses and housekeeping. But on this occasion his browbeating in absentia had the undesirable result of offending the one person he never dared to offend: Minnie. He realized that he had overstepped the bounds of decent behavior, and even Groucho was ashamed of what he had brought about. Yet he could not bring himself to offer an apology to Ruth or his mother, and in the end he sent Gummo, the family conciliator, to repair matters.

Groucho's unpleasantness could not stay *en famille* after this, particularly since the blowup had happened in front of invited guests—and, of course, his own son. The situation was hopeless and getting worse. Groucho had begun to fuse his onstage character with the real one, and Ruth was to head a long list of insultees who made the mistake of assuming that success had mellowed the comedian instead of giving him license to act with greater animosity and caprice. Indeed, the more prominent the Groucho fan, the more likely he was to be squelched at this time. Yet here the fallout from misbehavior could be turned to advantage.

"When we hit in vaudeville," Groucho recalled, "I used to get invited to parties in various cities. Often there were rich people and local politicians. I was deferential to them, and sometimes we would agree to have lunch. I always got stuck with the check. When *The Cocoanuts* became a smash it happened all over again. Only this time I decided, what the hell: I'll give the big shots the same Groucho they saw onstage—impudent, irascible, iconoclastic. They not only ate it up, they started picking up the tab."

Looking out over the footlights, he once asked anxiously, "Is there a doctor in the house?" When a prominent physician stood up and identified himself, Groucho asked another question: "How do you like the show so far, Doc?"

On election eve he remarked to Chico: "I see we have the Honorable Jimmy Walker." He addressed the mayor, then under investigation. "What are you doing here? Why aren't you out stuffing ballot boxes?"

The night that President Coolidge attended *The Cocoanuts,* he fared no better. Groucho interrupted the action to inquire, "Isn't it a little past your bedtime, Cal?"

The Prince of Wales was not sassed, but when His Highness came backstage Groucho exacted an invitation to visit Buckingham Palace should the Marxes ever be in the neighborhood.

Much as he delighted in abusing the famous, Groucho was fondest of the response he gave to an obscure playgoer from the old neighborhood. In one memoir he calls the man Leonard Dobbin; Arthur, in *his* memoir, refers to him as Herman Schroeder. And the Marxes' early biographer, Kyle Crichton, says he was George Heinkel. In any case, during the twenty years since Groucho and Leonard/Herman/George last met, the former slum child had excelled in school and in college, earned a law degree, and now worked for an established firm. According to family tradition, much elaborated over the years, he came backstage to see Groucho, and, incidentally, do a little boasting about his imminent partnership and his current salary: $9,000 a year. At the time Groucho pulled in ten times as much, but he said nothing as the unwelcome visitor droned on about the advantages of an honest job. "You're not a boy any longer," he pointed out. "It's about time you settled down."

"Do you really think so?"

"I certainly do. I'd start looking around for another line of work. Before you get too old to get into anything else."

Groucho stared in appreciative wonder. Here was a better straight man than anyone Kaufman had concocted. Assuming a long face, he took his listener for a ride: "But what kind of work do you advise me to get into? I don't know anything but show business. I didn't even finish grammar school."

The lawyer suggested a career in sales; the entertainer thought not. "You see, most actors steal, and I'm afraid I'd always have my hand in the till." Indicating a gold watch on the dressing table, Groucho confessed that he had lifted it from a stranger's pocket. "I wouldn't get too close to me," he warned. "I might steal *your* watch. And that gold chain, too! I've always wanted a gold chain."

"I'd better be going."

"So soon? We haven't decided on a business for me yet." Groucho hinted that he might consider a job at a legal firm. "I wouldn't ask for much at first. Say five thousand a year and all I can steal?"

"I'm afraid not." Clearly rattled, the old acquaintance departed with a sermonette. "Julius, it's not too late to mend your ways. Think over what I told you. And do me a favor. Don't steal anymore."

Groucho's reply was wistful. "I wish I could stop, but unfortunately, it's the only way I can make both ends meet."

Marx Brothers fans had 377 opportunities to see *The Cocoanuts* on Broadway. Toward the end of the run Chico and Harpo renewed an old argument. Years of bets and measurements had proved that Chico was one-sixteenth of an inch taller than his brother. But Harpo had better posture and appeared to have the advantage. Now he insisted that he really was the taller of the two. Chico, the compulsive gambler, took the bait: off went the shoes and socks, out came the measuring tape. Chico was crestfallen to find that Harpo was indeed a full half-inch taller. How could this be? He suspected trickery and summoned his brothers to take new measurements. But whatever instrument they used the result was the same. Harpo had the height advantage, and Chico had to pay up. Sometime later, according to Maxine, Harpo told Chico that he had gone to a chiropractor and had himself stretched for the previous twelve hours.

Having won the practical joke, Harpo encouraged Chico to conspire in another one—this time with the ticket holders as victims. During the final week, as Groucho spieled, Silent Sam and Willie the Wop changed places onstage, wearing each other's wigs and doing each other's shtick. The childhood lookalikes had pulled their stunt once again, and not a soul in the audience could tell the difference.

The producers, never too big to bend down and pick up the small change, knew that there was even more profit to be wrung out of *The Cocoanuts*. Soon after it closed in New York they took the musical on tour. The road company starred all four Marxes, but surrounded them with an underpaid and inferior chorus line—a group of women Groucho contemptuously called "road apples." The Brothers worked their way west, playing major venues, seeing old vaudeville friends, and posing for a picture in front of the Broadway Theatre in Denver. The photograph is of interest because it includes Uncle Al Shean, who was passing through town, and excludes Chico, who, according to Groucho, had better things to do, either at a poolroom or with a date.

The tour ended at the Biltmore Theatre in Los Angeles. On its last night the film director King Vidor, along with actor John Gilbert, Greta Garbo, and another actress, Eleanor Boardman, attended in black beards and funny hats. "We thought we would break the Marx Brothers up," Vidor said, "but we didn't. Groucho just started ad-libbing a lot of jokes about us. He looked down at us and said, 'I thought that was Greta Garbo in the audience, but it was General Grant.' We threw our beards up onstage, and they started throwing costumes and props down at us."

And still there were a few dollars more to be wrung out of *The Cocoanuts*. In the spring of 1928 the Marx Brothers, along with Margaret Dumont, toured the shrinking circuit of vaudeville theaters in "Spanish Knights," an abbreviated version of the show. When that was finished, they all took the summer off. They would need the breather; that fall they were to begin rehearsals for their third Broadway show, *Animal Crackers*. After well-publicized token protests, George S. Kaufman had contracted to write the book along with his new collaborator, Morrie Ryskind. Irving Berlin, however, meant it when he said he wanted nothing to do with a Marxian sequel. The composer wholly agreed with Ryskind's recollection of *The Cocoanuts:* "Berlin wrote some excellent music for our show, but those guys could ruin anything. They run around for fifteen minutes, and then the young lovers do a song. Nobody gives a damn if the boy loves the girl or not." This time the score would be composed by two songwriters with vaudeville experience, Bert Kalmar and Harry Ruby. The pair turned out to be as subversive as the Brothers themselves, short-changing the romantic leads in order to favor Groucho with two signature numbers, "Hello, I Must Be Going" and "Hooray for Captain Spaulding."

Rehearsals were briefly held up pending the arrival of Harpo, who had spent the summer in Europe, meeting celebrities in the south of France. Somerset Maugham took to him immediately, and George Bernard Shaw included him in a sight gag of his own. Approached on a nude beach, he and Harpo swiftly wrapped towels around their middles. Asked by strangers if he really was *the* Bernard Shaw, he nodded, simultaneously whisking the towel from Harpo and leaving him completely naked. "And this," said the playwright, "is *Mrs.* Shaw." Harpo also visited Italy, prompting Groucho to write Dr. Samuel Salinger, the family's long-time physician in Chicago, "Harpo is arriving home today . . . and I am sure that one of the things he won't declare at the Customs Offices will be a slight dose of Mussolini Gonorrhea." It was not the last time Il Duce would enter the Brothers' lives and correspondence.

Once Harpo was declared healthy the quartet settled down to work. Because they had invested some of their own money in the show, all four promised to rehearse with serious intent. The vows remained unbroken for about a week. It was not that they were emboldened by optimism and a sense of security in their own talents. They simply could not help themselves. It was the first real childhood for all the Brothers, and they looked at the stage as a vast toy store full of pretty girls, props, lights, straight men and women, and, the greatest plaything of all, a script to be tossed around and pieced together again.

The trouble was that for all of them the line between show business and life was, and remained, blurred. Harpo, at least, was unmarried, and he could pick up and dally with anyone he wanted. Groucho and Chico were husbands and fathers, yet in the end these facts seemed irrelevant to their deportment. Chico seemed to relish his reputation as Mr. Irresponsible. For him nothing had really changed since the days when he hocked his father's clients' pants and, by his constant pilfering, forced Harpo to remove the hands of his pocket watch lest it end up in the pawnshop. Unfaithful to Betty on their honeymoon, Chico continued to womanize without affection and gamble without winnings; after all, if he could outwit Groucho onstage, how difficult could it be to fool his wife and raid the family funds? If Betty were to cry because of all this, if Maxine were to pay a price, he could always make it up to them. Charm was his long suit. Chico had few articles of faith, but one of them was that not many women, young or old, could resist him when he shot the keys and flashed the 5,000-candlepower smile. And in this he was correct. Groucho, on the other hand, was no womanizer and he was certainly no spendthrift—friends used to say he clung to each nickel until the buffalo bleated. His difficulties arose from an inability to let go of the Captain Spaulding figure he had so painstakingly constructed. "I was kicked into acting by my mother," he stated, "and if I hadn't been I'd now be on relief." It was a fact he was not pleased to acknowledge. His mix of gratitude and resentment took the form of comic malice. Onstage, Margaret Dumont was the stand-in for Minnie. In real life, he went against any woman vulnerable to a wisecrack: fans, the wives of friends, and, most often, Ruth—until he became the father of daughters.

None of their sons' quirks disturbed the elder Marxes. For Frenchy it was enough that the boys paid the bills and came around, always kissing him when they came to call. For Minnie, it was enough that the boys had risen into the stratosphere. Unable to practice the con on theater managers anymore, she used her wiles on newspapermen, adding to the legend by portraying herself as not only the giver of life to the Marx Brothers, but the dispenser of fortune. Actually, she was less sentimental than her sons. One afternoon she walked into a neighborhood jewelry shop and left off a set of colored beads that needed restringing. She told the proprietor that these five-and-dime jewels were among her greatest treasures because they had been given to her by the boys when they were all poor. The jeweler promised to treat them with great care, and awaited the day the mother of the Marx Brothers came to pick up her prized possession. She never returned.

•

MARGARET IRVING, veteran of Sigmund Romberg's *The Desert Song* and Irving Berlin's *Music Box Revue*, joined the cast of *Animal Crackers* early on, as a high-society type. She remembered the preparations as "Chaotic. Those little devils . . . You could never get them together at the same time. Zeppo would be at his broker or Chico would be over at Jamaica Racetrack." Even Groucho, the most dedicated of the four, became impossible to deal with. On the eve of *Animal Crackers's* first tryout in Philadelphia, Irving pleaded with him: "We open in a few minutes. Don't you think we ought to rehearse these lines?" Groucho's answer was not reassuring: "Just go along with the gag and see what happens. We'll probably have a better show." And so they did. Emboldened, the Brothers added new routines and fresh practical jokes to almost every performance. To further torment Irving, one evening they had all the openings in her costume sewed up. Years later she could look back with a smile. "My cue was coming, so I just put the dress around me, across my bust, and held it on the back with a pin. I sidled on stage. Those four wrestled with me to get me to show my back to the audience. You might win against one, but against four? The audience was howling. I got through the scene. As soon as I got into my next costume, Sam Harris came over. 'Mag, what was the matter with the last dress? I didn't like it. I saw your bloomers sticking out.' "

In a later scene she was required to wear a hoop skirt. "I walked on in the spotlight, feeling very regal. I was on a second or two, and I heard somebody in the audience giggle. Had I picked up a brassiere on the hoop, or a pair of pants or something?" Bewildered, she attempted to sit down. A pair of hands emerged from under the costume. "The hoop was so big I hadn't sensed there was anyone under there before. It was Harpo."

Groucho looked down at his brother's hand. "Waiter, will you bring some ice water up to 10?"

And so it went all through the tryouts. Yet the Marx Brothers never wholly departed from the main plot, simply because it afforded them enough freedom to caper as they pleased—and enough form to give them the aura of Broadway professionals. *Animal Crackers* begins in the palatial home of a Long Island socialite. Mrs. Rittenhouse (Margaret Dumont) makes ready to greet the African explorer, Captain Jeffrey T. Spaulding (Groucho). To add zest to the party, millionaire Roscoe Chandler plans to exhibit a famous painting, Beauregard's *After the Hunt*—and, incidentally, make advances to the hostess. The real love interest is supplied by Mrs. Rittenhouse's daughter Arabella, and an impoverished and socially unacceptable artist, John Parker. Complications are caused by the theft of the painting; wrongful accusations; social climbers; Captain Spaulding's secretary Jamison (Zeppo); a musician engaged for the occasion, Emmanuel Ravelli (Chico); and his partner, the Professor (Harpo), as well as a number of servants and delinquents.

The tone is set with Groucho's entrance. His derogatory attitude remains unchanged from *The Cocoanuts*. Carried onstage by native bearers, the explorer steps from his pallet and asks about the fare. "What? From Africa to here, a dollar eighty-five? That's an outrage. I told you not to take me through Australia. It's all ripped up. You should have come right up Lincoln Boulevard."

Turning to Dumont, he beams: "You're one of the most beautiful women I've ever seen. And that's not saying much for you." Looking around, Groucho adds, "Well, I certainly am grateful for this magnificent washout—I mean turnout." Before anyone can reply, he launches into song:

> Hello, I must be going.
> I cannot stay
> I came to say
> I must be going.
>
> I'm glad I came
> But just the same
> I must be going.

This segues into a choral salute:

GUESTS

Hooray for Captain Spaulding, the African explorer.

GROUCHO

Did someone call me schnorrer?

GUESTS

Hooray, Hooray, Hooray!

DUMONT

He is the only white man
Who covered every acre.

GROUCHO

I think I'll try and make her.

GUESTS

Hooray, Hooray, Hooray!

When the music stops, Dumont welcomes her prize guest to "my poor home." Groucho replies, "Oh, it isn't so bad," but quickly reconsiders. "Wait a minute. I think you're right. It is pretty bad. You're letting this place run down and what's the result? You're not getting the class of people that you used to. Why, you've got people here now that look like you." He brightens. "Now, I'll tell you what we'll do. We'll put up a sign outside, '*Place under new management.*' We'll set up a seventy-five-cent meal that'll knock their eyes out. And after we knock their eyes out we can charge them anything we want. Sign here and give me your check for fifteen hundred dollars. Now, I want to tell you madam that with this insurance policy you have provided for your little ones and for your old age. Which will be here in a couple of weeks now, if I'm any judge of horseflesh."

For all the unscripted business, certain ad-libs were actually written in the script and made to appear accidental. An actor's mistake made in rehearsals became a regular part of the entertainment:

CHANDLER

Tell me, Captain Chandler—er—er—Spaulding.

SPAULDING

Yes, Spaulding. You're Chandler. You're Chandler and I'm Spaulding. (*Explaining*) It's the switching from the light to the heavy underwear.

CHANDLER

Tell me, Captain—er—er—

SPAULDING

Spaulding. You're Chandler and I'm Spaulding. (*To audience*) Could I look at a program for a minute? It might be intermission for all he knows.

As he went through these routines Groucho steadily worked on his stage character. By the time he uttered his curtain speech, the raffish and derogatory figure was indelible. Julius Henry Marx would play different characters in different shows, but the features would remain in place, a prime attraction for the next fifty years.

Other themes were set in *Animal Crackers*. Because Groucho was cast as a fraud and fortune-hunter ("You have got money, haven't you? Because if you haven't, we can quit right now"), he needed a counterpart who was villainous, lecherous, and even more of an arriviste. In *Animal*

Crackers this character is Chandler, a plutocrat whose aura of success cannot disguise his Eastern European intonations. Groucho is only allowed to suspect his rival. The exposure is done by Harpo and Chico in a scene revealing Roscoe T. Chandler to be Rabbi Cantor, originally from Czechoslovakia. Here Kaufman had something more than a mockery of immigrants in mind; he was satirizing the financier and art collector Otto Kahn, known for masking or denying his Jewish heritage. (One of Kaufman's favorite immigrant stories concerned the millionaire being driven through the streets of the Lower East Side. His eyes light on a tailor's sign: SOL KAHN, COUSIN OF OTTO KAHN. Commanding the chauffeur to stop, he barges into the shop, threatening the terrified owner with a lawsuit unless the sign is altered immediately. The next day Kahn orders his car to pass by the tailor's place. Sure enough, the lettering is changed. Now it reads SOL KAHN, FORMERLY COUSIN OF OTTO KAHN.)

The authors also went after Eugene O'Neill's expressionistic play *Strange Interlude,* with its stark, action-stopping soliloquies. In the middle of a flirtation with a pair of women, Groucho suddenly steps forward to muse aloud: "Here I am talking of parties. I came down here for a party. What happens? Nothing. The gods look down and laugh. This would be a better world for children if the parents had to eat the spinach."

Kaufman and Ryskind crammed twice as many puns into *Animal Crackers* as they had into *The Cocoanuts,* and these, too, became a part of Groucho's style. Still speaking to the two women, he makes a blanket offer of marriage. Dumont protests: "Why, that's bigamy!" Groucho agrees: "Yes, and it's big o' me too." In a reminiscence of Africa, he speaks one of his most famous lines: "One morning I shot an elephant in my pajamas. How he got in my pajamas I don't know." He elaborates: "We tried to remove the tusks. But they were embedded so firmly we couldn't budge them. Of course, in Alabama the Tuscaloosa. But that's entirely irrelephant to what I'm talking about."

With and against Chico he experiments in absurdity and plays a few more word games:

GROUCHO

What do you get an hour?

CHICO

For playing, we get-a ten dollars an hour.

GROUCHO

I see. What do you get for not playing?

CHICO

Twelve dollars an hour. Now for rehearsing we make special rates. That's-a fifteen *dollars* an hour.

GROUCHO

And what do you get for not rehearsing?

CHICO

You couldn't afford it. You see, if we don't rehearse, and if we don't-a play, that runs into money.

GROUCHO

How much would you want to run into an open manhole?

CHICO

Just-a the cover charge.

GROUCHO

Well, drop in sometime.

CHICO

Sewer.

Although Groucho was uncredited in the program, he contributed one long recitative to the proceedings. A few minutes were needed for a scene change, and he wrote a nonsense poem; it was delivered deadpan with one foot on the stage and the other planted on a kitchen chair:

> *Did you ever sit and ponder as you walk along the strand*
> *That life's a bitter battle at the best*
> *And if you only knew it and would lend a helping hand*
> *Then every man can meet the final test.*
> *The world is but a stage, my friend, and life is but a game;*
> *And how you play is all that matters in the end.*
> *For whether a man is right or wrong,*
> *A woman gets the blame;*

And your mother is your dog's best friend.
Then up came mighty Casey and strode up to the bat,
And Sheridan was fifty miles away.
For it takes a heap of loving to make a home like that,
On the road where the flying fishes play.

At this point he would remove his foot and drag the chair slowly off the stage as he concluded, "So be a real-life Pagliacc' and laugh, clown, laugh." Groucho found that the literate audiences would break up at his entr'acte. The less sophisticated would applaud respectfully, as if they were in the presence of a laureate. "To them," he wrote, "my recitation was a great piece of philosophy."

Harry Ruby and Bert Kalmar were capable of writing romantic ballads like "Three Little Words" and "I Wanna Be Loved by You." But they realized that unabashed sentiment would never work in the Marx Brothers context. In a fantasy scene, set in the time of Mme. Dubarry and Louis the Fifty-seventh (a restatement of the flashback in *I'll Say She Is!*), they helped the boys make a shambles of brotherly love:

> We're four of the three musketeers
> We've been together for years
> Eenie, meenie, minie (*honk*)
> We're four of the three musketeers
> We fight for the King, for the Queen, for the Jack
> And we're first at the front
> When the front's at the back
> The foe trembles each time it hears
> This motto ring in its ears
> It's one for all and two for five
> We're four of the three musketeers.

En route, the composers also trashed notions of sweetness and light. In the customary musical of the 1920s, the ingenue was all sugar and moonbeams. Here she would comment:

> All the boys I've known used to say
> I was made of stone
> I would always leave them alone in despair
> I was on the pan

I've been called an electric fan,
Told I'm even colder than Frigidaire.

Not only did the Brothers undercut plot and feeling in *Animal Crackers,*
they also thumbed their noses at authorities outside the show. In the
crush of opening night, when even Harpo had trouble scrounging up a
ticket for Woollcott's friend Somerset Maugham, the Shuberts thought
they would have an easy time barring a brash young columnist from the
Graphic. In their view Walter Winchell had panned too many Shubert
productions. "I don't mind missing the openings," Winchell sniped back.
"I can always go to the second night and see the closings." But the prohibition rankled, and he resolved to crash *Animal Crackers*—especially when
he learned that the musical had a minor character named Wally Winston
of the *Evening Traffic.* One way or another, he let it be known, he would
be inside the Forty-fourth Street Theatre when the house lights dimmed.
Jacob and Lee Shubert assigned nine press agents and two detectives to
make sure their venue remained Winchell-free. Predictably, the Brothers
sided with the outcast. At first Harpo supplied Winchell with a false beard
and stuffed an Algonquin Hotel towel into his suit jacket to give him the
appearance of a hunchback. When that failed to please either Harpo or
Winchell, the Brothers waited until the guards had passed, and then
sneaked the journalist in through a dressing room window. Once
Winchell gained entrance he was whisked backstage and made up as
Harpo. Groucho explained to security men that his brother suffered from
occasional seizures, and that a spare Harpo had to be kept on hand in case
of emergency.

From the wings Winchell saw a classic Marx Brothers musical, with no
cues missed and with laughter building from Groucho's entrance to the
curtain calls. A delighted Brooks Atkinson praised "the new fury of puns
and gibes," calling special attention to Groucho who, "delivering his madcap chronicle of an African exploration, touches on nearly every topic of
the day and makes some of the most insane verbal transitions since his
last appearance." The *Times* critic concluded: "These are nihilists—these
Marx boys. And the virtue of their vulgar mountebankery is its bewilder-
ing, passing, stinging thrusts at everybody in general, including themselves. . . . Those who remember Groucho as the Little Corporal will
know how comic he can be as the King." Percy Hammond decided that
Groucho was an "unruly clown" who jumps suavely "through the paper
hoops of the libretto, and as he does so he adds to our sum of nonsense."

Once again the Marx Brothers were in a smash hit, with scalpers asking as much as $100 for a pair of $10 seats. And once again the Marx Brothers did repeat business. Columnist Heywood Broun told readers of the New York *World* he had seen twenty-one performances of *The Cocoanuts*, whereas he had visited *Animal Crackers* a mere dozen times. Still, he added, "I hope to catch up, as the season is still young."

The frantic extempore style grew more elaborate as the season went on. Broun proudly wrote: "When Groucho examined the stolen painting, he said, 'It looks like an early Broun.' It earned a loud, proud laugh from [me], but the rest of the audience sat stony wondering what an 'early Broun' might be. I believe the line was dropped after that and that it is restored only on such nights as I stand in the wings."

The Brothers promised Harry Ruby a bathrobe for his birthday. When the day came and went without any gift, Ruby cast the stagehands in a revenge play. One evening the chorus sang "Hooray for Captain Spaulding" and, as usual, presented him with a treasure chest, referred to by the Captain as "A matchbox for an elephant." The top swung open and the composer emerged. "Where's my robe?" he demanded, standing his ground until someone whisked him away. Such gambits grew contagious. On another evening Dumont innocently opened the chest—and leaped back as a parade of Grouchos passed in review. Every one of them was a stagehand or musician, emerging from a trapdoor appropriately moustached and cigared for the occasion.

Arthur Marx had no illusions about becoming an actor, but he enjoyed watching his father from the wings. On a whim Groucho would occasionally let his son ride with him onstage, lifted on the shoulders of "Nubian slaves." Nothing in the program, or in Groucho's lines, ever explained the boy's presence; audiences simply accepted it as one more instance of Marxian eccentricity. Arthur remembered "standing there when Groucho would be getting into his sedan chair. To give me a thrill, if he was in a good mood he would sometimes say, 'Hop in and take a ride with me,' and then he'd pull me into the chair with him. I'd ride out onto the stage and have to sit there while he went through his routine with the Nubian slaves. Much to the audience's bewilderment, the routine would contain no reference to the little boy in short pants, who remained in the sedan chair, gaping worriedly out into the sea of faces, until he was carried back into the safety of the wings again."

When Sam Harris returned from a holiday in Florida, the Marx Brothers invited him backstage during a performance. While waiting for their cues they began talking about hot stocks. "There's a gold mine in Arizona," Harpo said. Chico added: "The gold is there on the ground just waiting to be picked up." Groucho demurred: "You didn't tell me you have to lean over to pick it up." Before Harris could offer his opinion he was shoved onstage. Everything had been darkened for a scene change. Suddenly the spotlight snapped on and the cue sounded for the Brothers' song. "We're four of the three musketeers," chanted the men in plumes and tights. The fifth of the fourth of the three was an incongruous sunburned producer in a Palm Beach suit. Ticket holders took no notice; at the Forty-fourth Street Theatre, coherence had been barred since opening night.

But back of the backstage, things were not so amusing. Groucho remained unhappy with what he saw as Chico's unprofessionalism, and for once Minnie agreed with him. It happened that the night she came by to wish her sons good luck, Chico was nowhere to be found. When he entered she slapped him in the face and demanded, "How dare you come in late! That's cheating." Chico ran his fingers across his cheek. "Minnie, that hurt," he told her, and doubtless it did. But not as much as he claimed; the eldest son knew that Minnie would never have slapped Groucho, no matter what his transgressions. You always hurt the one you loved.

Betty Marx, Chico's wife, had much to say on this subject. Although Minnie had relocated to Queens, closer to Manhattan but some twenty miles from Great Neck, Groucho made an effort to see her every day. Chico had to be prodded to visit his mother. Yet when he did go, he would hand over whatever cash he happened to have on hand without a word. If Groucho presented Minnie with a hundred-dollar bill, the gift was invariably accompanied by a lecture on thrift. Small wonder that he grew cranky the day that Minnie complained about her failing health: "I think I'm closing up shop soon. The show is almost over." Groucho snapped at his mother: "Don't be silly. You'll outlive us all." Now that he had found a way of forcing Minnie into the role of a dependent child, *der Eifersüchtige*—the jealous one—was not going to let his mother slip away that easily.

•

TIMING, a comedian's greatest asset, lay behind the Brothers' next leap. They had already failed in silent film; "Humorisk" could not capture a shadow of their appeal, and it was assumed that their careers would be spent on the stage. But in 1927 Al Jolson electrified audiences by breaking into song in *The Jazz Singer.* New job categories—sound man, vocal coach, studio musician—came into being, and the search for melody, dramatic eloquence, and vocal comedy was on. It seemed logical to the Marxes' agency, William Morris, that their clients would be ideal for celluloid. After all, went the reasoning, 75 percent of the act talked, and the silent one honked a horn and dropped noisy silverware. Morris received an encouraging feeler from United Artists, but no one could agree on a price for bringing *The Cocoanuts* to the screen. The agency then shopped the property and talent to Paramount. The asking price was $75,000 for the package. Walter Wanger, later to become a producer famous for his aphorism "Nothing is as cheap as a hit, no matter how much it costs," was then in charge of the studio's New York office, and he liked what he saw. With some trepidation he took the offer to Adolph Zukor. The studio chief shook his head: too much money for an untried team. Yet Zukor did not refuse a deal outright. Wanger sensed that if he shaved the price he might be able to get *The Cocoanuts* on screen after all. To that end he set up a meeting with the executive, the agency, and Chico.

Here Chico the professional gambler took over. As good as he was in card games, he invariably stayed too long and frittered away his winnings in search of a bigger jackpot. Dealing with the act, however, he was usually balanced, charming, and shrewd. At the meeting with the Paramount chief his main weapon was flattery. In awed tones he spoke of the deep personal thrill he felt just to be in the company of America's leading showman—a legend and yet a philanthropist, always looking after his performers.

Zukor wondered what could possibly hold back the career of such a discerning man.

Chico explained. It was a small matter of fees, actually. He and his brothers had worked for years to make this film the best it could be. Now they wanted a return for all that investment of time and effort. Not too much return, of course—say $100,000?

Zukor nodded. He allowed that was an agreeable price. Now it was Wanger's turn to be awed. He told friends that he had never seen anyone wrench an additional dollar, let alone an extra twenty-five grand, from Zukor. Then again, he had never seen Chico in action.

As a result of the Paramount meeting, the Marx Brothers would each be earning $2,000 a week in *Animal Crackers,* and more than twice that amount for moonlighting in the movie of *The Cocoanuts.* It was no wonder that Groucho felt as if prosperity would never end. He had amassed savings of some $250,000, joined an exclusive country club in Great Neck,

Minnie's parents, Lafe and Fanny
Schoenberg (1898)

Minnie at nineteen (1883)

Groucho begins his career
as a singer (1905)

The Four Nightingales (*top
to bottom*): Groucho, Harpo,
Gummo, Lou Levy (1909)

Sherlocko, the Monk

By GUS MAGER
Copyright, 1911, by Journal-American-Examiner

No Mystery Is Too Baffling for Him

"Sherlocko, the Monk"—the comic strip that inspired the Marxes' nicknames (1910)

Minnie Palmer (her showbiz name) promotes the acts she's producing (1912)

MINNIE PALMER
Chicago's Only Lady Producer Presents
4 MARX BROTHERS & COMPANY
with
GEORGE LEE and PAUL YALE
INCLUDING A CAST OF 19 PEOPLE

The company is breaking all records on the Western Vaudeville Managers Association

MISS PALMER ALSO PRESENTS THE FOLLOWING SUCCESSES
"Six American Beauties," "Golden Gate Girls" and "After Twelve O'clock"

Groucho in New Orleans (1917)

Groucho as Napoleon in *I'll Say She Is!* at the Walnut Street Theatre, Philadelphia (1923)

Zeppo, Chico, Groucho, Lotta Miles, and Harpo in *I'll Say She Is!* (1924)

Groucho without moustache or glasses (1920s)

At Sam and Minnie's house
in Richmond Hills: Ruth,
Frenchy, Chico's daughter
Maxine, Harpo, Groucho,
Arthur (1920s)
(Maxine Marx Collection)

Stage Version of *Animal
Crackers*: Groucho as Captain
Spaulding (1929)
*(The White Collection, Performing
Arts Research Center, The New York
Public Library at Lincoln Center)*

Stage version of *Animal Crackers*: Dumont and Groucho (1929)
(The White Collection, Performing Arts Research Center, The New York Public Library at Lincoln Center)

and bought a classic Packard Runabout with tooled leather upholstery and burled walnut dashboard, and he continued to invest in the burgeoning stock market, certain that if trends continued he would double his earnings by the end of the year. The Marxes' schedule was about to be burdensome, but even here Paramount was pliant. *The Cocoanuts* would be filmed four days a week, with Wednesdays off so that the boys could play matinees. Having fallen behind Warner Brothers in the changeover to talking pictures, Paramount scheduled fifteen features and fifty short subjects for the calendar year of 1929, and *The Cocoanuts* led the way.

It would be shot at studios in Astoria, on Long Island. Most Paramount features were being shot and edited in Hollywood, but the New York facility remained useful for Broadway stars unable to leave town; W. C. Fields had filmed several shorts and features on the premises. Robert Florey and Joseph Santley were signed to direct, beginning in February, with Santley handling the choreography and Florey the action. Florey, a French filmmaker, immediately crossed swords with Groucho, to his eternal regret. The greasepaint moustache, he decreed, would have to go: "The audience isn't accustomed to anything as phony as that and just won't believe it." Groucho pointed out, "The audience doesn't believe us anyhow. All they do is laugh at us and, after all, isn't that what we're being paid for?"

No amount of arguing could persuade him to change; his only compromise was a small dusting of talcum powder to diminish the glare. After the first day's shooting, Paramount producer Monta Bell made another decision. "Groucho," he said firmly, "you can't step out of character and talk to the audience."

The opposition only seemed to make Groucho more recalcitrant. He had no proof to back up his opinions, and no experience in commercial film. He took the position as much out of perversity as comic instinct: Groucho thought he had seen the last of capricious and dictatorial vaudeville managers, and here they were again, in a new guise. Later he would tell anyone who would listen that Robert Florey could barely understand English and had no sense of humor (both false: he had been in the United States since 1921 and was fluent in English, and Chaplin admired his work). Groucho also said that Monta Bell had retired from filmmaking "for the good of the industry" (the producer / director actually went on to make films until the post–World War II period).

Bell countered by refusing to allow any shots to be made in Florida. "Why are you concerned with real backgrounds," he asked Florey, "when one of the leading characters wears an obviously fake moustache?" The director did what he could under arduous conditions. As difficult as Groucho may have been to work with, he at least showed up on time. Chico, Florey complained, "had found an Italian restaurant whose owner produced homemade wine" against the laws of Prohibition, "and that's where we would find him most of the time. Zeppo would also frequently be missing. Actually, they seemed to take turns and I'd always have to send assistants all over the place to look for the missing member. Until the brother was found there was little we could do but sit around."

Nearly forty years afterward, cinema historian Paul D. Zimmerman wrote that the camera work in *The Cocoanuts* "showed all the mobility of a concrete fire hydrant caught in a winter freeze." This is at once accurate and unfair. Filmmakers like Charlie Chaplin and Buster Keaton moved as they pleased, because the grinding of cameras would go unheard by audiences. Directors of the talkies could take no such liberties. On the sound stage, microphones amplified the rustle of newspapers and charts until they sounded like detonations; Ryskind found that "the buzzing of a fly sounded like an airplane." To solve this problem Florey ordered all the paper props to be soaked in water. This gave them a slack, subaqueous look, but by this point realism had been jettisoned. Shutting out the grinding noises of the camera was a more difficult matter. Each cinematographer was forced to remain in place, enclosed in a cumbersome soundproof box. Only the lens peeked out. As a result, all work had to stop from time to time so that the cameramen could step outside and catch their breaths. With all the difficulties Florey experienced, he still managed to invest his musical—the first full-length one to be shot in the United States—with a certain personality and verve, shooting some of the dance numbers from overhead in a style that Busby Berkeley would emulate, and attempting to wring some interest from the moribund love story.

None of the Brothers was allowed to view the final cut, and they were working the night that *The Cocoanuts* opened in New York. Two days later, when they attended a matinee, Groucho was inescapably reminded of "Humorisk." The show was sparsely attended and children ran up and down the aisles, wholly indifferent to the characters on-screen. "We're going to have to buy back the print," he whispered to Chico. "This will ruin our careers." Chico disagreed, and to Groucho's loud chagrin and secret pleasure, his brother was correct. In the *Times*, Mordaunt Hall praised the film, accurately noting: "Fun puts melody in the shade." The out-of-town papers fell in line. Rather than discouraging patrons because of its rapid dialogue, *The Cocoanuts* forced them to go back a second and third time to catch the gags. When Paramount confidently predicted that the Marx Brothers' movie would be one of the top grossers of 1929, Groucho finally permitted himself to see the glass as half full. William Morris had made entertainment business history by booking the Marxes into the Palace for $7,000 a week, the largest salary that theater had ever paid to an act. *Animal Crackers* had proved to be their third Broadway smash, and the film was thriving in theaters across the country, with bookings planned for England.

So secure did Groucho feel that he published a piece about his Wall Street adventures. "I come from common stock," he wrote in a light-hearted *New Yorker* piece, and went on about his new obsession. "Between the ages of sixteen and twenty-six my interests were devoted to the drama, music, painting, literature, and the Arts. I was a dilettante, a classicist, a philosopher, a bookworm. For years I read no farther back in a newspaper than the sporting page. To me, the financial sheet was only a page to remove mud from my shoes. No more. I use the editorial page now. The financial sheet is sacred."

Groucho told the truth with a slant. He had indeed plunged headlong into the market. And why not? Practically all of his show business colleagues were similarly enchanted with the prospect of increasing their holdings exponentially every month. The Broadway producer Max Gordon spoke for the lot when he and Groucho played golf at a Long Island course on a sunny spring afternoon. "This is the life," Gordon rhapsodized. "Here I am, a nobody. My real name is Salpeter, and I'm just a kid from Rivington Street. But I can spend a fine day playing golf because I already made $3,000 dollars in the market this morning." Groucho shared Gordon's euphoria. A line by their mutual friend Ira Gershwin seemed perfect for the occasion: "How long has this been going on?"

CHAPTER SIX

Listen to the Mockingbird

DURING THE RUN of *Animal Crackers* Groucho's former neighbor visited him once again backstage. The lawyer gave him credit for eschewing a life of crime, but went on to complain, "I was out front tonight and you were still doing the same silly, ridiculous things you were doing before."

"Well, wasn't it funny?" Groucho challenged him. "Didn't you hear the audience howl with laughter?"

"Yes I did. And I even got a snicker or two out of the show myself. But you're thirty-seven now. Aren't you embarrassed, at your age, acting like a nut and making a public fool out of yourself?"

Groucho changed the subject. "How are you doing these days?"

"I've got news for you. I didn't get that twenty-five-dollar raise I expected. Instead they raised me *fifty* dollars! And it won't be long before I'll be making two hundred dollars a week. Imagine! At my age, getting two hundred dollars a week!"

"Being a kindly man," Groucho was to write, "I didn't have the heart to mention the six thousand a week I was collecting. I just sat there and let him rave on. Except for throwing in a few even more stuffy phrases, he delivered the same lecture he had given me two years before. When he finally ran down I said, 'Leonard, you've convinced me! . . . Any fellow who can pull down a hundred and fifty a week at your age makes me realize the foolishness of my ways. You are a shining example of young America on the march, and *Animal Crackers* will be my swan song in the theatre.' "

The forecast was more accurate than he knew. Once this production closed, he and his brothers would never again perform in a Broadway show. For within a few months they would suffer a double loss—of their savings, and of their source—and these losses would radically alter the team's direction.

The sorrows began on a pleasant September evening in 1929. After 171 performances, *Animal Crackers* closed and, dangling the promise of big money, Sam Harris persuaded the Brothers to go on tour. Just before the troupe departed for Boston, Frenchy and Minnie dropped in on a rehearsal. The visit came not long after Minnie's unpleasantness with the one brother outside the act. Gummo's new wife, Helen, had been married before. During an acrimonious divorce, she had given up her infant daughter Kay to her in-laws. Now she claimed that she had been unduly pressured, and sued to get the child back. Her new mother-in-law was furious at Helen for relinquishing Kay in the first place. "You can't tell me she didn't know what she was doing," Minnie said. The suit was long and difficult, and even though it eventually went Helen's way, Minnie could not bring herself to forgive the woman. Perhaps as a counterpoint to the resentment, she turned to her boys in show business. Appraising the new singers and dancers, she flirtatiously announced that she was available for the chorus line. The boys refused Minnie outright; they told her she was too young. As consolation, she and Frenchy were invited to dinner chez Zeppo. Chico begged off; he had a previous appointment to visit Adolph Zukor's estate. The other boys joined their parents in an old-fashioned, multicourse dinner.

"While we ate and ate," Harpo remembered, "everybody caught up on everybody else. The state of Frenchy's wardrobe. (He could match the Prince of Wales, suit for suit.) The state of Gummo's business. (He was now a successful dress manufacturer.) What Groucho had published lately. (His squibs and vignettes were appearing in all the big columns.) Chico's latest acts of generosity. (To his favorite charity, the Impoverished Pinochle Players of America.) Zeppo's latest idea for an invention. (He was scheming and conniving to get out of show business.) My status as a bachelor. (The family never gave up trying to marry me off.)"

During the dinner Minnie became anecdotal, summoning up the train rides and the one-night stands in Texas and Mississippi, the hick audiences, the managers and boardinghouses, the hens and guinea pigs. As she spoke the decades seemed to fall away; she sprang up and joined the boys in some old songs, ending with seven choruses of "Peasie Weasie." By that time everybody was hungry again, and the family sat down to consume the leftovers. They worked off the second sitting by playing round-robin Ping-Pong, with Minnie shrieking every time her new blond wig slid over her eyes.

Suddenly it was past the old folks' bedtime. The boys summoned the chauffeur, kissed their parents good-bye, and sent them off to Long

Island. As the senior Marxes approached the Queensboro Bridge, Minnie complained that she was not feeling well—it must have been those second helpings. Her face froze. A moment later she gasped and slumped forward in the seat. Frenchy took unaccustomed command, ordering the driver to stop, leaping from the car, and halting both lanes so that the automobile could make a U-turn. They headed back where they had come from; Zeppo would know how to handle this.

But all their youngest son could do was put his mother in the guest room and phone for emergency medical aid. Presently a doctor arrived, examined the patient, and softly told the sons what they already suspected: the sixty-four-year-old had suffered a massive stroke. If their mother made it through the night they could take her to a hospital. She was too unstable to move just now. No one was to be at her side for more than a few minutes at a time. At two in the morning, as Harpo awaited his turn, the doctor told him to go in quickly. There was no more that medicine could do.

Minnie stared at Harpo with sightless eyes. He tried an old trick: "I've come to pin the carnations on Mr. Green's cottage, Minnie." For a moment her lips trembled, and she focused on Adolph, the blond one, the son who had looked so much like her when she was young, who played the harp like Mama in the old country. Forty years old and unattached, still fooling around with the girls like a schoolboy. She smiled indulgently and tried to say something, but no words came. Circumstances forced her to replace language with gesture—the mime talking to the mime. Harpo had no trouble understanding his mother. "I knew what she was trying to say. I reached over and straightened the new blond wig she had bought especially for tonight. The smile came back for a second. Then it faded, and all the life in Minnie faded with it. I took her into my arms. I don't remember what I said, or thought. I only remember I was crying. Minnie was dead."

She was buried at the vast cemetery of Woodlawn in Queens. Frenchy seemed dislocated; the force and energy of his household had gone, leaving him in the dark. He was not to recover from the loss, and from the funeral onward he was wholly dependent on the boys to pay his bills and guide his life. All five brothers were in attendance, and the wives and a handful of friends—but not the children. Chico kept Maxine away; Groucho also felt that funerals were for adults, and saw to it that Arthur and Miriam stayed home. As the company walked through the Jewish burial grounds Alexander Woollcott spotted a headstone bearing the name O'Flaherty. "There's a spy in this cemetery," he whispered to

Groucho. Chico appreciated the line: "I better get as good a laugh when I go." Harpo was also amused, and hated himself for snickering. Was this all Alex could do—crack wise on a sad day? But Harpo had underestimated his friend. The next issue of *The New Yorker* carried a fulsome obituary amplifying the party line the Brothers had been pushing ever since they cast Minnie out as their chief financial officer. Woollcott wrote that the mother of the team "had done much more than bear her sons, bring them up and turn them into play actors. She had *invented* them." She had indeed brought them into this world, she had kept them off the streets and pushed and coaxed and bullied them into performance. But just as each of the boys was part of an ensemble, so was Minnie. If any individual could be said to have "invented" the Marx Brothers it was Al Shean, Minnie's brother. Left to their own devices, and Minnie's, they would have remained an obscure, ragtag act. Another few years and their names would decorate the long list of forgotten magicians and jugglers and baggy-pants comedians, headliners who faded along with vaudeville itself. Uncle Al was the one who showed the boys that comedy was more than schoolboy clowning, that it required form and substance, timing and careful, scrutinized dialogue. But Woollcott was uninterested in the whole truth; he had made his fortune out of exaggeration and the myth of celebrity, and Minnie's demise offered him yet another opportunity to wax eloquent. "They were just comics she imagined for her own amusement," he gushed. "They amused no one more, and their reward was her ravishing smile. . . . She died during rehearsals, in the one week of the year when all her boys would be around her—back from their summer roamings, that is, but not yet gone forth on tour. Had she foreseen this— I'm not sure she didn't—she would have chuckled, and combining a sly wink with her beautiful smile, she would have said, 'How's that for perfect timing?' "

In the next few weeks Harpo was the most visibly affected mourner, unable to join in the Round Table raillery. Gummo and Zeppo kept their own counsel; Chico went on what his daughter called a "heart- and mind-deadening gambling spree, his only way of dealing with the loss of the mother who was so much like himself." By all accounts Groucho seemed less mournful than his brothers. A letter to a friend was melancholy but distant, as if written for publication: "In the afternoon she was at the theater watching a rehearsal joking and laughing. Four hours later she was gone. The only grain of comfort, if there can be one, was the fact that it was merciful. . . . It's a thing we all have to face, but to each one it's a harrowing experience." Publicly he saluted Minnie as "a great dame," but

Woollcott's appraisal, like Woollcott himself, was more than Groucho could bear. "Sure," he was to tell his son, "Mom gave us a little push. But *we* did all the work. *We* were the ones with the talent."

Whatever their individual reactions, the Brothers had little time for lamentations. A week after their mother's funeral they were in Boston playing *Animal Crackers* to sellout crowds. For all four, laughter proved to be the best medicine, coupled with the sensation of well-being that comes from financial prosperity. The stock market had been stumbling since September, but Wall Street spokesmen, economists, and the government issued bullish predictions. Groucho was not so sure and consulted his broker. The assurance he received was patronizing in the extreme: "Mr. Marx, you may not realize it, but this has ceased to be a national market. We're now in a world market. We're receiving buying orders from all the countries in Europe, South America and even the Orient. Only this morning we got an order from Hindustan to buy one thousand shares of Crane Plumbing." An abashed Groucho bought three hundred shares of Crane. When he paid a visit to Eddie Cantor's dressing room, the star was so flattered he gave away a closely guarded stock tip: Goldman-Sachs was "the most sensational investment and holding company on the big board." Groucho immediately acquired a chunk of stock in the company, even though he knew less about Wall Street than Cantor did.

And then came October 24, 1929. That Thursday morning, following several days of backslide and recovery, the calamity began. In a single day Montgomery Ward toppled from 83 to 50, Radio from 68¾ to 44½, U.S. Steel from 205½ to 193½. The great banks, Morgan, Chase National, Bankers Trust, played King Canute for a couple of weeks; then the bad news washed over them all. On November 2, the *Commercial & Financial Chronicle* wrote the finale to an epoch: "The present week has witnessed the greatest stock-market catastrophe of all the ages."

Groucho had no need of such official notices; several days before, he had received a call from Max Gordon. In four words the producer encapsulated the situation: "Marx, the jig is up." Indeed it was; Groucho's entire life savings had washed away in the Panic. "I was a wealthy man on the eighteenth hole of a golf course," he stated bitterly. "By the time I got to the club house I was destitute." In this he was hardly alone, of course, and unlike most of his countrymen he had the promise of future employment. But his worst fears had been confirmed; all he possessed outright was the house. From here on, wherever he moved, whatever dwelling place he owned at the time would become a symbol of security, as important to him as a shell is to a hermit crab. Chico increased his brother's misery by overturning the fable of the grasshopper and the ant. "Look at it this way," he said cheerfully. "You lose your money in the market. I toss mine away on dames and gambling. Who had the most fun?"

Entertainers, taking their cue from *Variety*'s headline, WALL ST. LAYS AN EGG, tried to smile away their bad luck. Cantor spoke about an uncle who had died too young. "He had diabetes at forty-five." The comedian shook his head. "That's nothing. I had Chrysler at 110." Groucho told friends that "the drop-in on Cantor cost me thirty-eight grand." He threw fresh ad-libs into the recipe for *Animal Crackers*. "Drab, dead yesterdays shutting out beautiful tomorrows," began one of the O'Neill send-ups. "Hideous, stumbling footsteps, creaking along the corridors of time." Groucho added, "And in those corridors I see figures, strange figures, weird figures. Steel 186, Anaconda 74, American Can 138." But the banter did little to restore his spirit. Images of death haunted him; he wrote a friend that he was "teetering on the edge of a pauper's grave." He slept fitfully if at all, and for the first time since the early days in vaudeville, suffered from stage fright. One evening, neither the stage manager nor Sam Harris could persuade him to leave his dressing room. As ticket holders whistled impatiently, Harpo, Chico, and Zeppo tried to amuse them with some old routines. These were not what the crowd had paid for. Harry Ruby, who happened to be in the audience, slipped backstage and confronted the holdout. "You can't do this. The audience is out there waiting for you. They paid to see you and you've got to give them a show."

"What for?" Groucho responded glumly. "What's the use of working and making money? I'll only lose it again."

Ruby had not only written the songs, he had sat through enough rehearsals to memorize every word and gesture. "If you don't go out there," he declared, "I'll play the part myself." Groucho remained in place, his head in his hands. The songwriter nodded grimly, seized a grease pencil, and began decorating his own upper lip with a wide black moustache.

Groucho watched him in the mirror. Then he put on Captain Spaulding's pith helmet and surrendered. "You win. No audience deserves to look at you for a whole evening."

The insomnia would not be dealt with so easily. He tried all the conventional methods, from peaceful music to hot Ovaltine, from wrapping himself in a night coat to retiring nude. Nothing worked. In desperation he consulted Robert Benchley, a notoriously light sleeper. "If I don't get some sleep soon," Groucho muttered, only half-joking, "I think I'll kill myself." The humorist recommended a hot bath scented with a special pine needle solution just before bedtime. Groucho was willing to try any-thing; he bought a bottle of the scent, dumped it into the tub, climbed in, and shut his eyes. Ten minutes later, Ruth heard gurgling noises, charged into the bathroom, and pulled her husband's head out of the water.

Bewildered, he asked her what was going on.

"You nearly drowned," she shouted. "Don't you ever try this again."

Groucho looked on the sunny side. "At least I'm sleepy."

By the time he got to bed, though, he was wide awake. The next time he ran into Benchley he complained about the almost fatal pine needle solution. Benchley's cheeky reply was worthy of Groucho himself: "Who said it was an insomnia cure? You said if you didn't get some sleep you wanted to kill yourself. I was just expediting things."

The persistent shortage of sleep, added to the shock of Minnie's death and the economic malaise, eroded Groucho's attempts to be the most mature of the Brothers. Difficult at home, he became insupportable on the road. Perhaps because Margaret Dumont represented the onstage symbol of female authority, he made her life a hell. As the troupe settled into an Indianapolis hotel, security got word that a prostitute was plying her wares upstairs. The room number was Dumont's, and as she approached, the detective was at her side—just in time to see Groucho emerge in his pajamas carrying a douche bag.

"You sneak!" he exclaimed, feigning shock at seeing his date with another man. "I don't know why I put up with this."

With haughty dignity Dumont tried to minimize the prank, but she was on the verge of tears. "Well, that's Groucho. He does these things. It just hurts me terribly."

Worse was to come. Groucho had egged on his brothers, and upon entering the room Dumont ran into Chico. "Oh," he said to the actress. "You got another guy. Well, I'll be back in half an hour."

No sooner had he left when Zeppo emerged from a linen closet, clad in a hotel towel. "Just because I'm the youngest," he complained, "you take my money but you never get around to me."

As he vanished, Dumont tried to explain the situation. "He's right. He is the youngest. They're making him do these things. You know, there are four of them."

The detective had only counted three. "Where's the other one?" He did not have far to look. Water was running in the bathroom, and upon investigation he found a man in a blond wig sitting in the tub. Harpo emerged from the water and exited, silent as always, nude save for a col-orful Windsor-knotted tie around his genitals.

By now a small crowd had gathered in and around Dumont's room, but the official guest was no longer in the vicinity. She was downstairs, mortified and weeping as she checked out. She spent the night in the local railroad terminal, and that was where Groucho came across her the next morning. Before he could say a word she burst into tears. "Ah, Maggie," he said. "Don't be mad. You know we'd never do anything to hurt you." He knew and she knew that this was a lie. But more important, he knew and she knew that she loved the work, that she was irreplaceable, and that she needed the job. The scene in the station played itself out with Groucho acting contrite and Dumont allowing herself to be coaxed back to work. It was the first of many such confrontations; during a train trip, the brothers deprived a conductor of his trousers and threw him semi-nude into Dumont's sleeping berth. "You never heard such screaming in your life," Margaret Irving said, recalling that night and many others on tour with *Animal Crackers*. "Maggie, bless her heart, she would quit the show every night of her life, and they'd coax her back. She couldn't get wise to these boys and the treatment she was getting. Because of them she got thrown out of so many hotels. I told her 'Don't resent it. Tell them to do it some more and that you love it.' But she could never bring herself to say that."

With a combination of mischief and irascibility, Groucho sought to avoid an obsession with the economic catastrophe enveloping the United States. But for him it was like the family's Old World recipe for curing headache: go around the house refusing to think of a white bear. His mind kept circling around and landing on the subject. It seemed to him that the painfully accumulated lessons of childhood were repeating themselves on a larger stage, with much the same results. The good son had done everything his mother had demanded, jettisoning a chance to have a respectable career in one of the professions, going on the road by himself, learning about life in the harsh school of experience—only to see Chico keep his spot as the favorite without lifting a finger to please Minnie. And now, after consulting with experts, after carefully assembling a conservative portfolio of investments, Groucho was broke and miserable, and Chico was broke and jaunty. It wasn't right. It wasn't just. But then, he tried to comfort himself, neither was life. Ruth, who had no skills except the minimal ones she had acquired as a chorine, cheerily volunteered to go back to work. Groucho would not hear of it. There were two kids to raise. Somebody had to stay home and take care of them, and it was not going to be him. Ruth was not Minnie and Groucho was not Frenchy; a man had to go out and earn money—big money—for his family. And so, three days after he was entirely wiped out, Groucho went on at the Maryland Theatre in Baltimore, show business as usual, knowing that these gags, this costume and makeup, were all that kept him from going under.

Fretful in the best of times, apprehensive in these lean years, Groucho could not know that the Depression would be the making of him. Not because it built his character (most survivors could say that in the coming years) but because it changed his audience. Despite the customary jeering of the avant-garde and the expatriate Lost Generation, the mass of Americans still respected their national institutions. "The chief business of the American people is business," said Calvin Coolidge in the middle of the 1920s, and the people believed him. The government, the military, the university, society, commerce—all the national bulwarks commanded respect, however grudging, until late in the decade. Prohibition was bad enough, turning a nation of social drinkers into criminals, and career criminals into millionaires. But worse was to come: overconfidence in a bubble economy, financial tremors, and, finally, an economic collapse beyond the means of the private sector or the government to correct. The Establishment on Pennsylvania Avenue, Wall Street, and Main Street was no longer to be trusted. Such sweet, soft-edged comedians as Harold Lloyd and Buster Keaton would have a harder time in this era; aggressive, impertinent personalities like W. C. Fields, Mae West, and the Marx Brothers—Groucho in particular—would flourish by assaulting the powerful, anytime, anywhere.

•

GROUCHO HAD two key roles in the early 1930s, one as a comedian struggling to reestablish himself and his bank account, the other as paterfamilias. The former he played with remarkable consistency and concentration. The latter was problematic. Although Harpo was known as the lovable Marx Brother, Groucho could be endearing as well—but almost always to his children. Whenever a major decision was to be made, Ruth took second place to the prepubescent Arthur and his little sister Miriam. The exigencies of show business, for example, demanded that the Brothers take to the road again. In Groucho's view, professional commitments and family schedules were entirely compatible—the family would simply tag along. Ruth argued that while Miriam might be trundled along without damage, Arthur would have problems being dipped in and out of schools like a tea bag in hot water. Groucho countered that a father's advice was worth a hell of a lot more than that of some grade school teacher's in Chicago, Cleveland, or Los Angeles. As usual in domestic negotiations, Ruth lost. In a way, so did Arthur, whose scholastic difficulties were made more acute by his parents' incapacities. They meant well, but neither of them had finished school, and they were ill-equipped to help their son with his math and social studies homework. Yet neither of them—Ruth through naivete, Groucho through parsimony—thought to hire a tutor.

When the tours were finished the family returned to Great Neck. There the indifferent student staged sporadic rebellions as a protest for all that he had endured on the road. Groucho handled these in his customary style. One morning, for example, Arthur was confined to his bedroom for a mild transgression. The boy lowered himself from the window to the garage roof à la Tom Sawyer, loaded his little red wagon with such vital supplies as a peanut butter sandwich and his baseball glove, and headed for town. By late afternoon he was pressing his nose against a candy store window and wishing he had remembered to take cash with him. From close by he heard the voices of his parents. Groucho got out of the car and confronted him. But there was no harshness in his voice. Instead he offered the boy a dollar because it was improper to run away without spending money. Arthur got in the backseat without further ado.

The time Ruth caught her son smoking was just as anticlimactic. She wanted to spank Arthur; Groucho wouldn't hear of it. He thought the best punishment would be to take away something the kid valued. Like his cigarette lighter. That finished the subject of punishment.

On the topic of sex, one would think Groucho an expert, entertaining lecturer. Actually he was useless. One time, speaking graphically, he spoke about the manner in which bulls impregnated cows. His listener didn't believe a word. To Arthur, the description sounded as surreal as something in a Marx Brothers picture. He concluded that Father was just being funny again.

On balance, however, the early 1930s was a golden time for the young Marxes. Even Chico's daughter Maxine, who would weary of Uncle Groucho's arbitrary moods, had nothing but good to say about him at this time. It was Ruth who suffered from neglect and misunderstanding. Groucho, attempting to provide the intimate and indulgent upbringing he had never known, did so at the cost of his wife's authority and, eventually, her affection. Undercut at all times, she retreated into herself as the children watched. At the time Miriam was too young to understand anything about the Depression, too old for diapers, and just right for chucking under the chin by all concerned. As far as the preschooler was concerned, fathers were permissive men who traveled around and put on funny costumes, uncles were thoroughly silly and adoring, and mothers were pretty blondes who did little except argue with daddies. In her case Mommy did not argue well, and Miriam was led to feel what she could put into words only much later: Groucho and Ruth "really weren't meant for each other from the start. They never should have been married in the first place." Yet there they were, and there they would remain for many years. The only thing to do, Miriam concluded, was to enjoy her father's approach to life, and the unique scene he built around his offspring. As it happened, the child enjoyed it far too much. She was never to find anything or anyone as glamorous on the outside.

•

PARAMOUNT EXECUTIVES drew the line with *Animal Crackers*. No more offscreen nonsense from the Marx Brothers, they decided firmly, and they assigned a tough director to oversee the new feature. Victor Heerman, the son of British theatrical costumers, had been involved with American films since 1914, when he broke in as an editor in Mack Sennett's Keystone Company. But Paramount was less interested in his comic instincts than in his reputation as a disciplinarian. The Marxes' wild history was the talk of show business, and Heerman's principal task was to rein them in. He was also supposed to control the ingenue, a talented singer who, at the age of twenty, already had a reputation for throwing tantrums on the set. She had been given the role by the new head of West Coast production, B. P. Schulberg, and he did not consider it a reward. "One night," wrote Lillian Roth in her confessional autobiography, *I'll Cry Tomorrow*, "as I danced with Mr. Schulberg at a party given by David O. Selznick, he said casually, 'You haven't been easy to handle lately, have you, Lillian?'

" 'What do you mean?' I asked uncertainly.

"Well, he went on as we danced, each of us smiling and nodding to others, it appeared I had once deliberately walked off the set; I had complained about Mr. DeMille, I had caused a scene over an insult, real or fancied, in a close-up shot; and I was temperamental and difficult.

" 'We're sending you back to New York to be kicked in the rear by the Marx Brothers until you learn how to behave,' he concluded casually.

"I was stunned. I left him standing on the floor and ran crying into another room. But his word was law."

So was Heerman's—at least to Roth. The Brothers operated under another legal system. Groucho took one look at the director and tried to discomfit him. "Here we expect a long lean Jew and instead we get a little fat Gentile." Heerman was not to be intimidated. He criticized *The Cocoanuts*: "You could see the picture going all over the place. There was nobody in charge." Groucho needed no translation. The Marxes' last picture had two directors; *Animal Crackers* would have only one, but he would be in full control. Heerman was tested many times during the filming, an experience Roth called "one step removed from a circus." She described a typical day: Zeppo sauntered into the studio at nine-thirty. At ten someone remembered to call Chico and wake him. Harpo arrived, noticed that some of his brothers were missing, and strolled off. Later he would be found asleep in his dressing room. Then Chico finally came in. Somewhat later Groucho, who had been golfing, entered with his familiar bent-kneed walk, removed his cigar, "and with a mad, sidewise glance, announced, 'Anybody for lunch?' Work resumed at midafternoon, and then it was five o'clock, and they were finished for the day."

On the rare occasions when the Brothers appeared on schedule and well rehearsed, other difficulties presented themselves. Roth recounted a scene with Groucho that needed at least ten retakes. "In this instance I was the culprit. We were supposed to be hunting a thief who had stolen a valuable painting. My line, when we stumbled on a fake painting, was, 'Oh, if we could only find the real painting!' Groucho's line was, 'I know who the thief is. Here's his signature.' 'Who is it?' I asked. 'Rembrandt,' he said. 'Don't be silly, he's dead,' I retorted. Groucho snarled, 'Then it's murder.' I burst into giggles every time he said that, ruining the take. The line itself wasn't so hilarious, but I knew Groucho was going to say it with the big cigar jutting from his clenched teeth, his eyebrows palpitating, and that he would be off afterwards in that runaway crouch of his; and the thought of what was coming was too much for me." (The fact that Groucho pronounced the word "moider" in his inimitable East Side accent served as the coup de grâce.)

Aside from her laughing jags, Roth behaved herself on the set. All four Brothers came to respect Heerman as well, although it took some time. The director had analyzed the stage version of *Animal Crackers* and felt it would not translate to the screen. To him the musical numbers were interruptions in the comic flow, and as he began editing he saw places for wholesale cuts. "I already have ten reels of film with these funny scenes," he told the Marxes. "We don't need the music." They disagreed; the juxtaposition of melody and comedy had always earned them big laughs. Why tinker with a successful formula? Ryskind, Kalmar, and Ruby sided with them, and the tension mounted. It took days of negotiation before the Brothers agreed to test Heerman's theory.

Demanding "a clean performance just the same as you do on the stage," Heerman filmed a series of routines and titled the series: "Scenes from the Forthcoming *Animal Crackers*." Sans fanfare the experimental footage was sprung on an audience at the Paramount Theater at Broadway and Forty-third Street. Filmgoers greeted the title with desultory applause, but once the comedy began they broke into smiles, then loud and sustained laughter. The director had made his point. Objections were withdrawn and Heerman went back to sculpting the movie his way. His authority became so noticeable that Roth told her friends about a jail, constructed on the set, to keep the Brothers in place during the shooting. The tale got out of hand, and Heerman was later forced to issue a denial: "These were adult men, and they didn't have to be locked in. There was a jail left over from another picture, and we used it as a makeup room or for the actors to lie down in. It was never locked." Still, the fact that so many people found the story credible enhanced the director's reputation for rigor. The Brothers would have to take their chaos theory elsewhere; Heerman was not subscribing.

In the end, most of the production numbers vanished and almost all of the surefire gags remained. There were a few alterations even in these holdovers: the Czech rabbi was now exposed as Abe Kabibble, a former fish peddler. Harpo engaged in a little cinematic fantasy, shooting at a statue that came alive and returned fire. And Groucho and Zeppo found a verbal equivalent to their brother's antics in a letter-writing routine:

GROUCHO

Jamison, take a letter to my lawyer. Honorable Charles H. Hungerdunger, care of Hungerdunger, Hungerdunger, Hungerdunger, Hungerdunger and McCormick, semicolon.

ZEPPO

How do you spell semicolon?

GROUCHO

All right, make it a comma. Gentlemen, question mark. Uhhh . . .

ZEPPO

Do you want that "uhhh" in the letter?

GROUCHO

No, put that in an envelope. Now then, in re yours of the fifth inst. . . . We seem to believe that it is hardly necessary for you to proceed unless we receive an ipso facto that is not negligible at this moment, quotes unquotes, unquotes and quotes. Hoping this finds you, I beg to remain—

ZEPPO

Hoping this finds him where?

GROUCHO

Well, let him worry about that. Don't be so inquisitive, Jamison. Sneak! Hoping this finds you, I beg to remain, as of June ninth, cordially yours, regards. Now read me the letter, Jamison.

ZEPPO

Honorable Charles H. Hungerdunger. . . . In care of Hungerdunger, Hungerdunger, Hungerdunger and McCormick.

GROUCHO

You left out a Hungerdunger. You left out the main one, too. Thought you could slip one over on me, eh? All right, leave it out and put in a windshield wiper instead. I tell you what you do. Make it three windshield wipers and one Hungerdunger. They won't all be there when the letter arrives anyhow.

Morrie Ryskind was fond of quoting his sister after she looked at the script of *Animal Crackers* for the first time: "If I hadn't already read all those lines, I'd swear Groucho was making them up as he went along." So would everyone else after viewing the film. Despite the many takes, the cut-and-slash editing, mismatched scenes, and unbalanced sound track, Captain Spaulding's delivery seemed to be invented on the spot, and so did the antics of his brothers. Critics overlooked the shortcomings of *Animal Crackers* and issued good notices. *Variety* described the new feature as "a dough film," predicting—accurately—that it would earn top dollar for Paramount. *Film Daily,* the business journal of the motion picture industry, acutely remarked that the Marxes' "popular brand of comedy pervades the picture. So much, in fact, that there is little footage left for a love plot of any importance. While most of the repartee is nonsense, it gets laughs, and that's what counts." In the *New York Times,* Mordaunt Hall, who had reservations about the Marx Brothers, nonetheless hailed *Animal Crackers* as a "further example of amusing nonsense." As an instance, Hall cited a routine in which Groucho and Chico discuss the idea of searching the house next door for the stolen painting. And suppose there is no house next door? The pair discuss plans for building one.

GROUCHO

What kind of house do you think we ought to put up?

CHICO

Well, I tell you, Cap, you see, my idea of a house is something nice and small and comfortable.

GROUCHO

That's the way I feel about it. I don't want anything elaborate, just a little place that I can call home and tell the wife I won't be there for dinner. . . .

CHICO

(*Pointing to the table*) What do you say, Cap, we building right about here?

GROUCHO

I'd like something over there if I could get it. I don't like Junior crossing the tracks on his way to reform school. I don't like Junior at all as a matter of fact.

The picture traveled well. British reviewers cheered *Animal Crackers* as a glorious follow-up to *Cocoanuts.* Only *Punch* sounded a minor sour note. After applauding three-quarters of the act, the critic vainly attempted to divine Zeppo's function. Perhaps he was "the cement that binds the brotherhood together, the power behind the throne." If not, then "how much more than fraternal of Groucho, Chico and Harpo to let him in on an equality." For the first time the Brothers were compared to the creations of Lewis Carroll: *Picturegoer* said that compared to the Marxes' world, "*Alice in Wonderland* is a serious book of reference." J. B. Priestley savored the day he stepped into a cinema on a rainy afternoon, came unbidden on the Marx Brothers, and, like many of his countrymen, "sat up, lost in wonder and joy." He saw Groucho as "urban America, the office executive, the speculator, the publicity agent, the salesman, raised to a height at which the folly of such men blazes like a beacon." He celebrated the team as "Rabelais caught in celluloid" and concluded with a comparison that would be repeated by lesser writers until it became a worldwide cliché: "Karl Marx showed us how the dispossessed would finally take possession. But I think the Brothers Marx do it better." On the Continent, Antonin Artaud would offer an equally high-minded appraisal. The playwright and critic had lauded Chaplin's defiance of natural law in the famous two-reelers; he had marveled at Buster Keaton's ability to leap from the screen to the audience and back again in *Sherlock Junior.* But these were productions of the silent era, when miracles were commonplace and words confined to title cards. The Marx Brothers contended with the contemporary world; they talked illuminating nonsense and made words mean what they wanted them to mean. Even their silence was clamorous. In his eyes *Animal Crackers* was an "extraordinary thing," bringing about a "liberation through the medium of the screen of a particular magic which the ordinary relation of words and images does not customarily reveal, and if there is a definite characteristic, a distinct poet state of mind that can be called *surrealism, Animal Crackers* participated in that state altogether." Naturally, *les américains* did not know what they had; the poor bourgeoisie would probably take the film "in a merely humorous sense." They would never guess that the Brothers had produced "a hymn to anarchy and whole-hearted revolt."

Such aesthetic commentaries were all right in their place. But they had no value to British theater managers, who measured success by the numbers at the box office. Pleased with what they saw, they invited the Marx Brothers to play the Palace in London, if everyone could agree on a fair price. As negotiations got under way the Brothers attended to their domestic bookings: a short tour of the Radio-Keith-Orpheum Circuit, performing old material for $9,000 a week, when even such high-priced talent as W. C. Fields and Fred Allen had earned less than $8,000.

As the Marxes made ready to go, Groucho got roped into a political campaign for Heywood Broun. The journalist had announced his candidacy for Congress on the Socialist ticket, hoping to represent the fashionable "Silk Stocking" district in Manhattan. There was much of the dilettante to Broun, whose knowledge of left-wing politics was derived largely from two books, Edward Bellamy's *Looking Backward* and George

Bernard Shaw's *An Intelligent Woman's Guide to Socialism*. Still, he attracted the support of Morris Ernst, Groucho's lawyer; Harpo; other members of the Algonquin set; and many notable outsiders including George Gershwin, John Dewey, Fred Astaire, Edna Ferber, and Helen Hayes. They all marched in lockstep, appearing at rallies, raising cash, and placing stories with the press—all, that is, except Groucho. His first comment took the form of an endorsement speech delivered on a New York radio station: "Man and boy I have known Heywood Broun for thirty years. He has known me for thirty years. That makes a total of sixty years and brings us down to the fiscal year of 1861, when conditions were much as they are now. My father was out of a job at the time, the farmers were complaining about the prices, and the Prices, who lived next door, were complaining about my father. . . . And so, pupils of the Pratt Street Grammar School, we have come together to observe Arbor Day and plant a tree in honor of the Polish explorer, Heywood Broun. Let us hope that one day the frozen Yukon wastes will give him up. Let us hope that something will give him up. Perhaps he will give himself up. I gave him up long ago."

The second blow was delivered at a September rally at the crowded Selwyn Theatre. Groucho was a self-described liberal Democrat, interested, in a way his parents and brothers never were, in economics and politics. But there was one thing he disliked even more than Babbitts and brass-collar Republicans, and that was hypocrisy. After listening to two hours of hortatory speeches about the candidate, he got into character. Lauding the "fine flower of the American theater" who had filled the arena in honor of the candidate, he added casually: "Before we leave I'd like to ask a question. How many people here live in Broun's district?" Everyone looked around. Only three hands were raised. Groucho's remark may have hit home more forcefully than he thought. Broun saw the election through, came in third in a three-man race, and two years later quit the Socialist Party for good. In any case, that night Groucho became in life what he was onstage, the mockingbird of American solemnity and celebrity.

In this he resembled a cartoonist and humorist whose work had begun to appear in *College Humor* and *Judge*. A publisher sent Groucho a copy of S. J. Perelman's first book, *Dawn Ginsbergh's Revenge*, hoping for a blurb. Groucho was happy to oblige. At first he offered "This book will always be a first edition," and when that was turned down, he submitted the acceptable "From the moment I picked up your book until I laid it down, I was convulsed with laughter. Some day I intend reading it." He *had* read it, of course, and found in it the kind of puns and absurdities that paralleled his own monologues: "A knock on the door roused Dawn from her lethargy. She hastily slipped it off and donned an abstraction. This was Dawn, flitting lightly from lethargy to abstraction and back to precipice again. Or from Beethoven to Bach and Bach to Bach again." When the two men had their first meeting, backstage at *Animal Crackers,* Groucho spoke about his latest interest. Would Perelman be interested in developing a script for a radio program starring the Marx Brothers? The twenty-seven-year-old writer protested that he had no knowledge of the demands and techniques of broadcasting, but to Groucho this was an asset—fresh talent, uncorrupted by experience. He put Perelman together with Will Johnstone and commissioned them to return in a week with something hilarious. The collaborators spent the next several days together without producing anything better than the notion of the Brothers as stowaways on a ship, each in his own barrel. With little enthusiasm they attempted to present their idea to the Marx Brothers at a lunch at the Astor. For most of the meal, Groucho related his misadventures in the market, Chico dashed out periodically to make calls to his bookie, and Harpo flirted outrageously with ladies dining at neighboring tables. Finally Perelman and Johnstone had their chance. "We expected the worst," Perelman said. "To our astonishment Groucho was transported: 'This is too good to waste on a radio show—it's going to be our next picture.' "

Paramount executives claimed that Hollywood was the best place to construct a movie about four men in barrels. Anxious to please their new masters, the writers made plans to relocate. While they were in transit, the quartet did a little traveling of its own. Groucho made the papers in October when the Chicago *American* gave out some distressing news: the Marxes were not giving their audiences full value. The man with the big black moustache was in fact Zeppo, who had stepped in for his brother. Groucho could be found in a bed at the Michael Reese Hospital, where he was recovering from an emergency appendectomy. "Actually," Zeppo stated, "some of his friends didn't even realize it was me. But it got pretty bad after a few days, because I never smoked cigars, and I'd smoke those goddam cigars every day. I used to vomit every day after the last show— four or five shows a day, and it was very difficult. But, anyway, I knew I could do it. And this frustrated me more, because I knew I could get laughs, but I wasn't allowed to with the Marx Brothers." For all his competitive nature, Groucho actually had no wish to cut his little brother out of the picture. He knew that Zeppo was a great storyteller, and that he could be adept with a prop or a straight man. Still, it was one thing to amuse friends, and another to break up an audience. In Groucho's opinion Zeppo needed experience to become a true comedian rather than the sappy love interest, and with vaudeville giving way to the cinema, there were no minor leagues to which he could be sent for seasoning.

After the operation Groucho cut back to two shows a day instead of the customary four. As a result the team was docked $800 from the weekly salary, and that made them all the greedier when it came to signing the London deal. In early December, Groucho wrote a friend that only one thing held up their overseas appearance: "The fact that we have made such absurd demands in the way of financial concessions that no manager with a spark of manhood in him could possibly comply with our insane requests. We are doing this purposely, as we do not care to go, but if we have to we will sell ourselves as dearly as possible."

The management of the London Palace was only too happy to play its eunuchoid role, and on Christmas Eve, 1930, the Marx Brothers boarded the S.S. *Paris,* bound for Plymouth. It was as incongruous a scene as anything in *The Cocoanuts* or *Animal Crackers.* On the street corners of New York unemployed men were hawking apples they had bought on credit, to be resold at five cents apiece. Meanwhile, Arthur and Miriam Marx were bidding farewell to their resentful cousin Maxine, who had to stay at home. Below, in Groucho's stateroom, Paramount lawyers and the Brothers, represented by Max Gordon, were busy negotiating a new contract. It would raise the Marxes' fee from $75,000 a picture to $200,000 plus 50 percent of the profits. By the time the lawyers left and the ship weighed anchor, even Groucho felt ebullient. As he put it, "Everything's coming up grosses." By then a hardcover collection of his satiric articles was in the stores. The acclaim of his friends would be more impressive than the sales of *Beds,* but that hardly mattered. Minnie had forced him to leave school in the seventh grade, and yet he had become a published author, a writer without a ghost. Getting even had its rewards, and not all of them were monetary.

•

TO GROUCHO shipboard life was anathema. He seemed to get seasick the moment the boat weighed anchor, and when he felt well he was asked to dress up, play in shuffleboard tournaments, and amuse the captain at dinner. Aboard the *Paris* he complained to Ruth every night and spent as much time as he could away from her and with the children. In short, the voyage was a microcosm of all that was going wrong in the marriage, acted out in formal attire.

A group of journalists boarded the ship when it docked at Southampton, where Groucho astonished the family by giving a series of congenial interviews. He was even pleasant to Ruth—an unexpected event, since they hadn't spoken in two days. The entente cordiale lasted until Groucho created a scene at the front desk of the Savoy, complaining loudly about the rates for his suite. Eventually chaos was restored and the Brothers made ready to perform their amalgam of bits from *Cocoanuts* and *Animal Crackers* for a London audience. Despite an air of nonchalance, the Marxes retained sharp and unpleasant memories of the last time they had played this city only to receive a shower of coins for their efforts. In a letter Groucho tried to play down the occasion: "I don't think they will laugh at me, but they will laugh enough at Chico and Harpo to put the act over, and that's all I care about." But he cared very much about his own success, and happily reported on January 5, 1931, "We opened here last night and were, surprisingly enough, a big hit." Because of their films, Londoners had become "sufficiently acquainted with our styles to get a fair idea of what we were doing." Evidently so; the critics went wild, headed by the *Daily Mail* reviewer who defied anyone to keep a straight face while these performers "made an art of absurdity," and apportioning out extra praise for Groucho, who "hurls more fun and puns at you in two minutes than most comedians would dare to deliver in an hour." In the next several weeks Groucho realized one of his dreams, attending parties where he held his own with Maugham, Priestley, and Noël Coward, and taking his son and daughter to see the sights of London, explaining to them that Henry VIII had his wives' heads chopped off because it was cheaper than paying alimony.

From London they toured Paris, a city where Groucho pretended to be uncomfortable, largely to unsettle Ruth. He retained a working knowledge of German from the years with Opie and Omie, but scarcely knew a word of his father's native tongue. Neither did Chico, a matter of regret on the afternoon the two hailed a taxi and stood at curbside, vainly attempting to make the cabbie understand that they wished to go to "le racetrack." Every gesture met with confusion until Chico got down on all fours and instructed Groucho to climb on his back and "make like a jockey." The Parisian considered their pantomime and brightened. He understood. The Marxes congratulated themselves and entered. The cab hied them to a large building. They emerged and looked around, bewildered. No betting windows were in view; no familiar aroma of horseflesh greeted their nostrils. The only odor they inhaled was that of automobile exhaust as the taxi pulled away. With good reason. They had been taken to a wrestling arena.

While the Brothers were overseas, the new movie cropped up in conversation. They all had second thoughts about the team of Johnstone and Perelman. Chico was assigned to cable Jesse Lasky at Paramount: "Feel that the writers in Hollywood are untrained, naive. Replace at once." Lasky advised those writers not to be upset. "Actors, you know—they're all a little unstable. I've already replied. I told them to stick to their vaudeville and we'd worry about the movie end." The "we" in that sentence did not include Lasky. He had shown the telegram to Perelman and Johnstone not to put them at their ease but to make them more insecure, and thus more anxious to please. He and Groucho would get along very well indeed.

Eager to begin working again, the Marx Brothers had no regrets about leaving Europe for the United States. Groucho went so far as to book passage on the fastest vessel in dock. The German ship *Europa* made the crossing in four and a half days. All went well until they reached New York harbor, where Groucho filled out the customs questionnaire:

Name: *Julius H. Marx*
Address: *21 Lincoln Road, Great Neck, L.I.*
Born: *Yes*
Hair: *Not much*
Occupation: *Smuggler*
List of items purchased out of the United States, where bought, and the purchase price: *Wouldn't you like to know?*

This did not sit well with the stony-faced inspectors. While the Marxes' fellow passengers moved through customs and went home, the Marxes were delayed for hours as officials fingered the contents of their luggage. Groucho had not declared an item subject to heavy duty, a combination watch and cigarette lighter purchased at Dunhills for $500. This he concealed in his mouth while Ruth fumed.

The word "zany" was not in the inspectors' lexicon. Groucho cost the family several more hours in customs, during which they were strip-searched before release. (The watch remained undetected.) "That was all the marriage needed," a friend remarked. "Groucho and Ruth were in parlous shape. The only thing that could save them was a change of scenery. Fortunately they got one. It was called California."

•

IN LATER YEARS Zeppo described the move as a relocation to Eden. "The sun was out, there was no smog, oh, it was just beautiful. It was so different from Chicago with the snowstorms, and New York with the rain and the snow, where we had been. We loved to come out on the Pantages Circuit, which covered from Vancouver and Seattle and came around to Frisco and Los Angeles. That was a regular vaudeville circuit that we played and we just adored it. We all wound up here."

Groucho's memories matched his brother's. "When we stepped off the train at Los Angeles the air was sweet with a heavy blend of orange and lemon blossoms. The rush to California had not yet begun and Hollywood still had that quiet, pastoral air about it." The booster of Great Neck transferred his allegiance wholesale. Now California was "a wonderful place in which to raise children."

Since Frenchy was at loose ends, he was invited to join the entire family on their three-thousand-mile jaunt, made at the suggestion of Paramount. The studio did not have to ask twice. In a piece about the stage versus the cinema, *Variety* had commented on the decreasing value of theater to the Marx Brothers. "Why *Animal Crackers* on stage at $5.50 when even the ruralities know they will see it later on the screen at 50 or 75 cents?" If any more hints were needed, Paramount announced the phasing out of its Astoria operation; after 1931 all of the studio's major films would originate in Hollywood, where the weather was reliable and the best talent and technicians were on hand. Furthermore, Broadway no longer seemed to be interested in comedians; W. C. Fields's *Ballyhoo* closed unceremoniously even though he was at the top of his form, and the great curmudgeon headed west. The Marxes saw the future, and it was at the thirtieth parallel.

As studio executives needlessly informed them, their careers had reached a new and dangerous corner. *The Cocoanuts* and *Animal Crackers* were essentially photographed stage plays. The Marx Brothers had been involved in only one purely cinematic project, "Humorisk," and that had been a catastrophe. The new one could simply not afford to fail. So they were edgy and trying not to show it when they gathered at the Hollywood Roosevelt Hotel to hear a reading of the script for their next film, *Monkey Business*.

Whenever Perelman wrote or spoke about this encounter he turned sulphurous—often at the expense of truth. The Los Angeles of 1931 was "a dreary industrial town controlled by hoodlums of enormous wealth, the ethical sense of a pack of jackals, and taste so degraded that it befouled everything it touched." Yet Perelman had no trouble returning again and again to accept the jackals' money. He claimed that while he and his partner ground out the scenario, the Brothers were bombing in Britain: "Music-hall audiences were not yet attuned to anarchic comedy, and they saluted the Marxes' whirlwind antics by jeering and pitching pennies onto the stage." But as we have seen, that London incident had occurred nearly ten years before; Perelman accidentally or deliberately confused the date in order to assign maximum humiliation to his tormentors. The studio-assigned "supervisor," Herman Mankiewicz, did not offer his writers much aid and comfort. He summed up their situation in four terse sentences: "The Marx Brothers are mercurial, devious and ungrateful. I hate to depress you, but you'll rue the day you ever took the assignment. This is an ordeal by fire. Make sure you wear asbestos pants." But Mankiewicz came with his own reputation for intimidating writers, and Perelman ignored him.

The reading was set for a Friday night at 8:30 p.m. It was not to be expected that the Marxes would enter on time or en bloc, and no one was surprised when the first arrival occurred at 9:15. It was Frenchy, accompanied by one of his favorite pinochle partners. A little while later Mankiewicz showed up with his brother Joseph, a fledgling scenarist. Next came Zeppo and his wife and the two Afghans they had purchased in England. Harpo followed, flanked by two blonds he had picked up en route. Chico and Betty entered, accompanied by their terrier, which immediately began a dispute with the Afghans. No sooner had the pets quieted down when Groucho and Ruth arrived with three writers. They were Arthur Sheekman, a bright young journalist who had helped Groucho with his prose style; Nat Perrin, a young New York gagman who had submitted a sketch that met with Groucho's approval; and Solly Violinsky, an ex-vaudevillian. Other friends and sweethearts came by; according to Perelman, by the time he cleared his throat and began to recite the first words, the room held twenty-seven people and five dogs.

Just before the evening started, the scenarists tossed a coin to see who would do the reading of the 126-page script. Perelman lost. His solo began pleasantly enough. Occasionally one could even detect a polite ripple of appreciation. This soon ceased, wrote the sufferer, and the attendees "became watchful—not hostile as yet, but wary. It was as if they were girding themselves, flexing for trouble." What Perelman could not know was that even back in New York the Brothers never laughed aloud at story sessions. Margaret Dumont once told an interviewer that "like most expert comedians, they involved themselves so seriously in the study of how jokes could be converted to their own style that they didn't even titter while appraising their material." But what awaited the writers was considerably worse than cold analysis. The roomful of listeners turned sullen, then resentful and, as Perelman saw it, vengeful. *"Some* of them got vengeful, that is; the majority got sleepy, for by then, I had stopped inflecting my voice to distinguish one character from another and had settled into a monotonous lilt like a Hindu chanting the Bhagavat-Gita." Sheekman later said that the reader deserved a medal of valor for his performance: "I would have shot myself on page twenty-five." By the time Perelman croaked "Fade-out," an hour and a half had passed. The only sound was the stertorous breathing of the dogs. After what seemed an eon, Chico stretched, revolved in his chair, and inquired, "What do you think?" With the deliberation of a diamond cutter, Perelman wrote, "Groucho bit the end off his cigar and, applying a match, exhaled a jet of smoke. 'It stinks,' he said, and arose. 'Come on.' "

This was the opening salvo in a long, complicated, and never-resolved relationship between the comedian and the essayist. Groucho Marx was fourteen years older than Sid Perelman, and light-years from him in accomplishment. Nevertheless, Perelman had been educated at Brown University, and he possessed a gift for parody, a rich vocabulary, and a radiant intelligence. Men with those qualifications gave Groucho a feeling of inadequacy, and he always felt the need to squelch them in some way—even when he needed them. And he needed Perelman, just as he needed the other writers. The next day he announced that the Marxes' judgment might have been a tad hasty. He told Perelman and Johnstone that some portions were usable after all, and sent them back to the typewriter. They would not be alone, however. Sheekman was hired to help Perelman with the comic narrative while Johnstone worked on sight gags. Perrin and Violinsky would augment the script with new routines and special material. Other names were peripherally involved: J. Carver Pusey, who wrote and illustrated a comic strip, "Little Benny," about a mute little boy, was hired to augment Harpo's act. Earlier, a writer named Bert Granet had submitted a shipboard idea for the Marx Brothers entitled "The Seas Are All Wet." He threatened to sue for plagiarism and was quieted with a Hollywood offer, although it was not on a Marx Brothers picture. Instead, he would collaborate with Sheekman on *The Big Broadcast,* one of Bing Crosby's first films.

As Perelman described it, the next five months were filled with drudgery, Homeric quarrels, ambuscades, and intrigues. "As far as their temperaments and their personalities were concerned, the Marx Brothers were capricious, tricky beyond endurance, altogether unreliable, and treacherous to a degree that would make Machiavelli absolutely kneel at their feet. They were also megalomaniac to a degree which is impossible to describe, despite the fact that they were not yet what they were to become." The writer confessed himself baffled by the man who had hired him. "I loved his lightning transitions of thought, his ability to detect pretentiousness and bombast, and his genius for disembowelling the spurious and hackneyed phrases that litter one's conversation. And I knew that he liked my work for the printed page, my preoccupation with clichés, baroque language, and the elegant variation. Nevertheless, I sensed as time went on that this aspect of my work disturbed him." Perelman was on the money; the old vaudevillian had spent too much time entertaining the multitudes, and he feared any line that might go over their heads. "What'll this mean to the barber in Peru?" was Groucho's persistent query. He was not referring to South America. He meant Peru, Indiana, and he envisioned a weary middle-aged Hoosier looking to the screen for diversion. Peru was perhaps an unfortunate choice of locale; more than one commentator pointed out that it was the birthplace of Cole Porter, America's most sophisticated songwriter. But Groucho's underlying point was well taken. Non sequiturs and wordplay were means; funny was the end that justified them.

In pursuit of the amusing, the writers were not materially aided by their producer. Herman Mankiewicz, Perelman wrote, "whose stormy Teutonic character and immoderate zest for the grape and gambling have been well delineated in connection with the authorship of *Citizen Kane,* was a brilliant man, but if he had any lovable qualities, he did his best to conceal them." Mankiewicz had a tongue like a rasp. He put down New York writers who deigned to come out to the Coast ("The part-time help of wits is no better than the full-time help of half-wits") and could barely contain himself when Perelman and Sheekman asked about the psychology of the Marx Brothers' screen characters. The producer responded instantly. "One of them is a guinea, another a mute who picks up spit, and the third an old Hebe with a cigar. Is that all clear, Beaumont and

Fletcher? Fine. Now get back to your hutch, and at teatime I'll send over a lettuce leaf for the two of you to chew on. Beat it!"

Nor were they given much aid and comfort by Paramount's new director, a former university light-heavyweight boxing champion and a pilot in World War II. Norman Zenos McLeod, a hero out of Frank Merriwell, asserted his authority in a subdued voice ("I'm as quiet as a mouse pissing on a blotter" served as his self-description), but he had a pronounced effect on Groucho and his siblings. They hazed him at first, appearing one morning on time and in costume—except that the costumes were on the wrong men. Harpo had painted Groucho's moustache on his own upper lip; Chico ran around in lunatic fashion, wearing Harpo's wig; and Zeppo spouted Chico's gags in a vaudeville Italian accent. McLeod was unperturbable, however, and the Brothers' deportment improved by the day. Instead of barring mischief, the director allowed and sometimes encouraged it. There were moments, he acknowledged, when the quartet would get "right out of hand and run away with a scene. They forget the business of the scenario and carry on making up the action on the spur of the moment. I always let these scenes run until they dry up, and sometimes the funniest part of a scene has never been in the original plan."

In vain Perelman, Johnstone, and the others protested that their work was regularly displaced by ad-libs, self-indulgence, and, they learned, outright nepotism. In the sunset of his career Uncle Al Shean had been hired as an uncredited writer of "additional dialogue." For $5,000 he proposed a single usable gag, and that one had whiskers. A woman complains, "Ever since I have been married, I have lived a dog's life." Replies Groucho, "Maybe he got a dog license instead of a marriage license." The writers groaned and went back to their hutches, consoling themselves the way Hollywood scribes have always done—by denigrating their occupation ("an experience no worse than playing the piano in a house of call," wrote Perelman), blowing their weekly paychecks on indulgences, and giving thanks. A lot of thanks. They knew only too well that one-third of the nation had no jobs to complain *about.*

CHAPTER SEVEN

Whatever It Is, I'm against It

NORMAN MCLEOD BEGAN his film career as an animator. S. J. Perelman had been a magazine cartoonist. Johnstone and Pusey still wrote and illustrated newspaper comic strips. They were all familiar with the fast setup and the big kinetic payoff; predictably, their scenario kept the pace of an animated cartoon. Strangely enough, this rudimentary approach found favor with Herman Mankiewicz. The man who considered himself the most sophisticated executive in Hollywood informed the filmmakers: "If Groucho and Chico stand against a wall for an hour and crack funny jokes, that's enough of a plot for me." The writers and director aimed to please; the final shooting script for *Monkey Business* contained more than a hundred jokes but almost no "back story." In the opening scene the Marx Brothers are presented simply as stowaways with no home other than the herring barrels in which they sit harmonizing "Sweet Adeline." (How the mute Harpo could sing tenor was left unexplained; they were the only sounds he ever uttered on film.)

At the time *Monkey Business* went before the cameras Frenchy was at loose ends. Still dapper, still an active card player, he had been romancing ladies of a certain age. One evening he expressed the idea that he might marry again. Minnie replaced by a stranger? The notion was more than the boys could countenance, and they devised a plan to sublimate their father's energies: he would be hired as an extra on their new movie. For reasons that were never fully explained, the continuity department chose this moment to suffer a mental lapse, and so Frenchy appears in two opposing scenes. First he plays a passenger disembarking from the ship. The film then cuts to a group onshore, where Frenchy again pops up, awaiting himself. This lapse was in tune with the asymmetric spirit of the film—as was the casting of Thelma Todd. To Groucho's way of thinking,

Margaret Dumont symbolized the vaudeville and stage comedy of yore. He wanted a more modern straight woman, and after considerable fuss and hurt feelings, he got one. Where Dumont presents the stately society matron, Todd is willowy. Dumont's stature and diction identify her as Old Money; Todd suggests the classic gangster's moll of the 1930s, a conniving blond out for a good time and a rich consort.

For all her flash, the former Miss Massachusetts was no casting-couch starlet. Todd had been a schoolteacher as well as a bathing beauty, and she had acted in a few serious features, among them the first sound movie of *The Maltese Falcon*. But this credit meant less to McLeod and Mankiewicz than her experience in short subjects, where she had played opposite the dithering comedienne ZaSu Pitts. They bypassed the other candidates and gave Todd the job of portraying Lucille, unhappy wife of gangster Alkie Briggs. For the first time in films Groucho was allowed to make sexual overtures to a female: "You're a woman who's been getting nothing but dirty breaks. Well, we can clean and tighten your brakes, but you'll have to stay in the garage all night." A bit later, he closes in for a smooch.

TODD

Oh, no, no, no, don't. My husband might be inside, and if he finds me out here he'll wallop me.

GROUCHO

Always thinking of your husband. Couldn't I wallop you just as well? . . . Oh, why can't we break away from all this, just you and I, and lodge with my fleas in the hills?—I mean, flee to my lodge in the hills.

Various sequences, like the "lodge with my fleas" exchange, pleased Groucho. But Perelman's overall approach disturbed him. "Groucho felt I was overliterary," the writer acknowledged. "I felt he had a wonderful talent for parody and literary turns of speech. For example, in *Monkey Business* we had a love scene in a conservatory, with Groucho reclining like Mme. Récamier. I wanted him to leap to his feet and say, 'Come, Kapellmeister, let the violas throb, my regiment leaves at dawn,' and then go into a parody of *The Merry Widow*, which was playing elsewhere with Mae Murray."

Groucho found the idea arch and ordered the scene eviscerated. All that remains is the "Kapellmeister" line, minor workman's compensation for Perelman. In another sequence, Groucho turns to a crook and assumes a cowboy drawl: "I ain't much on flowery sentiments, but there's somethin' I jes' got to tell yuh. Shucks, man, I'd be nothin' but a pizenous varmint and not fitten to touch the hem of yo' pants if I didn't tell you you've been treatin' me squar' mighty squar', and I ain't fergettin' it." Satirizing the pulp Western was one of Perelman's specialties. Some twenty-five years later he adopted the same voice and tone in a parody of a perfume ad, published in *The New Yorker:* "Pussonally, I'd ruther sniff the ozone a-blowin' through the mesquite than all this fool loco-juice. . . . Howsomever, the wimminfolks set rich store by sich fiddledeedee, so I'll be obleeged if ye'll jest draw me off a Mason jar of thet thar shemale nonsense, pardner." Groucho agreed to do the impersonation, but he was never really comfortable in any voice but his own. Over the next year he resisted most attempts to shoehorn edified shtick into traditional Marxiana. But he could never resist wordplay, provided that it made light demands on the audience. The line "Love flies out the door when money comes innuendo" was permitted to stay; so was the double entendre about a man who had "more women than you could shake a stick at, if that's your idea of a good time," and the comeback when the Captain threatens to throw him in irons. "You can't do it with irons. It's a mashie shot. It's a mashie shot when the wind's against you, and if the wind isn't, I am."

The university of vaudeville and theater had taught Groucho a central truth: every joke has an internal rhythm. Tap into it, and you can wring laughter from the most ordinary phrases. Miss it and you might spend a life on the Borscht Belt. The repetition of "mashie shot" is an instance of that hard-won lesson; so is the double use of "shy" in an exchange with Todd. She remarks that for a man who claims (falsely) to be a lawyer, he's very shy. "You bet I'm shy," comes the answer. "I'm a shyster lawyer." Other comedians would have been satisfied with the last four words; Groucho insisted on hammering home words and lines. The trope annoyed writers but pleased critics and audiences; the repetitions made Marxian dialogue easy to remember and quote.

Monkey Business was not especially difficult to shoot; the cinematographers enjoyed more freedom by 1931, and the on-deck chase scenes came off well. So did a set piece involving Harpo in a shipboard Punch and Judy show, as well as a scene in which Chico explains the inability of his "dem and duff" brother to speak. He also got another chance to annoy his moustachioed brother:

GROUCHO

One night, Columbus's sailors started a mutiny.

CHICO

Naw, no mutinees at night. They're in the afternoon. You know, mutinees Wednesdays and Saturdays.

GROUCHO

There's my argument. Restrict immigration.

As filming progressed, Groucho began to express a neurotic lack of confidence in *Monkey Business*. He doubted the quality of the writing, editing, and direction, and told anyone who would listen that the new ending was not nearly as effective as the original. Here he had a point. The first version was to have taken place at a brewery, with Harpo swimming in a vat of beer, Groucho menacing a group of thugs ("How would you like to be shot, sideways or in a group?"), and the Brothers ending back in the barrels. But the budget did not allow for the brewery props, and *Monkey Business* was forced to end in a barn, as Harpo and Chico battle with some malefactors. Groucho does a mock broadcast of the fight, peppering his commentary with wheezes unworthy of a top comedian ("Both boys are fiddling in the middle of the ring and I don't think much of the tune. . . . Now they're trying. Very trying—I copped that one from an almanac").

In a letter to his stockbroker Groucho refers to his newfound solvency, and then adds, only partly in jest, "The picture is coming along slowly, and I predict it will be the most colossal failure in the history of the movie industry." Another letter details his low opinion of that industry, describing a party where "Josef von Sternberg, with baggy wide pants and a cane [was] trying awfully hard to forget that he was born in Brooklyn and not Vienna. The place was afire with repartee, wiseys, who was the best director, what their next part was going to be, who was humping who, why this supervisor was fired, why Carl Laemmle Jr. [head of Universal production] was going to displace [Irving] Thalberg [head of MGM production] as the little Napoleon of the silver screen, and all the claptrap that goes to make a Hollywood conversation one of the dullest on earth." (Groucho had always regarded Marlene Dietrich's director as a one-joke man anyway. On lunch breaks at the Paramount commissary, the same remark—"Beware the Ides of Marx"—was murmured over Groucho's head every day. The speaker, who always moved on without identifying himself, was von Sternberg.)

Groucho's dyspepsia separated him from the rest of the quartet. Within weeks of the team's arrival in California Harpo had fallen in with the San Simeon crowd, and he spent weekends mixing with the party-goers at William Randolph Hearst's estate. Chico befriended fellow gamblers like Clark Gable and Babe Ruth, high rollers who joined him at the racetrack and casinos of Agua Caliente, a gambling town on the Mexican side of the border. Zeppo, consigned to the same old role of nice-looking straight man, was the least satisfied of the Brothers. He later described himself as "getting very neurotic at going on, doing stuff I didn't want to do. Taking money for which I didn't think I was deserving. I either had to get out and do something, or else wind up with a nervous breakdown." While he pondered his next move, however, he managed to live like a mogul, complete with yacht and decorative wife swathed in expensive furs. In contrast, Groucho shrank from the high life, making the socially ambitious Ruth even unhappier. First he put the family up in a bungalow at the Garden of Allah apartments, where he could hang out with New York writers. Then he moved them to a series of rented houses that were, in his son's view, "about as spectacular-looking as the gardener's place on Chico's estate." While Ruth pouted about the lack of a swimming pool, Arthur and Miriam swam at other people's estates, as well as various health clubs, some of them restricted, prompting Groucho's much-quoted remark that since his daughter was only half Jewish perhaps she could wade in up to her waist.

During this period Groucho considered returning to the stage. No doubt the notion got him through some bad nights, but it had little basis in reality. As he well knew, the combination of sound movies, radio, and the Crash was maiming Broadway and killing vaudeville. Not that stage producers had entirely forgotten the Brothers. Florenz Ziegfeld talked to reporters about an edition of the Follies that might star the Marx Brothers. Earl Carroll, Ziegfeld's great rival, actually offered the Marxes $10,000 per week to appear in his *Vanities*. The management of Loew's State topped that: they would pay $15,000 for a single week's work. Perelman wrote that Groucho's "passionate avocation" was "the collecting and cross-fertilization of various kinds of money," but the comedian evinced little interest in these proposals because they led nowhere. Guided by Groucho, the Brothers determined that they would only appear in a Broadway show that could be transferred to the screen in the manner of *Cocoanuts* and *Animal Crackers*. Ultimately 75 percent of the

Marx Brothers did do a star turn in New York—for two nights only. *Shoot the Works,* devised by Heywood Broun and his fellow Round Tablers, was a star-filled hodgepodge whose cast changed each night. Critic Percy Hammond considered the evenings "as full of fun as a Socialist picnic," but the show had a good cause, funneling proceeds to unemployed actors, an especially vulnerable group in those hard times. Considering its pedigree, *Shoot the Works* should have been better: *New Yorker* staffers Peter Arno, Dorothy Parker, and E. B. White composed the sketches; music and lyrics were from the likes of the Gershwin brothers and E. Y. Harburg. But the highlights came from performers who ad-libbed, or who exhumed some surefire routines from the past. The Marxes fell noisily into the latter category. Briefly reunited with Margaret Dumont, they went through a medley from *Animal Crackers.* "After several bows," reported the *Times,* "Groucho attempted to quiet the audience with a sly curtain speech in which he expressed gratification that the three brothers could get along without the fourth." That brief address conveyed two points of information—that Zeppo's days with the act were rapidly drawing to a close, and that Groucho, the perpetual outsider in the family, had become its public representative.

This was by default. A faun in private life as well as on-screen, Harpo had neither the interest nor the ability to represent the act. Chico's love of gambling allowed him to move among the powerful and well-known, and one day his social contacts would be of enormous value, but he was too restive for subtle mediations. Zeppo had the intelligence to make deals, but at thirty he was still considered the kid, too young to be taken seriously. That left Groucho, strutting like a natural leader but actually defenseless when it came to hard bargaining and fine print. To make matters worse, the team no longer had William Morris to represent them. Morris had been insisting on 10 percent of the Marx Brothers' $200,000 fee for *Monkey Business.* The Marxes stubbornly refused, maintaining that the agency contract had ended with *Animal Crackers.* Morris sued, and after a nasty court fight won its fee. Happily, Max Gordon rode to the rescue, aiding the Brothers in their battle with Paramount. Negotiations were not easy. The studio pointed out that the old contract had been written in flush times. The Depression had made deep inroads at every movie studio; all Paramount employees earning over $100 a week were forced to take a 5 percent pay cut. If every executive was willing to tighten his belt, surely the Brothers would agree to a reduced salary for their new film. Gordon reminded the studio that *Animal Crackers* had been a huge profit-maker. If the Brothers wanted to return to live performance, they would make top dollar on any stage in the States. Why should they take a step backward in cinema? Besides, they were a guarantee of box office success. They and Paramount would get rich together. Unless, of course, the Marx Brothers went to another studio.... The executives squirmed, demurred, protested. And in the end they agreed to the old terms.

Monkey Business got under way, taking on a new quarry—the American gangster film, and by inference the American gangster himself. *Little Caesar* and *The Public Enemy* had just ignited the careers of Edward G. Robinson and James Cagney, investing the street criminal with a new glamour and a fresh vocabulary. Bowing to the moral strictures of Hollywood's self-censoring Hays Office, these films saw to it that the criminal met with a violent comeuppance in the last reel. But by then he had enthralled millions with a gaudy wardrobe that few could afford and a racy argot that everyone could parrot. *Monkey Business* daringly bucked the trend, mocking the spirit of the entire genre. Particular attention was paid to attitude and vocabulary.

THUG

Beat it, I tell you.

GROUCHO

Pardon me. What did you say?

THUG

I said beat it!

GROUCHO

He said beat it. Gee, I wish I'd have said that. Everybody's repeating it around the club.

. . .

BRIGGS

Is there anything you've got to say before I drill ya?

GROUCHO

Yes, I'd like to ask you one question.

BRIGGS

Go ahead.

GROUCHO

(*Coy*) Do you think that girls think less of a boy if he lets himself be kissed? (*BRIGGS backs away and sits down as GROUCHO advances on him*) I mean, don't you think that although girls go out with boys like me, they always marry the other kind?

Groucho drolly remarked that *Monkey Business* "was released the same time as Charlie Chaplin's *City Lights,* which was acclaimed as an instant classic. Our picture was described by 'Sid' in *Variety* of October 13, 1931, as 'the usual Marx madhouse with plenty of laughs sprawling from a plot structure resembling one of those California bungalows which spring up overnight.' " Still, the bungalow had plenty of occupants. Across the country the film broke box office records, and Paramount's ad confirmed the news in *Variety:* "Harpo, Groucho, Chico, Zeppo SRO Everywhere." With the phenomenal success of their third film, the Marx Brothers rose above the status they had enjoyed on the stage. The first feature had made them cult figures with a dedicated following—one suburban theater booked *Cocoanuts* twenty-eight different times over the next two years. *Animal Crackers* had emphasized the team's ability to play the backwaters of America as well as selected cities in Europe. But with *Monkey Business* the Marx Brothers became authentic movie stars on two continents. Alone among their peers they had achieved that status without compromise. Other identifiably Jewish film actors projected an innocence and vulnerability (like Eddie Cantor), showed a yearning for the good life in America (like Al Jolson), or became wholly assimilated personae (like Edward G. Robinson and Paul Muni). In contrast, the Marx Brothers never pushed the soft pedal, never modified their approach or themselves. From the palmy days of *I'll Say She Is!* to the present tense of *Monkey Business,* their object was to scrawl graffiti on the walls of national institutions. Now the world saw them as they saw themselves—permanent outsiders, magically immune from retribution in their battle against dignity, power, and reason, feverish in their pursuit of gratification and money.

This was the fever that goaded the Brothers on, regardless; whenever they encountered roadblocks, they simply chose another route. The team had been considering a second go-round with outlaws. But in March 1932, criminals lost their status in a single headline: LINDBERGH BABY KID-NAPPED. For Groucho the abduction and murder came home a little too directly. He remembered that shortly after the news went out over the wires, an unfamiliar car motor sounded in the driveway. All Groucho could see from furtive peeks was an abandoned Ford. He called the police, who took the car away and told him nothing about its owner. Months later, he was approached by the lyricist Lorenz Hart. "Did you ever find out about that car in your driveway? It was me." Groucho failed to find the humor in Hart's practical joke, for the citizens of Los Angeles, like the people in every other city and town in America, had been transfixed and terrified by the Lindbergh murder. But unlike every other city and town, Hollywood's leaders decided to do something about it. Once Bruno Hauptman had been executed for killing the Lindbergh baby, Will Hays sent out a warning that resonated through the film studios: "To overemphasize the gangster's role in American life is undesirable." The Marxes got the message and looked elsewhere for laughs. They found them about as far from organized crime as it was possible to get: the campus of a fictive academy called Huxley College.

Horse Feathers required the talents of Kalmar, Ruby, Perelman, and Sheekman, plus those of an assortment of additional dialogue writers. By now, relations between Perelman and Groucho had taken a nosedive, and the two men rarely agreed on anything. Edmund Wilson's diary *The Thirties* provides glimpses of the comedian versus the writer: Groucho "gagging all the time, terrific vanity—Perelman finally had a showdown with him, said, That's not very funny! about one of his gags—Groucho said, Oh, so you don't think that's very funny, and gave him to damn well understand that he'd better think it was funny."

Perelman's collaborators damn well understood that Thelma Todd was as funny as Groucho said, and they were not surprised to learn that she was hired for the role of Connie, a flirtatious college widow. Groucho, former real estate swindler, raffish explorer, and stowaway, would get a social promotion in *Horse Feathers,* playing Professor Quincy Wagstaff, the new head of Huxley College. Zeppo was to be featured as Frank, his light-headed son; Chico as Baravelli, the ice man/straight man; and Harpo as Pinky, a dogcatcher full of moonbeams and mischief.

Even more than the previous films, *Horse Feathers* gives the audience no chance to get its bearings. Here college football is the Brothers' metaphor for American business—the incessant meetings, the hypocritical praise of sportsmanship contrasted with the vicious attempts to win at any cost. Scene 1 opens on a group of professors bearded and cloaked like Hasidim. They have gathered to welcome the new college president. In contrast, Groucho appears at the other side of the platform, suspenders down, shaving. A moment later he is introduced and begins his inaugural address. Its opening lines were to echo through the nation's campuses for the rest of the century:

GROUCHO

Members of the faculty, faculty members, students of Huxley and Huxley students. I guess that covers everything. Well, I thought my razor was dull until I heard this speech. And that reminds me of a story that's so dirty I'm ashamed to think of it myself.

The retiring president attempts to offer a proposal for improving the college. Wagstaff replies with a torrent of abuse. "Why don't you go home to your wife. I tell you what. *I'll* go home to your wife. And outside of the improvement she'll never know the difference." Suggestions by the trustees are met with a typically Grouchovian reply set to music:

GROUCHO

I don't know what they have to say.
It makes no difference anyway,
Whatever it is, I'm against it. . . .
No matter how they've changed it or condensed it
I'm against it.

As for faculty politics:

I soon dispose
Of all of those
Who put me on the pan.
Like Shakespeare said to Nathan Hale
I always get my man.

In his first confrontation with Zeppo, Groucho sets his most surrealist tone, crossing into territory marked by René Magritte. The painter specialized in reproducing the elements of bourgeois life and turning them sideways. In his work, men in conventional suits and bowler hats stalk each other like assassins, or fall from the sky by the thousands, like raindrops. One of his most famous paintings centers on a pipe but bears the inscription "This is not a pipe." What is it, then? A painting, of course. But something more: a comment on an object, and a satire of the word itself. "At one border," observes the art critic Robert Hughes, "Magritte's field of action touched on philosophy; on the other, farce." Just so with Groucho, whose writers were essentially gagmen, but subversive gagmen well aware of the modes and attitudes of the avant-garde.

GROUCHO

You're a disgrace to our family name of Wagstaff, if such a thing is possible. What's all this talk I hear about you fooling around with the college widow? No wonder you can't get out of college. Twelve years in one college! I went to three colleges in twelve years and fooled around with three college widows. When I was your age I went to bed right after supper. Sometimes I went before supper. Sometimes I went without my supper and didn't go to bed at all. A college widow stood for something in those days. In fact, she stood for plenty.

ZEPPO

There's nothing wrong between me and the college widow.

GROUCHO

There isn't, huh? Then you're crazy to fool around with her.

ZEPPO

Aw, but you don't—

GROUCHO

I don't want to talk to you again about this, you snob. I'd horse-whip you if I had a horse! You may go now. Leave your name and address with the girl outside and if anything turns up we'll get in touch with you—where are you going?

ZEPPO

Well, you just told me to go.

GROUCHO

So that's what they taught you in college. Just when I tell you to go, you leave me!

Horse Feathers attempts to knock down everything it encounters. Liberal arts education is devalued in a brief exchange.

GROUCHO

Have we got a stadium?

FACULTY

Yes.

GROUCHO

Have we got a college?

FACULTY

Yes.

GROUCHO

Well, we can't support both. Tomorrow we start tearing down the college.

FACULTY

But Professor, where will the students sleep?

GROUCHO

Where they always slept. In the classroom.

Again breaking through the wall between actor and viewer, Groucho watches Chico at the piano. "I've got to stay here," he reminds the audience. "But there's no reason you folks shouldn't go out into the lobby till this thing blows over."

Lovers' baby talk would never recover from an exchange between Groucho and Todd. Gamblers have bet all their money on Huxley's rival, Darwin College, and the blond has been enlisted to vamp the Professor. As their canoe drifts downstream, Groucho expresses concern.

TODD

You're perfectly safe, Professor, in this boat.

GROUCHO

I don't know. I was going to get a flat bottom. But the girl at the boat house didn't have one. . . .

TODD

Professor, you're full of whimsy.

GROUCHO

Can you notice it from there? I'm always like that after I eat radishes.

TODD

Is gweat big strong mans gonna show liddle icky baby all about those bad football signals?

GROUCHO

Was that you or the duck? 'Cause if it was you, I'm gonna finish the ride with the duck.

TODD

If icky baby don't learn about the football signals, icky baby gonna cwy.

GROUCHO

If icky girl keep talking that way, big stwong man gonna kick all her teef wight down her thwoat.

At a speakeasy (itself a mockery of the Eighteenth Amendment forbidding the sale of alcoholic beverages) Chico uses a funnel to pour the identical hooch into bottles marked SCOTCH and RYE. Upon hearing Groucho's admonition "You can't burn the candle at both ends," Harpo produces from his pocket a taper lit at either extremity. In the same spirit, when he passes by a poker game and overhears a player say "Cut the cards," Harpo obliges by producing an axe from his raincoat and chopping the deck in half. During Groucho's biology lecture, Harpo and Chico become the Lords of Misrule, complete with peashooters and hurled textbooks. This restatement of "Fun in Hi Skool" extends the attack on public education they had undertaken since the days at P.S. 86 on Lexington Avenue, when Chico cut classes and Harpo was thrown out of them bodily.

The battle of the Marx Brothers against self-improvement has one sour note. To amuse himself Harpo feeds one book into a glowing fireplace, then another and another until in a frenzy of pyromania he shovels scores of volumes onto the flames. The scene was filmed four years before the Nazi book-burning pyres in Nuremberg but it has left a bad taste and disturbed critics and historians ever since *Horse Feathers*'s 1932 release.

The picture also had some weaknesses in the writing—flaws that Groucho would point out years later when he discussed S. J. Perelman's contribution to the Marx Brothers: "He was not a playwright. He could write a funny line." The trouble was that the funny lines tended to stand by themselves. In one interlude, for example, a secretary enters a fast-moving conference, bringing plot and action to a halt. An administrator is tired of waiting to see Professor Wagstaff. "The Dean is furious," she chirps. "He's waxing wroth!" Groucho looks up. "Oh, is Roth out there, too? Tell Roth to wax the Dean for a while." The gag worked well enough when Perelman wrote it for *College Humor* magazine. Here it comes at the expense of narrative drive, something that rarely happened when George S. Kaufman was on the scene.

Early in the shooting Chico entered with a legitimate excuse for showing up late. He had shattered a knee and broken several ribs in a major automobile crash. Groucho regarded the incident as a personal affront. Writing to a friend he complained that the break would cause nearly two months of delay—a general nuisance, as he put it, "but so is Chico." The accident forced Paramount to halt production for nearly two months, and during the hiatus more distressing news came in. Enmeshed in a troubled Broadway revue, *Flying Colors,* the Marx Brothers' friend and consultant, Max Gordon, had suffered a nervous breakdown. After an aborted suicide attempt, he was sent to a sanitarium. A little too casually, Harpo dropped by one morning during a visit to New York, attempting to elevate Gordon's spirits. After an hour he strode to the door and, almost as an afterthought, reached into his pocket and withdrew a roll of bills. He tossed it on the bed, and exited. Gordon gratefully recalled the incident: "Four thousand dollars were scattered around—needed, helpful, reassuring." Groucho's sentiments paralleled his brother's, but it was not in him to make the rare quixotic gesture. He waited a day, then telephoned Gordon to assure him that Harpo did not act alone. "I want you to know I've got fifty percent," Groucho stated, "and there is more where that came from." He rang off before the producer could embarrass him with sounds of gratitude.

Forced to walk with a limp (which was temporary), Chico recovered sufficiently to resume close-up shooting in June. Save for a couple of scenes at the climactic football game, where a stand-in was unsubtly used, the infirmity was of no consequence. All went well until the filming of the finale. It, too, had been revised. The original script called for a victory bonfire in celebration of Huxley's gridiron win. The conflagration was supposed to spread to a campus building, where the Brothers would last be seen playing cards, undisturbed as the inferno rages and the ceiling crashes down around them. McLeod and Mankiewicz knew this denouement would exceed their straitened budget, and they demanded a less elaborate ending. The writers obliged them with the Brothers' most mischievous closer to date—a wedding with Todd as the bride, and Groucho, Chico, *and* Harpo as the grooms. Zeppo is not in the scene; he was deemed superfluous by the writers—and by Zeppo himself. Without informing anyone he began looking around for another line of work. The idea of becoming a talent agent appealed; after all, he had been around performers all his life. If he could find a job with an agency, fine. If not, he would do something else. Whatever the case, he decided, the next Marx Brothers movie would be his last.

Horse Feathers opened in the summer of 1932, and before the autumn the Brothers were the darlings of the in crowd, the bourgeoisie, and the intellectuals. Only Chaplin had enjoyed this breadth of recognition. In Paris, a writer for *Le Monde* joined his colleague Antonin Artaud in hailing the Brothers' comic approach. The Marxes, the critic wrote, are "exactly like ordinary people and act just as we should if social regulations did not prevent us from behaving that way." Watching their comic distortions, "one feels as if he were looking in a deforming mirror. The Marx Brothers lift us out of reality by exaggerating our peculiarities and aggravating our faults." In London, the critic for the *New Statesman and Nation* wrote that the Marxes had tapped into the word of dreams: "They introduced the psychological disturbance that is caused by seeing something that is mad and aimless . . . something which, if not utterly disconnected, depends for its connections on the workings of the unconscious." The British critics invoked the leaping congruities of dreams in *Alice in Wonderland,* and back home *Time* gave the Brothers its imprimatur, placing them on the cover of the August 13 issue, with all four crowded into an oversize garbage can. The magazine paid particular attention to Groucho's "unsquelchable effrontery."

The final arbiter, the public, had its say at the box office and made *Horse Feathers* an indisputable smash. Informed of the box office receipts, the Brothers made plans for elaborate vacations, interspersed with appearances at the best remaining vaudeville houses. This, they thought, would take the better part of a year; their fifth movie would go before the cameras early in 1934. But according to Chico's daughter Maxine, "Paramount couldn't afford to give them a year off. The picture division was $6 million in the red." The studio shuffled its executives: Emmanuel Cohen was in, B. P. Schulberg was out. (B. P. would never again assume command of a studio. Years later he would remind friends of a Marx Brothers character, examining a bookshelf and commenting on his adaptations, "I made this one. . . . I made that one," his eyes glistening with tears.)

Various stories went around, to the effect that Ernst Lubitsch was preparing to direct the Brothers in a parody of Balkan romances. These were no more than wishes in the form of publicity releases. But before the Marxes could get discouraged Cohen made concrete plans, assigning Sheekman, Kalmar, and Ruby to write the next Marx Brothers film. It was provisionally titled *Cracked Ice,* then retitled *Grasshoppers.* While the scenarists chipped away at the dialogue, the Brothers anxiously explored sources of additional income. Maxine recalled: "Maurice Chevalier had recently made a deal to do a radio show for $5,000 a week. Standard Oil of New Jersey, Pennsylvania and Louisiana wanted Daddy and Groucho to do a weekly broadcast for over $7,000 a week. [The eventual sum was $6,500—precisely what Greta Garbo received for her film work at that time.] Before any deal was made with Paramount, Groucho and Chico agreed to go on the air, but they were nervous." Groucho was unsure how his brand of outrageous puns and double entendres would go over in the puritanical world of radio. "However, he was never one to pass up a few easy bucks, and Chico *always* needed money to gamble. (Harpo got a weekly salary for *not* appearing—radio was obviously not for him.)"

The programs, produced in New York and Hollywood, were broadcast every Monday night on the National Broadcasting Company's Blue Network from 7:00 to 7:30 EST. Groucho played detective Waldorf T. Beagle. Chico, in his familiar Italian mode, played Beagle's assistant, Emmanuel Ravelli, a character taken bodily from *Animal Crackers.* Michael Barson, editor of the long-neglected scripts, reminds us that a few years earlier the two "had been presenting four shows daily in vaudeville; more recently it had been seven performances a week on Broadway. They were now being paid a princely sum to stand before a microphone each week for half an hour (less, really, minus the musical interludes and announcer spots) to read from a script they had barely bothered rehearsing." Most contracts required the stars to finish their skits with a personal endorsement: Rudy Vallee extolled the benefits of Fleischmann's yeast, Walter Winchell pushed Jergens lotion, and Groucho and Chico spoke glowingly of the gasoline made by Standard Oil. The scripts were written by Sheekman and Nat Perrin, new to radio, but veterans of two Marx Brothers pictures.

In its initial form the show was called *Beagle, Shyster, and Dismal.* By the time of the first broadcast in November 1932, the title had changed to *Beagle, Shyster, and Beagle.* Then came a complaint from a lawyer named Beegle. "As is always the case," Perrin later commented acerbically, "the studio panicked when they heard the word 'lawsuit,' so the name was changed to *Flywheel, Shyster, and Flywheel.*" Under that title, Groucho, now Waldorf P. Flywheel, and Chico, still Emmanuel Ravelli, recycled jokes and situations from their past. They also experimented with new ones that might be used in their upcoming film. Some very senior gags could be heard throughout the series, particularly in the seventeenth episode, which borrowed the stolen-painting plot from *Animal Crackers,* and the nineteenth, which repeated a routine from *Cocoanuts:*

GROUCHO

Now here is a little peninsula and here is a viaduct leading to the mainland.

CHICO

Awright. Why a duck . . . why-a no chicken?

GROUCHO

I don't know. I guess they never thought of it that way. This happens to be a viaduct, that's all. I never heard of a Via Chicken. You try to cross over there on a chicken and you find out viaduct.

CHICO

Why a duck? Why a duck?

GROUCHO

It's deep water. That's viaduct. Look, sap. Suppose you were out horseback riding and you came to that stream and you wanted to ford over. You couldn't make it. It's too deep.

CHICO

Well, whatta you want wit a Ford, if you gotta horse?

GROUCHO

Well, I'm sorry the matter ever came up. I don't care where you're from. It's a viaduct.

CHICO

Hey, look. I unnerstan why a horse. I unnerstan why a chicken. I unnerstan why a dis, why a dat. But I don't unnerstan why a duck.

GROUCHO

Well, I was only fooling. They're going to build a tunnel in the morning. Is that clear?

CHICO

Yeah, it's all clear, except why a duck.

GROUCHO

Now, if you'll come with me, I'll take you down and show you our cemetery. I've got a waiting list of fifty people at that cemetery just dying to get in. But I like you and I'm going to shove you in ahead of all of them. I'm going to get you a steady position, and I hope it's horizontal. . . .

The reputations of the Marx Brothers and NBC notwithstanding, *Flywheel* was given a shoestring production. The network owned state-of-the-art broadcast studios in New York, but none in California; there, empty sound stages were rented from RKO. Recalled Perrin, "We'd round up thirty or forty people to become an audience—they'd sit on folding chairs—and do the show in front of them. The boys liked playing to a live crowd, being from vaudeville. Once we finished the performance, the stagehands would come right in and start clearing the stage for whatever film needed it."

The program seemed to bring out the worst in radio reviewers. A show about a straying wife, for example, met with *Variety's* deepest disapproval. The paper, a defender of "family programming," complained: "That's fine stuff for children! Chances are that if the Marxes proceed with their law office continuity along lines like this they will never be able to hold a kid listener. Firstly, because parents don't want their children to hear about bad wives and divorces, and this isn't an agreeable theme to the kids. Which means that if the Marxes don't look out, whatever kid following they have on screen will be totally lost to them on the air."

But neither the kid following nor the critical appraisals were responsible for the short career of *Flywheel*. The fault lay with the NBC schedule. Only 40 percent of the audience listened to their radios before 8 p.m.; as a result the Marx Brothers program seldom rose above a 22.1 rating. The Texaco Fire Chief show, broadcast at the more popular hour of 9:30 p.m., regularly earned ratings of 44.8. The managers of Standard Oil felt that they got too little from the Marx Brothers, who delivered the unfunny commercials with a palpable insincerity:

GROUCHO

Yesterday, I went to visit Uncle Charlie and it made him very happy. And that wasn't all. An hour later I left, and that made him twice as happy.

CHICO

Yeah, I don't know what to do about Uncle Charlie. He's a case. He's such a crank.

GROUCHO

You mean a crank case. Well, Essolube, that famous hydro-fined motor oil, is the best thing in the world for a crankcase.

CHICO

Hey, you didn't say nuttin' about Esso, which is more powerful than any gasoline.

GROUCHO

Well, we can mention Esso next week. So—

BOTH

Good night, ladies. Good night.

Esso summarily terminated its sponsorship in the spring of 1933. By that time Groucho and Chico had fattened their coffers by some $70,000 each, and kept the Marx name before the public while the next movie was being prepared. Nonetheless, *Shyster* marked the Brothers' first real misstep since vaudeville, and served to renew Groucho's self-doubt and financial insecurity. More than forty years later the aftertaste of the cancellation still lingered. "Company sales, as a result of our show, had risen precipitously," he explained bitterly in *The Secret Word Is Groucho*. "Profits doubled in that brief time, and Esso felt guilty taking the money. So Esso dropped us after twenty-six weeks. Those were the days of guilt-edged securities, which don't exist today."

On the surface all seemed well; a contemporary photograph shows all the brothers to be hale. Groucho in particular looks younger than his forty-three years, lean and relaxed as he beams at his pretty, plump wife and his two bright-faced children. The family had moved into an impressive home on Hillcrest Road in Beverly Hills, and all of them seemed at ease in their new surroundings, as if this was where they truly belonged. "I fought this off as long as I could," Groucho wrote a friend, "but here I am, just another yokel. From now on you can expect nothing in my letters but climate." But all was not as it appeared—it never was, where Groucho was concerned. Arthur was to recall four features of that house: fourteen rooms, six baths, a three-car garage—and no swimming pool, because Groucho wanted to avoid freeloaders who might drop in for a swim and stay all day.

Something else was missing in the house on Hillcrest Road: marital accord. Relations had been souring for years; S. N. Behrman thought he could trace the dissolution to an evening when he escorted Ruth to the O'Neill drama *Mourning Becomes Electra*. "She watched the stage," Behrman wrote, "the unfolding crimes and perversions and deaths, with tremendous interest. I saw her pretty little profile, the little retroussé nose, watching, listening. I felt that the play totally absorbed her. Finally, the last great scene came, between the two surviving characters. Ruth spoke. Behind her hand she whispered to me:

" 'Tell me—do they have kitchenettes at the Beverly Wilshire?' "

Behrman repeated the incident to Woollcott, who printed it in his *New Yorker* column. "I didn't feel any better," the playwright confessed, "when I was told what Groucho said to Ruth when he read it:

" 'Now the whole world knows how dumb you are instead of just you and me!' "

After eleven years together, Groucho and Ruth separated physically if not legally, sleeping in separate bedrooms. Divorce was not an option for a man who taught his children that Henry VIII preferred decapitation to alimony. Groucho gave Ruth the material benefits and status she craved, paid scant attention to her almost-nightly bouts of heavy drinking, and separately pursued his own interests. These included the briefest of affairs; a true emotional involvement seemed beyond him. In later years Betty Marx confided in her daughter. Ruth's common complaint, she told Maxine, was not Groucho's occasional dalliances, but the fact that he was a brief and ineffective lover. That may have been a wife's vengeful commentary—particularly since Ruth knew that Betty could not say the same of her husband Chico. Or it may have been why Groucho preferred undemanding liaisons. In any case, his biographer and friend Hector Arce maintains that Groucho "never stopped having his one-shot encounters during his marriage," but that he "handled them with more discretion than his brothers. Any guilt he had about his infidelities would have to be added to the end of the long list of complexes with which he was already burdened."

When Groucho was not otherwise engaged, his leisure hours were spent in the company of writers and composers. For the first time, he felt at ease with them—and, on occasion, he picked their brains for new material. The work of one pair especially appealed to him: George and Ira Gershwin, fellow New Yorkers whose political satire *Of Thee I Sing,* with a book by George S. Kaufman and Morrie Ryskind, had just won the Pulitzer Prize. What if the musical were to be filmed? What if it were to become the Marx Brothers' next vehicle?

The dream was not as unattainable as it sounded. In February 1933 the Brothers had journeyed to Mexico to participate in the First Annual Motion Picture Golf Tournament at Agua Caliente. As befit their reputation, the quartet entered as one player, with Groucho making the drives and brassie shots, Harpo assigned the long irons, Chico the short irons, and Zeppo the putts. At roughly the same time, Paramount Publix Corporation, a subdivision of Paramount Pictures, went bankrupt. This was the company that held the Marx Brothers' contracts, and when the Brothers learned of the fiscal situation they broke off relations with the studio. According to the *New York Times,* the Marxes were "serving notice on the executives that they considered their contract breached because of assorted nonpayment of certain sums of money, as well as the transfer of their contract from one [Paramount] corporation to another." The truth was that *all* of Paramount was in perilous shape, and the Brothers feared that they had no future at the studio. In April they formed a corporation called The Four Marx Brothers Inc., to produce their own films. The Marxes' attitude toward business—even their own business—remained as iconoclastic as before. The parsimonious Groucho was named treasurer. Harpo, who knew nothing of finance, was president. Chico, who never prepared for anything, was secretary. And Zeppo, who was little more than a walk-on these days, was vice president. Their intentions were serious enough, though; The Four Marx Brothers Inc. announced plans to work with a new production company. Its first film would be the Gershwin musical *Of Thee I Sing,* starring the Marxes. Norman McLeod would leave Paramount to direct.

Renewed confidence in the Marx Brothers' careers, in Hollywood, and indeed in the future of capitalism, was the front Groucho displayed to the public. But that was all it was, a front. In fraternal conferences he expressed the idea that economic, political, and personal recovery might be a chimera. In a single day all their fortunes had vanished; there was no reason to think it couldn't happen again. The other Brothers protested that he was just being his usual morose self, but they never bothered to read the newspapers and journals he did, compulsively poring over them on sleepless nights. Particularly upsetting was President Roosevelt's declaration of a "bank holiday" early in 1933, to straighten out the muddled financial affairs of the lending institutions. Suddenly nobody had any money, even though everyone still needed to eat. Barter and scrip sprang up. An Oklahoma City hotel told patrons that they could get rooms in exchange for "anything we can use in the coffee shop." The cashier accepted vegetables, eggs, and a pig. A newspaper in the Middle West offered new subscription rates: one year, ten bushels of wheat; two years, eighteen bushels. It was hard to find humor in all this, but Robert Benchley tried. "I see no reason why there should not be a new theatrical season," he wrote, "providing my proposed plan for using pressed figs and dates for money goes into effect fairly soon." Thinking of the new cinema season, Groucho failed to crack a smile.

When the banks reopened, Jesse Isidor Straus, president of R. H. Macy, published his credo in the *New York Times:*

> I trust my government.
> I trust our banks.
> I do not expect the impossible.
> I shall do nothing hysterical.
> I know that if I try now to get all my cash I shall certainly
>   make matters worse.
> I will not stampede. I will not lose my nerve. I will keep my head.

At the time Macy's sold only for cash, and this, too, failed to amuse Groucho. Events in Europe confirmed more of his fears. There were hunger marches in London, fascist victories in Spain and Italy. And in the Marx family's country of origin, Adolf Hitler led his Nazi Party to victory, promising a campaign against the Jews of Germany. Whatever good was happening to the family looked temporary indeed, and as if to remind them of fortune's fragility, Frenchy suffered a major heart attack in the spring of 1933. On the first day his sons were allowed to visit him, Long Beach was hit by a major earthquake, the first they had ever experienced. Groucho needed no more reminders of how temporary security and life could be. Perhaps out of guilt for having trivialized Frenchy whenever reporters asked him about the Brothers' rise, he chose this time to compose an affectionate tribute to his father. It ran in the March issue of *Redbook*. "At dinner the other night, when the entire family was gathered at my house . . . Frenchy was the most dapper man at the table; there was scarcely a wrinkle on his face, and his appetite was better than mine." The author tried to laugh off the old man's hurtful attitudes: " 'Groucho is no good at pinochle,' said Frenchy rather sadly—much as Joseph Conrad might have sighed, 'My son cannot write.' " But much of the piece fondly recalled the vaudeville days when Frenchy hired claques and cooked for the family. It concluded, "As a businessman, his success was something less than sensational, but what of that? There is probably no one in the world who can produce kugel or biscuits like Father used to make. And I know of no one—not even Chico—who can make a better score at pinochle." Groucho could console himself two months later, when Simon/Samuel/Frenchy Marx suffered his third and last heart attack. The seventy-two-year-old died on May 11, and the body was brought east for burial. Approaching middle age, the Marxes were orphans in more than one sense of the word.

•

BY THE TIME of Frenchy's death his fourth son had become one more victim of the Depression: Gummo's once-prosperous dress business went under, forcing him to declare bankruptcy. His siblings closed ranks and brought him west to be their manager, although just what he would manage was questionable. Funding for *Of Thee I Sing* had not materialized, and the dispute with Paramount continued. In very late spring, money matters were finally settled and the Brothers agreed to rejoin the studio for their fifth picture, now officially titled *Duck Soup*. Groucho had his doubts about this one, too, but he also remarked on two changes that could revive the team's fortunes. For once, the Marx Brothers would have the services of a front-rank comedy director, Leo McCarey, the man responsible for teaming Stan Laurel and Oliver Hardy. (He was also responsible for the title; "Duck Soup" had been used by Laurel and Hardy in their 1927 two-reeler.) And Groucho would be rejoined by the woman he had scorned for the two previous films, Margaret Dumont.

A Paramount publicist later speculated about the dowager's comeback: "Groucho may have considered her a good luck object inasmuch as critics were calling the Hollywood-made films 'descents from the heights.' "

Duck Soup would allow the Marxes to regain the heights—but at a price. Up to now, Groucho, Chico, Harpo, and Zeppo acted in life as they did in their films: as if their self-contained world were hermetically sealed off from reality. In that unique arena you could wear a painted moustache, flourish a steaming hot coffee cup from a raincoat, speak with a bogus intonation, and no one, no matter how well dressed or well educated, would ever comment on your outfit or challenge your sanity. As far as they were concerned, the same held true on the outside. The economic catastrophes of the United States and Europe made little impression on men who were earning thousands of dollars a week, and whose names were better known to most moviegoers than those of their congressmen. In matters of politics and social conscience, Groucho was far ahead of his brothers, who espoused a vague liberalism, an appreciation of President Roosevelt's New Deal, and a belief in the improvement of the Working Man's lot. But all that was about to change. For the first time in his movie career, Harpo had trouble concentrating. Hitler's speeches were being broadcast, and twice shooting was suspended to hear Der Fuhrer rant.

Harpo expressed surprise when so few of his friends showed alarm at the events in Europe. "Nothing would really come of the dictator's threats, they said. He was all bluff and hot air. His act was nothing more than a bad imitation of that other comic, Mussolini." With Europe descending and Hollywood comatose, the Marx Brothers made *Duck Soup*, at once a political satire and an aimless farce, a reason for rejoicing and a grievous disappointment, an entry into a new world of filmmaking and an adieu both to a style that had established their names and to a studio that had given them everything but confidence.

CHAPTER EIGHT

No Sanity Clause

FOR HIS MYTHICAL nineteenth-century realm, novelist Anthony Hope chose the name Ruritania and furnished it with an appropriate protagonist: the Prisoner of Zenda. This worthy took the best-seller lists—and later the movie houses—by storm. The story of Rudolf Rassendyl, lookalike of the king, fascinated Americans. They could not get enough of the gentleman of leisure who heroically impersonated His Majesty, fell in love with Princess Flavia, rescued the king from lethal plotters, and then renounced his royal amour for the good of the nation. In the next generation, George B. McCutcheon dubbed *his* fictive country Graustark; it was an exotic unspecified region where princess and commoner could enjoy a sentimental tryst. By the early 1920s "Ruritanian" and "Graustarkian" had entered the English vocabulary as adjectives to describe an operetta world of castles and cafés, peopled by villains in swirling capes, noblemen in uniforms, and beautiful women whose gowns trailed gracefully along tessellated floors. With indecent haste the blood-soaked fields of Flanders were passing into history, obscured by the Jazz Age and the Depression. The escape artists of Hollywood no longer wished to examine the hollow men responsible for the Great War. Nor did they wish to gaze for long at current Europe, where a new breed of totalitarian leaders were conniving and murdering their way to power. Now and then a journalist wrote unflattering pieces about the personalities and policies of Benito Mussolini, Adolf Hitler, Joseph Stalin, Francisco Franco. But as Harpo noticed, the warnings generally went unheeded. The genre of Balkan romance—with or without music—found increasing favor as the real Continent descended into terror and despair. First came fantasies of espionage, then Erich von Stroheim's stylish *The Merry Widow* and such lighthearted works as the Marion Davies vehicle *Beverly of Graustark*. These led on to nonstop farces like the 1932 *Million Dollar Legs*, starring W. C.

Fields as the head of Klopstockia, a nation he led by Indian-wrestling his political opponents every morning.

So the Brothers' fifth film, for all its later reputation as a breakthrough antifascist movie, was actually in step with American cinema, circa 1933. Yet *Duck Soup* contains a cynicism so mordant and a pace so modern that it reaches beyond its time to join the classics of political satire. Leo McCarey was no Ernst Lubitsch, and Bert Kalmar and Harry Ruby were hardly Arthur Schnitzler and Bertolt Brecht. Theirs was a raucous, transparent form of humor, manufactured and packaged in the U.S.A. Still, iconoclasm came naturally to this group of filmmakers, and there are no bigger icons than heads of state. Years later Harry Ruby protested that what the team did was "strictly entertainment." But that was not the whole truth; the result far outran the intent.

For its basic humor, *Duck Soup* stresses McCarey's first tenet, "Do it visually," filling almost every scene with sight gags that make Groucho work harder for his laughs. During the first few weeks of work, the star expressed impatience with this Mack Sennett approach: "That idea of snapping your fingers went out with the Keystone Kops." But each of the Brothers was finally won over. Harpo was the easiest to convince. With his fondness for sight gags, McCarey allowed the mute to perform his shtick unhampered by instructions. Chico kept gambling with the director and losing, and the performer-director relationship seemed headed for a downfall until the morning that Chico came in with a bag of walnuts and asked McCarey how far he thought he could throw one. "Farther than you, I bet," came the reply. McCarey flung the object about a hundred feet. Chico reached into the bag, pulled out a walnut and threw it twice as far. McCarey paid up. (Chico never told him that he had filled his walnut with lead.) Finally, Groucho conceded that McCarey was "a good drunk"—a phrase denoting the director as convivial, approachable, and, in the end, a man who knew which routines only worked on paper, and which would be effective on celluloid. A Gilbertian number about sex and political ambition had struck Groucho's fancy:

> Of course you're all aware
> A king must have an heir
> Someone to pass the family name along
> Will someone tell me where
> I'll ever get an heir
> If a king can do no wrong?

McCarey decreed the song extraneous and added that the comic lead had plenty of other tunes. Groucho conceded the point. He also relinquished any chance at a suggestive love scene. There would be no reappearance of the Thelma Todd double entendres because there would be no reappearance of Thelma Todd. As Groucho saw it, his were the smallest sacrifices; both Chico and Harpo had to forsake their musical solos. Moreover, in *Duck Soup* Groucho was to receive his greatest leap in social status. Just as Woodrow Wilson went from the presidency of Princeton University to the presidency of the United States, the comedian rose from head of Huxley College in *Horse Feathers* to the leader of all Freedonia in *Duck Soup*. Rufus T. Firefly is installed at the insistence of the heiress Mrs. Teasdale (Margaret Dumont), whose money has been propping up the nation's shaky finances. Her new favorite makes his entrance by sliding down a fire pole into the inauguration ceremonies. Firefly greets his benefactor in the style of their earlier encounters:

DUMONT

As chairwoman of the reception committee, I welcome you with open arms.

GROUCHO

Is that so? How late do you stay open?

DUMONT

I've sponsored your appointment because I feel you are the most able statesman in all Freedonia.

GROUCHO

Well, that covers a lot of ground. Say, you cover a lot of ground yourself. You'd better beat it. I hear they're going to tear you down and put up an office building where you're standing. You can leave in a taxi. If you can't leave in a taxi, you can leave in a huff. If that's too soon, you can leave in a minute and a huff. You know you haven't stopped talking since I came here? You must have been vaccinated with a phonograph needle.

Much of the film's humor stays on a par with the other Marx Brothers pictures, half-stagy, half-cinematic, with an old, but brilliantly performed mirror sequence starring Groucho, Chico, and Harpo on either side of a nonexistent looking glass; contretemps with McCarey's favorite second banana, Edgar Kennedy, master of the "slow burn"; and Chico's indelible line "Who you gonna believe, me or your own eyes?"; plus, of course, the customary cascade of insults to Dumont. "Remember," Groucho reminds his compatriots, "you're fighting for this woman's honor, which is probably more than she ever did." (The "probably," which some wanted to eliminate, gave the line the necessary rhythm, and on Groucho's insistence, it stayed in.) Other remarks were more pointed:

DUMONT

This is a gala day for you.

GROUCHO

That's plenty. I don't think I could handle more than a gal a day.

There are also punning exchanges with members of the cabinet:

MINISTER OF WAR

Gentlemen! Gentlemen! Enough of this. How about taking up the tax?

GROUCHO

How about taking up the carpet?

MINISTER OF WAR

I still insist we must take up the tax.

GROUCHO

He's right. You've got to take up the tacks before you take up the carpet.

But with the entrance of Louis Calhern as Ambassador Trentino, scheming representative of the neighboring country Sylvania and Groucho's rival for Mrs. Teasdale's hand, the picture assumes a darker tone. Every time he and Groucho confront each other there are lapses of protocol, and these eventually lead to out-and-out war. At a crucial moment Trentino offers a truce, and Groucho is briefly mollified:

GROUCHO

It was silly of me to lose my temper on account of that little thing you called me.

TRENTINO

Little thing I called you? Why, what did I call you?

GROUCHO

Gosh, I didn't even remember what it was.

TRENTINO

Well, do you mean worm?

GROUCHO

No, that wasn't it.

TRENTINO

I know. Swine.

GROUCHO

Uh-uh. No, it was a seven-letter word.

TRENTINO

Oh, yes! Upstart.

GROUCHO

That's it! Upstart! (*He leaps up furiously and slaps the ambassador with a glove*)

TRENTINO

This man is impossible! This is an outrage. My course is clear. This means war! You runt!

GROUCHO

I still like "upstart" the best.

TRENTINO

I shan't stay here a moment longer.

GROUCHO

Go, and never darken my towels again!

TRENTINO

My hat!

GROUCHO

My towels! (*Exits*)

Further attempts to impose peace are futile. "It's too late," Groucho replies petulantly. "I've already paid a month's rent on the battlefield." At his right hand is Chico, former street vendor. He has received his latest assignment after a travesty of Senate inquiries:

GROUCHO

Now listen here. You give up that silly peanut stand and I'll get you a soft government job . . . but first I'll have to ask you a couple of important questions. Now, what is it that has four pairs of pants, lives in Philadelphia, and it never rains but it pours?

CHICO

'At's a good one. I give you three guesses.

GROUCHO

Now lemme see. Has four pairs of pants, lives in Philadelphia. Is it male or female?

CHICO

No, I don't think so.

GROUCHO

Is he dead?

CHICO

Who?

GROUCHO

I don't know. I give up.

CHICO

I give up, too. Now I ask you another one. What is it got a big black moustache, smokes a big black cigar, and is a big pain in the neck?

GROUCHO

Now don't tell me. Has a big black moustache, smokes a big black cigar and is a big pain in the . . . (*Suddenly enlightened*) Does he wear glasses?

CHICO

'At's-a right. You guess it quick.

GROUCHO

Just for that you don't get the job I was going to give you.

CHICO

What job?

GROUCHO

Secretary of War.

CHICO

All right, I take it.

GROUCHO

Sold. . . . Now that you're Secretary of War, what kind of an army do you think we ought to have?

CHICO

Well, I tell you what I think. I think we should have a standing army.

GROUCHO

Why should we have a standing army?

CHICO

Because then we save money on chairs. (*GROUCHO boots CHICO downstairs*)

Following the customary absurdities and plot twists, Chico is revealed as a double agent, spying for Sylvania. A new lampoon gets under way, making a mockery of courtroom procedure:

GROUCHO

Why weren't the original indictment papers placed in my portfolio?

ZEPPO

Why, I didn't think those papers were important at this time, Your Excellency.

GROUCHO

You didn't think they were important! Don't you realize I had my dessert wrapped in those papers? . . . (*Turning to CHICO*) I'll bet you eight to one we find you guilty.

CHICO

'At's-a no good. I can get ten to one at the barber shop. . . .

GROUCHO

When were you born?

CHICO

I don't remember. I was just a little baby.

GROUCHO

Isn't it true you tried to sell Freedonia's secret war code and plans?

CHICO

Sure. I sold a code and two pairs of plans. 'At's-a some joke, eh, boss?

GROUCHO

Now I'll bet you *twenty* to one we find you guilty. . . . Chicolini, give me a number from one to ten.

CHICO

Eleven.

GROUCHO

Right.

CHICO

Now I ask you one. What is it has a trunk, but no key, weighs two thousand pounds and lives in a circus?

COURT OFFICIAL

That's irrelevant.

CHICO

A relephant! Hey, that's the answer. There's a whole lotta relephants in a circus.

JUDGE

That sort of testimony we can eliminate.

CHICO

'At's-a fine. I'll take some.

JUDGE

You'll take what?

CHICO

Eliminate. A nice cold glass-a lemonade. (*To GROUCHO*) Hey, boss, I'm goin' good, eh?

GROUCHO

(*Addressing the bench*) Gentlemen, Chicolini here may talk like an idiot, and look like an idiot, but don't let that fool you. He really is an idiot. I implore you, send him back to his father and brothers who are waiting for him with open arms in the penitentiary. I suggest that we give him ten years at Leavenworth, or eleven years at Twelveworth.

CHICO

I tell you what I'll do. I'll take five and ten at Woolworth.

Then there is the matter of the conflict itself. Before the guns can fire, the home front must be propagandized. The four Marx Brothers make themselves into minstrels and sing the praises of armed conflict:

> They got guns
> We got guns
> All God's chillun got guns.
> We gonna walk all o'er the battlefield
> 'Cause all God's chillun got guns.

The fortunes of war get their comeuppance in dialogues with the military:

GENERAL

Your Excellency, our men are being badly beaten in open warfare. I suggest we dig trenches.

GROUCHO

Dig trenches? With our men being killed off like flies? There isn't time to dig trenches. We'll buy 'em ready-made. Here, run out and get some trenches.

GENERAL

Yes sir.

GROUCHO

Wait a minute. (*Holds his hand up at chin level*) Get 'em this high and our soldiers won't need any pants.

GENERAL

Yes sir.

GROUCHO

Wait a minute. (*Hand above his head*) Get 'em this high and we don't need any soldiers.

Even friendly fire is not immune from ridicule:

GROUCHO

(*Firing bursts from a machine gun*) Look at 'em run. Now they know they've been in a war.

ZEPPO

Your Excellency—

GROUCHO

They're fleeing like rats.

ZEPPO

But sir, I've got to tell you—

GROUCHO

Remind me to give myself the Firefly Medal for this. (*He fires another burst*)

ZEPPO

But Your Excellency, you're shooting your own men.

GROUCHO

Here's five dollars. Keep it under your hat. Never mind. I'll keep it under *my* hat.

Finally, as Harpo is sent out from headquarters, nobility, sacrifice, and patriotism are interred:

GROUCHO

You're a brave man. Go and break through the lines. (*A reassuring hand on HARPO's shoulder*) And remember, while you're out there risking life and limb, through shot and shell, we'll be in here thinking what a sucker you are.

Film historian Andrew Bergman makes a good case for calling these sequences "a vaudeville *All Quiet on the Western Front*." The Marxes, he observes in a study of Depression America and its films, "emerge in different costumes: as revolutionaries, redcoats, rebels, union men, frontier coonskinners, Allied Expeditionary Forces. Sides are irrelevant: the uniforms are obviously costumes, get-ups, rather than symbols of side or cause." The finale is reminiscent of that evening back in the 1920s when Groucho and Harpo staged a food fight during a double date: Ambassador Trentino is taken prisoner, Freedonia triumphs, and Mrs. Teasdale chants the national anthem, "Hail, Hail Freedonia." All four Brothers turn and bombard her with ripe fruit: nothing is sacred, not even victory.

Having taken care of patriotism, jurisprudence, officeholders, militias, envoys, diplomacy, and the Geneva convention—without a longueur from the opening scene to the fadeout—the Marx Brothers sat back to read the rave reviews and count the receipts. The first notice indicated that this might be their most profitable film to date. "Practically everybody wants a good laugh right now," said *Variety* in late November, "and *Duck Soup* should make practically everybody laugh. It is humorous in the typical Marx Brothers style, and a style that happens to be popular. Picture should draw and please all over." So it appeared, at first. "DUCK SOUP" IS OUTSTANDER reported the show business daily; and in the Midwest, "DUCK SOUP" HOT $20,000 LEADS MILD ST. LOUIS. The "serious" criticism disagreed with these early results. The *New York Times* found the film to be "extremely noisy without being nearly as mirthful as their other films." The *New York Post,* long a supporter of the team, picked up the political subtext, but stated that the Brothers "were not at their best when mocking the frailties of dictatorship." The *New York Sun* declared that in *Duck Soup* "the Marx Brothers take something of a nose dive," and the judgment of the *Los Angeles Times* was harsher: the team looked to be "washed up." The intelligentsia, who were expected to applaud the picture, gave it the back of their hands. *The Nation,* for example, reported that "pretty nearly everyone seems to have agreed that in *Duck Soup* the Four Marx Brothers are not quite so amusing," and that Groucho was "badly provided for." Hardly anyone invoked the name of Lewis Carroll; the crowning irony came when the Marxes' home studio, Paramount, released *Alice in Wonderland* during *Duck Soup* season. The film was more of a curiosity than a hit. But it caused intellectual chatter by showcasing the likes of Cary Grant, Gary Cooper, and W. C. Fields. Worse still, from the Marx Brothers' point of view, *Alice* was directed by the man who had guided their two previous films, Norman Z. McLeod.

For Paramount, as for all studios, public opinion was the final arbiter, and it was negative. *Duck Soup*'s fast start gave way to indifference and downright hostility; it had, in *Variety*'s term, "no legs." The manager of a Nebraska movie house filed a devastating report: "Even a small town knows when there is a flop. This was sure it." An Iowa manager agreed with the *Los Angeles Times:* he was "afraid these boys are washed up." And the man who ran an upstate Illinois theater summarized *Duck Soup* accurately as "a lot of gags and chatter that did not appeal to the masses." The postmortems commenced. With after-the-fact sagacity every executive— particularly every Paramount executive—had a reason for the failure.

Chief among them was the emergence of President Franklin Delano Roosevelt as the savior of the economy and of the United States itself. At first, official Hollywood looked at the New Deal with suspicion. But as soon as the motion picture business picked up in 1934, the executives changed their minds about That Man in the White House. This new outlook could be discerned in Darryl F. Zanuck's rewrite of a Warner Brothers film. The final scene of *Heroes for Sale* was to show the protagonist (played by Richard Barthelmess) dead, eulogized with four lines of dialogue:

BOY

He was a wonderful man, wasn't he?

GIRL

He loved everybody but himself.

BOY

Was there anybody else like him?

GIRL

Yes, another man—a man who died on the cross at Calvary nineteen hundred years ago.

The Zanuck finale expunged the religious tone and focused instead on two men talking:

TOM

It's not optimism—just common horse sense. Did you read President Roosevelt's inaugural address?

ROGER

He's right. You know it takes more than one sock in the jaw to lick a hundred million people.

Zanuck's instincts did not play him false. And the leaders of almost every other studio felt much the same way. The Marx Brothers made them uneasy. In the view of these men, the last thing audiences wanted to see was four slapstick comedians attacking authority in these delicate times. They added that the Brothers belonged to the vaudeville era, that the 1930s were ushering in a new kind of cinematic comedy. This was an unabashedly sentimental era, a time of working together to beat Old Man Depression. The Brothers were heartless and deliberately unromantic. Americans were in an isolationist mood, and a satire of Balkan despots was too exotic for their tastes.

The Marx Brothers had temporarily dispersed when these reports came in, and their reactions showed how very different they had become—and how similar they remained. In appearance, Chico and Harpo still bore a resemblance to each other; both had full faces reminiscent of Minnie's, both had receding hairlines and the settled look of businessmen in early middle age. Both were indoorsmen by nature, but because of a fondness for the California weather, they sported year-round tans. Groucho was taller by several inches, leaner and darker than his brothers, better-looking in family photographs, but with a neurotic edge, and little of the animal magnetism of Chico or the genial easy manner of Harpo. Zeppo was still the kid brother, a bodybuilder who radiated physical fitness and an indifference to trouble, economic or personal. Recently married, he hung around with Chico, a fellow gambler, cultivating the famous at card games.

Harpo, to his surprise, had become a most ardent New Dealer, and wanted to do something about his new passion. He was given a chance one afternoon when he received a call from his old admirer, Alexander Woollcott, in New York. The columnist had just learned that President Roosevelt was about to make good on a campaign promise to recognize the Soviet Union. Harpo said that was fine, and asked what else was new.

"Nothing," said Woollcott, "except you're going to Russia."

Harpo protested, "I don't want to go to Winnipeg, Manitoba, let alone Russia. I like California. I like the sunshine. I like the people. I like the language."

As usual, Woollcott was not paying attention. "Listen, you faun's behind," he went on. "I've already started pulling strings for you to get a visa. I suggest you be in New York no later than ten days from today."

In ten days Harpo was in Manhattan. A little over a month later he was at the Russian border, harp in hand. His reputation had not preceded him, and the suitcase full of props—silverware, horns, canes, etc.—came under close and suspicious scrutiny by the Soviet functionaries. Once he got past the border, the atmosphere changed. With a straight face Harpo informed journalists that the Marxes were Karl's distant cousins, causing widespread approval, and when he appeared at Leningrad's Music Hall the reception was galvanic. On opening night, Harpo's turn—a combination of harp numbers, gookies, and pantomime excerpts from *Cocoanuts* and *I'll Say She Is!*—earned him a twenty-minute ovation. The star knew exactly how to play his audience, and how to enlist its oppressors. After one performance he shook hands with Maxim Litvinov, then second to Stalin himself. A cascade of knives fell from a sleeve—Litvinov's. The onlookers, Harpo wrote delightedly, "exploded with one big shriek. The only time I ever played the straight man, I got my biggest laugh. And the comic was the Foreign Minister of the Soviet Union."

Back in the States, Chico admitted for the first time that he was discouraged about the future of the Marx Brothers. The only project he and Groucho had going for them was a radio show based in New York. *Marx of Time* was essentially a parody of the popular "March of Time" newsreels, featuring topical remarks by Ulysses H. Drivel (Groucho) and his colleague Penelli (Chico). The program's sponsor, the American Oil Company, gave up after eight weeks of indifferent ratings. This time Groucho was more philosophical: "We asked our listeners to write us and we got five hundred letters—four hundred in favor of studio audiences and one hundred against the Marx Brothers." Another defection occurred during this period, and it had profound results: Zeppo decided to call it quits. Significantly, he wrote his resignation to Groucho, who released the text to the press.

"I'm sick and tired of being a stooge," Zeppo confessed. "You know that anybody else would have done as well as I in the act. When the chance came for me to get into the business world I jumped at it.

"I have only stayed in the act until now because I knew that you, Chico and Harpo wanted me to. But I'm sure you understand why I have joined Frank Orsatti in his theatrical agency and that you forgive my action. Wish me luck."

Groucho understood. Zeppo's roles, he was to acknowledge in a memoir, were so unrewarding that "much of the time all he had to do was show up. It's not that he didn't have the talent, he simply had three older brothers ahead of him." In 1934 Zeppo looked to be far ahead of those brothers; as an agent, he would begin by representing George S. Kaufman and Moss Hart, among others. Meantime, Groucho, Chico, and Harpo were so much at loose ends that the *Los Angeles Times* ran a discouraging article: "Every indication points to the Marx Brothers being through with the movies for the time being. They played the game for what it was worth, but the screen is relentless in its exaction on comedians. It's their duty to be funnier in each succeeding picture, and . . . the same tricks can't be worked over and over again."

Unhappy with these judgments, and suspecting that they were right, Groucho fled the scene. In the summer of 1934 he took the family off to a well-appointed cabin in Skowhegan, Maine, some three thousand miles from Hollywood. Among other appealing features the place had eight rooms; he and Ruth and the children could play together in the daytime, and he and Ruth and the children could all be in separate bedrooms at night. He enjoyed swimming and playing catch with Arthur and reading children's books to Miriam, but after a while he recognized that he was not cut out to be a full-time father. And that is exactly what he feared he might become. A letter to a friend shows the state of his mind: "As you know I am up in the Maine woods, and it is lovely. There's a thrilling piece of news, and one that will probably set your heart to palpitating wildly. I am up in the woods. Hundreds of thousands of people are up in the woods. This is as insipid a line as anyone could write. If it is written to anyone who is in the city, it could only make them angry or envious, and if it is written to someone in the woods, it could only be received with apathy and boredom. At any rate I am up in the woods."

Across Lake Wesserunsett, the local playhouse had scheduled a season of Broadway revivals. The managers invited their neighbor to join the road show of *Twentieth Century,* a Ben Hecht–Charles MacArthur hit of 1932. To relieve his ennui and to remind himself and others that he was an actor by trade, Groucho agreed to appear in the starring role of Oscar Jaffe, a hyperkinetic Broadway producer. The audience was small and sympathetic, the cast relatively polished, the part actor-proof. Yet Groucho found layers of meaning in the experience. Although he had not been allowed a long rehearsal period, he brought the crowd to its feet night after night. He played sans moustache and got his laughs anyway. He was not supported by his brothers, and no one seemed to miss them. A *Time* correspondent caught the play and filed a report, noting that John Barrymore had played Jaffe in the movie version. "The audience agreed that Groucho compared creditably with his notable predecessor. This is one of the rare times when any one of the four Marx brothers has been seen on the stage without the others. . . . Now, at forty-five, he sails alone." After the very first performance Groucho informed the family that straight acting was "a racket." Being funny was far more difficult; it was the clown and not the king who ought to dominate the stage. For the first time in years he considered the possibility of becoming a legitimate actor, forsaking slapstick without a backward glance. After all, it seemed obvious that Paramount would not be heartbroken if the Marx Brothers broke up their act. In the old days B. P. Schulberg was an ally; the executive who replaced him, Emmanuel Cohen, had taken one look at the receipts of *Duck Soup* and reacted accordingly. "I'm just getting my feet under the desk here," he told the Brothers. "Everything's all right, but give me a little time to get things straightened out." The little time had stretched into many months, and still no contract arrived from the studio. Groucho battled anew with insomnia, and grew nostalgic for his lost comic career. The summer, which had begun so happily, degenerated into a period of anxiety and low spirits. One morning when Chico called from Hollywood Groucho could hardly contain himself—only to be crushed when his brother inquired, "What's new?" Groucho exploded. "I've been in the woods for four months, with a six-party telephone and a bunch of farmers. And you have the nerve to call me up and ask *me* what's new!"

But Chico was wandering in his own thicket. Even now he had no idea of Paramount's plans, or what action the Brothers should take if—as seemed likely—they lost the backing of their studio. Groucho bitterly commented that Chico was ebullience without substance. The man could recite the serial number on a dollar bill backwards a month after he had committed it to memory—but always forced the cast of *Duck Soup* to do retakes because he didn't know his lines. He griped about having his piano solo excised, but couldn't bother to practice. All he did before a performance was soak his hands in hot water for ten minutes—Chico's idea of warming up.

Restive and worried, Groucho took his family back to Los Angeles, expecting to confront his older brother yet again. He was in for a surprise. One of the most enthusiastic bridge players in 1930s Hollywood was a young man MGM considered its Boy Wonder—a title bestowed on him by a Universal screenwriter. (In a few years that scenarist, F. Scott Fitzgerald, would use Irving Thalberg as the model for protagonist Monroe Stahr in *The Last Tycoon*.) A slim, fragile figure, Thalberg seemed to have risen by walking forward. Disdaining to put his name on the credits ("If I have to tell them who I am, I'm not"), he had already produced such major films as *Grand Hotel, Ben-Hur,* and *Anna Christie.* S. J. Perelman, who hated to be in awe of anyone, particularly a film producer, thought that Thalberg's line "A writer is a necessary evil" summed up all that was wrong with Hollywood. ("I'm sure he meant weevil," Perelman added.) Yet the Marx Brothers' old scenarist could not help but be impressed by a visit to Thalberg's office where "eight of the most famous playwrights in America were in his anteroom, waiting to see him. It was my first intimation of what power means. In my mind, power is the ability to purchase people and make them wait for you." But with all of Thalberg's vaunted omnipotence, comedy was a genre that had eluded him thus far, and he was anxious to improve his resumé. Enter the cardsharp Chico Marx, with his customary timing and gall. He reminded Thalberg that the Brothers were at liberty. His bridge partner perked up. He had heard that Groucho was back in town. The other siblings were already here—why not have lunch at the Beverly Wilshire and talk things over?

The meal did not begin well. As Groucho remembered it, Thalberg opened with, "I would like to make some pictures with you fellows. I mean *real* pictures."

Groucho instantly flared up. "What's the matter with *Cocoanuts, Animal Crackers,* and *Duck Soup*? Are you going to sit there and tell me those weren't funny?"

"Of course they were funny," Thalberg responded. "But they weren't movies. They weren't *about* anything."

Harpo broke in. "People laughed, didn't they? *Duck Soup* had as many laughs as any comedy ever made, including Chaplin's."

"That's true, it was a very funny picture, but you don't need that many laughs in a movie. I'll make a picture with you fellows with half as many laughs—but I'll put a legitimate story in it and I'll bet it will gross twice as much as *Duck Soup*."

On behalf of his brothers, Chico took the bet a few days later—but not without a few demands. Acting as if he had a fistful of bids, the eldest Marx insisted that the act was more appealing without Zeppo than with him, that every studio in town was anxious to sign the Marx Brothers, that they would bring MGM such big audiences that 15 percent of the gross seemed a fair asking price. To the Brothers' delight, Thalberg agreed to these terms. For lagniappe, he offered a three-picture deal. But for all his agreeability, the producer was no pushover. He had his own terms, as well as some discerning analyses of the team's shortcomings. He wanted those understood before they came to work at MGM. In the first place, the Marxes were not kids anymore. When they first began making films, their superabundant energy gave them the illusion of youth. Five years later they were all settling into middle age. Chico was forty-seven, Harpo forty-six. The wigs and hats failed to hide the deepening lines around their eyes and mouths. If Groucho's moustache and eyebrows gave him an ageless quality, his step was not as lively, and his celebrated slouch occasionally suggested a hint of sciatica. Moreover, their harsh brand of comedy lacked appeal for the modern woman; questionnaires showed that she felt the trio's on-screen characters were grotesque and unsympathetic. Then there was the matter of tempo: the

Marxes' five previous pictures actually contained too many gags, and the audience reaction overrode the punch lines. In the old days people went to see a Marx Brothers picture two or three times to catch all the jokes. But as the box office receipts showed, today's moviegoers had decided that once was enough. The horseplay was too unfettered, the rowdiness too anarchic. To conclude, the Marx Brothers' films had ramshackle plots that no one could believe—hardly an asset at MGM, where writers were made to polish story lines until they could see their faces in them.

These were not easy truths to deal with, and the Brothers took some time to consider all that Thalberg had said. But there was never any real question about Groucho's reaction. *Monkey Business, Horse Feathers* and *Duck Soup* were bright, sometimes brilliant comedies, but they lacked a center and forced the Brothers to repeat themselves. They required a new approach and perhaps a new studio would provide it. If any doubts remained, Samuel Goldwyn dispersed them. He had no idea what to do with the Marx Brothers himself, but he thought Thalberg just might pull off a miracle. "If Irving wants you," he advised, "go with him. He knows more in one finger than I know in my whole body." Several weeks later the Brothers signed the necessary papers and moved into an office on the Metro lot, there to await conferences about their new film, *A Night at the Opera.* "You get me the laughs," Thalberg had promised, "and I'll get you the story." To that end he hired James McGuiness, a well-established writer who specialized in straight drama. McGuiness concocted a plot built around Harpo as the world's greatest tenor—but voiceless for the duration of the film. This was rejected out of hand, although Thalberg felt that some of the narrative had value. At Groucho's insistence Kalmar and Ruby were assigned to work on the first comedy version; they outlined the story of a flop musical oversold to its backers. Thalberg gave it a thumbs-down. The story of a comedy inside a comedy displeased him so mightily that the notion did not reappear in Hollywood until Mel Brooks's *The Producers,* more than thirty years later.

Of Kalmar and Ruby's efforts, all that remained were the character names of Groucho as Otis B. Driftwood and Dumont as the millionairess Mrs. Claypool. Thalberg then brought in Robert Pirosh and George Seaton, a promising young team. Groucho was quick to pronounce their work unsatisfactory. Well then, Thalberg asked impatiently, "whose work *would* you accept?" Groucho answered in five syllables: "Kaufman and Ryskind." The producer nodded. He knew instinctively that Groucho was right, and wired an offer to New York. Kaufman detested California, and Thalberg had to up the ante several times before the playwright broke

down and agreed to sign on for $5,000 a week, with a minimum guaran-
tee of $100,000. Ryskind, whose reputation could not compare with his
senior partner's, contented himself with $1,000 a week. Even then, Kauf-
man could not be kept in Hollywood for long periods. As soon as the
writers won approval of their story line he departed for some theatrical
business in Manhattan. That left Ryskind to hand over the opening dialogue to Thalberg. "When I gave it to him," wrote Ryskind, "he read
through its entire length without the faintest smile crossing his face.
When he was finished he handed it back to me and said, 'Morrie, that's
the funniest scene that I have ever read.' I've always wondered what his
reaction would have been if he hadn't liked it."

It was the last time anything on the project went smoothly. Thalberg
was a difficult man to see, and the Brothers continually found themselves
in the position of the man waxing Roth in *Horse Feathers*. The trio made
an attempt to be punctual, only to find the producer's office shut; he was
forever in story conferences on other movies. The Brothers ultimately
took matters in their own hands, lighting cigars, blowing gusts of smoke
under the door, and loudly yelling "Fire!" between puffs. A distressed
Thalberg emerged, saw what the Brothers were up to, and apologized for
the delay. But a few weeks later he kept them waiting again—this time
inside his office as he went down the hall to consult with Louis B. Mayer
on some non-Marxian matter. The negotiation took longer than antici-
pated, and when he returned he found the Brothers squatting nude, roast-
ing potatoes in his display fireplace. And still Thalberg could not give the
trio his undivided attention. Several weeks later he kept the group waiting once more. On this occasion they barricaded his door with heavy
filing cabinets. These took an hour to remove. Never again did the Marx
Brothers cool their heels in his waiting room.

Once Kaufman and Ryskind turned in their final script, MGM saw to it
that the "unsatisfactory" collaborators, Kalmar and Ruby, Pirosh and
Seaton, were quietly rehired to punch up the material. As befit the ethics
of 1930s Hollywood, neither team knew what the other was doing.
Another gagman was brought in late, and he became the key element in
the creation of *A Night at the Opera*. In his time Al Boasberg was something of a legend; since his death in 1937 he has become a mythic figure
among comedy writers. The son of a Buffalo, New York, jeweler, Boasberg had sold routines and jokes to a long list of headliners including
George Burns, Bob Hope, and Jack Benny, who paid him $1,000 a week
just to look over an already written script and improve the dialogue. No
day in his life went by without a joke, practical or otherwise. He liked to

claim that he was training a termite to sharpen his pencils, and once stood up in a theater and hysterically shouted, "Is there a Christian Scientist in the house?" When a lady raised her hand, he inquired: "Would you mind changing seats with me? I'm sitting in a draft." He was also the author of the classic show business joke about the actor who cries when his late wife's name is mentioned. "You must have loved her very much," says a friend. Replies the actor: "You should have caught me at the grave." Burns remembered the day the newly married Boasberg picked up his in-laws at the Los Angeles airport. En route he rented a limousine and donned a chauffeur's uniform.

"While driving home, the mother said, 'My daughter must be doing very well.'

"Playing it straight, Boasy said, 'Oh, yes, he's probably the best comedy writer in Hollywood.'

" 'Well, I've never met him,' the mother continued. 'What kind of man is he?'

"Boasberg answered, 'He's probably the finest man I ever met in my entire life. Maybe I shouldn't say this, but it's a shame what his wife's doing behind his back.'

"In a shocked voice, the mother gasped, 'What on earth is she doing to him?'

" 'Well, for one thing, she started sleeping with me even before she got married.'

"The rest of the trip was in absolute silence. . . . As soon as his wife saw the chauffeur's uniform, she knew he was up to one of his practical jokes. She patiently explained to her confused parents that Boasy was her husband, and after everything was straightened out, they all had a good laugh—that is, everybody except the mother. She never really did warm up to Boasberg."

In short, the gag writer had all the attributes of a Marx Brother except the genes. With some misgivings, Thalberg signed him to brush up the script of A Night at the Opera. For this film Boasberg staged a single practical joke, but it was a memorable one. A large, saturnine man, he liked to court the muse in a full bathtub, waiting for inspiration to strike. Somewhere in this period he became afflicted with gag writer's block. Day after day Thalberg waited for the expected pages; day after day he was disappointed. As the first week of shooting drew near, the producer snapped. He called Boasberg, demanding a look at what he had done so far. The writer surrendered. "O.K., Mr. Thalberg. I've got that material, but if you want it you'll have to come over to my office and get it. I'm going home and leaving it here."

Accompanied by the three Marx Brothers, Thalberg came over. The office had been abandoned. He and the trio searched everywhere. They found nothing on the desk, in the drawers, the filing cabinet, the waste-basket. Sighing, Groucho rolled his eyes upward, and there he saw what Boasberg had promised. The writer had composed a scene, snipped the dialogue into pieces one line long, and tacked them to the ceiling. "It took us about five hours to piece it together," Groucho claimed. "But it was worth it, for it turned out to be the nucleus of one of the most famous scenes we've ever done." That set piece occurs when Groucho, playing the manager of an obscure young tenor, comes aboard a ship and is assigned a minuscule stateroom. Once inside, he plays unwilling host to stowaways (Chico, Harpo, and the tenor), plus a band of stewards, a manicurist, a plumber, a woman searching for her Aunt Minnie, other passengers, and various drop-ins until some twenty people have jammed the place. Groucho sends out for food and the Brothers accept all comers ("Tell Aunt Minnie to send up a bigger room") until not even a broom straw could enter. At this point Margaret Dumont stops by, opens the door, and the crowd explodes out the door like pellets from the barrel of a shotgun.

The idea seemed promising enough, but neither the producer nor the comedians were certain of the audience reaction. A lot was riding on this film; if it failed, it would surely be the Marxes' last. Together, they hit upon a revolutionary method of testing the reaction. The picture would be taken on the road *before* it was filmed—the Brothers, along with the indispensable Margaret Dumont and the love interest, singers Kitty Carlisle and Allan Jones, would play some of *A Night at the Opera*'s key scenes in front of a live audience, shaping the comedy to please the crowd. The procedure was akin to the time when Morrie Ryskind sat in the Broadway audience of *Animal Crackers,* editing and deleting lines for the next show. For MGM, however, it marked a complete break from sound-stage tradition, and the Marxes were watched closely as they performed "Scenes from *A Night at the Opera*" in the West Coast theaters of the Fanchon and Marco Circuit. Included in the show were scenes in an open-air restaurant, a stateroom, a hotel room, and an opera house.

Groucho was out of practice, tense, and defensive. Unable to let down his guard, says Ryskind in an autobiographical piece, the comedian unconsciously committed one of the cardinal sins of performance: overcompensation. "He was so wound up that whenever he would deliver it was almost as if he were saying to the audience: 'This line is funny and you'd better laugh.' Faced with a militant challenge like that, very few of them did." The tour opened in Salt Lake City. Groucho came onstage and immediately misspoke. He was supposed to ask Dumont, "Well, Toots, how did you like the show?" The line came out, "Well, Tits, how did you like the show?" The explosion of laughter only increased Groucho's insecurity; after all, he had brought the house down by blowing his first line. Then new complications occurred when an antipathy developed between Ryskind and Boasberg; the last thing the tryouts needed was feuding gag writers. Ryskind, Groucho recalled, was "a very small man, and was standing by the cigar counter of the hotel and some shmuck comes into the hotel wanting to speak to the captain of the Japanese tennis team, who were also staying there. This guy happens to ask Boasberg who the captain is and Boasberg points out Ryskind, who was short and looked like he could have been Japanese. Ryskind never forgave Boasberg for that." A truce was finally worked out for the greater good of *A Night at the Opera*. "They certainly weren't a happy team, but Morrie had to use Boasberg's material because it was very funny." As each section improved, the laughs came more freely and frequently, and by the time the show opened in Seattle Groucho had begun to regain his form. Still, he expressed doubts about some sequences, and these were not prompted by insecurity. The stateroom scene failed to elicit the response everyone expected, and the writers voted to remove it from consideration. Consulted by phone, Thalberg overruled them. He always trusted his instincts, and they told him that the suspension of disbelief was too much for a theater audience. "You see a flat drop that's supposed to be a stateroom, and you can't make it look like it's crowded. In pictures, it will have an entirely different perspective." The sketch stayed and took on fresh ad-libs. Among them was Groucho's reply to the manicurist's "Do you want your nails long or short?" "You better make them short, it's getting crowded in here."

Clifton Fadiman, one of the pop polymaths who enjoyed writing about English literature, mathematics, philosophy, and film comedy, investigated the Marx Brothers at this time. Lest anyone suspect that he was going to contribute one of the "higher analyses" of the team, Fadiman told readers of *Stage* to relax. He would make no attempts "to trace the origin of the Marx Brothers' humor to the commedia dell'arte of the sixteenth century," and "their impertinent treatment of the social properties" would not be "construed either as a revolt against the constrictions of

American life, or as a proletarian propaganda." Furthermore, "Groucho's intransigent attitude toward his lady stooge" would "not be explained as a symbol of frustrated manhood crying out against female domination." He went on to discuss the making of the stateroom scene: "In the first part of the sequence, Groucho is outside giving a breakfast order to the steward. As he finished the order, Chico thought of adding, in stentorian tones, 'And two hard-boiled eggs'—and Harpo, not to be outdone, blew his horn. For some reason or other, this gag, expertly worked up, of course, made the whole scene jell. It turned something merely funny into something almost pitilessly hilarious."

Late in the tour Thalberg docked his yacht in Santa Barbara and dropped by to see one of the shows. "He had been making movies for many years in Hollywood," Groucho happily recollected, "but this was his first experience with live show business. Here he was sitting in the audience watching the people in his employ. He was impressed by this and had a wonderful time. And we were impressed to have a man as important as he was coming up to see the show. This was the first time he had ever been around comedians. He had always done different kinds of pictures. Mostly dramatic pictures such as the ones with his wife Norma Shearer, but this was the first time he was with comedians and he loved it. After Santa Barbara the show was ready for the cameras."

Thalberg's choice for director was Sam Wood, a disappointment for Groucho, who was just getting to trust his producer. Wood, former assistant to Cecil B. DeMille, had next to no experience with comedy. In addition he was a fervent conservative—an attribute that intensified Groucho's distrust. Had the director been a pleasant man, his politics might have been overlooked; Ryskind was also a hard-nosed Republican, but he had a light touch and kept his politics away from the sound stage. Wood was forever sounding off about his political beliefs, and his notion of rallying the cast was the constantly articulated line "All right, gang, let's get in there and sell 'em a load of clams." In addition Wood was obstinate and emotionally distant, more concerned about his ulcers than about the nuances of the script. The affable tenor, Allan Jones, who had no comic lines, remembered him as "a disagreeable guy, very insecure" who responded to actors' questions by saying, "I don't know. I don't know. Just do it again." Jones and Kitty Carlisle, then an untried singer, did as they were bid, going through as many as twenty performances of the same scene. To provide *Opera*'s love interest, the couple portrayed the relationship of an impoverished singer and a beautiful ingenue, thwarted by villains and encouraged by the Brothers in their new roles as eccentric

Cupids. Wood was well aware that this screen romance provided the spine of the film—and more significantly, that it had been put in at the insistence of Thalberg. To cover himself, he ordered scenes photographed from various points of view, giving the producer a choice of interpretations. To Groucho the gags seemed to diminish with each successive take. Thalberg thought otherwise, and encouraged Wood to use as much celluloid as he needed. Leery of contradicting the Boy Wonder, the comedians tormented Wood the way they knew best: with a fusillade of practical jokes. Chico stole five dollars from the director's wallet and, harking back to the vaudeville days, returned it in a sack containing five hundred pennies. Harpo pretended to lose consciousness after a bogus fall, holding up production for an hour. Groucho gave him such a hard time that the director exploded, "You can't make an actor out of clay." The response was immediate: "Or a director out of Wood!" Finally the Brothers had Wood's lunchtime milk—a necessity because of his ulcers—delivered in a baby bottle with a nipple. "Don't you guys have any sense of dignity?" was all Wood could mutter. There was no reply, and none was necessary. For insecurity could cut two ways. Carlisle remembered working conditions during the *Opera* filming: "Groucho would come up to me from time to time to ask, 'Is this funny?' Then, totally deadpan, he'd try out a line. I'd say, 'No, I don't think it is funny' and he'd go away absolutely crushed and try it out on everyone else in the cast. Chico was always playing cards in the back room and had to be called to the set. Harpo would work well until about eleven o'clock. Then he'd stretch out on the nearest piece of furniture and start calling at the top of his voice, 'Lunchie! Lunchie!' "

Below this roiled surface, however, the Brothers knew they were onto something big. Thalberg had not simply supplied them with a foreman; Wood knew how to give a professional gloss to his films and make certain that farce would not bury the "through line" of narrative. Moreover, the Marx Brothers were supplied with a great straight man in Sig Rumann, an expert German farceur, as the opera impresario; a backup troupe of talented singers; and the most detailed sets and costumes of their careers. So despite all their rowdiness and clowning they, too, went through twenty takes and, when word got out that they were unhappy, blithely assured the press: "Even if we're hard to get along with, anyone can get along with Wood. He's the top."

But Groucho had not performed the same service for Louis B. Mayer. The producer had been against the idea of the raffish Marxes at his elegant studio, where there were "more stars than there are in heaven," and

he made no secret of his detestation of Groucho in particular. One afternoon during the filming the two men crossed paths, and Mayer made the
mistake of asking how things were going. Groucho made the mistake of
answering, "It's no concern of yours." The autocrat coldly walked away,
biding his time for the day when the Brothers needed a favor. Meantime,
he wished the film ill, and sat with unamused countenance during *Opera's*
unannounced screening at a theater in Long Beach. To his private pleasure, the debut was catastrophic. People tittered at the titles, and then
became distracted, barely smiling for the next hour and a half. The pauses
put in for audience reaction became empty spaces, and the projector
could be heard grinding in the booth upstairs.

Thalberg had a feeling that this was not a typical audience, that the
age of the ticket buyers, or the timing of the afternoon show, or the
showcase itself, had somehow tainted the sneak preview. He had some fifteen minutes of cuts made, then ordered all six reels taken to a theater
across the street, where the whole process began again at a later time of
day. If ever there was proof of Thalberg's commercial instincts, this
unreeling provided it. Laughter built from the opening titles to the duels
with Rumann to the insults to Dumont. By the time of the stateroom
scene, the laughter was uncontained. Thalberg had a hit on his hands and
he knew it. So did Mayer, who withdrew and kept his own counsel.

Audiences in the major cities were unprepared for *A Night at the Opera,*
and so were the critics. They expected the Marxes' established style of
pandemonium, chutzpah, and eros; they witnessed something more and
something less. On the plus side, Kaufman and Ryskind provided a steady
flow of bright dialogue, and Wood, for all his overshooting, allowed just
the right spaces for audience reaction so that every gag was in the clear.
As Otis B. Driftwood, Groucho remained the swindler par excellence, and
as Mrs. Claypool, Margaret Dumont maintained her position as the
dowager queen.

DUMONT

Mr. Driftwood, three months ago you promised to put me in society. In all that time, you've done nothing but draw a very handsome salary.

GROUCHO

You think that's nothing, huh? How many men do you suppose are
drawing a handsome salary nowadays. Why, you can count them
on the fingers of one hand, my good woman.

DUMONT

I'm not your good woman!

GROUCHO

Don't say that, Mrs. Claypool. I don't care what your past has been. To me, you'll always be my good woman. Because I *love* you. There. I didn't mean to tell you, but you—you dragged it out of me. *I love you.*

DUMONT

It's rather difficult to believe that when I find you dining with another woman.

GROUCHO

That woman? Do you know why I sat with her?

DUMONT

No.

GROUCHO

Because she reminded me of you.

DUMONT

Really?

GROUCHO

Of course. That's why I'm sitting here with *you*. Because you remind me of you. Your eyes, your throat, your lips. Everything about you reminds me of you. Except you. How do you account for that? (*To audience*) She figures that one out, she's good.

The affronts continue when he speaks to his rival for Mrs. Claypool's money, impresario Herman Gottlieb (Rumann): "Nix on the lovemaking because I saw Mrs. Claypool first. Of course, her mother really saw her first but there's no point in bringing the Civil War into this." Gottlieb has arranged for a haughty, imperious tenor, Lasparri, to sing at the New York Opera Company. Groucho is appalled at the way Lasparri brutalizes his dresser, Harpo, but he is more disturbed by the salary Gottlieb is dangling. "You're willing to pay him a thousand dollars a night just for singing? Why, you can get a phonograph record of 'Minnie the Moocher' for seventy-five cents. And for a buck and a quarter, you can get Minnie." An obscure new tenor, Ricardo (Jones), appears, along with his inamorata Rosa (Carlisle), and Groucho gets an idea. Through a series of plot complications he negotiates with Ricardo's self-appointed agent, Chico.

GROUCHO

Could he sail tomorrow?

CHICO

You pay him enough money, he could sail yesterday. How much you pay him?

GROUCHO

Well, I don't know. . . . Let's see, a thousand dollars a night . . . I'm entitled to a small profit . . . how about ten dollars a night?

The two con men hammer out a contract.

GROUCHO

(*Reading from the paper*) "The first part of the party of the first part shall be known in this contract as the first part of the party of the first part shall be known in this contract—" Look, why should we quarrel about a thing like this? We'll take it right out, eh?

CHICO

Yeah, it's-a too long, anyhow. (*Both tear off the tops of their contracts*) Now, what do we got left?

GROUCHO

Well, I got about a foot and a half. Now, it says, "The party of the second part shall be known in this contract as the party of the second part."

CHICO

Well, I don't know about that.

GROUCHO

Now what's the matter?

CHICO

I no like-a the second party, either.

GROUCHO

Well, you should have come to the first party. We didn't get home till around four in the morning. I was blind for three days!

CHICO

Hey, look, why can't-a the first part of the second party be the second part of the first party? Then-a you *got* something.

GROUCHO

Well, look, rather than go through all that again, whaddya say?

CHICO

Fine. (*They rip out a second part of the contract*)

GROUCHO

Now I've got something you're bound to like. You'll be crazy about it.

CHICO

No, I don't like it.

GROUCHO

You don't like what?

CHICO

Whatever it is. I don't like it.

GROUCHO

Well, let's don't break up an old friendship over a thing like that. Ready?

CHICO

O.K. (*They tear another part off*) Now the next part, I don't think *you're* gonna like.

GROUCHO

Well, your word's good enough for me. (*Another part is torn away*) Now then, is my word good enough for you?

CHICO

I should say not.

GROUCHO

Well, that takes out two more clauses. (*And they are ripped out*) Now, "the party of the eighth part—"

CHICO

No, that's-a no good. (*Mutual tearing*) No.

GROUCHO

"The party of the ninth part—"

CHICO

No, that's-a no good, too. (*More tearing. Only thin slivers of paper remain*) Hey, how is it my contract is skinnier than yours?

GROUCHO

I don't know. You must have been out on a tear last night. But anyhow we're all set now, aren't we?

CHICO

Oh, sure.

GROUCHO

(*Offering his pen*) Now, just put your name right down there and then the deal is legal.

CHICO

I forgot to tell you. I can't write.

GROUCHO

Well, that's all right, there's no ink in the pen. . . .

CHICO

Hey, wait, wait. What does this say here?

GROUCHO

Oh, that's the usual clause. That's in every contract. That just says, "If any of the parties participating in this contract is shown not to be in their right mind, the entire agreement is automatically nullified."

CHICO

Well, I dunno.

GROUCHO

It's all right. That's in every contract. That's what they call a "sanity clause."

CHICO

Ha, ha, ha. You can't fool me. There ain't no Sanity Claus!

The stateroom scene, with its overcrowded, claustrophobic set, is one of the few Marx Brothers routines to prove more explosive on-screen than onstage. That ten-minute occasion, coupled with the big-league look and pace of an MGM studio movie; the send-up of arias and chorales; the romance of Jones and Carlisle; the hit song "Alone," composed by Arthur Freed and Nacio Herb Brown; and some new and surefire remarks from Groucho, helped put the film across. Within a day of its New York premiere fans were repeating exchanges like the one between Claypool and Driftwood on the gangplank:

DUMONT

Are you sure you have everything, Otis?

GROUCHO

I've never had any complaints yet!

Or the one between two of the brothers, when Chico is forced to give a speech:

CHICO

What'll I say?

GROUCHO

Tell them you're not here.

CHICO

Suppose they don't believe me?

GROUCHO

They'll believe you when you start talking.

Or the evasions of Groucho when he has to hide his brothers and Jones from a New York hotel detective:

DETECTIVE

I'm Henderson, plain-clothesman.

GROUCHO

You look more like an old-clothes man to me.

DETECTIVE

You live here all alone . . . ? I notice the table is set for four.

GROUCHO

That's nothing. My alarm clock is set for eight.

Most newspaper critics followed the lead of their New York colleagues. In the *Times* André Sennwald supplied the encomium Thalberg had hoped for: "The loudest and funniest screen comedy of the season." Thorton Delehanty's assessment in the *Post* increased Thalberg's pleasure and confidence in the team: "It is a dangerous thing to rate any Marx Brothers picture as their 'best,' yet even at the risk of having to eat my own words I would say that none of their previous films is as consistently and exhaustingly funny or as rich in comic invention and satire as *A Night at the Opera*." Few paid attention to *The New Republic,* where Otis Ferguson, sharpest of the intellectual critics, took exception to the general view. He compared the MGM comedy to a sieve and a leaky ship: "It seems thrown together, made up just as they went along out of everyone else's own head . . . it drives off with whole wagonloads of the Keystone lot without so much as putting the fence back up; it has more familiar faces in the way of gags and situations than a college reunion." Ferguson excepted Groucho, who "would be funny in still photographs," but summed up the hour and a half he spent at the theater as "both great and awful."

Ferguson's divided judgment was all but buried in the autumn of 1936. *A Night at the Opera* went on to do exactly as Thalberg had promised, becoming one of the studio's biggest hits and grossing some $5 million at the box office. Who cared about the opinions of one lonely critic? The Marx Brothers were back, and this time out they had not only satisfied the audience, they had widened it. Groucho took to showing friends a fan letter sent from Iowa: "Mrs. King was telling me about a little boy who was spending Thanksgiving at the Emrie Hatchery near the depot, and Mrs. Emrie took him to see the Marx Brothers in the picture, and he laughed so much he wet his pants. This occurred in Humboldt, and it seems to me that the best thing for you to do would be to send the boy a new pair of pants for the advertising is well worth the price."

The key portions of the letter had nothing to do with the little boy or his pants. They referred to the person who brought the child to the theater, and the one who told the story. Both were women. For the first time in the Brothers' cinematic careers, they had pulled in a large portion of female fans. The price for this widening appeal could not be fully calculated at the time. Only much later did the cost become apparent. In *A Night at the Opera* Harpo remained as silent as a stone, Chico kept his accent and his pianistic style, and Groucho still walked the walk and talked the talk. Some of their bits were among the funniest ever written and performed on screen. Yet a close examination shows that the old fire was banked. Instead of making sport of romance, they now facilitated it. Instead of whacking away at the powerful institutions of government or the military or education, they battled the toothless enemy of grand opera. At Thalberg's insistence the crew of maniacs had become hilarious but harmless uncles, like the later Laurel and Hardy. They were not outrageous anymore, they were only frivolous; they were not surreal, they were only foolish; they were not daring, they were only impolite. Not that the Brothers minded. They were the first comedy team to become a box office attraction in the sound era. MGM proudly announced plans to put them in another glossy vehicle, complete with ten-week road tryout. Thalberg had been proven correct on all counts, the Marxes were flush, and the receipts kept pouring in. And to top it all off, the U.S. economy was making a recovery.

At home, Groucho was a pleasure to be around—at least for his children. He took pride in the fourteen-year-old Arthur's new skills as a tennis player, and he was amused at Miriam's sassy attitude. At eight, she seemed absolutely fearless, especially of him. She told him to stay away from her birthday party because "You'll scare my friends," and refused to allow Ruth to arrange her hair Shirley Temple style, mostly to provoke Groucho. He responded predictably. "Don't be like that. Let your mother do your curls. Why, when I was a little boy I had curls right down to my shoulders." His daughter snapped, "Yeah, and I'll bet everybody called you a sissy." Ruth was displeased by Miriam's attitude; Groucho delighted in the fact that she was wisecracking beyond her years. "I was so envious of Groucho's kids," Maxine remembered. "They were so free." Miriam not only spoke her mind, she also read and saw whatever she wanted. In contrast, said Maxine, "My mother censored everything I read and saw. Groucho never censored anything. Any book was open to his children, any movie they wanted to see." An odd arrangement, but understandable. Chico, who knew the price of wildness, brought his daughter up with restraint. Groucho, the most circumspect Marx, the victim of numberless fears and sleepless nights, allowed his children to do as they pleased. Watching them flourish, he seemed to forget about marital skirmishes, and he pronounced this period one of the happiest of his life. A friend remembered Groucho's eupeptic mood at the time, and the way he permitted himself to sing one of Irving Berlin's most famous lyrics, "Nothing but blue skies from now on." If he had been gifted with a little foresight, another Berlin line, "Say it isn't so," might have been more appropriate.

CHAPTER NINE

His Life Was His Jokes

GROUCHO'S CHEERFUL expectations lasted well into 1936. Like Harpo, Groucho became an ardent New Dealer, taking heart in President Roosevelt's assurances that recovery was simply a matter of confidence and fortitude. The evidence was there for all to see. Studio receipts went up. True, movie houses had to entice customers with free dishware and discounted tickets, but the audiences were trickling back. Like the rest of Hollywood, he read the good news of "an about-face on prosperity road" in the *Film Daily Yearbook*. Like the rest of Hollywood, he knew that all major companies were running in the black for the first time since 1931. The Marx Brothers' status reached a new plane when Jerome Kern and Dorothy Fields used their names in the new movie musical *Swing Time*. As a heartbroken Fred Astaire discards his formal attire, he tells Ginger Rogers he's "never gonna dance": "To Groucho Marx I leave my cravat, to Harpo goes my shiny silk hat."

Yet the old fears and resentments would not be allayed. While Gummo joined Zeppo's company to become a major show business agent, while Chico gambled and Harpo entertained friends, Groucho examined and reexamined his bank account. Suppose FDR was wrong? What if the next picture bombed? Wary of brokers, he became known as an easy mark for insurance agents. One persuaded him to buy an annuity; it guaranteed $80 a week when he reached the age of fifty-five. High-pressure sales talk was unnecessary. Groucho knew at least a dozen former stars who had once earned weekly salaries upwards of $1,000 and who were now grateful for a walk-on in a Marx Brothers movie. It took little imagination for him to visualize an impoverished Julius H. Marx ten years distant, cadging meals and begging to participate in a crowd scene.

The insecurities manifested themselves in story conferences for his next movie, *A Day at the Races*. Robert Pirosh and George Seaton, abetted

by a number of additional dialogue writers, went through eighteen versions before they emerged with something acceptable. But more often
Groucho displayed his mood swings chez Marx or at the Beverly Hills
club. One morning he heard tennis pro Fred Perry telling a group of players, "I read a very funny story in an English magazine this morning."
Groucho snapped, "Well, it's about time." Perry took the reply personally; Groucho meant to put down either British humor or the pro's pre-
sumed illiteracy. Arthur overheard the exchange and winced; Perry was
someone he wanted very much to please. Indifferent in studies, the fifteen-
year-old had become not only the best tennis player in school but one of
the most promising young players in the state. But Arthur wanted to
please his father even more than to please Perry, and he said nothing. In
time he would make both men proud of him once more, as he starred on
the courts.

Miriam had no such method of gratifying Groucho, and she sought
his attention in all the wrong ways. Sunny Sauber, the daughter of a
Columbia producer, characterized her friend in that period as "a real
tomboy. She didn't dress like other girls. Her hair was short when it
wasn't in fashion. She wore blue jeans when girls didn't wear them." Even
with this reduced wardrobe, Groucho put his daughter on a strict clothes
budget. "He also played rough with her. He lashed out at her. I don't
remember Miriam doing anything that would put Groucho down, or
answering him back. Everything Miriam did was for his approval and
love. Groucho, in return, made her feel kind of klutzy." Even so, she was
an adoring child. Too adoring, some friends thought; at the age of nine
she was still encouraged by Groucho to take showers with him. "Freud,"
one of them said, "would have had a field day."

By this time Groucho's marriage had evolved into a series of private
arrangements and public humiliations. What had happened was yet
another rendition of the old Hollywood story: at nineteen, a young,
pretty, unworldly woman marries a man of thirty. Her emotions are on
the surface, he internalizes everything. She remains unsophisticated, he
reads widely. She is known only as a homemaker, he rises in his profession. One day they both look up and the breach between them is too wide
to repair. In the movie colony, the customary answer to such situations
was, as the columnists had it, Splitsville. But that was not Groucho's way.
Chico's wife Betty, who knew all about straying husbands, once spoke of
her brother-in-law's instructions to Ruth: "You go your way and I'll go
mine, but let's stay married." As Ruth saw it, she had very little choice in
the matter. With Groucho she had status in the town, a membership in

the club where she could meet agreeable people and run up a liquor tab, a large house, the company of her children all the time, instead of having to share them after some courtroom agreement, and the visits of amusing and famous guests.

A group of cronies singing along with Gilbert and Sullivan records was not Ruth's idea of excitement, but there were other nights when she took delight in the company her husband kept. Arthur Sheekman, for example, was an articulate writer, quick-witted but kind. Groucho had met him in Chicago a few years back, when Sheekman covered show business for the Chicago *Sun-Times*. The comedian wrote a guest column, the two hit it off, and Groucho encouraged Sheekman to try his hand at comedy writing. Now Sheekman was in Hollywood, doing some work for the Marx Brothers. Groucho had, he acknowledged, lifted him "from local to world-wide obscurity." Equally obscure, and equally diverting, was the young playwright and budding scenarist Norman Krasna, another Groucho protégé. Looking back at some of the dinner parties, Krasna, then in his twenties, said, "All the fun was around him, and everybody tried to gravitate around Groucho." "Everybody" included some unusual guests, like the guitarist Andrés Segovia and the pianist Arthur Rubinstein. Groucho introduced the latter to Krasna as "a fellow piano player." Flustered, Krasna protested that he was not a musician, that in fact he was "the most tone-deaf person in the whole world." Rubinstein instructed the young man not to be arrogant, saying that the most tone-deaf man in the world was his friend King Alfonso of Spain. "I might concede, however," he added, "that you are the *second* most tone-deaf man in the world."

Among Groucho's other guests were the top strata of Hollywood writers, including Moss Hart and George S. Kaufman, Nunnally Johnson and Harry Kurnitz, all refugees, like the Marxes, from New York. The one group rarely in evidence chez Groucho were the rest of the Marx Brothers. Chico, as always, preferred the company of gamblers and chicks, and Harpo, Zeppo, and Gummo moved in their own circle of friends. For the most part, the Brothers met on the set and preferred it that way. Occasionally, though, Harpo would show up at one of Groucho and Ruth's parties, a guest in tow. One night it was George Gershwin. The host yearned to have Gershwin play for the company, but was afraid to impose. Neither Groucho nor the composer seemed at ease for much of the evening. Finally Harpo went to his brother. "Listen," he said, "if you don't ask George to play pretty soon, he'll go home."

Groucho whispered, "I thought he would be insulted if I asked."

"He'll be insulted if you *don't*."

Groucho made the request, and Gershwin graciously agreed to play a few of his songs. He sat at the keyboard for the next five hours. It was the kind of event that led Kaufman to observe, "An evening with Gershwin is certainly an evening with Gershwin."

At certain intervals, Groucho felt that the life he led was too frivolous. After reading Somerset Maugham's defense of card playing as a method of thought, he wondered if perhaps Frenchy and Chico were right about card skill after all. It would not do to play pinochle; that was their game. But bridge had a certain cachet. He engaged a prim, spinsterish instructor and insisted that Sheekman, Krasna, and a few others learn the game. But after a few lessons the old Groucho asserted himself. Sheekman and his young wife had been openly affectionate with each other during a lesson, and after they had left Groucho remarked to the teacher, "It's too bad about the Sheekmans."

"What about them?" she asked. "They seemed to be very nice."

"I know, I know," he sighed.

"Just what is wrong with them?"

"They're brother and sister."

She never gave another lesson—at least not at Groucho's.

Ruth watched all of this with mixed feelings. She admired her husband's friends, but their talk of studio politics and their analyses of international politics were hard to follow.

In time she acquired her own coterie, people she had met at the tennis club or on vacation—people who enjoyed dancing and drinking. These individuals became the butt of Groucho's domestic insults and one-liners. The upshot was a continual Battle of the Dinner Guests: Ruth would want one of the instructors from the Arthur Murray Dance School in Beverly Hills, or perhaps Arthur and Kathryn Murray themselves; Groucho would want a couple of gag writers and their wives or girlfriends.

In some private fantasy, Groucho imagined that this war could go on indefinitely, allowing him to avoid alimony and child support, and, more important for his public image, to maintain the façade of a well-regulated home. He refused to see that his fifteen-year marriage was on its last five-year plan. So he went on as before, using Ruth as a straight woman and, as a kind of consolation prize for his incivility, paying her liquor bills without a gripe. Groucho's domestic insults tended to copy the style of the much admired George S. Kaufman, notorious for his insults to bridge partners: "I know you only learned to play this morning, but what *time* this morning?" As Ruth brought in the dinner Groucho would remark to their guests: "Oh, concentration camp fare again" or "I suppose you've never had vegetables like this before. But then, who has?" These grenades would be followed by questions addressed to the hostess: "What prison sent you the recipe for this?" and "I suppose the meat could be tougher, but will someone tell me how?" Guests tended to stare at their plates during Groucho's kvetches; sometimes they laughed. Frequently the children did. Once in a while Ruth tried to adopt Groucho's tactics in insult comedy. At a nightclub she asked her always beleaguered sister-in-law: "What a pretty necklace. Did you just get it out of hock?" Meant to be amusing, the line just hung in the air. Chico and Betty turned away as Groucho answered for them. "I wish I could say that you would hock something for me," he snapped at Ruth, "if I were ever in trouble."

Understandably Ruth took to spending more time at the tennis club than at home. If her Nordic, athletic looks were beginning to fade she was still attractive, and there were men who paid attention. Night by night, and then day by day, she slid deeper into alcoholism. More than once Ruth banged up the car in the driveway as she arrived home. Customarily, Groucho confined himself to snide reproaches made *en famille* when his wife was at her most defenseless and he could be at his most manipulative.

Groucho was playing the aggrieved party. It was a role for which he needed no rehearsal. A lifelong collector of gripes, many of them legitimate, he frequently went over his catalog on sleepless nights: third in the birth order, a disappointment to Minnie because of his appearance, pushed out of the nest before he was ready, abruptly deprived of the fortune he had so carefully amassed. . . . It was no wonder that he had never truly been at ease with anyone except with his brothers, and then only in a working relationship.

The locked door of Groucho's separate bedroom was the external expression of a long-held belief. From his experiences as a boy, an adolescent, and a man, to get close to a woman meant to be let down, to be forced into decisions before he had thought them through, to be made socially uncomfortable and financially and physically obliged. Not that his attitude always worked against him: it was what made his skirmishes with Margaret Dumont so effective and funny. But it was also what militated against trusting and intimate relations with the female, a category that would one day include daughter as well as wife. It could hardly be expected that Groucho would remain celibate during these final years with Ruth, yet the affairs he did have were infrequent and brief, limited to uninvolving one-night stands with the likes of a dancer in the stage company of *A Day at the Races.*

That company had been formed in the spirit and style of *A Night at the Opera.* As with the previous film, the cast performed various sketches from the upcoming picture, testing and reworking gags on the road. Originally titled *Peace and Quiet,* the movie centers on a sanitarium, a refuge for the hypochondriacal Mrs. Upjohn (Margaret Dumont). Like other institutions in Marx Brothers films, the place is on the verge of bankruptcy. Villains rub their hands in preparation for a seizure. The one person who can save the day—according to Mrs. Upjohn—is her former physician, Dr. Hugo Z. Hackenbush (Groucho). Why, she tells the staff, "I didn't know there was a thing wrong with me until I met him." Neither she nor anyone else is aware that her beloved Hackenbush is a doctor of veterinary medicine. Further complications depend on a racehorse, a romance between the beautiful sanitarium owner (Maureen O'Sullivan) and her boyfriend, a tenor (Allan Jones), and two unhelpful aides (Chico and Harpo). The road tryout lacked the romantic couple: O'Sullivan was busy playing Jane in a Tarzan picture, and Jones was finishing work in *Showboat.* But they had stand-ins, and the Brothers and Dumont were on nearly every night. That was more than enough.

The more disordered the scenes with Ruth, the tidier and more exacting became Groucho's performances on stage, as if they exemplified real life and his marriage a farce—a fair summation of the way things were proceeding. A Marx Brothers publicist, Teet Carle, remembered the way in which Groucho pored over a single word, trying different candidates for a punch line. In one scene he confronts Sig Rumann, veteran of *A Night at the Opera,* as the pop-eyed Plattdeutsch-speaking physician, Dr. Leopold X. Steinberg. Preparing to examine his patient, Dr. Hackenbush washes up. He removes his watch, glances suspiciously at Rumann, and then tosses it into a basin of water: "I'd rather have it rusty than missing." On the tour, Carle wrote, *"Gone* and *disappear* were each used forty-four times; *missing* got fifty voicings. Every time, the latter word brought the biggest laugh." In another sketch Chico tries to sell Groucho a discounted book: "One dollar and you remember me all your life." Groucho: "That's the most nauseating proposition I ever had." Adds Carle: "Among other words tried out were *obnoxious, revolting, disgusting, offensive, repulsive, disagreeable,* and *distasteful.* The last two of these words never got more than titters. The others elicited various degrees of ha-has. But *nauseating* drew roars. I asked Groucho why that was so. 'I don't know. I really don't care. I only know the audiences told us it was funny.' " Audiences also told them that statements were often funnier than interrogations. Al Boasberg contributed Groucho's line "Is he dead or is my watch stopped?" The response was tepid, but the rephrase, "Either he's dead or my watch has stopped," brought down the house.

In order to test the gags objectively, the Brothers hired a trio of vaudevillians to take their places for two weeks. As Harry Lash, Bobbie Dooley, and "Skins" Miller executed the Marx routines, Groucho, Chico, and Harpo sat in the orchestra watching these versions of themselves. With all the planning, there were some unforeseen difficulties: one evening in Duluth the stage horse took one step too many and tumbled into the orchestra. "He must have known where the real horse players were," Groucho told the cast. But if animals were allowed to ad-lib, the Brothers truly attempted to adhere to their lines, actually muting the routines when the laughter came too easily. Groucho led the pack by walking with much less exaggeration, and pulling back on his facial gimmicks. "I know I can get a laugh on almost any line with my eyebrows and my eyes," he told the writers. They got the message, stopped relying on his comic technique to carry a weak joke, and began the process of rewriting almost every comic scene. It was small wonder that one of the scenarists, George Oppenheimer, agreed with S. J. Perelman. Working for the Marx Brothers, he said, turned out to be "spiritually and mentally gruelling." But being a Marx Brother turned out to be an even more arduous chore.

•

IRVING THALBERG had never been physically strong. Cardiologists and pulmonary specialists regularly cautioned him against overwork. One predicted that with his long hours and stressful meetings the Boy Wonder would be lucky to attain the age of thirty-five. But Thalberg paid them no mind; he passed the dangerous milepost in 1934 and kept reaching for greater authority and rewards. In the summer of 1936 there was an aura of concentrated intensity about him, especially in his bright, nervous eyes. A deep California suntan overlaid his natural pallor, yet he never seemed truly robust, and when Labor Day arrived no one was surprised when he permitted himself a brief holiday. Thalberg and his wife, the actress Norma Shearer, joined Chico and Betty and some other cardplaying friends at the Del Monte hotel near Monterey. As they sat on the veranda an autumn breeze suddenly made Betty shiver. Thalberg took off his jacket and put it over her shoulders.

Two weeks later, when *A Day at the Races* went back before the cameras, Sam Wood appeared on the set with a long face. "The little brown fellow died," he told the cast. It took a few minutes for the Brothers to comprehend what their director had said. Details were tragically simple, spelled out in the next day's long and worshipful obituaries. The gallant gesture Thalberg had made on the veranda had amounted to a death warrant. He developed a head cold and a fever. By the end of the week he had come down with lobar pneumonia. On September 15, his heart failed. Filming stopped for the day at MGM; it was as if the president had died. Thalberg's funeral was attended by every major Hollywood personality. Sheilah Graham, F. Scott Fitzgerald's companion in the late 1930s, was there. Later she told the writer about the Marx Brothers "sobbing their eyes out . . . always making sure that they were within crying distance of the 'right' people." According to Graham, Fitzgerald's last, incomplete novel, *The Last Tycoon,* based on the career and personality of Thalberg, was to have featured a similar funeral scene. In it, the ghost of the deceased would come back to condemn such hypocrisies as "trash." But Graham only saw the surface of things: the Marxes were not crying solely for public relations purposes; whether they knew it or not, they were also in mourning for their future. "After Thalberg's death," Groucho later admitted, "my interest in the movies waned. I appeared in them, but my heart was in the Highlands. The fun had gone out of filmmaking. I was like an old pug, still going through the motions, but now doing it solely for the money." Harpo was affected in a different way. With the sudden passing of the Boy Wonder, intimations of mortality struck home; Harpo's own boyishness was a mask that fit a little more uncomfortably in each picture. He was closing in on the half-century mark, and, despite the fact that he was second only to Chico in romantic adventures, lived childless and alone, just as Minnie had feared. Within a fortnight of the funeral he announced plans for marriage to a woman he had been dating for a few months. Susan Fleming was a pretty, little-known actress whose best part had been in *Million Dollar Legs,* playing opposite W. C. Fields. They got married in the Santa Ana firehouse one afternoon, away from all show business connections. Harpo and Susan were to have many admirers, but none was as envious as Groucho, not only because of the manifest love the couple had for each other, but because of their skills as parents. "It was a very happy marriage," he was to say many times, always wistfully. "They knew how to do it. He and Susan adopted four children. And they raised them beautifully." The favorable appraisal was not always returned. Susan took her brother-in-law's measure early and late. "He destroys people's ego," she commented. "If you're vulnerable, you have absolutely no protection from Groucho. He can only be controlled if he has respect for you. But if he loses respect you're dead. He won't take off on me because I'm as fresh as he is. So he leaves me alone and loves me dearly on account of it."

Three months after their marriage, Susan and Harpo arranged to take in their first child, William. Before he arrived, the adoptive parents filled their swimming pool with soil to extend the backyard and turn it into a playground. The household would eventually include two more boys and a girl. Harpo explained to friends that he came from a large family and intended to duplicate the experience—minus the poverty: "I wanted to have a child at every window, waving to me when I came home." He got his wish.

That September, while one Marx marriage was consolidating, and another deteriorating, the Marx Brothers went back to work at MGM. They had a new producer, Laurence Weingarten, whose main qualification for the job was his lineage: he was Thalberg's brother-in-law. A pattern had been set by *A Night at the Opera,* and Weingarten used it as a template. If he varied so much as a frame, it was to accentuate Thalberg's formula. Did *Opera* feature musical solos? Very well, *A Day at the Races* would mount a series of overproduced numbers, including a water carnival scene. Another used dozens of wide-eyed, "Who dat man?" black singers, chanting in a hallelujah chorus that was insensitive even for the 1930s. (It evidently jibed with the director's worldview. According to Groucho, he and Sam Wood were watching a UCLA football game when a black player joined the huddle. "Imagine," the director grumbled to the comedian, "letting a nigger play on the same team with a lot of white guys.") Did *Opera* have a villain? *Races* would call for *two* wicked schemers. Was *Opera* marked by sentiment? *Races* would display a procession of lovers' quarrels, a weepy heroine, and the Brothers acting as sympathetic Cupids. For the first time Harpo was called upon to play charades with Chico, communicating through a series of child-pleasing visual puns.

HARPO

(*Whistling through his teeth and holding his fingers under his nose like a moustache*)

CHICO

Buffalo Bill?

HARPO

(*Slouches in a circle*)

CHICO

Buffalo Bill goes ice-skating.

HARPO

(*Begins slashing at the shrubbery*)

CHICO

Oh, Hack-in-a-Bush?

HARPO

(*Shakes CHICO's hand wildly, congratulating him for understanding*)

In *Opera*, Kitty Carlisle possessed a certain coolness that never interfered with the farceurs. In *Races*, Maureen O'Sullivan, an attractive personality in other films, was all warmth and vulnerability. Playing a colleen with quavering voice and winsome manner, she was given such lines as "Hold me tight. I'll be all right. (*She cries*)." The words melted the viewers' hearts—and applied brakes to the Brothers' momentum. *A Day at the Races* contained a mere handful of interludes that harked back to the Paramount days. One takes place in an infirmary, where Groucho is about to administer medicine to his patient, Dumont:

HOUSE DOCTOR

Just a minute . . . that looks like a horse pill to me.

GROUCHO

Oh, you've taken them before.

HOUSE DOCTOR

Are you sure you haven't made a mistake?

GROUCHO

You have nothing to worry about. The last patient I gave one of those to won the Kentucky Derby.

HOUSE DOCTOR

May I examine this, please? Do you actually give those to your patients? Isn't it awfully large for a pill?

GROUCHO

Well, it was too small for a basketball and I didn't know what to do with it. Say, you're awfully large for a pill yourself.

The Marx Brothers' seventh feature film also displays a dance by Groucho, in which he walks with bent-kneed energy around Dumont, and the "Tootsie-Frootsie" routine, one of the Brothers' most memorable uses of repetition, upended clichés, and comic timing. The con game, in which Groucho ultimately becomes Chico, occurs at the track. In need of money to save O'Sullivan's sanitarium, Chico pretends to be an ice-cream vendor. He closes in on Groucho at the betting window and dissuades him from betting on Sun Up.

For one dollar Groucho purchases a tip sheet with guaranteed long shots.

GROUCHO

(*Reading the sheet*) Z-V-B-X-R-P-L. I had that same horse when I had my eyes examined. Hey, Ice Cream. What about this optical illusion you just slipped me? I don't understand it.

CHICO

Oh, that's not the real name of the horse, that's the name of the horse in code. Look in your code book. . . .

GROUCHO

Well, I haven't got any code book.

CHICO

(*Opens ice-cream wagon*) Well, just by accident, I think I got one here.

GROUCHO

How much is it?

CHICO

That's free.

GROUCHO

Oh, thanks.

CHICO

Just-a one dollar printing charge.

GROUCHO

Well, give me one without printing. I'm sick of printing.

CHICO

Aw, come on. You want to win . . .

GROUCHO

I want to win, but I don't want the savings of a lifetime wiped out in the twinkling of an eye. (*Forks over a dollar*) Z-V-B-X-R-P-L. Page thirty-four. Hey, Ice Cream, I can't make head or tail out of this.

CHICO

Look in the master code book. . . . You no gotta master code book? Well, just by accident, I think I got one right here.

GROUCHO

Lots of quick accidents around here for a quiet neighborhood. Just a minute. Is there a printing charge on this?

CHICO

No. Just a two-dollar delivery charge.

GROUCHO

What do you mean, delivery charge? I'm standing right next to you.

CHICO

Well, for such a short distance, I make it a dollar.

GROUCHO

Couldn't I move over here and make it fifty cents?

CHICO

Yes, but I'd move over here and make it a dollar just the same.

GROUCHO

Say, maybe I better open a charge account, huh?

CHICO

You gotta some references?

GROUCHO

Well, the only one I know around here is you.

CHICO

That's-a no good. You'll have to pay cash.

GROUCHO

You know, a little while ago I could have put two dollars on Sun Up and avoided all this. (*Buys the master code book and begins reading*) "The letter Z stands for J unless the horse is a filly."

CHICO

(*Offscreen*) Get your tootsie-frootsie ice cream.

GROUCHO

Hey, Tootsie-Frootsie. Is the horse a filly?

CHICO

I don't know. Look in your breeder's guide. (*Offscreen*) Get your ice cream. Tootsie—

GROUCHO

What do you mean, breeder's guide? I haven't got a breeder's guide.

CHICO

You haven't got a breeder's guide?

GROUCHO

Shh! Not so loud. I don't want it to get around that I haven't got a breeder's guide. Even my best friends don't know I haven't got a breeder's guide.

CHICO

Well, boss, I feel pretty sorry for you walking around without a breeder's guide. Why, you're just throwing your money away buying those other books without a breeder's guide. (*A long wait while GROUCHO thinks about it*)

GROUCHO

Where can I get one, as if I didn't know?

CHICO

One is no good. You got to have the whole set. (*Offscreen*) Get your tootsie-frootsie. . . .

GROUCHO

Hey, you know, all I wanted was a horse, not a public library. . . . How much is the set?

CHICO

One dollar.

GROUCHO

One dollar?

CHICO

Yeah, four for five. (*Pulls out a stack of books*)

GROUCHO

Well, all right. Give me the four of them. There's no use throwing away money, eh . . . ?

CHICO

Here you are. (*Going to the betting window*) Six dollars on Sun Up.

GROUCHO

(*Decoding the book*) Z-V-B-X-R-P-L is Burns. . . .

CHICO

(*Peering over GROUCHO's shoulder*) Now you find who jockey Burns is riding and that's the horse you bet on. It's easy. (*Moving away*) Get your ice cream, tootsie-frootsie. . . .

GROUCHO

Oh, I'm getting the idea of it. I didn't get it for a long time, you know. It's pretty tricky when you didn't know it, isn't it, huh?

CHICO

It's not that book. . . .

GROUCHO

You've got it, huh? I'll get it in a minute, though, won't I?

CHICO

Get your tootsie-frootsie. . . .

GROUCHO

I'm getting a fine tootsie-frootsie right here. . . . How much is it?

CHICO

One dollar.

GROUCHO

And it's the last book I'm buying.

CHICO

Sure, you don't need no more.

GROUCHO

(*Hands him a ten-dollar bill*) Shoot the change, will you? They're going to the post.

CHICO

I gotta no change. I'll have to give you nine more books. . . .

GROUCHO

(*Totally encumbered by books, he holds some under his arms and between his knees as he limps to the betting window*) Good thing I brought my legs with me, huh? Tell me, what horse have I got? I just heard the fellow blowing his horn.

CHICO

Here it is: Jockey Burns—Rosie . . . oh, boy, look: forty to one. Oh, what a horse.

GROUCHO

I was going to bet on Sun Up at ten to one. I'll show them a thing or two. Hey there! Big boy, two dollars on Rosie, huh?

CLERK

Sorry, that race is over.

GROUCHO

Over! Who won?

CLERK

Sun Up.

CHICO

Sun Up! That's-a my horse. (*Collects his money*) Gooda-by, boss. (*Counts the winnings*) Ten, twenty, thirty . . .

GROUCHO

(*Surrendering to fate, he dumps all the books back into CHICO's abandoned ice-cream pushcart and moves it off, trailing books as he goes*) Get your tootsie-frootsie nice ice cream . . . nice tootsie-frootsie ice cream. . . .

But these moments are exceptions to the safe and saccharine content of *A Day at the Races*. In general, the film reduces the Brothers' mania to eccentricity, and their iconoclasm to fitfully amusing mischief. Some of the mistakes lay with Sam Wood. Without Thalberg to give him assurance at the end of the day, scenes were repeated until even the extras dared to complain. But Wood was not the only detriment. Groucho himself made a central error when he argued for the excision of "Dr. Hackenbush," a Kalmar-Ruby song that recalled the salad days at Paramount (he later performed the number at parties, as if to apologize for the oversight):

> For ailments abdominal
> My charges are nominal

Though I'm great for
I've a rate for
Tonsillectomy.
Sick and healthy,
Poor and wealthy
Come direct to me.
"Oh, God bless you," they yell
When I send them home well.
But they never, no they never send a check to me.

Groucho's character name arose from a legal dispute. Originally he was to be called Dr. Quackenbush, a monicker that pleased him mightily. Then several letters arrived from doctors with birth certificates bearing that surname. They guessed that any character played by Groucho would be a mountebank, and the group threatened to sue for the sake of their reputations. "I've already got Quackenbush painted on my shingle," Groucho arrogantly proclaimed. "Let them change their names if they don't like it." But studio lawyers refused to back him and, after a quick search of the national phone books, he was given the safe name of Dr. Hackenbush.

This episode did not sweeten his disposition, nor did an unrequited schoolboy crush on O'Sullivan. She was then married to John Farrow, a director famous for going on extravagant benders. Said a friend: "Groucho couldn't keep his eyes off her. She was a beautiful shicksa with doe eyes and soft hair, and given his home situation she couldn't have come along at a more opportune time. Alas, she was never anything other than sweet to him." Groucho convinced himself that Farrow was a wife-beater (an accusation O'Sullivan emphatically denied), and probably saw himself in the role of Frank Merriwell, rescuer of maidens in distress. In any case, O'Sullivan later recalled that the time for dalliance was not propitious. Perhaps had Groucho altered his style even a little, he might have enjoyed a different outcome. But he kept up the rat-a-tat monologues after shooting stopped. "It went on all day," the actress remembered. "Groucho and I would go out for lunch. After a while your face starts to crack. I was tired of it after the third day. I told him, 'Please, Groucho, stop! Let's have a nice quiet normal conversation.' Groucho never knew how to talk normally. His life was his jokes."

He tried to extend that life by becoming a scenarist. With his young friend Norman Krasna, Groucho wrote the script for a Warner Brothers movie, produced and directed by Mervyn LeRoy. Krasna remembered an instance of his collaborator's hypocrisy: LeRoy had added a bit about Coney Island, and "Groucho was offended that anybody would tamper with his lines—and look who's talking—he was the world's greatest tamperer." At a preview, LeRoy hoped to be congratulated by Groucho. Instead, the comedian stared at him and witheringly spoke two words: "Coney Island." Groucho was further dismayed when ads for *The King and the Chorus Girl* used his picture in an inset, underlined with the legend "He Wrote It!" There was, Groucho learned, no way to sever his identity from the man in the greasepaint moustache and large cigar. No matter how he tried, he would never be a writer who performed comedy; he would always be a comedian who wrote.

As the title indicated, *The King and the Chorus Girl* centered on a European monarch (played by the French actor Fernand Gravet) prepared to renounce his throne for the love of an American woman (Joan Blondell). The resemblance to Britain's King Edward VIII, abdicating "for the woman I love"—American divorcée Wallis Simpson—was unmistakable. The effort was treated lightly by the *New York Times* ("a buoyant farce-romance"), but most critics and filmgoers agreed with the assessment in *Life*: "easily the season's silliest movie." British journals were less generous. *Picturegoer* stated that "it is a painful shock . . . to find a reputable film organization indulging in such an outrage on good taste." The magazine paid special and censorious attention to the film promotion, particularly an ad in *Variety* captioned "Reign, Reign, Go Away." For public consumption Groucho said that he was sorry not to have thought of that pun himself.

The Brothers fared considerably better when *A Day at the Races* opened in April 1937. Their humor tamed, their attack blunted, the Marxes were now fit for wide public consumption. The editors of *Life* made the Marxes' latest work their Movie of the Week and *The New Yorker* delighted in Groucho's lines, particularly a warning to Sig Rumann: "Don't point that beard at me. It might go off."

Graham Greene filed a more perceptive review when the feature opened in London. Writing in the short-lived magazine *Night and Day*, he found admirable sequences in *A Day at the Races*. Yet he expressed a lingering affection for the Paramount films with their "old cheap rickety sets, those titles as meaningless and undifferentiated as Kipling's, *Duck Soup* and *Horse Feathers*." Greene also admitted to "a kind of perverse passion for Miss Maureen O'Sullivan" but inquired, "what business has she in a wild Lear world where a veterinary doctor is in charge of a sanitarium? Miss O'Sullivan is a real person [and] real people do more than retard, they smash the Marx fantasy. When Groucho lopes into the inane, they smile at him incredulously (being real people they cannot take him for granted), and there was one dreadful moment when Miss O'Sullivan murmured the word 'Silly.' Silly—good God, we cannot help exclaiming since we are real people too, have we been deceived all along?" The critic concluded by interviewing himself: "Are Groucho and Chico just silly and not poets of Edward Lear's stature . . . ? No, these revelers of the higher idiocy should not mingle with real people nor play before lavish scenery and an arty camera. Like the Elizabethans, they need only a chair, a painted tree."

Unburdened by high-toned nostalgia, the public disagreed. *A Day at the Races* brought in a $5 million gross, more than five times the cost of making the picture. It was the biggest profit of the Brothers' career. *Races* profits far exceeded those of any other comedy, including the ones made by W. C. Fields. His projects cost as much as the Marxes' and generally grossed less than $1.5 million each. The Marx Brothers could now be counted among MGM's elite group of popular stars, trailing such box office giants as Spencer Tracy and Clark Gable, but well in advance of Robert Montgomery and Edward G. Robinson. Louis B. Mayer had never understood the Marx Brothers' humor, and he specifically resented Groucho's offscreen attitude. But once the mogul checked the profit statements his mind broadened. After all, what was a little rudeness among colleagues? But the Brothers were having none of him. Through their agent, Zeppo, they cast about for other deals with rival studios. Up to now the Marxes had been in movies written and shaped for their talents. Now they considered a departure from tradition: appearance in a film adapted from a Broadway hit. The play was *Room Service* by John Murray and Allen Boretz, a slam-bang farce directed in New York by George Abbott. Spirited bidding by MGM, Paramount, Warner Brothers, and RKO kept driving the price up until only one studio remained. For $250,000 RKO bought the property, and, thanks to heavy bargaining by Zeppo, they bought the Marx Brothers for another $250,000 plus a percentage of the gross. This was a time for crowing; in a town where youth has been worshiped since the early days of the silents, three middle-aged men, Groucho, forty-eight, Harpo, fifty, and Chico, fifty-one, found themselves internationally famous and locally bankable. Their images popped up in animated cartoons from the Disney and Warner Brothers studios. A vogue started: theme parties in New York and Hollywood asked guests to come dressed as a Marx Brother; George Gershwin attended one as Groucho, only to find himself surrounded by other men with similar cigar, spectacles, and greasepaint moustache. Zeppo deservedly felt triumphant, and Chico and Harpo made plans to spend the money: Chico as usual, on gambling and women, Harpo on his new family. Only Groucho lived up to his name; the eternal pessimist expected bad news at any time—and in this he was not disappointed. A week after RKO bought *Room Service,* Al Boasberg died suddenly of a heart attack, depriving the Brothers of the best additional dialogue writer they would ever hire. A month later, George Gershwin failed to come out of a coma after brain surgery. The composer and the trio had never been close, but they had mutual friends in town, had attended many of the same social gatherings, and had made the long climb from show business obscurity at roughly the same time. The Brothers' sense of loss was acute. They reconsidered a film adaptation of George and Ira Gershwin's *Of Thee I Sing.* The book of the show had been written by George S. Kaufman and Morrie Ryskind, the ultimate in credentials. But it was not to be; the musical was never brought to the screen by them or anyone else.

Uncertain of his future and restless at home, Groucho agreed to make an effort at rekindling his marriage. He and Ruth booked a cruise to Hawaii, sans children. Reconciliation would have been unlikely in the best of circumstances, and the Marxes did not enjoy the best of circumstances. They had hardly unpacked in Honolulu when Groucho learned that he and Chico had been indicted by a federal grand jury in California. The crime: plagiarism. According to the lawsuit, the previous September the two brothers had broadcast a radio skit, "Mr. Diffle and Mr. Daffle," written by two other brothers, Garrett and Carroll Graham. The Grahams had not received credit, nor had they been paid, and they insisted on compensation. The Marxes' lawyers stated that the skit had been written by the late Al Boasberg, that the Grahams had been minor contributors at best, and that Boasberg had given Groucho and Chico his permission to use the skit as they saw fit. Originally, the defense had hoped to have the case dismissed as a nuisance suit. Now that Boasberg was dead, however, their position seemed untenable.

Never at his best away from the field of action, Groucho was tense and argumentative during the vacation. By the end of three weeks, both husband and wife were glad to head home. On the night before the boat was due to dock in California, Groucho retired early, as was his custom, leaving Ruth in the Palm Court with a dance instructor. When she failed to return by 3 a.m. he went in search of her. He found his wife with the instructor out by the lifeboats, enjoying a long passionate kiss. Ruth was drunk; her companion also had imbibed too much. His chin made an easy target for a right cross. While the instructor was down, Groucho furiously hustled Ruth back to their stateroom. And yet when they got back to Beverly Hills, the Marxes kept up a façade of amiability, as if nothing untoward had happened on their trip. The pretense went on for the children's sake, and for other reasons as well. Ruth knew that if she left, she would not only be abandoning Groucho, she would be forsaking a comfortable lifestyle for—what? The unknown was unpleasant to contemplate, for she would be wholly dependent on alimony payments. And if the Groucho of tomorrow was anything like the Groucho of today, she would get the most meager settlement possible. On the other side of the equation, Groucho guarded his money and clung unrealistically to the idea of the home as bulwark against the forces outside; after all, Frenchy and Minnie's union was hardly made in heaven, and yet they stuck it out to the end. He may also have had some premonitory feelings. Decades later, Norman Krasna remembered that even the last, difficult stretch with Ruth represented "the tag end of Groucho's golden years."

That end would not have been so golden save for a judge's lenience. Groucho had hardly returned to Los Angeles when the Grahams forced the Brothers into court to answer the plagiarism charges. Groucho and Chico put up a weak defense and within a week found themselves on the losing end of the case. Faced with a scene right out of Minnie's nightmares, a one-year jail sentence, Chico lied, "This is the first time I have ever been accused of stealing anything." His next statement returned to the factual. "Many other actors have used our stuff and we've never said a word." After due consideration, the judge bawled out the Marxes and then allowed them to pay a fine in lieu of imprisonment. Gratified, the comedians opened their checkbooks. In press interviews they changed their tone from defiant to candid. Chico: "That's a relief. We'll be glad, Groucho and me, to shell out a thousand each. But jail—say, that's a terrible thought." Groucho was, as always, Groucho. He might as well have been speaking about his marriage as about the judicial pronouncement: "Well, I was expecting the worst, so I'm well satisfied."

•

IRONICALLY, the Marx Brothers became most attractive to the Surrealists just at the time when their screen personae were being housebroken. Salvador Dalí, painter of erotic fantasies and melting watches ("the Camemberts of time and space," as he explained it), was always a favorite of the Hollywood art collectors. His self-promotion, his gold lamé trousers and long moustache, his accessible and pricey works, exerted a hypnotic effect on certain filmmakers, among them Walt Disney and Alfred Hitchcock, who mistook technique for profundity. Dalí professed himself thunderstruck by the inarticulate beauty of Harpo (Groucho was to say that Dalí, like Alexander Woollcott, "was in love with my brother—in a nice way"). The artist took it on himself to write an outline for a Surrealist film centering on Harpo but starring all three of the Marx Brothers. An excerpt from this effort should suffice to show why the movie was never made:

> Groucho comes out and sits at his desk. He takes out a magnifying glass and a palmist's book and scrutinizes each hand, one by one. In one of the hands he finds something which interests him but which he cannot see properly because of the light, so he tries to bring the lamp on his desk but this is a fixture. Impatiently, he pulls at [a girl's] arm but naturally cannot pull it far, so that in exasperation, he takes up a large pair of scissors from the table as if to cut off the hand.
>
> At this moment, Chico comes into the room, clothed in a rain-soaked mackintosh and calls to him, "Come and see the latest accessory on my car."
>
> Groucho lets go of the arm and the scissors. They go down to the street where Harpo is waiting in front of the car. Chico says to them, "I have just installed indoor rain."

Worthless as a scenario, it helped generate more publicity by being talked about. Dalí added to the Brothers' reputation by painting large ethereal canvases of Harpo playing music. Then Charlie Chaplin, the darling of the intellectuals, added his tribute. Embracing all the Brothers, but nominating a first among equals, he told Groucho, "I wish I could speak on the screen as well as you." That was all that aesthetes needed to hear. The Marx Brothers became their new favorites, and the Brothers returned the favor. More than any of his siblings, Groucho thirsted for the approval of artists and writers. He tried his best to emulate Chaplin, who made a point of entertaining prominent novelists and painters at his palatial home, where the swimming pool was designed in the shape of Charlie's bowler hat. Groucho cofounded the West Side Writing and Asthma Club, with a membership that included Robert Benchley, S. J. Perelman, Donald Ogden Stewart, and the playwrights Ben Hecht and Charles MacArthur. As he cultivated his old vaudeville colleague, Groucho was gratified to learn that Charlie also felt a deep insecurity, convinced that his celebrity and money could vanish overnight. At lunch the two comedians compared notes. "There we were," Groucho wrote, "two neurotics sitting and talking, completely terrified about life and their careers! You would think that by this time Chaplin would be more or less convinced that he had remarkable talent. But no! He was just as frightened as he had been when he first came to me and asked my advice."

When Charlie and Groucho met in another arena—a tennis court—matters were not so cordial. The event began well enough: a new clubhouse was being dedicated, and for the occasion a doubles match was set up with Groucho and the American champion Ellsworth Vines versus Chaplin and the English master Fred Perry. Chaplin prided himself on his tennis and on an acquaintance with athletes who were nearly as famous as he was. When newsreel photographers appeared he stepped up his game a notch. For Groucho, however, the cameras merely provided a fresh opportunity for clowning around. He had brought along a suitcase full of food and drink, certain that there would come a time to use the props for maximum effect. It occurred just after Perry and Chaplin won the second game as easily as they had the first. Playing to the crowd, Groucho announced a lunch break, opened the case, spread a tablecloth on the playing field, and passed sandwiches around. To the delight of onlookers he grandly suggested that Charlie join him in a spot of tea. The offer was declined. What Groucho failed to note in his memoirs was Chaplin's exasperated comment, "I didn't come here to be your straight man." Nevertheless that was the role he played. It was just as Harpo's wife observed: family, friends, rivals—all would be made into fall guys or girls if Groucho could possibly arrange it. Although Charlie smiled for the cameras, it took years for him to forgive the incident.

The two comedians diverged in other ways. Charlie, whose childhood was more deprived than Groucho's, was "a lifelong member of the left," according to his most thorough biographer. Kenneth S. Lynn notes how often Chaplin's political expressions jibed with those of the Stalinists. As we have seen, Minnie and Frenchy had no interest in labor politics even in turn-of-the-century New York. Forty years later Groucho had moved no further left than the New Deal. Like most people in the film colony he had seen the Hollywood Communists up close, and he dismissed them as "the kind of hypocrites who would sing 'Arise You Prisoners of Starvation' in between laps around their swimming pools."

Groucho and Charlie also differed in their attitudes toward women. After a slow start, Chaplin had become an intense voluptuary, and at the age of thirty-one had already been married and divorced twice. By forty his name had been linked with so many females in and out of the movie colony that gossip columnists lost count. Meanwhile, Groucho's affairs were few and brief, and in his late forties he seemed to have given up prowling altogether. Quite frequently, when a long-married couple is on the verge of breaking up, there is one last attempt to revive the romance by producing another child. That seems to have been the case with Groucho and Ruth—except that the decision was essentially one-sided. In her third month, Ruth suddenly and independently resolved to terminate the pregnancy. Arthur knew about the decision before Groucho did; the son called for his mother at the abortionist's office and drove her home. When Groucho learned what Ruth had done, he simply withdrew into himself even more. There were no loud recriminations; at this point he was forced to acknowledge that a new baby would not solve old problems, that what he had proposed was damaging and unrealistic. No more was said about the matter, and the fuse burned on.

Arthur and Miriam had difficulty choosing sides in the gathering conflict. On the one hand, it was impossible not to feel pity for Ruth when they saw her drunk and hopeless night after night. They had lost count of the sorry evenings when Groucho insulted their mother's cooking or banished her from the table. And then there was the business of private bedrooms. Groucho's impregnating Ruth for the last time was probably one of the couple's few intimacies in years. Ruth scarcely bothered to keep up appearances anymore; eventually she became indifferent to the needs of her children. One day in May, for instance, she agreed to attend Miriam's performance in a school ceremony, and then canceled at the last moment—something had come up. She did not specify the "something" and even the thirteen-year-old sensed that the excuse was bogus. In tears, Miriam begged her father to substitute for Ruth. Without a backward glance he canceled a business appointment and appeared at the school auditorium. Miriam's relief and gratitude were not to last long. The headmistress recognized her famous guest and asked him to say a few words. Groucho took the microphone and predicted that most of Miriam's classmates would be collecting alimony by the time they reached the age of thirty. The reaction was frosty and embarrassed. The headmistress professed herself shocked to the core and demanded that Miriam take her father home. That she did—and refused to speak to Groucho until her next allowance came due. That was fine with the speaker; his daughter's sassy attitude was a source of pride. Like her aunt Susan, Miriam had discovered the way to earn Groucho's respect. Her alcoholic mother was another problem entirely. Neither Miriam nor Arthur could figure out a way to solve that one.

•

AS A REFUGE from marriage, the set of *Room Service* proved invaluable to Groucho, even though the results of the filming were not up to the Marxes' usual standard. RKO had spent half a million dollars on the property and the talent, and they refused to let scenarist Morrie Ryskind tamper with a proven Broadway hit. Therefore, Ryskind noted, "Ninety percent of the story was taken up with Groucho's stalling tactics to avoid being evicted from his hotel room. A theatrical audience will accept a story that takes place in one setting; in fact, fewer settings usually enhance a play's charm by shifting the emphasis toward the quality of the dialogue. But with movies tending to be primarily a visual medium, a one-set story can seem claustrophobic before the end of the first reel." Ryskind was able to wring a few funny moments from the proceedings, but in general, the scenarist acknowledged, *Room Service* "was a cramped, badly paced miscalculation dismissed by the critics and ignored by the public, which gives me the distinction of having written the best and the worst of the Marx Brothers' movies." Ryskind's recall was inaccurate; if *A Night at the Opera* was at or near the top of the line, *Room Service* was far from the bottom. Films with that distinction had yet to be made.

The plot of *Room Service* contains certain parallels to the Brothers' early experiences in the theater. A producer proclaims his eagerness to back Groucho's production—if room is made for a certain chorine. This is reminiscent of an actual proposition made by the producer of *I'll Say She Is!* back in the 1920s. The Brothers attempt to wring some comedy from the situation, but no routine in the film works for more than a joke at a time. Chico is miscast as a Broadway director, his vaudeville accent rendering him unbelievable from the first entrance ("The rehearsal she's-a wonderful. I still think it's a terrible play, but it makes a wonderful rehearsal"). Harpo has no discernible function except to hang around, point to things, and serve as the victim of Groucho's put-downs ("This is the brains of the organization. That'll give you some idea of the organization"). Throughout, Groucho sounds one flat note of connivance. To render matters even less amusing, the script was modified on orders from above. Donald MacBride, who specialized in choler and sarcasm, had played the part of the hotel manager on Broadway. He fills the same role in the film, but where once he fulminated with "God damn it!" upon his exits, he is now reduced to "Jumping butterballs!" Once or twice the Brothers rise to their old heights: in a manic luncheon scene the starving Harpo hunts peas like a spear fisherman, pausing only to catch some salt when Chico upends the shaker and jiggles it over his right shoulder for luck; and in an interlude when the Marxes vainly try to catch and slaughter a wild turkey ("Well, there were no cranberries anyway," Groucho says afterward in his best sour-grapes manner).

But *Room Service* could not be rescued, either by the trio or by their supporting players. Among these were the adolescent Ann Miller, who gave not the slightest hint that she would become a lead dancer in musical comedy, and a raw newcomer, Lucille Ball, whose comic gifts were never put to the test. A foreman rather than a director, William A. Seiter took just five weeks to film the entire movie. The hurried quality of his work, coupled with the routines of an uncomfortable Groucho, Chico, and Harpo, practically guaranteed a box office disappointment. Yet Groucho never registered a complaint, on the set or off. The money was too good, and the script set in stone, thanks to RKO's edict. The best thing, he concluded, was to recite the lines as best he could, and cash the paychecks as fast as they came in. When the movie was released, he was astonished to read the first reviews; they were nowhere near as negative as he expected. In New York, the *Post* described *Room Service* as "hilarious entertainment" and the *Journal American* pronounced it "fast, loud and funny." The *Times* offered a mild dissent: the film was to be "laughed at moderately if you saw the play, immoderately if you missed it." In England, the British Film Institute's monthly *Bulletin* went so far as to say "there is no falling-off in the power of the Marx Brothers to raise laughs." Groucho was considerably less kind and more accurate about this latest work of the Brothers'. "It was the first time we tried doing a play we hadn't created ourselves. We can't do that. We've got to originate the characters and situations ourselves. Then we can do them. Then they're us. We can't do gags or play characters that aren't ours. We tried it and we'll never do it again."

That said, what would their next film be? The Brothers had no idea. RKO reported that *Room Service* had earned about 7 percent less than the studio's average films, making the Marxes a very cold property at the studio. They would be forced to return to MGM, where their contract still demanded another two pictures. But it was a very different place from the days of Thalberg. Louis B. Mayer was in charge now, and Groucho assumed that "he wanted us to bomb." Perhaps so. Mayer was a vindictive executive with a long memory; he would not be above taking a wound or two, as long as his opposition had a chance of getting permanently maimed. With little choice in the matter the Marx Brothers came back to the studio nonetheless, prepared to do battle with a script, a director, a producer, and the studio itself. Middle age had descended, and the odds against them were getting longer than the ones against Sun Up.

•

AS FILM HISTORIAN Joe Adamson noted, the idea of placing the Brothers either at a World's Fair or a circus had been circulating ever since *A Day at the Races.* Producer Mervyn LeRoy decided that the Marxes were a circus in themselves, and that therefore they would be ideal within the confines of a carnival tent. On all counts his reasoning was faulty. The Marx Brothers, particularly Groucho, realized their best potential when they appeared in the most incongruous settings: a college, a courtroom, an opera house, the seat of government. In a circus they would simply be another act. LeRoy might have realized as much, had the Brothers been allowed to take their material on the road. But Mayer was in no mood to allow the Marxes that luxury. They would perform from a shooting script, like every other performer at MGM. Reluctantly they agreed, and *At the Circus,* their ninth film, started them on the drastic downhill course from which only one would return.

During the early days of shooting, a small incident symbolized the entire production. A pivotal scene called for the appearance of a gorilla—that is, a man in a gorilla suit. The takes were long, and the pelt was hot. Periodically the impersonator would have to remove his disguise and take a breather. To relieve his discomfort, he punched holes in the skin. These were discovered by the costumer who owned the monkey suit. He walked off the job, threatening to sue, and taking his damaged goods with him. A frantic search followed his departure. Three days later, Groucho recalled, a man with a usable orangutan skin was located in San Diego. "Even a child knows that an orangutan is much smaller than a gorilla, but strangely enough the ape man didn't and he impetuously bought it without trying it on. We gave him every chance to squeeze himself into the skin but it was hopeless. When he finally realized he was too big for the pelt he broke down and cried like a baby gorilla. However, this was no time for sentiment. We were faced with reality, and also with the head of the studio." There was a picture to be shot, and MGM was obliged to hire a smaller monkey man who specialized in impersonating orangutans. "Moreover," concluded Groucho, "because of the demands of the union we had to pay the original ape man standby salary, portal to portal, and psychiatric treatment."

To underline their shabby status at MGM, the Brothers would no longer have the services of front-rank comedy writers. Irving Brecher, the scenarist assigned to *Circus,* was best known for supplying one-liners to the brash standup comedian Milton Berle. No one was happy with the choice—including Brecher. "Groucho," he recalled, "had a quality of doing things when you were in public, such as in a restaurant or even in somebody's home for dinner. He would often bug the help and ride them." To some extent, Groucho's conduct reflected his basic unhappiness with home and career. But that does not mitigate his lack of tact, or his aggression toward those unable to fight back. No one else in the family had ever been unkind to underlings, not that there were many in Minnie's days; in his callousness, Groucho was unique. One night at the Brechers' a maid became so upset by the things he said that she dropped a big tray and exited in tears. "I always felt, and I told him a couple of times," Brecher continued, "that they were not fair game for him. He admitted this was true, but he couldn't resist going after the underlings."

In fairness, Groucho also went after the *übermenschen. Circus's* director, Edward Buzzell, was a bantamweight song-and-dance man who had also come out of vaudeville. On a few occasions he had shared a bill with the young Marx Brothers. Given their common background, he and Groucho should have meshed easily. Instead, the comedian found ways to disconcert the man in charge. Early in the proceedings Buzzell suggested, "Now, let's really act this scene." Groucho responded, "The Marx Brothers will do anything but act. If you want dramatics, hire our stand-ins." The director was tempted, but held his tongue. In time Groucho came around, confiding in a letter to his friend Arthur Sheekman that Buzzell was "smarter than I imagined. . . . I think the picture will be better than I thought."

At least one of the reasons for his upbeat prediction was a song designed for his talents. It adroitly harked back to the African explorer of *Animal Crackers* and the parodic classroom lectures of *Horse Feathers,* slipped double entendres past the censors, included an incongruously Jewish name, and mentioned the New Deal's most popular accomplishment. This time out, Groucho would not make the mistake of excising the number. From the first hearing, he knew he could dine out for decades on "Lydia the Tattooed Lady."

> Lydia, oh, Lydia, say, have you met Lydia,
> Lydia the tattooed lady?

She has eyes that men adore so,
And a torso
Even more so.
Lydia, oh, Lydia, that encyclo-pidia,
Oh, Lydia the Queen of Tattoo.

When her robe is unfurled
She will show you the world,
If you'll step up and tell 'er where,
For a dime you can see Kankakee or Paree
Or Washington crossing the Delaware.

For two bits she will do a mazurka in jazz
With a view of Niagara that nobody has
And on a clear day you can see Alcatraz.
You can learn a lot from Lydia.

Come along and see Buff'lo Bill with his lasso,
Just a little classic by Mendel Picasso.
Here's Captain Spaulding exploring the Amazon;
Here's Godiva—but with her pajamas on. . . .

Here's Nijinsky doing the rhumba;
Here's her Social Security numbah.

She once swept an Admiral clear off his feet
The ships on her hips made his heart skip a beat
And now the old boy's in command of the fleet
For he went and married Lydia!

References to Nazi Germany were tacked on afterward, to the wild approval of military audiences ("When she stands the world grows littler / When she sits, she sits on Hitler"). The composer and lyricist had created the song in the style of Groucho's beloved Gilbert and Sullivan. Doubtless the writers could have done more if their schedule had permitted, and if Metro-Goldwyn-Mayer had been open to more music for *At the Circus*. It was not. Studio executives transferred Harold Arlen and E. Y. Harburg to a picture with a higher budget and greater promise: *The Wizard of Oz*, starring Judy Garland, a kid on her way up. In MGM's view, the Brothers were running in place.

CHAPTER TEN

You Lose Either Way

LIKE THE MARX BROTHERS, Buster Keaton grew up in vaudeville. He started out as the Human Broom, held by his heels and whisked around the stage upside-down by his father. On his own, he won recognition as the Great Stone Face, a stunt comedian with an expression of implacable woe. In theory Buster should have been a friend of the Brothers'; he played many of the same venues, went to Hollywood at about the same time as Chaplin, and for a period in the late 1920s and early '30s was considered Charlie's equal as performer and filmmaker. But that day had passed, due to the advent of talkies, changing public taste, and Keaton's losing bouts with alcoholism. By 1939 the director of *Sherlock Junior* and *The General* was on his uppers, a slumping, melancholy "advisor" reduced to a tiny office at MGM. The man who once earned $150,000 a year now made $100 a week grinding out gags for *At the Circus*. If Buster regretted the arrangement, the Brothers hated it outright. To Groucho the luckless silent movie star seemed an emblem of bad times in show business, and he led his brothers in a boycott. Buster suggested a visual about a midget being handed a balloon and promptly rising in the air; they dismissed it outright. A few days later Buster offered another routine. What if Harpo sees a circus camel, but not the animal's keeper? Some feed spills out of the camel's bag and Harpo replaces a single straw. As he does, the keeper bends down to pick up a match, accidentally pulling the camel to its knees. Harpo thinks this is the straw that broke the camel's back and removes it—just as the keeper straightens up and the camel resumes his upright posture. "When I acted this one out for the Marx Brothers," Keaton told his biographer, "Groucho asked with a sneer, 'Do you think that's *funny?*' Chico and Harpo just stared at me in disgust." Keaton, the long face even longer, responded, "I'm only doing what Mr. Mayer asked me to do." Attempting to mollify them he added, "*You* guys don't need any help."

Buster was mistaken. The Marx Brothers needed a great deal of help, and on this picture they received almost none. Impolitic as he might have been, Groucho was essentially correct about Keaton's offerings: they smacked of the 1920s, and only the Great Stone Face could have brought them off. But Groucho should have been equally leery of Irving Brecher's writing and Edward Buzzell's direction. The scenarist understood that in *Horse Feathers* and *A Day at the Races* Chico nimbly fleeced the con man, Groucho. What he failed to notice was the whimsical logic and careful structure of those scenes. The railroad interlude in *At the Circus* encapsulates the show's fatal defects. In order to save the circus from creditors, Chico sends for Groucho, a shady lawyer he has known from previous chicaneries. Groucho arrives on a rainy evening, just as the circus train is about to pull out of the station. As the skies open, Groucho attempts to clamber aboard, only to be stopped by Chico: "Nobody get on-a da train unless dey gotta badge." Harpo sidles up, leading a performing seal. He displays a dozen badges, one of them on the tail of the animal. Chico permits both Harpo and companion to come aboard, but keeps Groucho in the rain. Ultimately Chico sells him admittance—but still refuses to allow Groucho to board because "That's last year's badge." In the end, Chico clambers onto the train, pushing Groucho down into a puddle where he sits until the fadeout, wet and humiliated ("If I were any drier, I'd drown"). What was supposed to be a loony negotiation has been turned into an instance of motiveless sadism. To compound the blunder, Groucho pops up in the next scene inexplicably warm and dry.

In fairness to Brecher and Buzzell, they had worked out a sequence to explain his appearance. Harpo was to have stretched out from the caboose with a fishing rod, snagging Groucho and reeling him in. Producers ruled the gag wasteful of money and effort, and excised it from the shooting schedule. Since this was a Marx Brothers picture, they argued, continuity was unnecessary. They made another mistake with Groucho's costume: for the first time in his life, he sported a black toupee. By 1939 Groucho had a receding hairline, and MGM executives decided to do something about it. After all, Harpo and Chico had been performing under wigs since the days of "Peasie Weasie." Why should Groucho alone show the effects of time? Unhappily, the labors of the MGM makeup department did not take twenty years away from him; the cosmeticians made him look like a forty-nine-year-old man hiding under a rug. (The image of Groucho was now so manufactured that on one occasion, when he was unavailable for a team photograph, Brecher put on the requisite makeup and posed with Harpo and Chico. It was the writer's face and body, not Groucho's, that looked out from a poster for *Go West*.)

The trio finally made peace with their situation by pretending this was a job like any other, with a time clock, a boss, and a schedule. As if to emphasize their new attitude, they began to behave more like their old selves. At a restaurant Chico was handed a check, put salt and pepper on it, and ate it. Standing in front of a hotel, Harpo saw a dignified woman leaving a taxi. She reminded him of Margaret Dumont and he impulsively picked her up in his arms and carried her to the front desk. "Register us quickly!" he ordered. During a Hollywood party a magician made the mistake of asking Groucho to pick a card. He selected one, pocketed it, said "Thanks," and left the premises.

On a handful of occasions the trio ignited the old humor on-screen. Playing opposite them, the reliable Margaret Dumont appears in her familiar role of society matron, allowing Groucho to count Newport's elite Four Hundred as they arrive for a formal dinner: "397, 398, 399. . . . Everybody showed up. Looks like no second helpings." Once again the fortune hunter is master of the non sequitur, although this time the dialogue provides only a shadow of their previous encounters:

GROUCHO

Oh, Hildegarde!

DUMONT

My name is Susannah.

GROUCHO

Let's not quibble. It's enough that you've killed something fine and beautiful. Oh, Susannah! (*Singing*) Oh, Susannah, oh, won't you fly with me? For I need ten thousand dollars 'cause the sheriff's after me!

DUMONT

Get out of this room or I'll scream for the servants.

GROUCHO

Let the servants know! Let the whole world know—about us!

DUMONT

You must leave my room. We must have regard for certain conventions.

GROUCHO

(*To camera*) One guy isn't enough. She's got to have a convention. (*Back to DUMONT*) Oh, Susannah! At last we're alone. Couldn't the two of us be—oh, how should I say it—uh, a man and a woman? There, I said it. Oh, Susannah! If you only knew how much I need you. Not because you have millions, I don't need millions. I'll tell you how much I need. Have you got a pencil? I left my typewriter in my other pants.

Another moment briefly recalled the salad days. Playing a stunt acrobat, the tart-tongued Eve Arden stashes $10,000 in her bodice. Groucho longingly appraises her bosom and addresses the audience: "There must be some way I can get that money back without getting in trouble with the Hays Office." The way, he decides, is to persuade the performer to walk upside-down in her suction-cup shoes. Gravity will be his accomplice. When she outfits him with a similar pair of shoes, he demurs: "I have an agreement with the house flies. The flies don't practice law and I don't walk on the ceiling."

Every time the comedy attempts to take flight, however, Buzzell and Brecher ground it with repellent love scenes between Kenny Baker, a puffy radio tenor clearly uncomfortable before the camera, and Florence Rice, whose emotional range is limited to broken cries of distress and murmurs of relief. More offensive is a scene of black children and adults, in awe of Harpo as he plays a number called "Swing-gali." In tracing the history of African Americans in 1930s films, historian Donald Bogle mentions a haphazard progression of the black character from "field jester to house servant to domesticated servant to humanized servant to posthumanized eccentric." The chorus in Harpo's number is composed almost entirely of those eccentrics—the kind of wide-eyed, grinning exaggerations who disfigured the end of *A Day at the Races*. Manifestly, MGM had learned nothing in the intervening years. Neither, apparently, had the Brothers. All of them had seen, and rued, the days of segregated vaudeville. En route to the U.S.S.R. Harpo had seen the Nazis' anti-Semitic policies taking effect and called them "this evil thing festering in Germany." The quartet was appalled when the Daughters of the American Revolution denied the black singer Marian Anderson the use of its auditorium in Washington, D.C. And yet the Marxes quietly went along with the racial caricatures, mistakenly assuming that what worked in the past would play today, and that a gag was a gag no matter who was its victim. It was only one of many miscalculations, most of them fatal to the film. Only the final moments of *At the Circus* recall the great Paramount features. A society orchestra, performing on a floating platform, is cut loose by the Brothers. Unaware, the musicians play on, as if American film comedy itself were going to sea.

When the film was finally wrapped, and Buzzell announced plans for a vacation in Europe, Groucho, Chico, and Harpo took him out to dinner at the Trocadero. At the restaurant they insulted the help and were insulted by them, left in high dudgeon, stopped to order soup at a sidewalk restaurant, halted again at a café, then pushed on to ringside seats at the Hollywood American Legion Stadium. There they ate dessert and watched professional wrestlers slam and groan for a few rounds. "We wound up," Buzzell remembered, "having coffee in a mortuary." The symbolism of the locale made them all uneasy; it was a little too apropos.

Critics gave *Circus* a mixed greeting. *Variety* led the enthusiasts, remarking on the picture's high-budget production values and praising the Brothers' return to the "rousing physical comedy and gag dialogue of their earlier pictures." In the *New York Times*, Frank Nugent took an opposing view. To him the Brothers' latest film was "a rather dispirited imitation of former Marx successes." Howard Barnes, the *Herald Tribune's* man at the movies, summarized *At the Circus* as "neither particularly fresh nor funny." He could find "almost none of the split-second timing which marked their great films of the past. The comic Brothers have set too high a standard in the past for in-and-out clowning." The most dismissive appraisal came from Groucho himself. In a letter to his friend Arthur Sheekman, he reported that he had seen *At the Circus* and "didn't much care for it." He wrote: "I realize I'm not much of a judge but I'm kind of sick of the whole thing and, on leaving the theater, vowed that I'd never see it again. I don't feel this way about all of our pictures: *A Night at the Opera,* for example, I always enjoyed looking at and, to a lesser degree, *A Day at the Races,* but the rest sicken me and I'll stay clear of them in the future."

For a man "sickened" with his on-screen image, yet anxious to keep his place in show business, one avenue remained: radio. That medium would not work for the team; beyond a few guest-shot beeps of his horn, Harpo had no suitable role. He also entertained no regrets. Marriage agreed with him, and he had invested wisely. With adopted children to raise, he seriously considered the part of stay-at-home father. Chico also made noises about quitting, but his claims amounted to fantasy. Even after his brothers had set aside some of his income his debts continued to mount. (Enclosing a check in Chico's name, Groucho wrote his broker, "By strategy, force and persuasion we've withheld this much . . . the beginning of a nest egg for that all-time sucker.") The compulsive gambler would always need a steady cash flow, and as he saw it, radio could provide the income without the labor—no elaborate rehearsals, no special costumes, no ungodly hours. As usual Groucho nursed ambivalent feelings, intensified by his fear of failing in broadcasting yet again. Interviewed by the press, he made sure to burn his bridges *before* he got to them. "I'm not really interested in radio," he assured a reporter. "I'm waiting for the Smellies or the Tasties. I want to crash through to the unseen audience in six assorted perfumes and flavors." But after being courted by CBS for several months, and entreated by Chico while *Circus* was being shot, Groucho underwent a public change of mind. In November 1939, the two brothers made their debuts on an hour-long program called *The Circle*. Each would receive $2,000 a week for sitting around a table with other celebrities, commenting on the week's events, and occasionally breaking out in song. Ronald Colman served as president of the group. Cary Grant was beadle; Carole Lombard, resident feminist; Groucho, the heckling treasurer; and Chico, the heckling assistant treasurer. Seated with the Marxes, Grant took the occasion to recall his first trip to the United States. As an ambitious cockney named Archie Leach, he tried to Americanize himself: "I'd been to the Palace to see the Marx Brothers, billed as the 'Greatest Comedy Act in Show Business, Barring None.' I noticed that Zeppo, the young handsome one, the straight man, the fellow I copied (who else?), wore a miniature, neatly tied bow tie. It was called—hold onto your chair—a jazz bow. Well, if that was the fashion, it was at least inexpensive enough for me to follow."

Other regulars and guests included such notables as Madeleine Carroll, Alexander Woollcott, Noël Coward, Merle Oberon, and Basil Rathbone. Groucho found Lombard especially intriguing. Marriage to Clark Gable had added to her already considerable glamour without diminishing her tart conversation. After one show Groucho sociably inquired, "How are you and Gable getting along?" The actress told him, "He's the lousiest lay I ever had in my life." With admiration bordering on awe, Groucho told a friend: "She talked like a man, words men use with other men. She was a gutsy dame. She was a real show business girl."

The gutsy dame did not elicit the same approval when she dropped out of *The Circle*, in part because the Brothers were running away with it. Cary Grant sang all the verses of "Mad Dogs and Englishmen" by his friend Noël Coward, whereupon Groucho and Chico attempted to top him with a Kalmar and Ruby–style number. Chico insisted that last week's paycheck was $15 short. Groucho eventually handed him the money, but not before doing a turn complete with chorus and full orchestra:

GROUCHO

I will admit
I use my wit
To hoodwink my competitors,
On some far beach I love to sit
Evading all my creditors.

But what I do I must do well
That's always my ambition,
And fifteen bucks is a bagatelle
To a man in my position.

This man now stands where fine folks tread,
I saved him from the gutter.
I tried to make the rat well bred,
He wants both sides with butter.

For helping out a pal I'm sued,
That's fine that is, that's funny.
I can't face such ingratitude
Besides, he's out of money. . . .
One buck, two bucks, three bucks, four bucks—

CHICO

Sorry, boss, but I gotta have more bucks.

CHORUS

Before he runs amuck
Advance the guy a buck.
What's a ducat?
A drop in the bucket. . . .

CHICO

I want my fifteen bucks.

GROUCHO

Say, hold that guy, you clucks.

CHORUS

He swings—but Groucho ducks!

GROUCHO

Here's your fifteen bucks.
(*Big orchestral finish*) Oh, mama, here's your fifteen bucks!

This Gilbert-and-Sullivan pastiche failed to enchant their fellow performers, and it indicated to the listeners at large that Groucho and Chico had hired their own writers. From that point, they operated with a rehearsed madness denied to the others, and on occasion improvised on their calculated ad-libs. One evening the Brothers engaged in a mock battle with José Iturbi, the Spanish pianist and conductor, finishing with a song reminiscent of the "I Want My Shirt" routine from *The Cocoanuts*. In a rare display of temper, Rathbone complained to the producers about Groucho's infuriating departures from the script. *Variety* took note of such frictions, and agreed that Groucho's "increasing ad-libbing" was "butchering the routine and effectiveness of the show. Constant heckling was funny when it was funny, but it's now so forced it's merely an audience-irritant. Under the circumstances, such straights as Madeleine Carroll and Lawrence Tibbett can hardly be rated fairly. . . . As a whole, there's hardly 60 minutes of entertainment in the big-budget Kellogg hour." Colman dropped out after a month, to be followed by Grant. Ratings slipped, and then tumbled to new lows. Many of the other participants soldiered on to the end, twenty-six shows later. *Variety* calculated *The Circle* to be a $2 million flop, the largest in broadcasting history. The Marx Brothers expressed few regrets; by that time they were involved in their tenth film, one Groucho called "another turkey" even before he saw the menu.

•

UNSURPRISINGLY, the children showed the effects of their parents' deteriorating home life. Miriam drew even closer to her father. "I think Miriam didn't want to leave Groucho alone," recalled her friend Sunny Sauber. "She was very worried when Groucho had to fly anywhere. She was always putting sugar in his sleeping capsules, because she thought he might take an overdose." When she did leave her father for the day, she assumed his style. Hospitalized for an appendectomy, she registered her religion as Druid. Canvassing the neighborhood for contributions to an Eleanor Roosevelt charity, she made an early appearance at Norman Krasna's house. "How much money are you giving?" she demanded. Taken aback, Krasna reminded her, "First you say 'Good morning' or 'Hello' or 'Would you like to give—' "

Miriam wasted no time. "You fascist!"

In later years Krasna dismissed her actions as youthful folly. But he made notes and in time he would base a character on her. Just then the writer was amused: in her childhood, little Miriam "kissed me before she went to bed. And now I was being called a fascist—on Rodeo Drive." Miriam never saw it that way. "For whatever reason, Norman Krasna didn't make a donation. I was furious and disappointed and gave him hell," she said. "But that didn't make me a young irresponsible radical. I was simply my father's daughter, that's all. Which was one reason why at that time I was the one woman Groucho took seriously." She had a point; at that juncture, and for the rest of his life, he tended to see women as makers of trouble or gratifiers of desire, not as people capable of discussing political or social issues. Miriam was a notable exception, and, all too briefly, a source of parental pride in her orneriness. That was before she entered a truly rebellious and self-destructive puberty.

Arthur turned nineteen in 1940; his battles for tennis trophies brought Groucho a lot of pleasure as well as bouts of tension and sleeplessness. Unlike Miriam, Arthur could remove himself from the domestic fray by entering out-of-town tournaments. Groucho wrote to his son frequently, signing his letters "Padre." In July of that year, Padre referred to a new Marx Brothers film: "*Go West* has again been postponed. I don't know why the studio doesn't come right out and say they are afraid to make it. . . . My attitude is, take the money and to hell with it. I had my hair darkened to match my greasepaint moustache, but it has been so long since the scheduled starting date that the dye has faded and now I will have to have it done all over again. So you see my theatrical career has dwindled to being fitted once a week for a pair of early American pants and having my hair dyed every three weeks. This is a fine comedown for a man who used to be the Toast of Broadway."

Another letter confesses, only partly in jest: "It's not so hot being the father of a tennis player. Hundreds of people to whom I wouldn't talk normally, rush up to me and immediately begin a long, involved conversation, explaining why you either won or lost in the last tournament. As you know, I'm deeply interested in your athletic progress, but not to the degree that I want to discuss it twelve hours a day." Then, as if he wondered whether his comments might be taken the wrong way, Groucho underlined his facetious tone: "Now whenever anyone asks me how you're doing at whatever tournament you happened to be in, I say, 'Don't you know? He's quit the game and taken up squash.' This baffles them. A lot of people have only heard of squash as a low-grade vegetable and they can't understand why anyone should want to stand in a cheap restaurant and throw vegetables."

That summer Groucho did receive one piece of good news. He, too, could get out of town for a while. The film's new producer was Jack Cummings, Louis B. Mayer's nephew. Cummings had no more affection for Groucho than his uncle did, but he sensed that a return to the old ways might make the Marx Brothers profitable once more. He found room in the budget for road tryouts in Chicago, Toledo, and Detroit. Pleased but wary, Groucho predicted that the process would be as complicated as possible, but even he could not have foreseen all the difficulties. Before the tryouts the screenplay underwent three massive rewrites. ("*Go West* is being constantly postponed," Groucho griped in another letter. "I've read the script and I don't blame them.") Bert Kalmar and Harry Ruby submitted a plot and dialogue. They had been favorites of Irving Thalberg's, but Thalberg was long dead, and the studio seemed hell-bent on removing traces of his influence. All that remained of their work was a title song. It failed to make the cut, but Groucho kept "Go West, Young Man" from obscurity by entertaining partygoers with his favorite verses:

> Before you go to Buffalo,
> To Baltimore or Borneo,
> To Eastern Pennsylvania or Japan,
> Go West, Young Man.
> If you go to that land, Sonny,
> You will have a lot of money,
> If you bring the money with you when you come.

One set of rhymes was to have special meaning for the singer:

> The judges there are very fair; they always are, of course.
> A cowboy and his missus went to court for a divorce.
> The cowboy got the children and the missus got the horse.
> Go West, Young Man!

Following the rejection of Kalmar and Ruby, the team of Irving Brecher and a bright new prospect, Dore Schary, tried its hand. Their effort, too, was thrown in the wastebasket. Other gagmen were approached; they spurned the offer. Brecher then worked alone. His version won studio approval.

For the first time, the Brothers would play out of their own time, in an "oater." By then, the comedy western had already enjoyed a long tradition. Chaplin and Keaton and Harold Lloyd had all made costume farces, and only two years before, Laurel and Hardy had done some of their best work in *Way Out West*. Their well-received and profitable feature was built around a purloined mine deed. Foiling malefactors, turning difficulties to their advantage, the stars restore the paper to its sweet and vulnerable owner. Not coincidentally, *Go West* employed much the same plot. The prior comedy wasted little footage on a subsidiary love story. In contrast, *Go West* ceded precious time and space to its drab romantic couple, Diana Lewis and John Carroll. With a little help from the studio, the Brothers might have compensated for this burden, but in a perverse moment MGM decided that while the services of director Edward Buzzell were required, those of Margaret Dumont were not. Without her, Groucho lost his edge. The film did employ Walter Woolf King as the unctuous villain. King had played the Harpo-abusing tenor in *A Night at the Opera,* and he needed no training to understand the Marx style. And to Brecher's credit, the scenarist produced a better script for this film than he did for *At the Circus*. Nat Perrin joined the troupe during the road tryouts; he punched up the gags and added dozens of new ones. These improved the script without elevating Groucho's spirits. More than his brothers, he found himself depressed by what was happening outside the studio. The headlines were uniformly dire. The Nazis had invaded Scandinavia, Holland, and Belgium; FDR had asked for a record $1.8 billion for defense; and only isolationists still clung to the belief that there would be no war in Europe. Germany and the Soviet Union had signed a nonaggression pact, shocking the leftists in Hollywood, and further embittering

Groucho. An editor of the Screen Writers Guild smirked, "Certain glamour boys and girls, famous writers and directors, were on their knees at the shrine of the crossed hammer and sickle when the bombshell fell. It hit them like a dropped option." Disgusted with it all, Groucho fired off a letter to Arthur Sheekman. It cataloged Groucho's global, fiscal, and professional worries: "I'm not able to sleep any more. You probably ask, 'Why can't he sleep? He has money, beauty, talent, vigor and many teeth'—but the possession of all these riches has nothing to do with it. I see [Nazi] Bund members dropping down my chimney, Commies under my bed, Fifth Columnists in my closets, a bearded dwarf, called Surtax, doing a gavotte on my desk with a little lady known as Confiscation. I'm setting aside a small sum for poison which I'm secreting in a little sack under my mattress."

As the Brothers had filmed *At the Circus* they could only guess which lines and routines would work in movie theaters. In general, their hunches played them false; they had been away from live performance too long. Performing "Scenes from *Go West*" in vaudeville houses, they were happily reminded of the old days when they could gauge responses on the spot, reshaping their comedy as they traveled. One sequence, planned for the first scene, introduced Groucho as the frontier swindler S. Quentin Quale. (The name is a measure of the film's wit: "San Quentin Quail" was then a California term for underage prostitutes.) He spent the next ten minutes attempting to fleece Chico and Harpo, cast as the greenhorn brothers Joe and Rusty Panello. Ticket buyers failed to respond at the appropriate moments, and Brecher and Perrin quickly retooled the dialogue to make Quale the loser, undone by the Panellos. Those pages evoked more mirth than their predecessors, and Buzzell was wise enough to open the film with them. He was not so judicious about other matters. Film historian Joe Adamson describes the on-set atmosphere of *Go West* as arid, with Buzzell convinced that he could hold the Marxes in check only by keeping a straight face no matter what they said or did. "When he suggested to Groucho that he needed more makeup on his nose and Groucho answered, 'Don't quibble. What I need is a new nose,' the only reaction he could think of was not to laugh. As a comedian with a past, Buzzell knew that to an attention-hungry performer laughter was license." Unhappily, the director's style became infectious. The rushes showed that Buzzell "had calmed his comedians, all right, and he had kept all three of them in viewfinder range. That was about all you could say for it."

Groucho's disdain for silent film comedy notwithstanding, the movie commences with a printed title; the legend might well have come from a two-reeler circa 1925: "In 1851 Horace Greeley uttered a phrase that did much to change the history of the United States. He said, 'Go West, young man, go West.' This is the story of three men who made Horace Greeley sorry he said it."

Following this, Brecher and Buzzell attempt to capture the spirit of the Marx Brothers' early and middle films. The efforts are fitfully resourceful:

CHICO

Is this the right way for my brother to get on the train for the West?

GROUCHO

(*Appraising HARPO's greenhorn wardrobe*) Not unless they're throwing a masquerade party out West, it isn't. . . . (*Perking up*) So you two gents are heading West, eh, partner?

CHICO

Not me, just-a my brother. . . . When he gets off the train he's gonna pick up some gold and send it to me. They say the gold is layin' all over the streets.

GROUCHO

The way he's dressed it looks as if *he* was layin' all over the streets. He's a tenderfoot.

CHICO

You wear those shoes you gotta tender feet, too.

GROUCHO

Oh, those were shoes! I thought that was fungus with buttons.

Until the last reel, the comedy is burdened with romantic and plot details. These are occasionally punctuated with vaudeville routines, informed by a bizarre social conscience:

GROUCHO

White man red man's friend. White man want to make friends with red man's brother.

CHICO

And sister, too.

INDIAN

Beray! Beray! Kulah! Kulah! Cocho! Rodah! Neitzche! Pardo!

GROUCHO

Are you insinuating that the white man is not the Indian's friend? Huh? Who swindled you out of Manhattan Island for twenty-four dollars?

CHICO

White man.

GROUCHO

Who turned you into wood and stood you in front of a cigar store?

CHICO

White man.

GROUCHO

Who put your head on a nickel and then stole the nickel away?

CHICO

Slot machine.

For the most part, though, the japes echo the Brothers' previous films, to meager effect. In an overcrowded stagecoach, meant to be a miniature of the stateroom scene in *A Night at the Opera*, the Brothers attack King. Bumping into fellow passengers, they disarrange his papers, ruin his clothes, and lose his hat. What must have seemed humorous on stage is wrecked by close-ups, reducing the humor to mugging and incoherent gestures as the scene bounces downhill from vaudeville to second-feature burlesque. When a woman complains that her baby is crying because of "the jerks in the coach," Harpo and Chico assume that she means them, a standard-issue gag for the Three Stooges.

Anachronisms, last resort of the weary gag writer, abound. Groucho expresses his preference for a motel instead of an Indian reservation, makes mention of the *Pot of Gold,* a popular radio program of the 1930s, and in a reference to *The Story of Alexander Graham Bell,* a film produced the previous year, Chico mentions a telephone. Groucho corrects him. "This is 1870. Don Ameche hasn't invented the phone yet." In a frontier bar, there are flashes of the Groucho of yesteryear ("Ah, Lulubelle. I didn't recognize you standing up"). These vanish when he attempts a romantic paean, addressed to a lady of the evening: "Foolish, foolish child. It's madness, this thing that's happened to us. It can never be. We come from different stock. Suppose I brought you to my country place at Drooling on the Lapel?" Playing opposite Mrs. Teasdale or Emily Upjohn, Groucho might have ended his solo at that point. But because Dumont was missing, Brecher and Buzzell attempted to beef up the ludicrous with the obvious. The speaker continues: "What would my people say?" A drunk at the next table belches on cue. "Well," Groucho muses, "they'd phrase it more delicately." He concludes with a mot shamelessly recycled from the Algonquin Round Table, "Time wounds all heels." It is not Groucho's finest moment, and there is even shoddier stuff for him to do and recite.

The comedian who was merely knocked over in *At the Circus* is thrown downstairs by bullies in *Go West.* Groucho ripostes weakly, "I was going to thrash them within an inch of their lives, but I didn't have a tape measure." In that moment he turns from amusing coward into abject victim, a role totally foreign to his persona, and he never recovers. At another point, Chico and Groucho actually become drunk, and have to receive assistance in order to walk. In all previous Marx Brothers pictures, women and enemies are the helpless ones. Now the Brothers themselves are the casualties of circumstance. With these alterations and distortions of character, *Go West* should have been a complete washout. Yet Buzzell and Brecher both possessed the same valuable asset: each knew how and where to ransack. Seizing control of the locomotive, the Marxes tie up the engineer and cover his mouth. Groucho turns to the audience: "This is the best gag in the picture"—only a slight exaggeration. Mystified about the train's operation, the Brothers peruse some printed instructions:

CHICO

Maybe that book's-a no good.

GROUCHO

Of course it's good. It's an engineer's manual.

CHICO

But-a supposing the engineer's name ain't Manuel?

GROUCHO

Then he's got to change his name. He can't make a fool of this book.

From here on, *Go West* becomes a series of well-staged cinematic quotes from 1920s movies, ranging from the hairsbreadth escapes of Harold Lloyd to the chase scenes of the Keystone Kops. The Brothers overstuff the furnace and pick up too much speed. Chico shouts "Brake!" Harpo, predictably, does what he is told and breaks the mechanism. He thinks to slow the train by throwing water on the fire—only to discover that he has tossed kerosene—and attempts to subdue the flames by tossing corn on them. It is, of course, popcorn, and the resultant blizzard nearly buries them all. As two cars unlink, Harpo grabs one with his hands and the other with his feet, stretching and narrowing like a rubber band until the cars recouple. Another mishap drives the train off the rails, and Harpo off the train. The cowcatcher picks up a house and steams toward him. Harpo miraculously passes through the front door and out the back, unscathed, a sedulous aping of Buster Keaton's narrow escape in *Steamboat Bill.* Toward the close, the train runs out of fuel and begins to slow down, narrowing the gap between the pursued and the pursuers. The day is saved when it occurs to the Brothers that the cars are made of wood; they start vigorously chopping them up to provide fuel, reducing the rolling stock to a mobile lumberyard, and borrowing from Keaton's *The General* en route.

Not many critics caught the allusions, but most were kind enough to notice an upswing from *At the Circus.* Otis Ferguson, who had been disenchanted with the Marxes' last effort, complimented this one with his left hand in *The New Republic:* "There are more things happening than you can keep track of. (In a way this is all to the good; some of them are not funny.)" But "the all-in sequence of the race with the train achieves the perfect spontaneous world of madmen." *Variety* felt that the vaudeville tour, "Scenes from *Go West*," had made all the difference; these performances helped the Marxes to "handle their assignments with zestful enthusiasm." Even though the *New York Times* found much of the film resistible, it also praised the train wreck, and it is that scene that gave the British press new reasons to cheer the team. *The Cinema,* an influential publication, lauded "one of the maddest and merriest climaxes ever devised for the screen," and the *Monthly Film Bulletin,* not given to hyperbole, located the Marxes "in their element in a plot which affords excellent opportunities for their special brand of fooling." Nevertheless, with war now dislocating Europe, *Go West* fared poorly overseas, and domestically it merely got by. Brecher subsequently dismissed the team's performance as "old men trying to be pixies," a phrase that was at once distorted and on the money. In an actuarial sense, men in their fifties could hardly be senescent even in Hollywood, where youth has always been prized above talent. W. C. Fields was sixty at this time, and he was busy writing and acting in *The Bank Dick,* released within weeks of *Go West.* But Fields was a different sort of performer. In his typical role as a harassed, scheming alcoholic, surrounded by those who would do him in, his age worked for him rather than against him. The Brothers were high-energy types, men who practically had to burst through the scenery and defy the plot in order to get their jokes across. That was all very well in the early 1930s, when they provided a bridge from vaudeville to sound films. Equipped with Irving Thalberg's new formula, they got their second wind at MGM and briefly reached a new plane. The momentum had carried them past *A Night at the Opera,* but not for long. Broad commedia dell'arte mugging had worn thin, and audiences were currently losing themselves in the scope and sentiment of films like *Gone With the Wind, Goodbye, Mr. Chips,* and a real sobersided western, *Stagecoach.*

No one was more realistic about the situation than Harpo. He and Susan had been making preparations for his retirement throughout the last year. Even though there would be six mouths to feed, Harpo assumed they could get by on the income from his investments and real estate holdings. Chico, sensing that his own number was up, finally made good on his threat, selected musicians for "Chico Marx and His Ravellis" and took the aggregation to New York to work the night club circuit.

That left Groucho. For him, Larry Hart's two-year-old lyric about "the sleepless nights, the daily fights, the quick toboggan when you hit the heights" had a special meaning. Only a few years ago the Marx Brothers were at the top of the heap; now MGM was holding the team at arm's length, with no enthusiasm for the one Marx comedy still owed to the studio. The quarrels Groucho had with Ruth were only a part of his dissatisfaction with life in general. Weighing the possibility of leaving show business entirely, he bought ten acres in the San Fernando Valley and made noises about becoming a gentleman farmer. When his friends gave him patronizing smiles, he challenged them. Why shouldn't he quit the scene? Save for the climate, he had never really liked Hollywood, never palled around with the movie stars, never gone for the big, phony house or the fleet of cars. He had amassed a sizable stock portfolio over the years since the Crash. What better way to spend his retirement than in doing what Minnie never could: getting pleasure from milking cows and raising chickens? He proclaimed this as his next move to his brothers and to the children. They didn't believe him either, and for good reason. Groucho Marx was no more equipped to farm at fifty than he had been at eighteen, and some part of him was well aware of his shortcomings. That is why he stayed around Beverly Hills, grumbling about marriage and circumstances, and, in between complaints, looking for something to do after the next and, he predicted, last picture. He felt the necessity to work, if only for the psychic income. He had been a headliner for too long, and now that his fingerprints were firmly embedded in the cement in front of Grauman's Chinese Theater he felt that the entertainment business owed him something. The trouble was, no producer, no impresario made an offer. He was unwanted as a team member or as a single. If the Brothers had cooled off, Groucho was ice-cold.

The only feelers came from magazine editors, aware that Groucho's earlier writings had amused Robert Benchley and James Thurber, and that college boys could still be seen wearing greasepaint moustaches and glasses at fraternity parties. Writing solo was not something that Groucho did comfortably, and he sought out a collaborator. Aided by the uncredited Arthur Sheekman, he published brisk comic pieces in *This Week* and *Variety.* The two would collaborate on Groucho's second book, *Many Happy Returns,* the title a satirical comment on the Internal Revenue Service. (It seems likely that Groucho was influenced by the success of W. C. Fields, whose gag book *Fields for President* had sold briskly in an election year. In it, the comedian printed his unique campaign speech: "I shall, my friends, offer no such empty panaceas as the New Deal, or an Old Deal, or even a Re-Deal. No, my friends, the reliable old False Shuffle was good enough for my father and it's good enough for me." Part of Fields's shuffle was a war against the graduated income tax. He titled one chapter "How to Beat the Federal Income Tax—And What to See and Do at Alcatraz.")

Meantime, Groucho and Norman Krasna chipped away at a stage comedy, provisionally titled *Time for Elizabeth.* The idea had come from a magazine ad that caught their mutual attention. Under a caption that read, "You too can live like this for $220 a month," an elderly man and a pretty girl posed beside a yacht. There was something false and funny in this situation, and they thought to spin a tale based on it. In addition, Groucho and Irving Brecher worked on a situation comedy for radio, centered on a middle-class family, the Flotsams. No one needed to ask who would play the father.

The admiration Groucho had for so many writers, combined with his new literary aspirations, naturally influenced the children. In his first year at the University of Southern California, Arthur made himself a campus celebrity by becoming an intercollegiate tennis champion. His academic studies failed to keep pace, and he made it clear to Groucho that he intended to leave school and try his luck behind a typewriter. Strangely enough, Groucho looked upon this next move with equanimity, Arthur recalled; but he extracted a promise. His son had to put in as many hours at the typewriter as he would have attending classes at USC.

Every day, shortly before noon, Marx Senior would put on a sweat-shirt, Bermuda shorts, and a blue beret and enter Arthur's room with the same announcement: "Okay, Hemingway—time to take a break." With Duke, their German shepherd, trailing along, they would peddle through Beverly Hills, with Harpo's house as their customary destination. Though Groucho might denigrate Harpo's comic style, he had never lost his fondness for the man—an affection that was always returned. The two brothers chatted about their mutual acquaintances in the movie business before getting down to the main topic: Chico's inability to stay out of trouble. The most recent example of his misbehavior was suggested by a headline in the *Los Angeles Times:* CHICO MARX SUFFERS HEART ATTACK AT LAS VEGAS NITERY. The two men immediately flew to Chico's bedside. The patient looked suspiciously hale. "I didn't really have a heart attack," he whispered. "But I have to get out of this contract somehow. I'm losing more money at the tables than I'm making with the band." Groucho made an angry exit: "You're a great brother. You give us a heart attack worrying about your heart attack, which you didn't even have the decency to have!"

After lunch, father and son would retire to an upstairs study, where Groucho pored over everything that had been written that morning. After much trial and error—mostly error—Groucho professed satisfaction with Arthur's progress and grilled his friends about the young man's future. Sheekman saw evidence of talent, and Groucho wrote back with such paternal concern that he almost forgot to put on his clown mask: "I am glad you are enthusiastic. Arthur's . . . letters had always struck me as being amusing but I was suspicious of my own judgment. Being a parent yourself, you know how it is—we like almost anything our children do.

However, many people, including Ed Sullivan, Morrie Ryskind, Dore Schary, Brecher, and yourself, have told me that they think Arthur has an incipient talent for writing, and who am I to back my opinion against all of yours?"

•

"THE AMOUNT OF WORK, politics, intrigue and chicanery involved in assembling even as important a triviality as a Marx Brothers' comedy is appalling!" Groucho wrote to Sheekman as the last MGM film took shape. "It's really unbelievable—all the meetings, conversation and arguments that have to be gone through with before one of these turkeys is completed! If I were to take it seriously I'd probably kill myself but once I get away from the meeting and the studio, it all recedes into a shadowy insignificance and I play the guitar and think of other things."

One of three things he thought about continually was an official separation from Ruth; her imbibing was now an open scandal. Word reached him that Arthur had left a party when the drinking got out of hand. "I can't stand this sort of thing," he had told his date. "My mother's an alcoholic. Let's get out of here." The second thing that occupied much of Groucho's time was the upcoming political election. Groucho refused to endorse Franklin Delano Roosevelt this time around; he disliked the notion of a man making himself president for life, and wrote to Sheekman, "I'll probably vote for [Wendell] Willkie—I'm dead against a third term." Groucho later turned around and kidded his own stance: "These are my principles. If you don't like them I have others." The third thing he thought about was the Marx Brothers themselves. Harpo had been hauled out of semiretirement, and looked to be the embodiment of Henry IV's remark about Falstaff: "How ill white hairs become a fool and jester." Chico, who had faked his heart attack, was nonetheless in poor health. He suffered from incipient hardening of the arteries, walked much slower these days, and had a diminished look. Groucho was no youth either, but his complaints were not so much physical as intellectual. Harpo had virtually no demands on his memory. He simply entered as usual, emptied his pockets on cue, and did his faun bits the rest of the time. Chico had to recall certain key straight lines, but most of the time he relied upon his instinctive timing and the fact that his big scene was always centered around a piano. Only Groucho bothered to work on the script; only Groucho had to memorize long speeches, with complicated non sequiturs and puns. He made no secret of his envy of Jack Benny, the performer he had known since vaudeville. With no makeup, and wearing street clothes, Benny had created a miserly character so real that he could get laughs merely with pauses as he counted his money. Groucho began to talk about his own on-screen character in the past tense. "I had no character as a Marx Brother—I wasn't real. I just talked fast, and the jokes better be good." He went to work on those jokes for the Marx Brothers' eleventh film, provisionally called *Bargain Basement*. Groucho knew enough about journalists to demand an immediate change of title. He could see the stories now: IN "BARGAIN BASEMENT" MARXES GO FROM PENTHOUSE TO CELLAR. *Step This Way,* an alternative title, won few votes, and the Brothers and MGM ultimately settled on *The Big Store*. The mise-en-scène was to be a major emporium, owned by the widow of Hiram Phelps. The plot, such as it was, concerned the wealthy Mrs. Phelps and a schemer who countenances a morganatic alliance, theft, even murder, to gain control of her department store. For some time, Groucho had been after his friends to hire Margaret Dumont in some acting capacity. "She's at liberty," he informed a screenwriter. This was "not an unusual condition for her, and I imagine she'd be very appreciative of anything that fitted her, and wouldn't expect too much of a salary." Another letter pleaded, "What about Dumont? Is there a part for her? I don't want to phone her unless I'm certain there's a good chance that she might get it—and boy she does need it!" After a one-film hiatus for Dumont, MGM succumbed to his lobbying and hired her for the role of Martha Phelps, unmarried sister of the late Hiram. The decision came just as the Dumont myth was gaining credibility, and it aided both the actress and Groucho. The two had been so effective together that some fans, and at least one newspaper, believed that they were married. Throughout his career Groucho, who had been embarrassing Dumont since the days of *The Cocoanuts,* insisted that she was humorless. As proof he offered the *Duck Soup* finale: "We're alone in a small cottage and there's a war going on outside and Margaret says to me, 'What are you doing, Rufus?' And I say, 'I'm fighting for your honor, which is probably more than you ever did.' Later she asked me what I meant by that." Maureen O'Sullivan burnished the legend when she stated that Dumont "had no idea why *A Day at the Races* was funny, or even that it *was* funny. When we started she told me, 'It's not going to be one of *those* things. I'm having a very *serious* part this time.' " But the image of a society-woman-turned-actress, wholly unaffected by the *mishegaas* around her, appears to have been the richest jest of all, Dumont's ultimate joke on Groucho and company. She was a close reader of her own reviews, and knew the truth of

J. B. Priestley's observation that she could be shot out of a cannon without disturbing her dignity. Out of Groucho's hearing she gave an accurate self-description—"I'm not a stooge. I'm the best straight woman in Hollywood"—and made a very keen analysis of what she did for a living: "There's an art to playing straight. You must build up your man but never top him, never steal the laughs from him." Now that she was back in the picture, Dumont had no intention of altering her image. Only once did she let her guard down, when she confessed to a reporter: "I was afraid I was being taken for granted. Missing Go West was the best thing that could happen to me."

As preparations for The Big Store got under way, the great straight woman supplied almost all of the enthusiasm. The Brothers seemed to be listless and uninterested, as if the project were doomed from day one. Their new producer, Louis K. Sidney, tried to rally them from the sidelines. In addition to Nat Perrin, writer of the Flywheel, Shyster, and Flywheel radio show, he hired three new gag writers, Hal Fimberg, Ray Golden, and Sid Kuller. The last two had experience working with a brother comedy team; unfortunately, that team was the Ritz Brothers, a group of undemanding nightclub comedians who specialized in exaggerated slapstick and gross double takes. (Miriam once made the mistake of seeing one of their films and then telling her father it was "really funny." With a show of not-quite-mock outrage he snapped, "If that's the way you feel, let the Ritz Brothers buy you that new bike you want." He finished with a little homily: "I used to have a line in Animal Crackers: 'You have to be a parent in order to find out how much your children hate you.' How true, how true!")

Upon completion of the writers' first draft Sidney sat down to address the Marxes. "Your last two pictures lost money," he reminded them. "I have never had a loser. We are not going to lose money. And we are going to have a good picture. I want all of you to promise your undying cooperation." Groucho could not work up more than a nod. Harpo made a wordless gesture of approval. Only Chico gave voice to his opinion. The confidence man assumed the role he knew best. "L.K., you're a great man, you're a great showman. I love you! I'm going to be with you all the way, I'm going to help on the story, I'm going to help on the gags, I'm going to go all the way with you, all the way." Reassured, Sidney signaled one of the gagmen to read from the work in progress. Chico closed his eyes in order to concentrate. As page 15 was being read, Groucho observed that at least one thing had not changed since the Paramount days. His brother was asleep.

MGM assigned Charles Reisner to direct *The Big Store* principally because of his background. The stocky journeyman had started as a vaudeville comedian, worked his way to Hollywood, and performed in silent comedies before going to the other side of the camera. To ingratiate himself, he went out of his way to be an easy laugher and a pleasant, unhurried overseer. Better still, because MGM had ruled against the "preproduction extravagance" of a live tryout, Reisner argued for a kind of workmen's compensation, and won the right to a sixteen-week shooting schedule. The result was a more relaxed and amiable movie than the two previous misfires. Yet it, too, suffered from a richness of embarrassments. The most egregious of these is the romance between Tony Martin and Virginia Grey. Martin plays Dumont's nephew, an aspiring singer and composer. In the previous Marx Brothers films for MGM the songs were not particularly speedy, but here the numbers act as an emergency brake on the comedy, and one of them stops the picture cold, when Martin warbles "Tenement Symphony." For this Melting Pot flapdoodle the writers had no one to blame but themselves; Golden and Kuller supplied the doggerel for Hal Borne's saccharine tune: "The Cohn's pianola / The Kellys and their Victorola / all form a part of my Tenement Symphony. . . . The songs of the ghetto / inspire the allegretto / You'll find them in my Tenement Symphony / . . . O Marie / O Marie / You'll be late / For your date with Iz*ee*. . . ." Their ode to diversity is swiftly undone by a gallery of racial and ethnic stereotypes: chattering Asians, overbreeding Italians, stoic American Indians, and the mandatory pop-eyed black choristers. It was this number that prompted cinema historian Joe Adamson to set up a "Nausea Rating" listing every one of the Marx Brothers' romantic leads, ranging back to Oscar Shaw in *The Cocoanuts,* and including Zeppo, John Carroll, Kenny Baker, and Allan Jones. Tony Martin was awarded first place.

Still, no picture with Margaret Dumont and Groucho can be without its redeeming moments. Violence is done to Martin, and Dumont consults the Yellow Pages. Under "Gumshoes" she finds Wolf J. Flywheel and pays him a visit. Attended by his faithful amanuensis, Harpo, Groucho states his fee: $20,000. She balks, and he begins to haggle. He agrees; the stated price *is* excessive. "Only a cheap chiseler would ask that much." How much is she willing to pay? $500? "Oddly enough, I'm prepared to take it. Shall we bind the deal with a kiss—or five dollars in cash? You lose either way."

At the scene of the crime, Phelps Department Store, Groucho is introduced to Grover, the store manager—and, secretly, the villain who still plans to do away with the young heir, wed Dumont, and claim her wealth and property. Douglass Dumbrille, who had played a corrupt racetrack owner in *A Day at the Races,* is a foeman worthy of Groucho's steel. Their first meeting parallels the collisions of old:

DUMBRILLE

How do you do?

GROUCHO

That's rather a personal question, isn't it, old man? How I do and what I do is my concern. (*To DUMONT*) And if you marry me, your concern will be my concern.

DUMBRILLE

What experience have you had in a department store?

GROUCHO

I was a shoplifter for three years. . . .

DUMBRILLE

(*At the boil*) We will assume that I am a customer. I am returning a baby carriage.

GROUCHO

Are you married?

DUMBRILLE

Why, of course not!

GROUCHO

Then what are you doing with a baby carriage? This man is a cad! A yellow cad!

DUMBRILLE

The whole thing is utterly ridiculous! Now I'll ask you a simple question: It's Bargain Day. The store is crowded, a woman faints. What do you do?

GROUCHO

How old is she?

DUMBRILLE

What difference does it make?

GROUCHO

You hear that? A woman's life is in danger and he asks, "What difference does it make?" And that charlatan is running your store? Martha, I'd fire him immediately.

DUMBRILLE

If Miss Phelps were not my fiancée . . .

GROUCHO

(*To DUMONT*) You mean that a woman of your culture and money and beauty and money and wealth and money would marry that imposter?

Alone with Dumont, he closes in:

GROUCHO

Martha dear, there are many bonds that will hold us together through eternity.

DUMONT

Really, Wolf? What are they?

GROUCHO

Your government bonds, your savings bonds, your Liberty bonds. And maybe, in a year or two after we're married, who knows? There may be a little baby bond.

DUMONT

Oh, that would be wonderful. Tell me, Wolfie dear, will we have a beautiful home?

GROUCHO

Of course. You're not planning to move, are you?

DUMONT

No, but I'm afraid after we've been married awhile, a beautiful girl will come along and you'll forget all about me.

GROUCHO

Nonsense! I'll write you twice a week.

Viewing the rushes, producer L. K. Sidney saw nothing funny in that last riposte and instructed his staff to leave it on the cutting-room floor. They agreed. Some weeks later, at the official MGM preview, he was appalled to see that the line was still there. Sidney confronted Kuller in the lobby, and the writer was still protesting his innocence when Louis B. Mayer advanced toward them. Harpo tried to intervene. It was just a matter of one line, he explained softly. Mayer wanted to know which particular line, and Harpo informed him. The great man rendered his verdict—"Greatest line in the picture"—and exited. Overruled, Sidney confronted the Brothers and their writers. Who was responsible for sneaking in the quip when he was away from the set? While Groucho modestly lowered his eyes, Chico broke the tense silence: "Let's just say the God of Comedy put it in."

The Big Store could have used more of that Dionysian spirit. It lurks and flickers through the picture, but the Marx Brothers were simply too jaded and unhappy to supply it with any consistency. Chico's unruliness lay at the heart of the dissatisfaction. In earlier times, his wildness could simply be overlooked; the profligacy and devil-may-care attitude were part of the package: you bought Chico, you bought his compulsions. But lately the man had become more than Groucho or Harpo could handle. With his consent they had been handling his paychecks, giving him enough to get by, but forcing him to save for his retirement. Almost $300,000 now sat in Chico's bank account, where he could not touch it without their signatures. While the dollars piled up, however, Chico had been running up gambling debts to mobsters. Afraid for his life, the debtor begged his brothers for money, and when they refused, went out and hired an attorney to sue for the cash.

With this as the background for the Marx Brothers' latest teamwork, an explosion was inescapable. Between takes, Groucho griped to a reporter from the *Los Angeles Herald:* "When I say we're sick of movies, I mean the people are about to get sick of us. By getting out now, we're just anticipating public demand, and by a very short margin. Our stuff is simply growing stale. So are we." Chico and Harpo listened as he continued his testy analysis. "What happened to us is that we were defeated by our own specialty. The fake moustache, the dumb harp player and the little guy who chased the ladies, all were funny at first. But it became successively harder with each picture to top the one before. We couldn't get out of the groove, without getting out of the movies. So we decided to get all the way out." Splitting up a team of brothers "means a certain amount of sadness. But everything passes, sadness included. Anyhow, I prefer never to work again than to make another Marx Brothers picture." Then he and his brothers went back to work. Whatever the bitterness between them, they had been professionals for too long to slough off their final assignment. Their timing was still expert, and they did what they could with shoddy material. Still, there were no stand-ins for the standard comic scenes, and in these the Brothers' weariness shows through. Groucho had discarded the toupee for this film, but his hair is dyed an incongruous jet-black to match his painted moustache; from under their customary wigs, the lined faces of Harpo and Chico resemble those of apple dolls dried in the sun. A sense of valediction hangs over the picture, and that is what saves it. Groucho is still limber enough to slouch through one of his surprisingly lithe athletic dance numbers. Harpo appears in seventeenth-century coat and breeches; two mirrors reflect his image before joining him in an imaginative Mozartean trio. And Chico and Harpo play piano duets in the ebullient and appealing style of the young Leonard and Arthur Marx.

None of this had any effect on MGM. By the release date of June 1941, the daily headlines had turned grim and the world was preoccupied with Allied losses and with fears of American involvement in the war overseas. To the studio, *The Big Store* now seemed totally irrelevant, a waste of staff and celluloid. Indeed, Metro thought so little of the Brothers that it gave Tony Martin equal billing with Groucho, Chico, and Harpo, hoping to lure some pop music lovers into the theaters. Yet all was not lost; a few sentimental critics recognized the contribution the Marx Brothers had made to the history of humor. Perhaps because this was thought to be the Brothers' last bow, *The Motion Picture Herald* rated *The Big Store* as "one of the funniest ever made by the Marx Brothers." The *New York Times* came closer to the truth when it recognized them as "still the most errant maniacs this side of bars," and summed up the entertainment as "An old Marx Brothers design. But as the last remnant on the counter it's a bargain." In Britain, the *Spectator* took the long view: "Among the players who have contributed to cinema history only Chaplin ranks higher than these three clowns . . . no pretentiousness ever survived the friendly investigations of Harpo and Chico, and no social political or economic skullduggery ever found Groucho at a loss for a nimble oration." Years later, a young comedy writer, Sidney Zelinka, ran across that review in Groucho's scrapbook. He paused to consider what he had read. Was this the nation that had tossed pennies at the Marxes in the 1920s? Had the Marxes been killed in some sort of mass disaster? "The praise was so generous," he remarked, "I thought for a moment I had stumbled onto an obituary." And in a way, that is exactly what he had done.

CHAPTER ELEVEN

Marx's Dust Bowl

THE ATTACK ON Pearl Harbor on December 7, 1941, was followed immediately by the dark farce of Japanese diplomats exiting the United States. They left safely under U.S. military guard, as specified by the Articles of War, accompanied by the curses of Secretary of State Cordell Hull: "Scoundrels and piss-pants!" Something of *Duck Soup* clung to this moment—a comment made at the time, and then quickly washed away by the brutal and disheartening headlines from the Far East. Such observations would not be revived until the antiwar movement more than thirty years afterward.

Comedy seemed beside the point as World War II began, and Groucho congratulated himself for leaving the party at the right time. For him the season was composed of farewells. Just before the year ended Ruth made arrangements to quit the Marx home and set up her own apartment. California law stipulated that husband and wife were entitled to equal shares of their property, and Groucho readily agreed. "They divided everything down to the silver in the house," Chico's wife Betty stated. "That's how honest he was." Honest, but also evasive. He wanted no public airing of the couple's mutual infidelities, and for that reason agreed to a generous settlement.

The children were the least affected physically. Given her choice of which parent to live with, Miriam unsurprisingly chose to stay with Groucho. During the last stages of the marriage Arthur was living in New York and working as a gag writer for the Milton Berle radio show. Before the assignment was over, he enlisted in the Coast Guard. At a naval base he read Padre's version of the marital denouement: "Obviously this uncomfortable set-up couldn't continue. I said good-bye to her before she drove off in her car. It was one of those awkward, half-serious moments, and I didn't know quite what to say. Finally, I put my hand out and said,

'Well, it was nice knowing you, and if you're ever in the neighborhood again, drop in.' Your mother seemed to think that was a funny line—so for once in my life I got a laugh when I wasn't trying for one.

"The house is pretty quiet now with just Miriam and me rattling around the fourteen rooms. Well, it's better than fourteen people rattling around in two rooms. I'll let things drift along—anyway, for the present."

In a letter to Sheekman the jaunty approach faltered: "I have a couple of radio things brewing, but the heat under them is very low and God knows what will become of me. At this point, the chorus of 110 voices sings the whole choral arrangement of Beethoven's Ninth. My social life is negligible. I play anagrams, pool, pinochle and listen to music. I smoke constantly and have a mole on my left shoulder. Would like to meet a sociable widow, around fifty-five, object wet nursing."

The relationship of a fifty-two-year-old man and his teenage daughter has been the basis of many a summer movie; in real life it had aspects that were not so charming. To Miriam the situation was an adolescent's dream realized. Like many girls her age she had not been getting along with her mother; suddenly she was emancipated from all maternal restrictions and criticism. Groucho affected to see nothing wrong with these new conditions and claimed that no one else in the family did, either. But admiring as Betty was of her brother-in-law, she had no fondness for the arrangement. That house, she said, was "no place for a fifteen-year-old." With Ruth out of the way Groucho felt free to bring women home, and to hold soirées for his friends. On these occasions Miriam acted as "hostess to these sophisticated men and women, sitting around and hearing remarks that weren't suitable for a girl her age." If the guests saw anything untoward about the arrangement they kept it to themselves. Most of them were highly amused when Miriam put down her father's latest date—a blond—as "Harpo in drag."

In this period, Groucho did more entertaining for guests than for paying customers.

His brothers faced their unemployment in different ways. Harpo actually tried to volunteer for the armed forces. The recruiting officers, he reported, found him "overaged, undersized, and devoid of any military skill. I had no business in olive drab or navy blue. The only uniform I was qualified to wear consisted of a plug hat, red wig, raincoat and baggy pants. The only weapons I could be trusted with were a rubber-bulb horn, a harp, a clarinet, and two sleeves' worth of knives." These he used to entertain the troops at installations all around the country. Change the uniform and the ordnance, and what was true of Harpo held for Chico.

The musically illiterate pianist went on the road with his Ravellis, travel-ing solo, waving a baton strictly for show, clowning at the keyboard, and squandering his week's wages as soon as they were in hand. "We began our tour in Flatbush," he said. "Every fifteen seconds I'd think I was hear-ing Harpo blowing that automobile horn, and every other fifteen seconds I'd wish he was." In 1942 Betty became the second Marx wife to end her marriage. Groucho remained fond of his sister-in-law, and when he learned of the impending divorce bestowed a gift of more than $100,000 in securities. Betty was not as happy with the gift as she might have been, because Groucho chose that moment to give a lecture about Chico's profligacy and self-indulgence.

Once he handed over the money, Groucho suffered a philanthropy hangover. Such quixotic gestures were not like him, and he immediately sought to replace the missing dollars with some new ones. To do that he would have to go to work again, this time without the trappings he had come to resent. He told *Newsweek* of a planned comeback, sans "mous-tache, slouch clothes, Chico or Harpo." The next move was unspecified, because no one had yet made him an offer worth taking. Groucho under-stood that he had a talent to amuse in a very specific manner, and that at present his brand of comedy was not in demand except at army bases and bond rallies. One of those fund-raising efforts took place in Washington, D.C., with Groucho aboard the Hollywood Victory Caravan. The assem-blage contained some of the biggest names in Hollywood: Charles Boyer, Claudette Colbert, Cary Grant, James Cagney, Bing Crosby, and fellow comedians Bert Lahr, Stan Laurel, and Oliver Hardy. Groucho hoped to be appreciated for himself alone, and not for the clownish disguise he had left at the movies. He was about to receive a sobering lesson. When the Caravan pulled into town the stars disembarked single file. A crowd was on hand, greeting each one with rousing cheers. When they saw a slen-der, middle-aged man in a dark suit, they failed to respond. Who was he, an agent, an accountant, a factotum? Groucho climbed down in silence, anonymously worked his way to the rear of the car, got on again, hastily assumed a greasepaint moustache, eyebrows, spectacles, and cigar, and walked off the train with bent knees. "Doesn't anybody want little old Groucho's autograph?" he inquired loudly. "You know, I'm somebody, too, even if I *am* out of work." The audience awarded him with a great round of applause. So much for putting Dr. Hackenbush in mothballs.

That day he wrote to Miriam in his old manic style: "Tomorrow we are having tea at the White House. I hope they have pumpernickel." He maintained that tone when he met the peripatetic Eleanor Roosevelt. She flashed her familiar toothy smile and greeted him warmly. Aware that the visit was only to include a light afternoon snack, he asked his hostess, "Are we late for dinner?" A Marine band blared in the background. He reacted sympathetically: "Now I know why you travel so much." Groucho and the First Lady watched the comedienne Charlotte Greenwood execute a high kick. "You could do that," he whispered, "if you'd just put your mind to it." After the show a general entered the room, searching for the president's wife. She had already left to attend another ceremony. The guest pointed to the ceiling: "She's upstairs filing her teeth." The general glowered and moved on. That was no way to talk about Mrs. Roosevelt.

Groucho had barely returned to his home when Ruth's divorce papers were officially filed. She already had everything she'd asked for, and he was shocked to find himself officially accused of inflicting "physical pain and mental anguish." He was willing to acknowledge that he hadn't been easy on Ruth these last few years, but the first charge truly upset him. At Chasen's restaurant he had seen Humphrey Bogart smack his first wife, Virginia Mayo, during one of their many contretemps. "Bogart," Groucho told his biographer Hector Arce, was "a great actor but a coward. I've never hit a woman—except in self-defense." It seems unlikely that Groucho ever physically abused Ruth. No doubt she had in mind the number of times she banged up her car or fell down, and had rationalized these as something other than self-inflicted wounds.

•

GROUCHO'S SECOND BACHELORHOOD commenced with the war. He claimed to be ecstatic in his new freedom from marital obligation; the evidence contradicted him. Bert Granet, a comedy writer and Beverly Hills neighbor, considered the first two years of the war "the lowest point in Groucho's life." The Granets lived nearby, and Groucho would take his German shepherd, Duke, for a walk, tarrying in front of their house. More times than she could count, Granet's wife Charlotte took pity on the loiterer and invited him to dinner. The table seated sixteen, and there were often that many guests, many of them writers. Groucho always took over, holding court at the head of the table because, he pointed out, "I'm the oldest."

He hired a secretary and kept an office in downtown Beverly Hills, but this was mainly for show. In the mornings he worked on the book for a musical, pacing around the room as his collaborator, Norman Krasna, sat at the typewriter. Partway through the first act, they decided that songs were superfluous. Pleased with this decision, Groucho wrote to his old Chicago friend, Dr. Samuel Salinger: "If we write it well, I expect to play it in New York with none of the familiar accoutrements . . . it's a straight play with some comedy, I hope." The rest of the time Groucho spent in make-work. In 1942 gasoline rationing began. His only car was a Cadillac that guzzled more fuel in a week than the ration board allotted ordinary civilians for a month. The driver could have claimed that he was no ordinary civilian, that he deserved extra privileges because of his war bond tours. But Groucho wanted no special dispensations and also refused to buy on California's flourishing black market. A bicycle became his major source of transportation. He made a habit of rising early and shaving with an electric razor. This gave him a feeling of patriotic pride: he no longer required much-needed steel for blades, or expensive soap for lather. As a bonus, because he no longer had to worry about cuts and nicks he could abandon the mirror and read books while he shaved. "I get five o'clock shadow around one in the afternoon," he commented, "but look how well informed it keeps me." Like most homeowners in the neighborhood, he had a Japanese gardener, and like all such Japanese gardeners, this one was sent to an internment camp for the duration. Groucho took over the task of weeding and planting. An attempt at vegetable gardening resulted in something he dubbed "Marx's Dust Bowl." Tending it, he was subject to the periodic gawking of tourists who recognized the bespectacled gentleman doing his own yard work. Groucho much preferred the occasions when he went unrecognized. One afternoon a Beverly Hills dowager, evidently deprived of her own Japanese servant, hailed him from her car. "Oh, gardener, how much does the lady of the house pay you a month?" Groucho straightened up. "Oh, I don't get paid in dollars. The lady of the house just lets me sleep with her."

Once the chores were done he would telephone his secretary, Rachel Linden, former amanuensis to Herman Mankiewicz. Some mandatory facetiousness would be followed by a sober dictation of letters over the phone. Upon their completion Groucho would put on his traditional uniform—shorts, sweatshirt, sneakers, and beret—and pedal to his office in downtown Beverly Hills. The building had no elevator, and he was customarily overheated and out of breath upon arrival. Rather than ascend the stairs he would whistle insistently until Rachel raised a window on the second floor. According to their well-established routine, she would then lower a basket tied to a rope. In it were letters and bills that needed the Marx signature. For the next twenty minutes Groucho would stand on the sidewalk, playing to passersby, perusing papers, and dictating an answer or two by shouting them up. The task finished, he would get back on his bike and shop for the day, visiting groceries and bakeries, placing his purchases in a hamper attached to the handlebars. This routine reminded him of the old days in New York and gave him unanticipated pleasure. When the marketing was over he pedaled homeward.

The aerobics kept Groucho physically hale, but did little to boost his morale. In some vital way he felt that his timing had gone off. For years he had toyed with the idea of a book entitled *Wags,* chronicling the history of practical jokes. This came to nothing, but the literary itch persisted. His kvetch about the Internal Revenue System, ornamented and edited by Arthur Sheekman, was published by Simon & Schuster. They dubbed the little book *Many Happy Returns.* The humor between hard covers was little better than the punning title. Early in 1941, *The Saturday Review of Literature* ran a condensation of *Many Happy Returns;* one portion serves to illustrate the tone and temper of Groucho's second book:

> March used to mean the beginning of spring; now it's the end of your bankroll. . . . You're probably saying to yourself, "Why do I have to pay an income tax? What does the government do with my money?"
>
> This is a pretty dull routine and I'd advise you to change it if you expect to get anywhere with yourself. What do you *think* the government does with your money? Spends it on a woman? Gets drunk? Or plays the ponies? That's what *you* might do with the money, or, if you have to get personal, what *I* do; but I can assure you that the government is not just out for a good time. . . .
>
> I want to explain what happens to your tax dollar. Your tax dollar goes right to Washington, where, contrary to popular impression, it is not thrown across the Potomac River and caught by a dollar-a-year man who bites it to see if it is counterfeit. Nobody bites your dollar. The bite is put on you.

Whimsy and bile rarely mix well, but even in the best of times *Many Happy Returns* would not have jumped off the shelves. And this was the worst of times; the war raged on two fronts, and daily bulletins carried news of Allied losses and retreats. To boost morale, the Office of War Information ceaselessly assured civilians that their taxes—some $10 billion worth by the end of 1942—were being used to effect an Allied victory and bring the boys home. A criticism of the IRS was the last thing citizens wanted to read—even with the publisher's superficial nod to the war effort. (The book's cover illustration showed Groucho attacking Hirohito, Hitler, and Mussolini. His weapon was a mallet labeled INCOME TAXES.) Meant as an impulse item to be bought on the way out of a bookstore, the volume lay unread and unsold. Groucho refused to confront the evidence; he became Margaret Dumont to Simon & Schuster's Chico: "Who you gonna believe, me or your own eyes?" To promote his effort he carried on a shameless one-man publicity campaign. A letter to *Variety* read, "You undoubtedly have had to dig down for Uncle Sam, and it seems to me that a copy of my book, *Many Happy Returns,* should be your constant companion. . . . Briefly, I have been plugging for your throwaway for many years and it's about time you turned around and helped boot this book of mine into a best-seller."

A couple of months later he wrote to *Variety* once more. By now he had collected a score of reviews, most of them as strained as the one in *The New Republic:* "Groucho Marx in print is not so funny as he is in person, but anybody other than Groucho Marx who was as funny as Groucho Marx in person would have been bounced into the receiving ward at Bellevue long ago." He mused, "It seems to me I spend most of my time defending myself against attacks by trade-paper Pulitzers, journeymen hacks and fly-bitten critics. I had no idea when I first embarked on a shady literary career that there were so many posts to defend. I imagined that once having written a classic it was done with and I could then rest on my literary oars and gracefully float into the harbor of the ten best-sellers. How do you like my metaphors?"

Nothing could induce the public to buy *Many Happy Returns.* Fewer than five thousand copies were sold. Groucho tried to make light of the disappointment: "I only write first editions," he told a reporter. His jaunty epilogue ran in the *Hollywood Reporter,* in the form of an open letter to Simon & Schuster. Whose idea was this book in the first place? Groucho reminded them. "There I was, sitting in the Warwick Hotel, and somebody from the S & S fox-hole contacted me (repulsive expression) and, in syrupy tones, pleaded with me to dash off a comic classic that would not only stupefy the critics but sell at least 100,000 copies. As a matter of fact, I'm glad I did the book—it proved conclusively that there's no interest whatever in this country in income taxes or Groucho Marx. I think, in the future, it might be wise to confine my literary efforts to the cheaper and more gullible magazines. The pay is good, the work is dignified and I get Thursdays and Sundays to myself."

And for the next several years he did busy himself with humorous pieces for *This Week,* the magazine supplement to the *New York Herald Tribune; Variety; The Saturday Evening Post;* and *Liberty.* They paid well according to their lights—sometimes more than $1,000 a piece, but hardly enough to support Groucho in Beverly Hills style. His real, if sporadic, income came from what he called "the squirrel cage of show business"— radio. His agents, Zeppo and Gummo, booked him as a drop-in on the Bob Hope and Bing Crosby shows, where he could pocket a $1,000 fee for an evening's light work. In time he became a fairly regular member of the Rudy Vallee–Joan Davis program for Sealtest. A few reviewers took notice of his sly delivery and John K. Hutchens, the influential cultural critic of the *New York Times,* went out of his way to call Groucho a "great man . . . one of the most comical, surely, in all the world." Of course, Hutchens allowed, the radio comedian "is better seen than merely heard. The frock coat, the cigar, the phony moustache were uproarious props, and the gliding loops that took him around a stage or a movie set were wonderful to see. Well, you can't have everything and besides, he himself foreswore those items when he retired from the screen by—as he put it— public demand."

But high-toned encomiums were of little help when Zeppo and Gummo tried to sell Groucho as a major star on radio. The Marx Brothers films were rapidly becoming a thing of the past, seen only at campus festivals and in the occasional rerun at places like the Laffmovie in New York. Abbott and Costello were the hot new comedy team now; the graduates of burlesque had a loud, unsubtle approach, but they were young and full of beans and their "Who's on First" baseball routine made ticket holders forget the Marx Brothers' word games of the past. But competitors were not the only factor to keep Groucho from prime time: he had failed too many times on radio. He was about to settle into the role of permanent guest when, early in 1943, the Marx agency got some heady news. The deal hanging fire for months had finally been consummated. The Pabst brewery would take a chance and make Groucho Marx the centerpiece of *Blue Ribbon Town,* a half-hour variety show. Groucho could scarcely believe the fee: $2,500 per program. The kid brothers, the nonperformers he rarely socialized with, had come through in a way that Harpo and Chico never did and never could. He recognized that Zeppo and Gummo were the true inheritors of Minnie's acumen, and he said so.

It is impossible to exaggerate the authority of a radio sponsor in that period. Bob Hope cloaked the truth in jest. His guest, Sidney Greenstreet, gave a throaty command: "Gaze into my eyes. You are in my power. You will do my bidding. You will fulfill my slightest wish. You will obey my every whim." Hope addressed the audience: "This guy's crazy—he thinks he's my sponsor!" Comedians were willing to go to any lengths, including out-of-town meetings with a sales staff, in order to flatter and cajole the company that was paying their bills. Groucho fell in line, eager to redeem himself as a single, without the use of greasepaint, Chico, or Harpo.

His mainstays on the show were Kenny Baker, the tenor from *At the Circus,* and a shapely singer, Fay McKenzie, both of whom accompanied Groucho when he went on tours of army camps. On the air and in person he used them as props for his monologues. These were very much in the established wartime mode—suggestive one-liners strung together with topical references. In one of them he spoke about his film career:

> I haven't made a picture recently. They tested me for the part of the man who makes love to Betty Grable in the picture version of *They Knew What They Wanted.* But they turned me down—they knew what *I* wanted. . . .
>
> I did do a little work in Hollywood. I worked at my draft board as a model. Don't laugh. I really was a model. Anyone who came in and looked like me was automatically rejected. . . .
>
> My experience with women has been very limited, though. As a matter of fact, I come from a very strict family, and I didn't go out with girls until I was twenty-one because my mother objected. After I was twenty-one, the girls objected!
>
> Even then, when I had a date, we always had to have a chaperone. You know what a chaperone is—that's a French word meaning, "Brother, are you in for a dull evening!" . . . I don't want you to get the impression that I still can't get a date, because back in Hollywood there are plenty of girls who are ready, willing, and able to go out with me. That is—I'm always ready, but the girls that are willing aren't able, and those that are able aren't willing. . . . The way I've been talking about women so much you're probably thinking that that's all I'm interested in—women. But that's not true. There are any number of things I'm interested in besides women. For instance, there's uh . . . that is, uh . . . darn it, I could have sworn there was something! . . . Ah, wonderful women! Just give me a comfortable couch, a dog, a good book, and a woman. Then if you can get the dog to go somewhere and read the book,

I might have a little fun! . . . And right now I want you to meet a girl who is always fun—the ingenue of Blue Ribbon Town—Fay McKenzie!

This routine showed just how much Groucho had yielded to the times. Any competent comedian could have performed it. The man had made his reputation as an outsider, a surrealist, a mocker of every totem and stricture he could lay his wits on. And now, without a backward glance, he had turned himself into a "character," speaking like some local humorist—a barber, say, from Peru, Indiana.

•

IN 1943 Arthur told Groucho of his plans to marry Irene Kahn, daughter of the late songwriter Gus Kahn. Groucho had nothing against his son's prospective bride—the two had been going out since their high school days—but he was not enthusiastic about the event. Among the reasons was his fear that the couple would make him a grandfather. The Pabst people were aiming for a young audience of beer drinkers; they didn't need an old man as spokesman—at least according to Groucho. Since Groucho had just laid a pile of expensive securities on Betty, his son reasonably assumed that a monetary gift was imminent. He was wrong. Groucho had no intention of giving any more away, even to a blood relative.

With Ruth and Arthur gone, Groucho saw no point in retaining a fourteen-room residence. It had seen happier times, and so had he. The big place on Hillcrest Road was sold with barely a twinge of regret, and he moved into a smaller home in Westwood. Miriam made the adjustment easily; as long as she remained the mistress of the house, it scarcely mattered where the house was. Gag writer Nat Perrin was one of several friends who finally began to see "something strange" in the father-daughter relationship: "We had this very small poker game, and Miriam would call Groucho five or six times during the evening. The attachment seemed a little unhealthy to me." Looking back, Arthur suggested that his sister had become hopelessly smitten. By the time she was eighteen, Miriam had developed into an extremely attractive young woman. "She had inherited most of her mother's looks, and much of her father's wit, sense of humor and native intelligence. At Beverly High she was extremely popular and could get anybody she wanted. But in her estimation, none of her boyfriends could possibly measure up to her own father when it came to stimulating companionship. Miriam adored and idolized Father—both as a comedian and a parent—and probably would have been content to remain single and go on living with him for the rest of her life."

Her rivals were few. For a time the only one to take seriously was Virginia Schulberg, the ex-wife of writer Budd Schulberg. Convinced that he had found the ideal woman, Groucho wrote Arthur about his intention to marry again. But a few letters later Arthur was notified that the romance had been called off. Groucho claimed that it was unseemly for a man his age to marry a twenty-seven-year-old woman. The fact that Schulberg was intelligent and independent went unmentioned, but it seems likely that Groucho had second thoughts about wedding a woman who could match him in I.Q. points.

And then came Kay Gorcey. Miriam so disliked being away from Groucho that she accompanied him to the *Blue Ribbon Town* studio, hanging around the greenroom with other relatives and friends while the show went on the air. One of Groucho's cast members was Leo Gorcey. In his late twenties, the actor still looked and sounded like the New York slum teenager he had played in *Dead End*, back in 1937. Since then Gorcey had been in more than a dozen B pictures, and in every one he played a bantam punk. That was the persona he brought to Groucho's program, addressing the host as "Marxie" and dispensing malapropisms and advice from the side of his mouth. The January 29, 1944, broadcast turned out to be a strange compound of postmortem and prophecy. The setup (entirely fictional) had Groucho ready to announce his engagement to comedienne Vera Vague, another member of the cast.

GORCEY

I hoid the news of your enterin' the blissful state of holy deadlock. . . . Ah, love. I love it. Wonderful to be in love. Especially when you're in love with someone you like.

GROUCHO

Leo, that's a very astute remark. And I might add that it comes from a very astupid person.

GORCEY

Marxie, you're takin' a very bitter altitude.

GROUCHO

Gorcey, you don't understand. I thought I was marrying a good housekeeper. But instead I'm stuck with a woman who isn't interested in anything but romance.

GORCEY

Gee, that's compressin'. You gotta do something drastic to get rid of that dame. Hey, I got it. She wants romance. Be insultin' to da dame. Boin her up. Be da kinda guy dat's no good at love makin'. Make her think you're a useless joik.

GROUCHO

No, I'd just rather be myself.

GORCEY

That's what I mean.

In reality Gorcey was the one with the bitter "altitude." He liked to drink, and when he had a surfeit of liquor he turned mean, picking on the nearest individual who was smaller or weaker than he was. Kay met just such specifications. In his vanity press autobiography, the actor writes about his ex-wife in a passage reminiscent of Chico's amorous adventures. "Once, while on a personal appearance tour, she saw me talking to a strip dancer. She came up behind me, tapped me on the shoulder, and when I turned around she kicked me in the sex department. When Kay and I got back to the dressing room, I decided she had a couple of slaps coming, so I slapped her. She picked up a hat pin which was a prop in the act, and jabbed me in the keister. I picked up a chair, with the full intention of bashing her brains out. The chair missed her but bounced back and broke my nose."

Another night, "I was rudely awakened and reaching for the gun that always adorned my nightstand, I found that Kay had beaten me to it. She had this gun pointed at my head with one hand and in the other hand was waving a lipstick-stained handkerchief. I had learned to load a revolver so that the first chamber coming up was empty so I lunged at her and recaptured my equipment.

"Since that night, I have never liked lipstick. Incidentally, this lipstick was deposited on my lips by her mother, who was slightly more demonstrative than her daughter."

In no sense was Kay a match for her volatile husband. Yet the pretty, petite actress could never bring herself to leave him. On his orders she accompanied Leo to work, waiting meekly until the broadcast was done. It was on those occasions that she and Miriam began to chat. The six years that separated them proved no barrier to intimacy; Kay's emotional distress made her seem much younger, and Miriam had an unripe sophistication that made her appear to be Kay's contemporary. The roles gradually reversed, the battered wife confiding her secret to the young listener.

Miriam persuaded Groucho to offer her new friend a refuge. At first, Leo Gorcey blustered and threatened; then he realized that he could not intimidate Groucho or persuade his wife to return. Kay settled into her own room in the Westwood house, and made herself useful. She and Miriam grew closer still, continuing to gossip and share intimate details of their lives. At times Sunny Sauber joined in, and thought the diminutive Kay "like one of us kids." And then one morning Miriam made a discovery that outsiders had long suspected. The guest's bed was always neatly made because she had stopped sleeping in it. She was spending the nights with her host. As Miriam tried to cope with this, Groucho faced another career crisis. In January, with much promotional hoopla, Pabst commemorated its hundredth anniversary. The main celebration took place in the company town of Milwaukee, and as Pabst's radio representative Groucho gave a command performance. Several stories about this calamitous occasion were floated afterward. Groucho's version states that he and the CEO, Edward Pabst, went to a bar. Groucho did the ordering. "Mr. Pabst was a fine old gentleman, almost eighty at the time. He wasn't much of a drinker. Later it was discovered that the beer I'd been forcing down Mr. Pabst was Miller High Life. Before you could say 'convertible debenture,' I was canceled from the show and a rising young comedian named Danny Kaye was hired to replace me."

Arce repeats a story that may or may not have been true. At the time many people found the incident credible because it involved Groucho's quick tongue. Supposedly, one of the Pabst family invited Groucho to his palatial home to play a game or two in the billiard room. The boy made a nuisance of himself, forever interrupting or getting in the way. Fuming, Groucho turned on him and muttered all too audibly, "Fuck off, kid." Pabst overheard him and took steps to see that such rudeness was not rewarded with another contract.

Yet another tale had Groucho follow young Pabst to the bathroom. Groucho quickly returned, but the youth remained cloistered for half an hour. When the host wondered aloud what could be keeping the boy, Groucho said: "He'll be gone for quite a while. I taught him how to masturbate."

Whatever the validity of these anecdotes, and they were burnished and elaborated over the years, Groucho lost his slot in June when the brewery, citing below-average ratings, refused to renew his contract. No other sponsor came forward to make Groucho Marx a radio star. As his career braked to a full stop, other parts of his life went on at maximum speed. He and Kay outlined a plan to marry as soon as her divorce papers came through. Miriam made ready to go off to Bennington College in Vermont, three thousand miles away from her misery. At roughly the same time, Norman Krasna put the last touches on *Dear Ruth*, a comedy scheduled to open on Broadway. The mise-en-scène was supposed to be a household in the pleasant neighborhood of Kew Gardens, New York. To anyone who knew the principals, however, the play clearly reflected the Groucho Marx family of Beverly Hills, California, circa 1940. The wife, Edith, is not much of a drinker, but she has Ruth's passive, oblique quality. The dour father, Harry, is a judge rather than a comedian, but his replies are strictly Grouchovian. When someone asks him how he slept he replies, "Like a top. Spun all night," and when he is offered Sanka, replies, "You're welcome." Miriam—actually named Miriam in the play—is portrayed as a young radical. Unbeknownst to her father, she has signed him up for a contribution to the blood bank. Later she chortles as he settles down, wan from the bloodletting:

MIRIAM

Dad, I'm crazy about you.

HARRY

Then stop signing my name to things.

MIRIAM

It's nothing for most people to contribute, but for you it was an effort and sacrifice—and you made it gladly.

HARRY

Not gladly.

MIRIAM

Was it hard for you?

HARRY

There were twenty women in the room and I was the only person who had to lie down and have a blanket. I hope the kid that gets my blood doesn't need it bad. I haven't got much confidence in it.

He is not so pleasant when Miriam starts sounding off about love:

HARRY

Have you ever had anything to do with a man?

MIRIAM

Father, sometimes I wonder how you've been raised.

EDITH

Miriam! You're talking to your father! . . .

HARRY

The child's perverted! And you're to blame, Edith! You're the keeper of my home, the moulder of my children! And I'm not satisfied with the moulding!

While Krasna worked, another writer became inspired because of Groucho—although not in a manner that would help the unemployed. Idly watching a short Hal Roach film, "The McGuerins of Brooklyn," Irving Brecher was suddenly reminded of *The Flotsam Family*. No sponsor had ever been found for that prospective radio show, and looking back he concluded that he had miscast the leading man. While the tryout "got a lot of laughs—the audience loved Groucho—it did not ring true because he was playing a man of flesh and blood. And Groucho's character is not—when you paint a moustache on with burnt cork, it's not really flesh and blood." The head of the McGuerin family was impersonated by William Bendix, a performer with a gruff but curiously sympathetic manner. Brecher hired him, retitled the show *The Life of Riley*, and made a fresh audition record. Months later, sponsored at first by the American Meat Institute and then by many other companies, *Riley* began a phenomenal run that took it into the television era.

At this point Groucho seemed to be the thing he once mocked, a souvenir of better times, fondly remembered but as obsolete as Buster Keaton. He tried to wangle an invitation on the Jack Benny show, one of the most popular programs in America. The Marx Brothers had known Benny for more than forty years; surely the two comedians would strike sparks on the radio. But Groucho insisted on using his own material, and Benny, whose comedy was as circumscribed as a minuet, would have none of it: Groucho would use the Benny writers and only the Benny writers. Both comedians remained firm, and the invitation was never offered. The best Zeppo and Gummo's agency could get Groucho were appearances on Dinah Shore's *Birdseye Open House,* where he played second banana and spritzed wild gags ("If you're going out of your head, leave your ears. We're short of ashtrays"). He also joined Vincent Price and Robert Benchley in Norman Corwin's verse play for radio, *The Undecided Molecule.* Cast as a mean-spirited judge, Groucho decides to annihilate a molecule when it refuses to become anything. The arbiter objects to those who describe him as mean-spirited:

> Why, I am so benign I hardly ever beat my wife
> My children bow before me
> I'm much admired by rattlesnakes
> And birds of prey adore me
> I'm tender and I'm sensitive and anti-insurrectionist
> I wouldn't hurt a cobra. And I'm anti-vivisectionist.

Try as he might, though, the judge is undone by the defense attorney, who points out that matter cannot be destroyed. Groucho replies, Dr. Seuss–style:

> Gadzooks, it is, I had forgot, we can't destroy a particle.
> It seems we're in the power of this clever young upstarticle.

Groucho regarded the highly praised guest shot as an audition, proof that he could play someone other than himself. Critics agreed, and showfolk went out of their way to congratulate him, but Shore was the only one who made an offer for further appearances. He resigned himself to performances on her program, and at entertainment-starved army camps. There, at least, he remained a favorite. The boys remembered the early Marx Brothers movies, even if their younger brothers and sisters now preferred the one-dimensional clowning of Abbott and Costello. The high moment in Groucho's act always came at the end, when he asked the soldiers where they hailed from. As the name of a hometown was called out the comedian summoned up an anecdote about it, naming specific streets, stores, and local personalities. No matter how small or obscure the hamlet, the Brothers had played it in their vaudeville days.

Every so often a producer, conscious of Groucho's popularity among the GIs, aware of Chico's touring band and Harpo's availability, longed for the vanished lunacy of the Marx Brothers movies. Why not bring the Brothers back for one last horselaugh? But the talk subsided as fast as it had begun—until one convinced himself that he could put together a package that just might work. David Loew knew that satire is a parasitic form of entertainment, no stronger than its host. But what if the host was *Casablanca,* the Warner Brothers hit of 1942? The Marx Brothers' comeback would be called *Night and Day*—no, better still, to jibe with their features it would be titled *A Night in Casablanca*—and it would send up Rick and Ilse and all the other personae of the Warner film. It couldn't miss, Loew argued. Returning to civilian life, the young veterans would be anxious to pick up where they had left off. Their wives and sweethearts would also hanker for emblems of the old days: plentiful gasoline, nylon stockings, rubber tires, sugar, butter, the Marx Brothers. At loose ends, Groucho needed only a little push. Chico, forever in need of money, agreed to go along, and Harpo fell in. The news about the Marxes' comeback went out over the wires in April 1945, and was immediately swamped by the bulletin of April 12: President Franklin Delano Roosevelt was dead.

Even this shocking, world-numbing event was not beyond the reach of Groucho's tongue. His life was indeed his jokes, as Maureen O'Sullivan had said. "I was getting $3,000 an appearance," for the *Open House* shows, he reminisced. "The day Roosevelt died, we didn't have a show. I got paid anyway. I never saw that kind of easy money. I thought to myself, there are not enough people dying."

No major production company extended a welcome to the Marxes, so they formed their own corporation, Loma Vista, and made the customary preparations. The auspices could not have been better for a team whose average age was fifty-five, and who had been absent from the screen for the entire duration of the war. David Loew was the son of Marcus Loew, a cofounder of MGM. The scenarist was to be Joseph Fields, himself the son of a famous New York producer and former vaudevillian, Lew Fields. Bearing in mind the success of his siblings in military installations, Harpo came up with the idea of an inexpensive preproduction tour to test out the script. They would play scenes from *A Night in Casablanca* before men in uniform—a more appreciative audience could not be imagined. The basics were found acceptable to the army as well as to the Marx Brothers, and bookings were arranged.

Groucho became his old self again—dour, peevish, hypercritical. He launched into a major attack on the scenario as written. Fields had parodied Humphrey Bogart and his new amour, Lauren Bacall, with the use of characters named Humphrey Bogus and Lowan Behold. The dialogue suffered from a similar banality. Since Groucho was, in effect, his own coproducer, he called in reinforcements. Loew signed two radio writers, Howard Harris and Sidney Zelinka; a former animator and inventor of sight gags, Frank Tashlin; and Roland Kibbee, who had furnished gags for Groucho's radio shows, and who would eventually shape the final screenplay. Groucho supplemented their work, and in his spare time acted as an unpaid publicity agent. What was needed now, he thought, was a gimmick, some sort of controversy that would get the film some space in the papers. Several carefully chosen columnists reported that there was doubt about whether the name of Casablanca could be used only four years after the Bogart movie. Groucho's friend Dr. Samuel Salinger said as much in a letter, remarking, "So you can't call it 'A night in Casablanca.' Why not 'History makes its Marx,' or 'the Marx of Time'?" Groucho responded: "In your letter you mention that we cannot call our picture *A Night in Casablanca*. This, apparently, is one of your own judicial decisions. We spread the story that Warners objected to this title purely for publicity reasons. They may eventually actually object to it, although I don't think so. Not being the giant legal mind that you are, I wouldn't venture a decisive opinion but my hunch is that any court would throw out such a case as an absurd one. It seems to me that no one can forbid one from using the name of a city. There have been a number of pictures with Paris, Burma, Tokyo, etc. etc. used in the title. At any rate, the publicity has been wonderful on it and it was a happy idea. I wish they would sue, but as it is, we've had reams in the papers."

Warners did better than sue. The studio's legal department wrote a letter to Loew demanding to know whether the Marx Brothers film would violate their property rights. "Let me handle this," Groucho told the producer, and thus began one of the great epistolary battles of 1940s Hollywood.

"Dear Warner Brothers," he began. "I had no idea that the city of Casablanca belonged exclusively to Warner Brothers. However, it was only a few days after our announcement appeared that we received your long, ominous legal document warning us not to use the name, Casablanca. . . .

"I just don't understand your attitude. Even if you plan on re-releasing your picture, I am sure that the average movie fan could learn in time to distinguish between Ingrid Bergman and Harpo. I don't know whether I could, but I would certainly like to try.

"You claim you own Casablanca and that no one else can use that name without permission. What about 'Warner Brothers'? Do you own that, too? You probably have the right to use the name Warner, but what about Brothers? Professionally, we were brothers long before you were. We were touring the sticks as The Marx Brothers when Vitaphone was still a gleam in the inventor's eye, and even before us there had been other brothers—the Smith Brothers; the Brothers Karamazov; Dan Brothers, an outfielder with Detroit; and 'Brother, Can You Spare a Dime?' This was originally, 'Brothers, Can You Spare a Dime?' but this was spreading a dime pretty thin, so they threw out one brother, gave all the money to the other one and whittled it down. . . ."

Groucho turned his attention to the Warner brothers themselves: "Now, Jack, how about you? Do you maintain that yours is an original name? Well, it's not. It was used long before you were born. Offhand, I can think of two Jacks—there was Jack of 'Jack and the Beanstalk' and Jack the Ripper, who cut quite a figure in his day.

"As for you, Harry, you probably sign your checks, sure in the belief that you were the first Harry of all time and that all other Harrys are imposters. I can think of two Harrys that preceded you. There was Light-house Harry of Revolutionary fame and a Harry Appelbaum, who lived on the corner of 93rd Street and Lexington Avenue. . . ."

The writer concluded benignly: "I have a hunch that this attempt to prevent us from using the title is the brainchild of some ferret-faced shy-ster, serving a brief apprenticeship in your legal department. I know the type well—hot out of law school, hungry for success and too ambitious to follow the natural laws of promotion. This bar sinister probably nee-dled your attorneys, most of whom are fine fellows with curly black hair, double-breasted suits, etc., into attempting to enjoin us. Well, he won't get away with it! We'll fight him to the highest court! No pasty-faced legal adventurer is going to cause bad blood between the Warners and the Marxes. We are all brothers under the skin and we'll remain friends till the last reel of *A Night in Casablanca* goes tumbling over the spool.

"Sincerely, Groucho Marx."

Unsatisfied, Warner's humorless legal department demanded to know the plot of *A Night in Casablanca*. Groucho obliged them, this time referring to Paul Henreid, who had dramatically lit Bette Davis's cigarette in the suffering-in-mink Warner film *Now, Voyager*.

"Dear Warners:

"There isn't much I can tell you about the story. In it I play a Doctor of Divinity who ministers to the natives and, as a sideline, hawks can openers and pea jackets to the savages along the Gold Coast of Africa.

"When I first meet Chico, he is working in a saloon, selling sponges to barflies who are unable to carry their liquor. Harpo is an Arabian caddie who lives in a small Grecian urn on the outskirts of the city.

"As the picture opens, Porridge, a mealy-mouthed native girl, is sharpening some arrows for the hunt. Paul Hangover, our hero, is constantly lighting two cigarettes simultaneously. He apparently is unaware of the cigarette shortage.

"There are many scenes of splendor and fierce antagonisms, and Color, an Abyssinian messenger boy, runs Riot. Riot, in case you have never been there, is a small night club on the edge of town.

"There's a lot more I could tell you, but I don't want to spoil it for you. All this has been okayed by the Hays Office, *Good Housekeeping* and the survivors of the Haymarket Riots, and if the times are ripe, this picture can be the opening gun in a new world-wide disaster."

This time Groucho signed his message "Cordially."

Even now the Warner lawyers failed to recognize that they were being played like tarpon on a line. Another letter came, insisting upon an outline of the film's content. Pleased beyond measure, Groucho fired off his third missive.

"Dear Brothers:

"Since I last wrote you, I regret to say there have been some changes in the plot of our new picture, *A Night in Casablanca*. In the new version I play Bordello, the sweetheart of Humphrey Bogart. Harpo and Chico are itinerant rug peddlers who are weary of laying rugs and enter a monastery just for a lark. This is a good joke on them, as there hasn't been a lark in the place for fifteen years.

"Across from this monastery, hard by a jetty, is a waterfront hotel, chockfull of apple-cheeked damsels, most of whom have been barred by the Hays Office for soliciting. In the fifth reel, Gladstone makes a speech that sets the House of Commons in an uproar and the King promptly asks for his resignation. Harpo marries a hotel detective; Chico operates an ostrich farm. Humphrey Bogart's girl, Bordello, spends her last years in a Bacall house.

"This, as you see, is a very skimpy outline. The only thing that can save us from extinction is a continuation of the film shortage."

Now it was "Fondly, Groucho Marx."

All three letters gained wide circulation, the brothers Warner became the laughingstock of Hollywood, and the writer congratulated himself for a put-on well done. He walked with a jauntier step these days, not only because of his latest comic triumph, but because he was about to take a new bride. On Arthur's birthday, July 21, Groucho Marx, aged fifty-four, and Catherine Marie Dittig Gorcey, twenty-four, made their union official. "I think this was supposed to be some sort of tribute to a wandering son," Arthur mused from afar.

The era of good feeling was not destined to last. Immediately after the Japanese surrender in August, Arthur was sent stateside from the Philippines and honorably discharged. The young veteran had no wish to sponge off his mother or his uncles, and he would rather have reenlisted than be indebted to Groucho. When Grace Kahn offered accommodations at her spacious Mediterranean-style house in Beverly Hills, Arthur and his bride were only too glad to move in. Groucho responded coldly, but said little. There would be time for a proper response. His opening came about a month later when Arthur tried to break into print.

The veteran's first effort was an autobiographical feature. It concerned an unemployed ex-serviceman who did household chores while his wife went out to work in an office. Groucho dismissed the piece as unsaleable. When *Esquire* magazine sent a letter of acceptance offering $50, Groucho acknowledged that he had been mistaken about the literary marketplace but refused to change his opinion about Arthur's financial prospects. In his view, a piddling reward of fifty bucks was for losers, not writers.

Having alienated his son, Groucho turned his inattention to his daughter. A letter to Miriam in the late fall of 1945 shows a parent out of touch with his child, blind to the reasons why she has been acting out her resentments, and barely able to address her without losing his composure. Miriam and Kay had been at odds, and information about the discord had been printed in a gossip column. "I am trying to make a go of this marriage," Groucho reminded the eighteen-year-old, "and it is very difficult for many reasons: age, temperament, intellectual basis and so forth. The addition of a feud between you and Kay certainly doesn't help things any. I am going to be frank and say that I think you are far more at fault than Kay. Kay, I have seen, has tried to be friends with you but you fight her off. You yourself had admitted that you have told Sunny [Sauber] all the details of my domestic life and I am sure that you also confided in . . . many others.

"This I consider an unforgivable breach of confidence and conduct. You wrote Kay that you missed me but that you dreaded ever returning to the house and what it (to you) represents. I miss you too but I certainly don't want you to return unless you realize that I am married and are willing to help to make this marriage succeed.

"I remember when Arthur married Irene. One day he just left and moved over to the Kahns. I felt hurt at first, but I gradually realized that he was married and that he had a right to do with his life as he pleased. You must let me do the same with mine. There are many details of this I could discuss, but there isn't much point to that. I purposely am not pulling any punches, for it is important that you clearly understand how I feel. It isn't very good for my peace of mind to realize that half of Hollywood knows so much about my private life and I trust this is the last of that. . . ."

Something stirred in Groucho and he tried to mitigate the impact of his words. His effort only complicated matters. "After reading this far you probably loathe me. I have been in bed many nights thinking this over, so don't think this letter is the immediate result of a bad lunch. I want to love you and be a good father to you but I don't think you have been a good daughter to me. I hope the school and its associations will help in knocking some of the cantankerousness out of you."

With a new and already difficult marriage, and two alienated children, Groucho took more than the customary refuge in his work, plunging into rewrites of rewrites of *A Night in Casablanca*. The tryouts elicited the kind of response the Brothers hoped for. But Groucho was above all a realist, aware that soldiers—particularly soldiers who were a few months away from being discharged—would laugh at anything. Whether ticket buyers would respond the same way was moot. Doubts surfaced, and word got around that the Marx Brothers were insecure about their new movie. Groucho tried to make light of them in letters to Sam Zolotow, chronicler of film and theater for the *New York Times*:

The first read: "My plans are still in embryo. In case you've never been there, this is a small town on the outskirts of wishful thinking. At the moment, I'm deep in the heart of *Casablanca*, and it is thrilling work. I arise at seven every morning, kick the alarm clock in the groin and speed to the studio. I always get a nine o'clock call, which means I shoot promptly at three in the afternoon. There's no use protesting—this is the way the movie business is geared and I suspect that's the chief reason why so much bilge appears in your neighborhood theater."

The second marked no improvement in disposition: "Today for the first time since the last of September, I emerged from my molehill at General Service Studio and saw daylight." Groucho went on to compare his life to those of the minor performers in Swain's Rat and Cat Act. It consisted of six rats, dressed as jockeys, perched on six cats, dressed as horses, galloping furiously around a miniature racetrack. "Of course," he assured Zolotow, "I get more salary than Swain paid his actors; as a matter of fact, they didn't get any salary. Swain paid them off in cheese. . . . These rats didn't have an agent—they knew their own kind and booked themselves independently. They didn't even have to shop for their cheese—they just sat in their dressing room and waited for Swain to throw their salary over the transom.

"If *A Night in Casablanca* turns out disastrously, and there is no reason it shouldn't, I am going to look up Swain and ask him if he would be interested in reviving his act with me playing one of the jockeys."

The upcoming year gave him more than enough reasons to wish that Swain and vaudeville were still in existence.

CHAPTER TWELVE

Parodies Lost

THE LIST OF DEFECTS began with the cast. Margaret Dumont, disappointed that no interesting parts had come her way for the last several years, announced her retirement from the screen. Chico's daughter was in New York at the time and called her. Dumont remembered the young lady and asked Maxine Marx to lunch. The grande dame arrived in high style, wearing long gloves and sporting a lorgnette. After the first course, she brought up the subject of the Marxes.

"The boys r-r-r-ruined my car-r-r-r-eer-r," she trilled.

Maxine apprehensively asked how that was possible.

"Oh, my dear, nobody took me seriously as a dramatic actress. People always thought they saw Groucho peering from behind my skirt"—Emily Upjohn to the end. Alas, she meant what she said about quitting the screen, at least as far as the Marx Brothers were concerned, and *A Night in Casablanca* was the poorer for her absence.

It was also impaired by Archie Mayo's direction. Cynical by nature, he once revealed his method for evoking a tearful performance from a child actress: "Tight shoes." No one said he was unskilled; Mayo had been responsible for *The Petrified Forest*, which featured Humphrey Bogart in his breakthrough role; he had directed John Barrymore in *Svengali*, and Al Jolson and Ruby Keeler, then man and wife, in *Go into Your Dance*. Obviously he was on intimate terms with many genres, from dramatic to musical. But comedy was not among his accomplishments, and he lacked the ability to handle spoken and visual gags. The Marxes could have insisted on any number of directors from Hollywood's second rank, but Mayo had been Groucho's neighbor in the old days and seemed an authentic fan of the Marxes' films. That was good enough for Groucho. In Mayo's defense, it should be added that even if he had been able to persuade Kaufman and Ryskind and Perelman to do rewrites, no one could have summoned up the Brothers' old energy. The once irresistible flippancy and fire had diminished in all of them, and in Groucho most of all.

Burdened with aging and less than enthusiastic players, Mayo placed great emphasis on the plot. Visiting the set, a reporter was told that the film in production was "a darned good yarn that stands up by itself without the special, high-powered comedy scenes." As the finished film unreeled, a viewer might almost think that encomium was true. *A Night in Casablanca* has a convoluted plot, and it has few truly effective gags. One of them, suggested by the uncredited Tashlin, opens the picture. Harpo leans against a house, apparently up to no good. A policeman approaches. "Say, what do you think you're doing?" he growls. "Holding that building up?" Harpo nods. The policeman takes him in custody. Harpo and the building separate—and the structure collapses. Unhappily, what follows is never as quick and rarely as funny, but there are occasional glints in the rubble. Nazis remain the principal villains in this postwar production, and there was no better Deutsch farceur than Sig Rumann, one of Dr. Hackenbush's victims in *A Day at the Races*. Dan Seymour, the only actor to play in both *Casablanca* and *A Night in Casablanca*, is cast as a corrupt police chief and shares the joke with the audience. Post-crime, he advises his minions, "Round up all likely suspects," a sly reference to Claude Raines's instruction at the finale of *Casablanca*, "Round up the usual suspects." As Rumann's rebellious valet, Harpo has more to do than usual, casually outdueling a Nazi swordsman, pantomiming with Chico, and, of course, soloing on his instrument. What he does not have is his usual affect. The makeup artists decreed that while Groucho and Chico could keep the same costumes and makeup, Harpo's voluminous wig would have to be modernized. Barbers would create a weave, using the pantomimist's real, albeit thinning, hair, and dyed red tresses. Their work produced exactly the wrong effect. Harpo had always been an ageless sprite. Now he wore the face of a distressed Ariel.

In this condition he carries the film until Groucho's late entrance, made after the exposition has been heavily laid in. (The Nazis are after valuable artwork secreted somewhere in the hotel; they have already killed several hotel managers who tried to hinder them in their search.) On comes Ronald Kornblow (Groucho). The president of the Yellow Camel cab service appraises the new arrival:

CHICO

They'll never let you in.

GROUCHO

Do they let you in?

CHICO

Sure.

GROUCHO

I'll put a stop to that. I'm the new manager.

In keeping with tradition, Groucho is thoroughly capricious. The hotel employees await instruction from their new boss. "Never mind the staff," he proclaims. "Assemble the guests. I'll tell them what I expect of *them*." For one thing, the clientele must learn that "a kind word will get them further with a bellboy or a chambermaid than a couple of drinks. Of course, a kind word *and* a couple of drinks will get them still further. And if it gets them any further than that, it'll get them kicked out of the hotel." Another alteration is suggested: "We're going to change the numbers on all the rooms." A staffer cautions him, "Think of the confusion." Groucho nods and waggles his eyebrows. "But think of the fun." Curious about the service, he is informed that his laundry will be picked up once a month. "You wait that long," he snaps, "and you won't be able to pick it up."

Hardly has he settled in when his straight woman enters. According to Groucho, United Artists "had plans to make Lisette Verea the greatest European import since the Volkswagen." As it happened, "*A Night in Casablanca* may have been the only movie she ever made." Her truncated career was no accident. She was comelier than Margaret Dumont, but nowhere near as heated or humorous as Thelma Todd. Other than a coy manner and an indefinable accent, she had little to offer to the film, and nothing to offer Groucho. Nevertheless, he plays on, as if the material were equal to his delivery. An agent for the Germans, she introduces herself:

VEREA

I'm Beatrice Rheiner. I stop at the hotel.

GROUCHO

I'm Ronald Kornblow. I stop at nothing. . . . You know, I think you're the most beautiful woman in the whole world.

VEREA

Do you really?

GROUCHO

No, but I don't mind lying if it'll get me somewhere.

VEREA

I'm singing at the supper club later. Won't you join me?

GROUCHO

Why, are you coming apart? (*VEREA saunters off. He watches the regular swaying of her hips*) That reminds me. I must get my watch fixed.

He is equally brusque at the front desk. A harrumphing executive and his dreadnaught wife attempt to check in.

GROUCHO

Have you got any baggage?

EXEC

Of course. It's on its way over from the airfield.

GROUCHO

In all the years I've been in the hotel business, that's the phoniest excuse I've ever heard. I suppose your name is Smith!

EXEC

No, it's Smythe—spelled with a "y."

GROUCHO

Oh, that's the English version. Mr. and Mrs. Smythe and no baggage! Let me see your marriage license.

EXEC

What! How dare you, sir?

GROUCHO

How do you like that? Puts a "y" in Smith and expects me to let him into the hotel with a strange dame!

EXEC

Str—Strange dame!

GROUCHO

She is to me. I've never seen her before.

EXEC

Sir, you may not be aware of it, but I am President of the Moroccan Laundry Company.

GROUCHO

You are? Well, take this shirt and have it back Friday! Mr. Smythe, or Smith, this is a family hotel and I suggest you take your business elsewhere.

EXEC

Sir, this lady is my wife. You should be ashamed!

GROUCHO

If this lady is your wife, *you* should be ashamed.

EXEC

My attorneys will be here in the morning!

GROUCHO

Yeah? Well, they won't get a room either, unless they've got a marriage license.

Between these echoes of the old comedy, Harpo mimes desperate messages and Chico acts as interpreter: "Eat-a chop suey? Eat-a rice. Eat-soup. Soup. Rice. Souprice. Surprise. You gotta surprise for Kornblow!"

Harpo crashes against his questioner. Chico immediately understands. "Somebody's gonna bump him off." Further gestures indicate that the assassination will take place in a lady's hotel room. Which lady? Harpo imitates a bomber. The B-29 is abbreviated to a simple B. He manipulates Chico's arm. "B-twist. Bea-twist. Beatrice!" Chico conveys the information to the manager. Groucho grumbles, "I don't mind being killed, but I resent hearing it from a character whose head comes to a point."

The narrative allows Groucho only a few more opportunities at insult comedy. Beatrice attempts to lure him yet again: He pays a call, flowers in hand.

VEREA

Ah, roses. I shall keep them forever.

GROUCHO

That's what you think. I only rented them for an hour.

VEREA

Oh, Mr. Kornblow.

GROUCHO

Call me Montgomery.

VEREA

Is that your name?

GROUCHO

No, I'm just breaking it in for a friend.

During the filming Groucho worked on Miriam, and on himself, selling the idea that *A Night in Casablanca* was bound to revitalize all the Marx Brothers' careers. "The picture may turn out surprisingly well," he wrote her. "We have scenes that I don't think Chico would ever have learned had we not played the stuff on the road. We have been getting along famously with Archie Mayo—he's no genius, but he's far better than Buzzell. Buzzell tried to graft his personality on us and it just didn't work." He went so far as to sign the euphoric letter "Ronald Kornblow." As filming entered the final period, he dared to say he considered himself "Fairly happy . . . the picture is almost over and I think it's going to be good.

Kibbee thinks it's going to be the best. That I don't agree with but I think it will be a whole lot better than the last three we made at MGM." At the end of the year he saw the completed film and reported, "the general feeling is that it's going to be good. Audiences laughed a lot at the stuff on stage so I'm sure they will when they see the picture. The last reel is a wild chase, apparently a basic requisite for a comedy. I think it's quite ingenious and pretty exciting." Mid-January 1946, the old Groucho reappeared. "I was terribly depressed at the preview. We had worked so long and hard on this, and thought we had it so solid and tight, and then to see reams of it emasculated by that fat idiot [Mayo], well it was heart rending." A week later he filed a stronger denunciation: "Although the picture has some good stuff in it, it still needs a world of fixing with perhaps some reshooting. Mayo's work was just hideous. He has managed to take some of the best scenes we did on the stage and wring them dry. David Loew, who originally was so strong for him, after the second preview sadly confessed that he had made a mistake and that Mayo's direction was shockingly old-fashioned. We are now running it in the projection room, clipping and cutting and pasting together, and it may eventually be all right but it's going to take a lot of work. Some of the damage is irreparable."

There was more damage on the home front. This was Miriam's first long stretch away from home, and Groucho wrote weekly letters to the Bennington freshman. They included all sorts of information, about the dog, about Hollywood, about her uncles—about everything except for the most important news of all: Kay was pregnant. It was obvious to anyone who knew him that Groucho had at last found a sexually compatible partner. It was difficult enough for Miriam to accept that the rival for her father's affection had won out. Even more painful was the knowledge that Groucho had not bothered to tell her that she would shortly have a stepsister; she gleaned that information from a newspaper column. Miriam blasted her father in a letter, and for once he rushed to apologize. Thereafter, he tried to keep Miriam informed of his domestic life—she was one of the first to know about the new house, for example. Groucho and Kay had put the Westwood place up for sale; in a few months they would move to 1277 Sunset Plaza Drive. But Miriam had been wounded too deeply by this time, and kept an emotional distance from her father and the stepmother who was once her crony. A new flurry of letters offered a double portrait of two affectionate, neurotic individuals who knew exactly how to prey on each other's vulnerability. Miriam's sparse letters prove the validity of Lord Halifax's observation that love is presently out of breath when it has to travel uphill from the child to the parent. Groucho's wavered between affection and irresponsibility. Now that he had a new and successful marriage, he could allow himself to be solicitous about his ex-wife. In one message he expresses concern for Ruth, advising Miriam, "See if you can't shake her out of this alcoholic haze. She needs someone strong to rely on"—as if Miriam had the objectivity and skill to treat an alcoholic. Nevertheless the freshman made an attempt during her winter break from college, staying with Ruth at the Gramercy Park Hotel, then heatedly moving out on New Year's Day, 1946, because the two were at each other's throats. Groucho barely alludes to this incident as he takes on different tones. He can be inappropriately coy: "I look at your picture every day in my bedroom, or does that sound like an old maudlin beer song? At any rate, you're not a bad looking girl. Would you like to exchange photos?" In a couple of messages he becomes an authentically worried parent. Addressing himself to Miriam's radical politics, yet hesitant to impose his own, he mentions a planned dinner at the Marx home. "Your dream girl Dorothy Parker will be there, and I told her all about you. As a matter of fact, I never speak to her that she doesn't inquire about you. I told her about your attending a Communist meeting in the big City . . . and that seemed to make her very happy. I don't want you to be a Communist; all I expect you to be is a good liberal American, and I am sure that you have enough sense for this. I certainly have no objection to your attending any kind of a meeting that interests you, and I think that is the only way you can decide what you want to be."

In a follow-up letter, Groucho's relief is palpable: "I read with considerable interest that you have retired from the Communist party and that the mantle of Emma Goldman is flung from your shoulders and that you are no longer warmed by the heat from the Stalin candle. As you know, I am in complete accord with you in this and have at times made myself extremely unpopular with certain groups out here with whom you are familiar. To them, Stalinites can do no wrong. Despite the fact that they are gobbling up half of Europe and a good hunk of Asia, they are just as stoutly defended by these fanatics as though it were a small kingdom in the Balkans completely surrounded by enemies. You know that I have never tried to persuade you one way or another because I knew that your common sense would convince you that there is only one way—and that's the American way—for us. This sounds trite but I can't help it— these kinds of phrases are grabbed upon by charlatans and used for their own purposes."

Without warning, however, Groucho can seize on his daughter's insecurities: "Perhaps it's the excess weight that you've put on that's responsible for your pessimism." Kay "is getting fat and will soon equal you except that you are not having a baby, I don't think." "Keep dieting— remember, you still have to catch a man." On the subject of sex he first adopts a lighthearted manner: "I am happy to hear that the man you are going with at the moment is not a fairy; I should have known this—I am sure that no one on the Luce publications is anything but virile." Then he switches to innuendo: "What about a boyfriend—do you have anyone or are you reduced to just going around with women? You don't say much about this side of your life so you are either hiding a dark secret or Mr. Right . . . hasn't come along yet."

Threading through these letters is another Groucho, acting as Jewish father, half-serious, and wholly guilt-producing: "I was deeply disappointed when your lover the mailman arrived today without a letter from you in his sack. Apparently our correspondence only blooms when you need something (like money, for example)." "Your letter was very disappointing. It seems to me that after an intermission of three weeks you could think of something more interesting to write about than an MGM musical." "I don't know why I should write to you again. This is the third letter and no mail from you. . . . For a few days, I seriously toyed with the idea of not sending you any more money but the picture of you being arrested for vagrancy in the swamps of Vermont melted my stony heart; hence the check."

Kay's pregnancy did little to elevate Groucho's spirits. En route to the birth of her first child she suffered from bronchitis and tooth trouble. The dental work afforded a glimpse of episodes to come. The Marxes gave a dinner party, Groucho wrote, at which Kay's dental pain "grew increasingly worse, she had two drinks and was plastered and was staggering around the library like a chicken with its head chopped off." Then came the exhausting business of the film itself. No miracle had taken place in the editing room. Groucho saw the final version and held his head in his hands; rather than improving *A Night in Casablanca,* Mayo's editing had emphasized its faults. "The scoring is bad, the direction is putrid and the photography (maybe that's all for the best) is dark," Groucho summarized. Loew "keeps saying, 'Don't worry, it will make money.' Of course it will, what the hell wouldn't in these times, but it would make even more had it been a great picture. Well, live and learn. But unfortunately I never do. I will be just as stupid next time."

Thus Groucho was genuinely surprised when the Brothers' twelfth movie opened across the country—the good reactions were more positive than he had any right to expect, and the bad were nowhere as pejorative as they might have been. Abel Green, the editor of *Variety,* filed an early review praising "Groucho's madcap antics" and predicting that the picture would be "appealing to the fans familiar with their style and will be wholly new to the next generation." Like most magazines, *Newsweek* acknowledged that "this is not the best picture they have ever done, but it is the Marx brothers, and that in itself should satisfy a great many people." The *New York Times* dragged its feet: "The world should be noticeably happier this morning considering that the Marx Brothers are back on the screen, after a five year absence, in *A Night in Casablanca,* which arrived Saturday. But the sad truth is that this battered old world is not much merrier than it was, say, on Friday, for the spark seems to have gone from the madcap Marxes. They are still wonderfully funny when hitting on all six, but too often the gags sound as wheezy as an old model T Ford panting uphill on two cylinders." But if the journalists had lost their enthusiasm for the Brothers, the high-toned critics remained in place. *Theater Arts* observed, "Whether throwing a hotel dining room into consternation with their frantic endeavors to rearrange the furniture, or confounding a packer by invisibly emptying his trunks faster than he fills them, they piece together the complicated mechanism of absurdity with as delicate a skill as ever." In England, the *New Statesman and Nation* had good news: "After five years, all one asked of them was that they should do it again. They've done it again. *A Night in Casablanca* does little more than mimic its predecessors, though retaining some pristine qualities. But it's very funny at times, and one forgives much merely because they're back." Groucho was especially pleased when James Agee, writing in *The Nation,* treated the comedian as a fellow intellectual: "Groucho, working with extremely sophisticated wit rather than comedy, has always been slowed and burdened by his audience, even on the stage. He needs an audience that could catch the weirdest curves he could throw, and he needs to have no anxiety or responsibility toward even a blunter minority, let alone majority. . . . Because there is no sufficient audience for the use of the brain for fun's sake, I suspect that we lose, in Groucho, the funniest satirist of the century."

Nearing fifty-six, Groucho was too old to have his head turned by such flattery, but it made him more amenable to be around. A good thing, too; the week that *A Night in Casablanca* opened in New York, Kay gave birth to a baby girl in California. They named her Melinda; all of Minnie's granddaughters—Harpo's Minnie, Chico's Maxine, Groucho's Miriam—were given a name beginning with *M* in her honor. Groucho was head of a family again, and little Melinda drew husband and wife together, even as she gave Miriam another reason to stay away from home. It was difficult enough to vie with Kay for her father's affections. There was no way she could rival a sibling in diapers.

•

THE EXPECTED OFFERS from film studios failed to materialize. Harpo stayed in semiretirement, doing an occasional personal appearance. Chico toured with his piano and band. Nearing sixty, he prided himself on his reputation as a bon vivant. He delighted in the backstage sign at the Roxy Theater in New York, placed there by the director of the chorus line: ANY GIRL FOUND ON CHICO MARX'S FLOOR WILL BE IMMEDIATELY FIRED! Groucho had neither the thrill of the chase nor the satisfaction of a theatrical paycheck. No one was interested in his amorous activities; no one wanted to see him play the guitar or front for a band. Offers from radio programs were sparse, and for a long while only the Dinah Shore program offered him regular employment. There he sang duets with the hostess, swallowed his pride, and recited cornball routines that he would have been loath to do as a boy in vaudeville:

GROUCHO

I'm a son of the old west. I'll never forget my horse, Old Paint. But he up and died.

DINAH

What did he die of?

GROUCHO

Old paint. I got so many cows I don't know how many cows there are.

DINAH

Didn't you ever count their heads?

GROUCHO

I couldn't. They was always facing the other way.

"It's a living," he explained to colleagues; at least it enabled him to kid the script, puncturing the dialogue with ad-libs like "Don't forget, Dinah, I can't compete with you. I haven't got your equipment," and, interrupting himself when he hit a high note, "I'll lay an egg any minute now." Only once did he let slip his real feelings, when he complained to Arthur, "I just don't understand it. I think I'm as good as Benny and Bob Hope and the rest of those guys. As a matter of fact, I was once much bigger on the stage than they've ever been. And yet I lose every sponsor I get, and they go on year after year with the same sponsors. What's wrong with me that I can't click on radio?" Neither Marx could supply a credible theory.

Groucho's other source of income through the mid-1940s came from product endorsements. The advertisements helped him in two ways: they paid his bills, and they kept his name and image before the public. Groucho's face had a way of popping up unexpectedly in major newspapers, and in such large-circulation magazines as *Life, The Saturday Evening Post,* and *Collier's.* There seemed to be nothing to which he would not lend his name: Stratford Regency pens, Arrow shirts, *Reader's Digest,* Blackstone cigars, Old Gold cigarettes, Blatz beer, Personna razor blades ("so sharp it could take the beard off my jokes"). If the company paid, Groucho enthused about the merchandise.

Still, these ads took up space, not time. For full effect Groucho needed to move bent-kneed across a room, to speak lines to a lady that relied on timing and intonation, not merely the size of the typeface. So when United Artists producer Sam Coslow dangled a large part in *Copacabana,* he leaped at the chance. His costar would be the South American personality Carmen Miranda, celebrated for wearing hats made of tropical vegetation and singing Portuguese lyrics at phenomenal speed. Groucho would play her shady agent, twice peddling his client to the Copacabana club, first as a vivacious piece of exotica, then as the veiled and mysterious Madamoiselle Fifi. He would also get to sing the Kalmar-Ruby song from *Go West,* and, as an added attraction, Kay would have a small part.

Just as Groucho forecast, self-deception clouded his judgment from first to last. He admired Miranda's talent and generosity—"She seemed to have hundreds of relatives back in Brazil," he commented, "all of whom she supported." What he failed to see was how grotesque she could be as a performer, and how much room she took in every scene. Anxious not to impersonate Hugo Z. Hackenbush, the on-screen Groucho became, in the memorable term of lyricist Johnny Mercer, Mr. In-Between. He wore a business suit rather than his customarily raffish formal wear, but he spoke, or tried to speak, in the cascading style he had made famous. He sported a moustache, but not the one made of greasepaint or one that he had grown himself. This was a paste-on affair, too abbreviated for a guardsman, too bushy for a popinjay; looking in the mirror he was reminded of Frenchy. He involved himself in the composition of the picture, saw to it that three writers were fired, and then complained about the new ones. When the shooting was done Groucho talked himself into another bout of Pollyannaism. "We previewed *Copacabana* the other night in Glendale and for a first preview it was astonishingly good," he wrote Miriam. "You must remember that they had no story and no names and no money (this last fact I wasn't aware of until we had been shooting two weeks) and we were surrounded by incompetents." Still bitter about Chico's threat to sue if he didn't get the money his brothers had put aside for him, Groucho added, "The only reason I took the job is because it was the only one offered to me, except for making a Marx Brothers picture, something I have no more desire for or interest in."

By and large the American critics were kind. They quoted one of the few memorable lines, spoken by Groucho in response to the question "Why are you always chasing women?": "I'll let you know when I catch one." They scarcely mentioned Alfred E. Green's uninspired direction and tried to find positive things to say about the comedy. "Its only notable distinction," said the *New York Times*, "is the fact that it has Groucho Marx. To the credit of the dauntless comedian, it must be said that he does his level best with the limited loopholes toward diversion that the situation affords." *Time* cheerfully dubbed Groucho "the face that launched a thousand quips," and *Newsweek* stated that "*Copacabana* manages a number of lively moments, most of which are provided by Groucho Marx." The British press was in no mood for flattery. Typically, the *Standard* found that Groucho gave "only a shadow of his old performances," and the *Spectator* went out of its way to denigrate the comedian's "little waxed moustache." Yes, the periodical granted, "from time to time his enormous gift for wisecracks comes triumphantly to the fore, but even so the breathless speed of delivery has been cancelled out; every joke is laboriously built up to and is followed by a ghastly pause for laughter. . . . Poor Groucho remains a rather sad wanderer in search of his vanished brothers." As usual, Groucho's postmortem was the most succinct: "I played second banana to the fruit on Carmen Miranda's head."

•

IN THE STRANGE and consequential year of 1947, Groucho got a chance to show Miriam what he meant by the term "good liberal." The House Committee on Un-American Activities had determined that Hollywood was a hotbed of subversive activity, and it began a highly publicized investigation into the political affiliations of producers, directors, and performers. A group of nineteen Hollywood professionals came into their crosshairs, refused to cooperate, and were immediately given the title of Unfriendly Witnesses. Taking a leaf from Groucho, director Billy Wilder said that only two of the nineteen were talented; the rest were just unfriendly. The kidding stopped when battle lines were drawn. On the right, a handful of show business personalities cheered on HUAC. One of the most vocal was Sam Wood, director of *A Night at the Opera* and no favorite of the Brothers. Speaking of the people he regarded as dangerous, he informed the congressmen, "If you mention that you are opposed to the Communist Party, then you are anti-labor, anti-Semitic, or anti-Negro, and you will end up being called a Fascist, but they never start that until they find out you are opposed to the Communist Party; but if you wanted to drop their rompers you would find the hammer and sickle on their rear ends, I think."

The attacked—liberals, free speech advocates, and full-throated Party members—agreed on one point. These irresponsible investigations were terrifying the town and encouraging a blacklist. They would have to be stopped. To that end, directors William Wyler and John Huston and scenarist Philip Dunne organized the Committee for the First Amendment. "Any investigation into the political beliefs of the individual," stated its press release, "is contrary to the basic principles of our democracy. Any attempt to curb freedom of expression and to set arbitrary standards of Americanism is in itself disloyal to both the spirit and the letter of the Constitution."

Variety described the group's tactic as a way to "backfire against the House Un-American Activities Committee via a drive to battle the top headlines out of Washington each day." Groucho was flattered to be asked to join the First Amendment group; within days he saw his name in the papers alongside those of Frederic March ("Who do you really think they're after? They're after you"), Humphrey Bogart (HUAC "is not empowered to tell Americans what to think"), and Danny Kaye ("Most fair-minded Americans hope the Committee will abandon the practice of merely providing a forum to those who for political purposes or otherwise seek headlines they could not otherwise obtain").

But in keeping with tradition, Groucho was uncomfortable with his new affiliation. The problem was that some of the people he was required to defend were the very ones he had cautioned Miriam about—those who had warmed themselves by the heat from the Stalin candle. Screenwriter John Howard Lawson, one of the nineteen, had made no secret of his Party membership; he wrote about it in *New Theater* magazine back in 1934. Albert Maltz, another screenwriter and onetime Communist, later admitted, "I felt the Party was the best hope of mankind." In the end Groucho decided to become a protester because of his loathing of the probers, not out of any affection for the accused. Friends suggested that the hearings resembled nothing more than a Marx Brothers routine, and that was the way Groucho came to regard them. And, at several points, they did seem to be an extension of something performed by Groucho, Chico, and Harpo. Bertolt Brecht, for example, had been a man of the left on two continents. But he made monkeys of the investigators by acting the part of a confused émigré. To aid him in his ruse, the playwright and sometime scenarist brought a translator whose German accent was even thicker than his own. Blinking amiably, he answered questions in a style that would have done credit to Chico and Groucho:

INTERROGATOR

Have you attended any Communist Party meetings?

BRECHT

No, I don't think so.

INTERROGATOR

Well, aren't you certain?

BRECHT

No—I am certain, yes.

INTERROGATOR

You are certain you have never been to Communist Party meetings?

BRECHT

Yes, I think so.

INTERROGATOR

You are certain?

BRECHT

I think I am certain.

INTERROGATOR

You think you are certain?

BRECHT

Yes, I have not attended such meetings, in my opinion.

Not to be outdone, writer/director Herbert Biberman attempted to avoid answering the question of whether or not he was a Communist. In the process, he and the Committee chairman, J. Parnell Thomas, engaged in a duel that might have been performed during the palmy days at Paramount:

BIBERMAN

It has become very clear to me that the real purpose of this investigation—

THOMAS

(*Pounding gavel*) That is not an answer to the question—

BIBERMAN

—is to drive a wedge—

THOMAS

(*Pounding gavel*) That is not the question. (*Pounding gavel again*)

BIBERMAN

—into the component parts—

THOMAS

Not the question—

BIBERMAN

—of the motion picture industry.

THOMAS

Ask him the next question.

HUAC supporters fell into the same disordered spirit. Morrie Ryskind said of screenwriter Lester Cole, one of the Hollywood Ten, "If he isn't a Communist, I don't think Mahatma Gandhi is an Indian." Director Leo McCarey noted that his own film, *Going My Way*, had not won favor in the U.S.S.R.

INVESTIGATOR

What is the trouble?

MCCAREY

Well, I think I have a character in there that they do not like.

INVESTIGATOR

Bing Crosby?

MCCAREY

No, God.

"It's a shame," Groucho remarked later, "that we never had a chance to do a picture about the Hearings. They would have made a hell of a subject for us." That they would have; but the three Marx Brothers were not to be reunited on film for many years. And for a frightening moment, it seemed that they would never work together again. All through the spring of 1947 Chico had been suffering from chest pains. Cardiological exams, rudimentary in those days, were indefinite and he went back on the road, gamely making jokes about his lack of funds. "Groucho and Harpo are rich men," he told a British journalist, "but me, I'm in England." Then, while performing in Las Vegas, he suffered a real heart attack—a major one. He had been traveling with his latest amour, a woman named Mary DeVithas. Originally, Maxine eyed her father's latest flame with suspicion. But when she realized that Mary was the only person who could persuade Chico to retire, the two became friends. As soon as Chico was released from the hospital Groucho tried to effect his own reconciliation. He took to dropping in on his elder brother, mainly to gossip about the old times. In a way it kept Groucho from worrying about himself all the time; Chico was older and sicker and lived in a much smaller house. Indeed, when an accountant asked the reprobate how much he had lost over the years, Chico said he could tell him to the penny. "How much money does Groucho have in the bank?" he said. "That's how much money I've lost gambling." But schadenfreude was only good for a while, and Groucho went back to fretting about his diminished career. As was his custom, he began to use his home as a pressure valve. Little Melinda was excused from his outbursts; he made her the center of his day, breaking off business meetings to run home and spoon-feed her meals or give her a bath. In the process Kay was displaced, just as Ruth had been elbowed aside when Arthur and Miriam were small.

The congruence of the Marx Brothers' comedy and the goings-on in *Alice in Wonderland* had been noted over and over in the Marxes' professional lives. What went unnoticed was the growing similarity between Groucho and Lewis Carroll himself. The American comedian was a more complete person than the English spinner of dreams. Yet there were eerie parallels: both men were emotionally stunted, happier in the company of the very young, who were eager to follow and who offered no real challenge, sexual or intellectual. Virginia Woolf's appraisal of Carroll's psyche could easily have applied to Groucho's: "His childhood was sharply severed. It lodged in him whole and entire. He could not disperse it. And therefore as he grew older this impediment at the center of his being, this hard block of pure childhood, starved the mature man of nourishment." Minnie had taken Groucho's childhood away long ago, and he had been in search of it ever since. In a way, his older brothers had been, too. Harpo found it by becoming a boy himself, first onstage and in films, and now in joining his adopted children on their level.

Through the years Chico maintained his own youthful outlook by a simple subterfuge. He dressed and talked like a grownup—and stubbornly refused to change one iota, acting as recklessly in middle age as he did when he was an irresponsible East Side kid. More mature fiscally and in his intellectual outlook, Groucho never stopped pressing his nose against the windows of childhood's estate. He was forever fascinated by innocence—the kind missing from his early years. One of his favorite routines was to address little girls as miniature adults. "Are you married?" was a standard interrogation; the inevitable puzzled denial proved to him how very young and untainted they were. As soon as the child—any child—grew up, however, his interest waned. Arthur and Miriam had reached their majority, and now Melinda took their place. If Groucho ran true to form, she would be his new romance, making her mother insignificant as time went on.

Susan, Harpo's wife, remembered this period, and how Kay, "the lovely and eager young bride, cooked beautifully, and would make interesting little things. She knocked herself out and then all these celebrated people would come to dinner and Groucho would manage during the evening to make her feel like a fool. So that all her efforts were destroyed." Decades before, Ruth had started out strong, and she had held herself together for decades until alcohol got the better of her. Kay had no such reserves to fall back on. She was physically and psychologically fragile, and she and the marriage withered quickly under Groucho's sarcasm and threats. Sunny Sauber was present when Kay disagreed with her husband on some minor household matter. "If you don't shut up," he snapped, "I'm going to throw you out in the gutter where you came from!" To complicate matters, Miriam chose this time to begin hitting the bottle. She looked back on this time with rue: "My mother had the gene that most alcoholics do, and I inherited it. Of course, Groucho didn't help matters. Women were never his strong point."

During all the various family crises and political complications, Groucho continued to make his radio appearances, taking his accustomed refuge in comedy—any kind of comedy. His spirits fell so low that he did something he had never done before—audition as a successor for another comedian. The man he was trying to succeed, Phil Baker, was the MC of the popular $64 Question quiz show. Groucho was turned down. Fearful of losing status, he began to accept any job that came along. Working at anything was better than collecting dust. When a radio producer, Manny Mannheim, dangled a one-shot on the Walgreen radio show, Groucho instantly accepted the offer. There was nothing to mark that program as special; it was to feature many stars including Bob Hope and Art Linkletter, a preeminent quiz-show master of ceremonies. The night of the broadcast, Hope was on mike for most of the program. Groucho was expected to come on in a comedy skit immediately after the thirty-minute break. Other guest appearances ran long, however, and he waited with mounting impatience for Hope's cue, "Why, Groucho Marx! What are you doing way out here in the Sahara Desert?" Groucho was supposed to identify himself as a traveling salesman, but his temper took over. "Desert, hell!" he fumed. "I've been standing in a drafty corridor for forty-five minutes." Hope went limp with laughter and the script slipped from his hands. Groucho put his foot on it. For the next twenty-five minutes the two comedians improvised their exchanges, much of them taken up with references to a notorious Los Angeles madam, and all of them amusing to the people in the seats. Mannheim enjoyed the comedy as much as they did. The show was transcribed; later he would excise the blue material and save the rest for commercial purposes.

The element of chance, always significant in Groucho's life, played a vital role that night. Backstage was a young packager of prime-time audience participation shows, including Linkletter's. John Guedel paid a visit to Groucho's dressing room after the Walgreen show was done. "Tell me something," he requested. "How come you don't have a show of your own?"

"If you must know," Groucho told him, "I haven't got a sponsor. And when I get one, I can't keep one."

"Do you want to know why? I can tell you."

"Yeah?" Groucho responded belligerently. "Why?"

"Very simple. On all the shows I've ever heard you on, you were tied down to a script. In my opinion, you never quite came off on a script show. Lots of people can read lines better than you. But nobody can touch you when it comes to ad-libbing. You should be doing a show without a script so you can utilize the thing you do best."

Groucho calmed down. "Well, if I had a good idea for one, and I could get a sponsor, I'd be glad to."

Guedel volunteered to go home and think of one. Three days later he presented a page-and-a-half proposal. Groucho looked it over doubtfully. He had trouble seeing himself as the host of a quiz show: "I don't know if I can do the glad-hand bit, and be sincere." He showed the outline to friends and to his family. Then he faced down their demurs and decided to take the risk. After all, John Guedel had enjoyed an enormous success with the MC Art Linkletter. With smiling faces and private trepidation, Groucho and Guedel signed a fifty-fifty partnership deal including $125 each for the audition record; booked time at NBC; and arranged for the necessary engineer and announcer. Word went out, and among other publications, *Newsweek* printed a report: "Top-rank comics are mapping new-type audience participation shows. Groucho Marx has one called Betcha Life."

Later, Groucho could afford to admit that he "wasn't particularly proud of doing a quiz show. It was like slumming." In this view he was not alone. Marx fans were willing to overlook mistakes like *At the Circus* and *Copacabana*—even clowns have to eat. But to think of Captain Jeffrey T. Spaulding, Professor Quincy Wagstaff, and Dr. Hugo Z. Hackenbush melted down and turned into a Rotarian MC—that was too dire to contemplate. Likening the comedian to a champion racehorse, *Newsweek* described this latest career move. It was "like selling Citation to a glue factory."

CHAPTER THIRTEEN

Two Soft Rackets

NEITHER ABC, CBS, NOR NBC EVINCED much interest in broadcast-ing John Guedel's quiz show, but that was before the producer made a Holmesian deduction. About a month after Groucho cut the audition record, a provocative item appeared in the *Daily Variety*. It noted that Al Gellman, president of the Elgin-American compact company, was com-ing to the Beverly Hills Hotel for a brief stay to sign Phil Baker as MC of a new quiz show, *Everybody Wins*. "The story," Guedel noticed, "said 'com-ing to.' That meant he hadn't signed him yet. So I called him up at the hotel and told him, 'I have a record of Groucho.'" Gellman brightened at the name. "Groucho Marx. I remember him in *The Cocoanuts*."

He agreed to listen to the recording and liked what he heard. Guedel treasured the memory. "Gellman didn't know Groucho had flopped four times on the radio, so he bought the show. Then we took it to the Ameri-can Broadcasting Company, and that's how it happened to be on ABC. Phil Baker, I understand, fired his publicist for putting that item in the gossip column before the deal was actually signed. I don't blame him."

The show was designed with the utmost simplicity. Groucho asked questions in four categories, $100, $90, $80, and $70. Contestants came on in pairs; they would be allowed only one answer between them, and they could win as much as $440. The couple that won the most money that evening was allowed one crack at a final, difficult question for a $100 bonus. Groucho was pleased with the format until Bernie Smith advised him to assume a frock coat and painted moustache for every broadcast. "The hell I will," Groucho responded testily. "That character's dead." Smith protested: "But the public won't know who you are. We've got to have you in something. Will you *grow* a moustache?" That Groucho agreed to do. He also went along with the idea of using writers to punch up his interviews with the guests. Five men would make contributions: Smith (listed as a director, but actually the chief writer), Elroy Schwartz, Ed "Doc" Tyler, Howard Harris, and Hy Freedman, who commented later, "Sometimes Groucho wouldn't even have to say a line. A pretty girl would come out and up would go the eyebrows. It was a great show for a writer, an easy and pleasurable show to do."

Too easy and too pleasurable, at first. *You Bet Your Life,* as it was officially billed, debuted in October 1947, as a semiscripted program. Staffers screened the contestants, picking up biographical details, before Groucho dallied with them. With these details as a basis for gags, the writers went to work. Since the show was transcribed, Groucho could make mistakes and double entendres with impunity. They would all be weeded out. The host and his editors did their best to make the proceedings seem unrehearsed; even so, the half-hours seemed to drag. In the *New York Times,* critic Jack Gould was one of the first to find fault: "Among radio's unresolved problems is the full utilization of the talents of Groucho Marx, a man of brains and capital comic ability. . . . Trouper that he is, Mr. Marx works hard and does his best, but the show never really comes off. Somewhere along the line the delightful silliness of Mr. Marx's act has been confused with the exhibitionistic absurdity of the average radio quiz. Radio Row to the contrary, the two are not the same. One happy day Mr. Marx will break into radio; he will be assigned a program without a stylized format."

You Bet Your Life made some brisk changes in approach and style. It was decided that the show needed a stronger air of spontaneity, even if the host had to fake it. Audiences could see that Groucho knew too much about his guests beforehand, and his prebroadcast interviews were shortened. To add spice to the proceedings a "secret word" became part of the fare: if a contestant unwittingly said that evening's choice of common noun—"chair," "egg," "shoe"—there would be a $100 reward. Groucho hated the proposed idea of sirens sounding when the prizes were given. What if a comely model brought it out? True, the home audience would be denied a glimpse, but the studio audience could see her, and they would set up an air of merriment. Even in 1947 this was thought to be a cliché, and the producers turned it down. He made another suggestion. How about getting laughs from money instead of the other way around? Recalling the "Why a Duck?" routine from *The Cocoanuts,* Groucho proposed that a bird decoy could be dangled from above, carrying currency in its beak. Everyone liked that idea, and a bespectacled wooden duck became the show's emblem. Before the first month was out, there arose the Loser Problem—the quiz was legitimate, and many contestants, having failed to answer the question, walked away with nothing. "When people go broke up there, I'm embarrassed," Groucho told his colleagues. "I feel they ought to have something, to give the thing an up note when they leave. Can't we ask a simple question like, 'Who's President of the United States?' or 'Who's buried in Grant's Tomb?' or something?" The Grant's Tomb question won instant favor with audiences.

And still some vital ingredient was missing. Groucho had always needed a foil—Chico, Margaret Dumont, a character actor against whom he could bounce his lines. George Fenneman would play that part. Originally hired to read ad copy about Elgin compacts, the personable young announcer amused Groucho from the start. "I did my first commercial," Fenneman remembered, "and he thought there was something in the lines I said. Something about, 'Have you looked at your compact lately?,' some romantic thing with violins going. He said, 'Who is this man? Is he a man?,' and he went on and on. I obviously said some of the right things back and each week he interrupted me more, and before I knew it, I was doing the whole show." As Groucho sagely observed, "There never was a comedian who was any good without a straight man. And George was straight on all four sides." Whenever Fenneman stumbled over a line or failed to add the prize money correctly, Groucho zinged him with a wisecrack. "It blossomed into this give-and-take," Fenneman testified, "with me always on the receiving end. In the beginning I guess I took some of the humor personally. I know I wasn't stupid, but when I finished the show I wasn't sure."

During the first season the staff and host worked out an infallible formula. From a group of good-looking women in the audience, the most extroverted were selected to appear on *You Bet Your Life*. Other guests were chosen for their personalities, with special attention paid to foreigners with pronounced accents; their intonations and hesitant answers made them Groucho's ideal prey. When he got too sharp, the producers advised him to let up a little, introduce his newest child to the show, let the audience know he was human. The interlude, in Guedel's words, "doesn't have to be full of big laughs. The main purpose is to show the people in the studio that you have a little girl, that you love her very much, and that underneath that cold-blooded exterior of yours is a very devoted father and warm person. That'll make them like you, they'll want to laugh all the more when you say something funny during the show. And that feeling will carry right over the air waves too." As soon as he made his point, Guedel experienced twinges of guilt. Who was he to tell a great comedian how to get laughs? He backtracked: "Don't pay any attention to what I said. Just go out there and do what you feel like doing. You were bigger in show business once than I'll ever be." For once, Groucho gave in. "I've lost every sponsor I've ever had," he remarked sadly. "All your shows have been successful." Following the producer's counsel, Groucho moderated his onslaught and made a point of bringing Melinda onstage. After such occasions, Guedel recalled, the MC would scrape for praise: "Wasn't I warm tonight?" or, referring to the altruistic star of a soap opera, "Wasn't I the Jewish Dr. Christian?" That he was—but the real Groucho could not be suppressed for long. The same week he was ingratiating himself with studio audiences, Guedel added, "he'd go out on the street and a woman would come up to him and he'd say, 'Get lost.' And she'd think it was so funny, and he's really telling her to get lost. Anybody else they'd slap in the face."

Ratings for the first few weeks provided little in the way of encouragement. *You Bet Your Life* came in ninety-sixth overall. But the statistics were misleading. Rather than reflecting Groucho's popularity, the number indicated the weakness of his venue: ABC was the smallest of the three networks, with lackluster programming throughout its schedule. The real proof of the show's impact came when the sponsor withdrew for the last five weeks, not because of Groucho's inability to draw audiences but because Elgin-American had sold all of its compacts. The company saw no point in advertising until the stock could be replenished.

With Groucho back in the news, mention was made of yet another farewell film for the Brothers. Early in 1948 two producers, Lester Cowan and former silent star Mary Pickford, announced plans to bring the Marxes back to the screen. *Diamonds in the Sidewalk,* based on an outline by Harpo, would be scripted by Ben Hecht. The notion of Harpo writing anything more complicated than a grocery list amused Groucho, but the fact was that the man who had once written "You are ded" during a game with Alexander Woollcott had come a long way. Harpo's son Bill described his father as "a happy agglomeration of surprises and contradictions." The man who never got through *McGuffey's First Reader* "went on to read, and savor, Tolstoy and Dickens. His favorite words were 'perspicacity' and 'penultimate.' When challenged he could reel off the correct spelling of 'chrysanthemum' or 'antidisestablishmentarianism.' "
Some vestiges of the old days could not be expunged; Harpo's private list

of stage props never failed to include "sizzers," "karit," "dimund ring," and "telliscoap." Proud of Harpo's accomplishment, and bearing in mind Chico's omnipresent need for another payday, Groucho agreed to make the film. Still, *Diamonds* was low down on his agenda; secretly he had a feeling that it might never be made. Ben Hecht was in great demand; the scenarist of *Wuthering Heights* and *Spellbound* would not be free anytime soon.

Tops on Groucho's to-do list was the completion of a stage comedy. He and Norman Krasna had been refining *Time for Elizabeth* for a dozen years, and in the spring of 1948 the magic word "Curtain" had finally been typed. Backers were recruited, actors auditioned and hired. *Time for Elizabeth* would open in the fall, directed by Krasna. All along, Groucho had planned to star in the play, but the demands of his quiz show made that impossible. Paul Lukas, one of Hollywood's dependable romantic leads, agreed to take the part, practically guaranteeing a box office smash. On the domestic side, Groucho was not only the father of a baby girl, he also became the grandfather of a baby boy: Irene, Arthur's wife, gave birth to Steven Marx just ten months after Melinda was born. Groucho experienced some lingering trouble with the idea of grandfatherhood. He failed to visit Irene when she was in the maternity ward of Cedars of Lebanon, allegedly because a friend of his had died at that hospital. Once she and the child were home, however, he became effusive, the quintessential baby-talking elder—except that this elder, unlike most men in their late fifties, was enjoying a career renaissance.

In the seesaw relationship of private and professional life the Marx women plummeted as Groucho rose. Ruth's heavy drinking continued and she remained a burden on those she had left behind. In a letter to Miriam, Padre overplays his side of the situation, placing the student between two warring parents: "I received a notification from Bennington that tuition was due for the next year. I told you last year that I had paid two years and that your mother should carry you the rest." Ruth had chosen to marry again, this time to a professional stage manager, which was fine with Groucho. What was not fine was Ruth's insistence on receiving payments to the end of time.

"When we separated I gave her over $200,000 and insurance policies. . . . I am now supporting your mother and a strange man. I overlook the point that she should have pride enough to refuse this money, but I can't overlook the point that since you are her daughter as well as mine, and the kind of a financial settlement she made, she should contribute toward your education. I am therefore returning the papers from Bennington for you to send your mother." Little wonder, given this background, that Miriam's own alcoholism led to angry, disordered behavior on and off campus. Her father had already brought her up short when he heard rumors—false, as it turned out—of a dalliance with Ed Sullivan, then a *Daily News* columnist: "I like Sylvia and Ed and it would hurt me to have anything happen to change that relationship. Plus this, it would then be very difficult for me to get my name in his column. I think you have given him quite some encouragement, and I hope you realize that it is always easier to lure a married man than a single one. So don't take too much credit for that conquest." Thornier problems arose, like the time when Miriam was driving under the influence in Massachusetts. As she remembered the incident: "I was visiting a college friend. I was drunk, and got stuck on the [railroad] tracks. My friend and I were able to jump out of the car before it was hit, but the car was badly damaged. I hadn't told my father anything about it until Walter Winchell mentioned it on the radio, at which point I had to give Groucho my own edited version of the events." At times she attempted to please her father—like Arthur, she sought a career as a writer, publishing some promising short stories in *Silo,* an undergraduate magazine. More often she was in some difficulty or other, on campus or off. Additional warnings were issued by Groucho, and by the Bennington deans. These were ignored, and "*l'affaire* Miriam," as her friends called it, ended with expulsion from college only a few weeks before she was scheduled to graduate. "I got the education but not the diploma," she was to say, but it would take decades for this intelligent, sensitive woman to give up drinking and find an altruistic career. After she left college, her eccentric behavior continued for quite some time. Miriam was attractive and responsible enough to land a job as college editor for *Mademoiselle.* She was irresponsible enough to become a local character in Greenwich Village, notorious for her hostile and sometimes fearful glare and the baseball bat she wielded on evening walks.

•

BROADWAY HAD always been kind to the Marx Brothers. Groucho had every reason to expect that *Time for Elizabeth* would add yet another set of raves to his scrapbook. He provoked laughter every week in prime time; Norman Krasna had already proven himself in New York with the hit comedies *Dear Ruth* and *John Loves Mary;* and an excellent midtown theater, the Fulton, had been booked for a September opening. But matters and mores had changed since the Brothers wowed the town in *Animal Crackers,* and rehearsals did not go well. Lukas dropped out, to be replaced by character actor Otto Kruger, best remembered for portraying the elegant villains of *Saboteur* and *Murder My Sweet.* Friends who read the script failed to react positively. "It's astonishing how many people dislike this play," Groucho commented sadly, "but Krasna and I are putting our own money in it as a gesture of nose-thumbing and defiance." The money amounted to $13,000 each, a considerable sum in those days. Still, Groucho preferred to gamble it on Broadway than spend it on his daughter. His priorities were made clear after Miriam and Ruth had a long reconciliation lunch at Chasen's restaurant in Los Angeles. Evidently wine flowed freely; Groucho received a bill for $67.55. He fulminated in a letter to Miriam: "You have a hell of a nerve. I am good and angry about it. I have no intention of letting you get away with this and I am deducting this from your next month's check." Both sides entered apologies in the weeks to come, but the damage was irreparable.

The contentious Groucho, so familiar to Miriam and a few intimate friends, was strangely absent from *Time for Elizabeth.* The play could have used a little heat and spite. In essence, it follows the fortunes of a middle-aged New York businessman, Ed Davis, who quits his demanding job and takes his family to Florida. Once ensconced in his bungalow, the retiree is driven half-mad by the monotony of his schedule and the Babbittry of his neighbors. In the end he heads north to his old job; the grass was greener on his side of the fence after all. There was nothing inherently wrong with the story; it simply needed fewer Krasnian pleasantries and more Grouchovian insults. At the conclusion of act 1, in the presence of his family, Davis tells off his stuffy employer.

SCHAEFFER

Have you gone crazy?

DAVIS

No, I just caught myself in time.

SCHAEFFER

Davis! Get your things and get out!

DAVIS

You mean I'm fired?

SCHAEFFER

You're damn right, you're fired!

DAVIS

You're going to have to pay me two weeks' salary. It's a State law.

SCHAEFFER

You're fired, do you hear me?

DAVIS

Certainly I hear you! They hear you in Yonkers, you big loud-mouth!

SCHAEFFER

Get out of here before I throw you off the premises!

DAVIS

Let's see you do it. Let's see you and your brother-in-law do it.

SCHAEFFER

You're fired!

DAVIS

(To his family) Repeats himself, doesn't he? *(Walks to desk and picks up fountain pen. To SCHAEFFER)* My fountain pen. *(He picks up framed picture)* My wife and daughter. You don't mind?

SCHAEFFER

You're fired!

DAVIS

After twenty-eight years! That's big business for you! Twenty-eight years? Say, I've got a watch coming. *(He takes watch from the desk, looking for some objection from SCHAEFFER. None is forthcoming. He starts out, stopping below armchair to wave at SCHAEFFER before he exits)*

What seems so atypical is the quality of insults: "You big loud-mouth!" "Repeats himself, doesn't he?" Lines like these could have been written by hacks, and indeed *were* written by hacks over the next forty years, as they ground out assembly-line sitcoms. The ending of *Time for Elizabeth* is particularly suggestive of the rigged dialogue and pink-ribbon finales of television half-hour comedy. Here the boss envies his ex-employee's lifestyle and tries to win him back.

SCHAEFFER

I've got one heck of a nerve asking you to give all that up, but I want to make you an offer. If you sign for ten years, I'll give you a piece of the business! Twelve and a half per cent!

DAVIS

Twelve and a half?

SCHAEFFER

Okay, that was my first offer! Fifteen! Shake hands, partner. We've got a deal . . . ! (*Looks around*) My respect grows for you every minute! You certainly know how to live. I pictured you in a big house with servants! But no! You're too smart! A little nest, care-free and cozy. . . . I've had a hard time these past few months! I'm all run down! You owe me something. Why don't you let Lily and me have this for a while? You and the family can take the yacht back to New York. . . .

Any objective observer could have predicted the critical reaction, but Groucho was scarcely an objective observer. He could not come to terms with the fact that his originality was confined to two personae: the absurdist of stage and screen, and the flippant quizmaster of television. When he ventured into the vast territory between these brackets he was always imitating someone: his magazine pieces smacked of Robert Benchley, playing the much put-upon "little man" hounded by larger forces such as the IRS; or S. J. Perelman, mixing slang and literary allusions. The Groucho of *Time for Elizabeth* was another copy, this time of a Broadway hack hoping to entice theater parties for a season or two. So he was truly astonished when the newspapermen of New York spoke in one disappointed voice. In the *Times*, Brooks Atkinson, long a Marx Brothers fan, tried to be gentle: "Mr. Marx wrote it several years ago at the time when he was retiring from the leer, lunge and grease-paint moustachio of his low comedy masquerade, thus depriving America of one of her greatest inventions." What he and Krasna produced was "strictly a perambulator frolic." Now, Atkinson went on, "Mr. Marx has everyone's permission to throw down the pen and put back the moustachio any time he pleases." Ward Morehouse, veteran theater man of the *Sun,* offered much the same complaint in his nineteenth-century baroque style: "I venerate Groucho Marx as a comic since he is one of the few clowns who has been able to make me bust a gallus with the look of his pan alone and before uttering a sound. In my classical book, those ferocious black eyebrows, those panther-glaring black eyeballs and that obscene black moustache, all screwed up into the semblance of a lascivious Tom cat on the precarious snoop for a canary, are the stuff on which dreams are made. But when the exemplary fellow tries his hand at play-writing, as he has in collaboration with Norman Krasna, I pronounce the curse of Cain upon him and bar him from my select society."

In the *Herald Tribune,* Howard Barnes observed: "The acting is far better than the material. Occasional laughter does not keep the latest arrival in town from being anemic." John Chapman, the *Daily News* reviewer, tried to be more comical than the author: "One of the first times I saw Groucho Marx he was slinking around the stage and telling somebody a story about an adventure in love from which he had had to flee. He had fled right out of the glass window, he said. To prove it he offered, 'I'd show you the scars only I know you don't smoke.' This killed me. Well, Mr. Marx has turned playwright in collaboration with another funny fellow, Norman Krasna, and their joint effort is . . . strictly magazine-fiction stuff, and I'd like to show Groucho my scars but I am beginning to fear that he has forgotten how to smoke."

Ring Lardner's son John had his say in the *Star:* "Mr. Marx and Mr. Krasna, having set out to write a routine, sentimental, timeless, plainfolksy—and presumably surefire—comedy of the old school, with here and there a pleasing jest, wind up with a pretty shabby piece of goods on their hands." The *Journal-American's* Robert Garland contented himself with a wisecrack: "*Time for Elizabeth* is no time, good, bad, or indifferent, for me." In the *Post,* Richard Watts gave the playwright reason to believe that he could never wriggle out of Hugo Z. Hackenbush's clawhammer coat. "There might have been more fun in *Time for Elizabeth* at the Fulton last night if Groucho Marx had played in it, instead of being merely its co-author. That is not to speak slightingly of Otto Kruger, who acts the leading role of a tired and rebellious business man with considerable ingratiating charm. The fact remains, though, that the new comedy is such a meek and uneventful little offering that the maniacal frenzy of a couple of Marx Brothers darting through the play's placid narrative is needed to save it from lassitude."

Nothing in fact could save it, and the show expired a week later. As was his custom, Groucho feigned nonchalance and headed home to California. But the reviewers had drawn blood. A month after the final performance he wrote to *Variety* editor Abel Green, "I am slowly recovering from the lacing we received from the New York critics." Labeling the group "a sorry lot," he cited passages from their writings. "Gibbs, for example, in the *New Yorker:* 'There wasn't a joke in the show.' Either he was stewed or he neglected to turn on his hearing apparatus. So many of the reviews were of a personal nature. Lardner, in the *Star,* lampooned me because I had co-authored a play that wasn't sardonic, sarcastic or bitter. Krutch, in the *Nation,* chided me for departing from the character I always portrayed on the screen and stage. Gibbs also had to drag in Hollywood. Judging from the fury with which most of the critics attack the authors, one would think that presenting a play in New York was a criminal offense.

"Well, the hell with them. I have two soft rackets, namely movies and radio, and they will never get another chance to slay me."

A letter to Miriam mixed curses, compensations, and tenses. "I am just beginning to recover from the effects of the pannings. I had no idea how deeply it had left its scars. Fortunately, I am so busy I have very little time to brood about them or the play. I think the critics are unfair bigoted bastards and I don't want any more of them. Let younger fellows take the whippings. Fortunately, I have other ways of making a living, and I don't want to be subjected to their not so tender mercies again. Tonight I have a radio record to cut, and when I am through with it no one compares me with Shaw or Sheridan, or even Molnár, but they all say how clever I was and what a witty man I am, and that's enough salve for my ego at my age."

That was not really enough, but it would have to do. Groucho was especially pleased at the end of his show's first season when *Life* ran one of its traditional features, "Life Goes to a Party." The men at the Hollywood affair were decked out in classic Groucho makeup—except for Groucho, who was made up as Chico. The event varied little from the ones in the 1930s, when George Gershwin and his friends dressed up as the Marxes; the importance, in Groucho's view, was that a national magazine considered him newsworthy. The costume party was significant for another reason. As it went on, Groucho wrote in retrospect, "I noticed a group of guests sitting in a corner. It wasn't until later that I discovered they were complaining about the upcoming Red purge of Hollywood. Of liberal bent and missionary zeal, some feared they'd unwisely lent their names to what were rapidly becoming unpopular causes. I confess I didn't worry too much about the situation at the time. I was happy at ending the first season of the show and looking forward to continuing it in the fall." Soon enough, he would have to confront that purge. But not quite yet; he was having too good a time.

Groucho's impudence not only appealed to listeners, it attracted the attention of the academy. In 1949, the University of Georgia School of Journalism presented him with radio's highest honor, the Peabody Award, as Best Entertainer. As expected, Groucho dismissed the whole thing out of hand. "What's so funny about me winning an award?" he asked an interviewer. "And by the way, who's this fellow Peabody?" Only to family and close friends would he admit that he was "enormously pleased."

Guedel was similarly pleased; he told Groucho that they had the makings of a blockbuster show—and that it would grow no larger if it stayed on the lagging ABC network. First, the producer stooped to pick up the small change. Like most programs, You Bet Your Life took the summer off. It was replaced by a cheaper production featuring a group of old vaudeville comedians, and the ratings fell precipitously. "We were quite concerned," recalled Smith. "Something had to be done or our time slot was going to be shot, and we'd have to start building it all over again in the fall."

Guedel had an inspiration. At a conference with ABC executives, he presented a set of impressive numbers. "Do you fellows know that the average listener hears a show only once out of every 3.4 times that it's on?" he asked.

"I never heard of such a thing," answered one of the vice presidents, "but it's logical and it makes sense."

"Well, that's the figure," Guedel persisted. "So I think it would be wise and it would be safe to run our show again."

The ABC team went back to headquarters to make the case. After they left, Smith asked Guedel, "Where did you get that figure? I never heard of this survey."

Allowing himself a small grin, Guedel answered, "I made it up."

His inventive fiction was persuasive enough for the higher-ups, and thus was born a fresh concept in broadcasting, the summer rerun. Yet even after Guedel factored in thirteen weeks of new income, he felt slighted. The other two networks were racking up larger audiences and higher profits. Why not go to one of them when the ABC contract was finished? The Columbia Broadcasting System had been following the progress of *You Bet Your Life,* and Groucho was welcomed aboard that network in October 1949. It was another good year for the comedian; he was named Best Quizmaster on the air by his colleagues. Bearing in mind Harry Truman's defeat of Thomas Dewey, he quipped, "It just goes to show that a man with a moustache can get elected."

In its first month at CBS *You Bet Your Life* rose to sixth place and stayed there for the season. Elgin-American gave way to a bigger sponsor, the De Soto–Plymouth dealers of America. Groucho's popularity made him quotable all over again. Instead of parroting phrases from the old movies, people spoke of his radio backchat—the query to a tree surgeon ("Have you ever fallen out of a patient?"), the come-on to a pretty contestant ("You've got a good head on your shoulders and I wish it were on mine"), the admonition to a woman with ten children who said she had so many because she loved her husband ("I love my cigar, but I take it out of my mouth once in a while"). The program's real director, Robert Dwan, deemed the last line too bawdy and excised it. Groucho's words made the columns all the same. Critics duly noted that Jack Benny had a jeweler's eye for group comedy, a mastery of the running gag and the momentous pause. And that Fred Allen had no peer when he described a town so dull that one day the tide went out and never came back, or a scarecrow so frightening that the crows returned corn they had stolen two years before. Yet Groucho had something as valuable, and more unusual. He could sit on a stool and speak with civilians—ordinary people with no show business associations—and wring explosive laughs in the studio and across the country.

All the same, Guedel did not rest easy. As the 1940s wound down, *You Bet Your Life* might have seemed as permanent as the medium that carried it. Groucho's producer knew better because he knew how to interpret the trade papers. It was true that only ten TV stations were on the air in 1947. It was also true that a mere 160,000 TV sets were manufactured that year. Budgets for television programs were the joke of the broadcasting industry; the producer of a new program, *The Author Meets the Critics,* had recently asked his small staff, "We have a hundred fifty for Thursday night. What should we do?" But by 1948 well over a million receivers were sold, 127 TV stations were broadcasting, and the Federal Communications Commission was receiving petitions for new stations every week. Something was up, and it did not bode well for those who made their livings strictly with their voices. Guedel worried about his hit show and how to translate it to television, but he did his worrying alone. Groucho had enough to think about.

One of the prime items was his rapidly deteriorating second marriage. At first, the attention Groucho lavished on little Melinda seemed to rejuvenate him and give Kay a purpose in life. But the era of good feeling did not last long. Just as he once undercut Ruth's authority when Arthur was an infant, he persistently elbowed Kay out of the way, cutting short business meetings to feed and bathe the child, taking over decisions about what to cook and whom to hire for housekeeping. Leo Gorcey's physical punishment had been bad enough; Groucho's indifference was more than Kay could handle, and she began to manifest the early symptoms of a nervous breakdown, crying easily and drinking more than she should. A neighbor remembered the evening that Kay drew her aside and burst into tears: "I get so mad at Groucho. He goes to Hillcrest for lunch. Jack Benny tells a joke, then Groucho tops him. Harpo tells a joke. Groucho tells one funnier. George Jessel tells a joke. Groucho tops him too. At the end of the day, do you know how I get him? He's gasping for breath!"

On a sadly memorable night, Kay hosted a Halloween party. Screenwriter Nunnally Johnson and his wife Dorris were in attendance. "She had gotten favors," said Dorris, "she had worked out games, and this surfeited Hollywood group had little interest in doing these things. I saw Kay grow more and more tense, and her face set almost in a mask of unhappiness. . . . The party broke up fairly soon. Kay said something like, 'Oh, take the prizes or something—do *anything!*' she was like a person who verged on hysteria."

The next morning Dorris called to apologize. Kay responded: "You don't have to explain *anything* to me. It's *your* friends."

Dorris knew what Kay meant: "She knew she'd never be a part of Groucho's *real* life: the contact with his friends. She was not one of that group. We had all made her feel that way, and I think it was quite inadvertent."

Groucho took the phone. "Kay's very upset," he said tersely. "She felt the party didn't go, and really feels out of control this morning. I'll talk to you another time." The other time turned out to be a chance encounter. "Kay is having psychiatric therapy," Groucho confided. "She's very much in need."

Groucho's professional life was becoming no less complicated. Against all odds, the Brothers' thirteenth film would be made after all. Groucho was deemed a box office draw, and even though Ben Hecht's name was no longer on the script the producers of *Love Happy*, as it was now called, convinced themselves that they had another hit in the making. A screenplay had been elicited from comedy writers Mac Benoff and Frank Tashlin and a shooting schedule set for the autumn of 1949. Groucho would play the comparatively small part of a detective, leaving Harpo and Chico to carry most of the plot and comedy. He was only too glad to let them steal the show. For the first time he stayed away from script revisions and editing. Cinema had no place in his life anymore; that medium belonged to the past. In his view, the action in show business had shifted to broadcasting. The evidence supported him. *Newsweek* had never been particularly interested in Groucho in the heyday of the Marx Brothers, but the magazine was fascinated by him as a broadcaster. On May 15, 1950, he made the cover, hailed as "A Sharp Knife in Stale Cake." The story followed his "turn back up an amazing comeback road," compared his face-offs with guests to a biology student examining frogs preserved in formaldehyde, and claimed that "his wit was bringing back entertainment to a medium whence entertainment had all but fled." A good deal of space was taken up with snippets of *You Bet Your Life*:

GROUCHO

Where are you from?

YOUNG WOMAN

I'm from Ralph's Grocery Store.

GROUCHO

You were born in a supermarket, eh? I thought supermarkets didn't make deliveries anymore. . . . Oh, you're the cashier? Now it begins to register.

. . .

GROUCHO (*To a congressman*)

How long have you been incongruous—I mean, in congress?

CONGRESSMAN

This is my third term.

GROUCHO

Better look out. One more offense and you'll get life.

Newsweek asserted that the show's popularity depended on two factors. The first was Groucho's suspiciously quick comebacks. The second was the choice of guests, especially in bizarre combinations—a window washer and a parachute jumper, a circus wardrobe mistress and a stagedoor man at a burlesque house, a fireman and a housewife, or the magazine's favorite, a little girl and a professional Santa Claus.

GROUCHO

How old are you?

GIRL

Six and a half.

GROUCHO

You don't look a day older than four. How do you keep looking so young? Santa, how old are you?

SANTA

Thirty-seven.

GROUCHO

I never thought I'd get to be older than Santa Claus. . . . (*To girl*) Is there anything you'd like to ask Santa Claus?

GIRL

How do you get through all the world in one night?

GROUCHO

(*After Santa's embarrassed silence*) Well, Dewey got all over being President in one night.

In passing, the cover also mentioned another, less publicized fact of Groucho's life. The psychiatrists had worked no miracles, and the Marxes had quietly agreed to separate. Lawyers were instructed to begin divorce proceedings.

Another negotiation went on at the same time. This one Groucho lost. The producers would pay him no more than $35,000 for his role in *Love Happy,* less than half his usual movie salary. To a star making close to $5,000 a week for ad-libbing, this seemed perilously close to an insult, and no one was surprised when he later summarized the film as "a terrible picture" and said, "I've tried to put it out of my mind."

There was one very different memory he could not excise. During a casting session, three voluptuous starlets sauntered across a stage. Lester Cowan asked him which he preferred for a small vignette in the movie. The actress would have but one line: "Two men are following me."

Groucho was then to look at the camera, wiggle his eyebrows, and say sardonically, "I can't understand why."

He took less than five seconds to make his choice. "There's only one, as far as I'm concerned. The blond."

As he remembered it, "The girl was signed for the part. For her scene she wore a dress cut so low that I couldn't remember the dialogue. Very soon other men throughout the world would be suffering similar fevers, for the girl was Marilyn Monroe."

Love Happy offered few such diversions. The idea for the screenplay had originated with Harpo, and it is really his picture. He pantomimes and gestures in a way that belies his age—sixty-two—possibly because he underwent cosmetic surgery before the filming. As if to underline the importance of his position as creator, Harpo is billed with the character name Harpo for the first time since *Cocoanuts.* (Chico goes by the name of Faustino the Great, and Groucho is Sam Grunion, Private Eye.) As usual, the mute is a total innocent who, with the connivance of his brothers, manages to win out over circumstance and villainy. In this case, the evil-doers are thugs working for the ruthless beauty Madame Egilchi (Ilona Massey). Groucho's original contract called for him to appear only at the beginning and the end of *Love Happy,* but the screenplay was so ragged that he had to be used for continuity, popping up at irregular intervals to explain the proceedings. Once in a while he spouts a gag reminiscent of better times: "I'm the same Sam Grunion who solved the famous Uranium Scandal. Scotland Yard was baffled. They sent for me and the case was solved immediately. I confessed." Otherwise he seems as uncomfortable as the plot. Before filming was completed the producers ran out of money, a fact evident in the last reel. Product endorsement was rare in 1949, and in that sense *Love Happy* was a breakthrough. Hasty negotiations with several corporations produced enough cash to complete the movie, and companies saw their investment pay off in the final reel. Pursued over the rooftops of Times Square, Harpo passes a Bulova watch sign, rides the blinking neon Pegasus of Mobil gas, hides in the Kool cigarettes penguin, and imitates the sleepy child in Goodyear's TIME TO RE-TIRE billboard.

As filming came to a close, Al Shean died. Along with his brothers, Groucho had pretty much lost track of Uncle Al. The last time they'd been together was three years before, when Groucho took the old man to see *Life with Father*: "He fell asleep in the first act, and didn't wake up until it was almost over. Come to think of it, life with my father affected Uncle Al the same way." But the boys never forgot Shean's rewrite of their vaudeville act. It had pushed them into the big time, and they acknowledged their obligation with monthly checks for more than twenty years. Uncle Al's death canceled the debt in full, emotionally as well as fiscally. The trouper was interred without their presence; none of the boys thought it necessary to go to New York for the funeral.

Save for the disagreeable work in *Love Happy*, *You Bet Your Life* occupied nearly all of Groucho's attention and energy. CBS wanted to retain the show; NBC was hungry for it. Dickering began. Early in the year Zeppo had departed the talent agency to pursue an entrepreneurial career manufacturing airplane parts. Gummo stayed on to engineer the deal of Groucho's life. By 1950, competition for hit comedy shows had become fierce. From Jack Benny to Fred Allen, almost all of them had started and flourished on NBC. Then CBS began to make inroads, offering larger salaries, emoluments, and an opportunity to star in the new medium of television. One by one the programs switched networks. According to Bernie Smith, "NBC was really up against it." Informants at the show's advertising agency, Batten, Barton, Durstine, and Osborn, he went on, "told me that one of the top people at CBS went up to Detroit. They went to the president of the De Soto division of Chrysler and put a check for a million dollars on his desk. They said, 'If you use your weight to have Groucho and Guedel put their show on CBS, that million dollars is yours.' They swore this really happened. De Soto knew they couldn't keep it anyway, and he couldn't operate that way or he'd get fired. So he just told the guy, 'I want to keep Groucho and Guedel happy. Whatever they say, I'll do.' Incidentally, the De Soto dealers were paying twenty-seven dollars out of each car sale to support the show."

William S. Paley, president of CBS, personally involved himself in the talent raids. One evening at Gummo's house in Beverly Hills, Groucho, Guedel, and Gummo were pondering their choices when Paley appeared unannounced. "We were being sociable," Groucho remembered. "I rose and excused myself. Paley rose and followed me, into the guest bath, and locked the door.

" 'Look,' he said to me, 'you're a Jew and I'm a Jew. We should stick together. You can't afford to sign with NBC.' "

Paley took exactly the wrong approach. In the first place, NBC, CBS's chief rival, was owned and run by David Sarnoff, himself a Jew. In the second place, Groucho loathed special pleading of any kind. Icily, he informed the head of CBS that he was displeased with the way the conversation was going. "There are certain things that are private and inviolate," he wrote in a memoir. "And that's why I got mad at Paley." And that was why he signed with NBC. Groucho made no sacrifice for upholding his code of deportment. The new contract guaranteed him $760,000 a year for ten years, plus a weekly salary of $48,000 for the thirty-nine weeks when the show was broadcast. Guedel, packager of the program, was also given a decade-long guarantee of some $250,000 annually, plus a $1,800 weekly payment.

For the TV version of *You Bet Your Life,* network executives again demanded a return to the Hackenbush makeup and wardrobe. Once more Groucho refused. Only one concession was made—the reforestation of his hairline. "If the sponsor and the network want to see me with a full head of hair," he declared, "there will be the devil toupée," and for all of his formal television appearances thereafter he wore a well-made hairpiece. Save for that *You Bet Your Life* was the same fixture as before: Groucho sitting on a stool, chatting up his guests, asking questions and distributing prize money. Out of the audience's sightline, a projector flashed the key phrases of Groucho's opening and closing gags, allowing him a little freedom to make them brief or to stretch them out, depending on the pace of the show. Control was tight, and grew even tighter as the show progressed. As he prepared for each taping, Groucho always consulted a cryptic reminder, scribbled on a folded piece of paper. It read "F.E.U. Prod. Look Ahead." These were reminders to Foul 'em Up—disconcert the contestants to keep them off balance, Prod them to reveal a personal incident or articulate a funny phrase, and Look Ahead to determine whether the interview might strike gold. If the guests seemed unpromising, he would cut off their chatter in the middle of a sentence, moving on to the next pair. Yet no matter how careful the planning, there was always an element of unpredictability from the guests as well as the host. Asked about his most embarrassing experience, one man told Groucho: "I was rooming with a three-hundred-pound fellow. And the bedroom caught fire. In my panic I put on the big fellow's trousers and shoes. I was coming down the ladder when a shoe came loose. I tried to retrieve it, and I dropped the trousers. There was a crowd of five hundred people below, and they could see my predicament." Even though this recollection was edited, the audience response was so intense that NBC editors preserved it on tape. Years from then the uproar could be still heard, "sweetening" the sound track of shows where the laughter came out of a can.

•

No one disliked *Love Happy* as much as Groucho did. The producers took so long to pay him that he had to take them to court. At no time did he show the slightest interest in promoting the film or even in seeing it. *Variety* regretted to report that "production numbers fail to come off because of their poverty-stricken appearance," and marked David Miller's direction as "not strong enough." A few reviewers wrote kinder words; most agreed with Bosley Crowther, the *New York Times* critic: "Does anybody have any idea whatever became of the Marx Brothers?" What happened was that the team had become soloists pursuing different avenues. Once in a while Chico persuaded Harpo to join him in a brief tour. In London the notices were ecstatic: "Fun and fantasy with something else," said the *Evening Standard,* "a mixture of worldly wisdom and naivete, of experience but also of an innocence never altogether lost, of dignity and absurdity together, so that for a moment we love and applaud mankind." The pair's club dates in Reno and Las Vegas met with great success; to the audiences, the absence of Groucho seemed to bring the two remaining brothers closer. But the onstage geniality was all an act. Chico would spend his off-hours wenching and gambling, driving Harpo to distraction. Upon their return home, Harpo complained to Maxine: "I can't talk sense to your father. He just laughs at me, or worse, agrees to lay off the wild nights and then goes ahead and does what he wants to do. I can't control him, and I don't want to hear about it anymore."

It was a dwindling pocketbook, rather than remorse, that changed Chico's course. In need of ready cash, he tried his hand at television, playing the proprietor of a soda shop in a half-hour song-and-comedy show called *The College Bowl*. It lasted one season. Harpo went solo, giving concerts when the spirit moved him.

Groucho, of course, had a national following every week. Everything about his professional life radiated an upbeat quality. It was his private life that edged close to dissolution. In the spring of 1950, he and Kay officially broke up. "I feel sad about it," he explained to Miriam, "but there isn't much choice. Kay wants it. Her analyst told me that the only way she could possibly become an adult was to be on her own." There followed some twisted logic: Groucho found Kay's frequent breakdowns intolerable, yet he raised no objections to letting her have custody of Melinda. "I couldn't stand her being alone. It would worry me too much. She has given me many scary nights in recent months. . . . I suppose if I were a young man I could survive these brainstorms, but I am fifty-nine and one doesn't bounce back so quickly at that age." It was he who filed the official divorce papers, claiming "extreme cruelty," but deliberately avoiding specific instances. He fended off reporters' inquiries by reducing a complicated situation to four words—"We're just plain unhappy"—and joked obliquely about the split on his show. (When a Marine general gave his status as "married," Groucho spoke up: "Oh, then you've seen plenty of fighting.") California was a community property state, and Kay might have made harsh financial claims. But she had neither taste nor inclination for combat, and agreed to abide by their prenuptial agreement—a very modest one, given Groucho's new wealth. It awarded her a residence in Westwood and some $13,000 a year for the next decade. He made his peace with the custody arrangement by becoming a consuming, almost obsessive presence in Melinda's life.

After Kay became a single mother, the child was encouraged to make more appearances on the show. "Being your typical proud and doting father," Groucho stated later, "I wanted to show off her gifts to the world. I might have been a bit smug about her talent, which was obviously inherited. I was tickled with the idea that a third generation of performing Marxes was being introduced to the public." He also wanted control. On camera, the six-year-old had to meet her father's high standards of performance, just as the Brothers were once expected to live up to Minnie's demands for a first-class show. Fenneman remembered Melinda "trembling backstage." "I used to sit with her and hold her hand," he recalled. "She certainly didn't want to make any of those appearances. She was a cute, nice little girl, but she never wanted to be in show business. Groucho desperately wanted her to, so she did it to please him." Looking back, Melinda had little fondness for those days. When she was small, she said, "I had fun singing and dancing, and I would have done it in an alley. But I quickly became aware of tremendous pressure. During later times it became very intense and uncomfortable and something I didn't want to do at all."

Then again, Groucho "never asked me if I enjoyed it or wanted it. . . . It was something that was expected of me: clean your room, do well in school, and give a good performance on the television show."

On this matter Groucho entered a plea of guilty, with an explanation: "I didn't sense until later that Melinda was unhappy being on the show. On the other hand I was quite aware that the sponsor was quite happy to have her."

From bright beginnings, Groucho's two ex-wives and his older daughter had taken hard falls. All three tried to please him, all three failed, and all three became substance abusers. His younger daughter was now well on the way to her own difficult time. If Groucho refused to discern the pattern in the carpet, others had little difficulty in seeing it and in privately questioning his motives. Was he so marked by Minnie's dominance, by her usurpation of his childhood, that he felt compelled to tyrannize and humiliate any woman who ventured too close? Was the alcoholism of Ruth and Miriam solely a matter of genetic heritage? Or was it exacerbated by the pressure from Groucho? What of Kay? She never let herself go in the way that Ruth did; at the time of the divorce she was as winsome as she was in the year of the courtship. If Groucho was drawn to her vulnerability in the radio days, why, when she was even more defenseless, did he find her so unattractive? Miriam, in one of her sessions with a therapist, thought she had found the key to her own misbehavior: "I do everything to fulfill my father's feelings about women. He hates them, and I prove him right."

Was it hate? There seems no question that Julius was confused by women from the beginning, and that the confusion often led to hostilities. As we have seen, Groucho could never please Minnie as easily as her other sons, particularly Chico—the main reason why she referred to young Julius as "the jealous one." Such praise as he was able to elicit from his mother came mainly in the form of adjectives in those early *Variety* ads. In his youth, few liaisons went well, and his first experience with a prostitute resulted in venereal disease. He may have been smitten with the women he married, but not for long. He simply had no idea how to include them in his life, to help them to ripen along with him. In addition there was the persistent image of himself as inadequate, placed there by

Minnie and reinforced by his own negative appraisal. When he said that he wouldn't want to join any club that would have him as a member, he was speaking the truth, as he always did, disguised as jest. Replace the word "club" with the word "woman" and all was revealed. Speaking of Groucho's relationships, Dorris Johnson found that he habitually took "more and more of the female role away from the female. He insisted on running the house, on being very absolute about money. . . . He removed all responsibility from them. He failed to let them grow in the sense of performing their roles. So he exacerbated their insecurities more and more. And yet, he was always attracted to girls that had *grave* insecurities. There was a continuing Groucho syndrome. The girl that had problems, who was young, who was pretty, was the girl Groucho was attracted to. And it's my opinion that when he took on the girls as wives, he removed their chance to grow and mature in self-reliance. . . . I believe Kay had need for a crutch, for shoring up her unstable psyche. She turned to drink for it. . . . As did Ruth, as did Miriam." From the underside—which is the way most children view their parents—Groucho might well have seemed a rancorous, misogynistic figure, ever on the attack when a female got within his range. But it was not women or girls as such who provided an ever-ready target, it was the insecure, the submissive, the powerless. Most of the time that meant wives or daughters, or those who might be interested in him romantically. But it could also mean men—including, as we shall see, his son. Weakness was what Groucho found intolerable. He had been weak himself as a child, fearful of the tough neighborhood kids, unable to resist his mother when she yanked him out of school, or the vaudeville managers and hotel owners and rude audiences who made his first professional years so miserable. Just as he sought to expunge the frailty within, he tried to destroy infirmity when he saw it, either with rude remarks or with contemptuous gestures. Of course, he might have accomplished the same thing with a kind remark or a benign gesture, but this would have been contrary to his experience and against the hard clown mask he had created, and now could not remove.

Outside of family and some close friends, few people knew of the troubled women around Groucho. He wanted it kept that way. But he knew that his image as a family man was being tarnished, and he must have been aware that his travails were the subject of many Hollywood cocktail parties. He badly needed some adroit public relations. These came clothbound in 1950, with the publication of Kyle Crichton's multiple biography, *The Marx Brothers*. Crichton, a disenchanted radical who once wrote for *The New Masses* under the pseudonym Robert Forsythe, kept the book mercifully free of politics. His principal subject matter is the Brothers' early rise, and he builds the story with an accretion of detail—much of it inaccurate. The biographer writes, for example, that *Animal Crackers* was filmed in Hollywood rather than in New York, and that Frenchy is seen waving to himself in *A Night at the Opera*, made two years after his death. Minor flaws of all five brothers, and of Frenchy, are merrily discussed. Minnie is canonized. Instead of taking a close look at this *monstre sacré*, the author takes up where Alexander Woollcott's valedictory left off (Crichton's original title had been *The Mother of the Two-A-Day*). In *The Marx Brothers*, Minnie Schoenberg Marx is a kind of artist without portfolio, a producer without a show, a molder of men, an angel of vaudeville, the animating spirit behind her sons' victories: "Their success had been built around her; their future would be secure because she had prepared them properly for it. She had feared the theater and they had shown few signs of talent for it; the result had been a strange and wondrous triumph of affection and determination. The world knew them as sophisticated buffoons, but in their own hearts they were still Minnie's boys. They left for Hollywood with the realization that it was their own life from now on."

The book is less a life history than an exercise in hagiography, cannily diverting attention from the Brothers' present-day affairs to their endearing and exuberant youth. Only if readers examined a small paragraph opposite the table of contents could they see the gears grinding. Customarily, the copyright of most books belongs to the author; in this case, it was assigned to "Arthur Harpo Marx, Chico Marx, Groucho Marx, Zeppo Marx and Gummo Marx. All rights reserved." Besides image-polishing, there was another reason for the Brothers to retain control of this work. They had the example of Al Jolson before them: the old star had received $3.5 million for *The Jolson Story* in 1946, even though he had only appeared on camera in one brief sequence. What if a movie were made about the Marx Brothers and how they grew? They leaked rumors that a film called *The Mother of the Two-A-Day* was being considered by several producers, and vigorously promoted the Crichton book. Chico autographed copies at Robinson's bookstore in Beverly Hills while Groucho flew to New York to rally Doubleday's sales staff. "The book is dirt cheap at three dollars," he told them. "Here's a book about five men. Broken down (and believe me there is no one more broken down than these five men) it comes to a measly sixty cents for each brother." The publisher gathered a garland of encomiums from newspapers and magazines ("You'll laugh reading about these goofy guys; it's like seeing them on the screen," *Variety*. An "extensive relation of their strange march to fame," *New York Herald Tribune*). As soon as these were in, George S. Kaufman contributed his own money quote in the *New York Times* ("Gaily amusing from start to finish"). Groucho topped them all: *he* reviewed the book for the *New York World Telegram*.

"This is a new and alarming trend in American letters," he wrote merrily.

> When I was a lad, biographers used to write about Napoleon, Dante and Byron's escapades through Italy.
>
> I can only attribute this literary decline to the fact that there is no one left to write about. Here are five nonentities crashing into a world that formerly belonged to the brothers Karamazov. By the way, have you heard about the Karamazov brothers' latest radio and TV show? That Groucho Karamazov (he's the one with the moustache) is a wow.
>
> Since Christmas is just around the corner (and, oh, how I dread it), and the shelves are going to be pretty bare of anything worth purchasing, you could do the literary world a great service by grabbing up these copies before they are all returned to the publisher and appear next year in the lending libraries as murder mysteries.
>
> Now enough of this kidding. I think *The Marx Brothers* by Kyle Crichton is the greatest book ever written. And that goes for Kinsey, Tolstoy, and Mrs. Kinsey.

That encomium helped to remind older people of what the Marx Brothers had done, and young people of what the Marx Brothers had been. To keep the family name current, Harpo chimed in. Only one Marx was truly active now, he pointed out in an article for *Coronet*. With the assistance of a ghostwriter, he recapitulated the family history and praised *You Bet Your Life*. The most important sentences came at the windup: "When the average American thinks of Groucho, he pictures him chasing a voluptuous blonde, bilking a gullible dowager, racing in that hilarious slinking crouch from one slightly fraudulent experience to another.

"Groucho with a real moustache is a new character. The new Groucho is actually the real Groucho, more sensible, wittier, warmer, and more believable.

"Actually, the Madman character that millions of stage and picture fans know is an imaginary character who needs the other three characters to give him substance. The Marx Brothers, as a complete unit, are no more. We all feel those days are done, and each is going his separate way." That they were, and Groucho's was the most separate of them all.

CHAPTER FOURTEEN

Just Don't Die

CHICO'S *COLLEGE BOWL* program faded from view after a single season. Harpo abbreviated a concert tour when advance sales fell short of expectations. Only Groucho retained his drawing power in the 1950s. He took a cameo role in the 1950 Bing Crosby film, *Mr. Music,* and the following year played the comic relief to Frank Sinatra in RKO's *Double Dynamite,* a title referring to the attributes of Jane Russell's impressive *poitrine.* Sinatra liked to dawdle in his dressing room, poring over the *Racing Form* while the cast waited. An hour later he would swagger onto the set, indicating that a man with powerful friends could keep his own schedule. But he strutted once too often on this set. Groucho had often bawled out Chico for unprofessional conduct. He was not about to tolerate it from a stranger. "I believe in being on time to work," he informed the singer. "The next time you show up late, you'd better be prepared to act for two, because I won't be there." Mob connections or no, Sinatra adhered to the shooting schedule from then on.

Groucho followed the first RKO film with another one, *A Girl in Every Port,* starring Marie Wilson. In the midst of his labors S. J. Perelman paid a call, reconstructing the visit in the pages of *Holiday.* In a way, "Weekend with Groucho Marx" was the writer's payback for humiliations suffered at the time of *Monkey Business* and *Horse Feathers.* Perelman's bantering article portrayed Groucho as self-involved, quixotic, and mingy. "The set to which I was directed, a faithful replica of a battleship, hummed with activity; hordes of extras in navy blue were absorbed in scratch sheets, electricians on all sides feverishly worked to draw inside straights, and high on a camera parallel, two associate producers, arms clasped about each other, were busily examining their pelts for fleas. Groucho, as was his wont, was in the very thick of the melee. He was sprawled blissfully in a director's chair, having his vertebrae massaged by Marie Wilson, a young lady whose natural endowment caused a perceptible singing in the ears. I promptly drew up a chair next to her and confided that I too was suffering from a touch of sacroiliac, but the fair masseuse appeared to be hard of hearing."

Perelman remarks pointedly, "I haven't met the young lady yet."

"No," retorts Groucho, "and you're not likely to, you sneak. I know when I'm well off."

Perelman turns his attention to the film's other comic lead, William Bendix, the man who owed his radio and TV career to Groucho's inadequacies. When a comedy called *The Flotsam Family* centered on the Jewish comedian, nobody wanted to buy it. The creator, Irving Brecher, turned the central character into an Irishman, Bendix took over, and *The Life of Riley* flourished. Groucho was not happy about it at the time, but by now professional jealousy had dissipated and the two got along well. Perelman joins them, attempting to project a geniality of his own. "You know, Mr. Bendix," he begins, "it must be hilarious, making a movie with a topflight comedian."

"Yeah," the actor agrees. "I'd love to do it someday."

"But I-I don't understand," Perelman persists. "You must roll on the floor when he gets off those repartees of his. . . ."

"It's a living," grunts Bendix.

Groucho breaks in, addressing his visitor. "Now, listen. From here in, it's strictly my treat. What about dinner at my place and a night ball game afterward?" Perelman readily agrees and Groucho ponders, "Where are your grips?"

"I left them with the cop at the main gate."

"Good. I've got a big, roomy house out in Beverly. Pick up the bags and take them to Schwabacher's used-car lot on Exposition Boulevard. You can sleep for nothing in one of their old jalopies."

"I have to clean up, take a shower," Perelman protests feebly.

"Who takes a shower to go to a ball game? Lot of cheap swank." Groucho scribbles on a card. "O.K., give this to my maid and she'll let you in the bathroom, but take it easy on the hot water—I'm not made of money."

Two statuesque actresses occupy the other chairs at Groucho's intimate dinner. "Hey, this meat is awfully dry," complains the one named Chiquita. "Isn't there any gravy?"

"Gravy, gravy!" shouts Groucho. "Everybody wants gravy! Did those six poor slobs on the *Kon-Tiki* have any gravy? Did Scipio's legions, deep in the burning African waste, have gravy? Did Fanny Hill?"

"Did Fanny Hill what?" Perelman inquires.

"Never mind, you cad. I'm sick to death of innuendo, brittle small talk, the sly, silken rustle of feminine underthings. I want to sit in a ball park with the wind in my hair and breath cold, clean popcorn into my lungs. I want to hear the crack of seasoned ash on horsehide, the roar of the hydra-headed crowd, the umpire's deep-throated 'Play ball!' "

"Golly!" enthuses Chiquita. "I feel like as though I had really witnessed the game!"

"So do I." Groucho yawns ostentatiously. "I'm pooped. I'll thank you two harpies to clear out and take that lush with you. I've got to be on the set at eight."

The narrative ends the next day, when Perelman returns to say goodbye. "My boy," Groucho mutters, his voice shaking slightly, "a very wise old man once said that there are two things money cannot buy—nostalgia and friendship. He died in the poorhouse. Don't forget to square that tab on the way out."

"He gripped my hand hard and was gone, a gallant freebooter who had made his rendezvous with Destiny. As his skulking, predatory figure faded from view, I bowed my head in tribute. 'Adieu, Quackenbush,' I whispered. 'Adieu, Captain Spaulding. No man ever buckled a better swash.' Then, through a mist of tears, I soberly signed his name to the check and went forth to a workaday world."

Groucho took the piece in better grace than Perelman expected, saving his resentments for a later day. The two had a complicated relationship, mixing admiration and displeasure, and it was to get no simpler in the ensuing decades.

Despite his cranky backchat, Groucho was as well off as he had ever been, and at last felt relaxed enough to reach out, at least tentatively, to his immediate family. He received word that Miriam still wrestled with a drinking problem, and persuaded her to return to Hollywood. There she could edit videotape for *You Bet Your Life*—and he could keep an eye on her. Once Miriam was on the scene, though, Groucho convinced himself that his daughter was on the mend, knocking back less and suffering fewer psychological distresses. Closing his eyes to an alcoholism as severe as Ruth's, he paid for Miriam's therapists' bills, all the while nursing a profound distrust of psychiatry. ("I don't doubt that analysis has done some good for a few people," he was to grumble. "I have no way of knowing, but I wouldn't be surprised if it's hurt more people than it has helped. If analysis did nothing else, it left a lot of people with a hell of a lot less money than they started with.") The problem of Kay was not so easily deflected. She had tried to raise Melinda on her own, but her mental health was precarious, and she suffered from a variety of bodily ills. To help raise the child, she called in a cousin. The women's combined efforts were not enough. Clearly the six-year-old was under stress, and badly in need of a stable home. Seizing his opportunity, Groucho petitioned the court and won temporary custody of his daughter. No further arrangements were necessary; Kay never got strong enough to reclaim Melinda.

In this period, Arthur and his wife, Irene Kahn Marx, were touched with a bit of fame by association. Warner Brothers bought the life story of Irene's father, the late songwriter Gus Kahn, from his widow, Grace. *I'll See You in My Dreams* would star Danny Thomas and Doris Day. Grace gave a portion of the Warner money to her daughter and son-in-law. It was enough for the couple to make a down payment on a house in Pacific Palisades. They and their burgeoning family—there was now a second son, Andy—were on their own. Grace had given Arthur charity, but made him dependent. Groucho had presented him with indifference, but caused him to be hungry for approval. This was Arthur's first real chance to break clean from the parental grip on both sides. He could wriggle free from his mother-in-law's influence easily enough. But just as Groucho learned that there was no fleeing from Minnie, even after her death, all his children were to find that there was no escape from their father, no matter how hard they ran.

•

WHAT CHIEFLY MATTERED to Groucho after the divorce from Kay was his romantic and professional life. ("Despite the fact that I regard myself as an extremely glamorous figure," he complained in a wry letter to comedian Fred Allen, "I rarely receive any mail that would indicate that the fair sex, as a sex, has any interest in me.") In contrast, his business schedule could hardly have been more crowded. Still smarting from the reception given to *Time for Elizabeth*, Groucho determined to show the world—at least that part of it in attendance at the La Jolla playhouse— that the New York critics were biased fools. In the summer of 1951, he took the part of Ed Davis, early retiree, only to be roasted à la Manhattan. *Variety*'s out-of-town reviewer characterized the play as "a flimsy soufflé with too many laughless lines to be a first-rate comedy and insufficient penetration for a study in irony." An ambiguous compliment followed: "Faced with an unreasonable handicap, Groucho's performance is all the more remarkable for its dogged devotion to his acting intent." Coauthor Norman Krasna was more to the point: "You're playing Walter Huston. It's fine, but it's not what the audience wants." Groucho gave in and reverted to his old surefire moves, wiggling his eyebrows and slouching across the floor. Sure enough, the laughter was produced as automatically as his mannerisms.

Britain had not been receptive to *Love Happy,* mostly because of its early association with Ben Hecht. The writer, a critic of the British presence in Palestine, had irritated the Court of St. James's and members of Cinematograph Exhibitors of Britain. So Groucho was grateful for a passage in the memoir *Thirty Years with G.B.S.* There, Blanche Patche, George Bernard Shaw's secretary, recalled an interview with her employer and one of his favorite performers: "G.B.S. once told Sir Cedric Hardwicke that he was the third greatest actor of our time, adding that Groucho Marx and [the music hall star] Lew Lake came in first and second."

But these were minor compensations. Groucho needed something contemporary to assure him that he was important for what he was doing now, not for bygone accomplishments. The laurel came late in the winter of 1951 when *Time* put him on its cover for the second time (the first had occurred nineteen years earlier when he shared the space with Chico, Harpo, and Zeppo, costars of *Horse Feathers*). His scowling image, complete with jutting cigar, ran over the line TRADEMARK EFFRONTERY. Inside, the magazine offered a thumbnail biography and showed up *Newsweek*'s naivete by pointing out that *You Bet Your Life* was "not exactly a simon-pure ad-lib performance. Contestants are chosen in advance, made to fill out questionnaires about themselves, and coached for an hour and a half before facing Groucho." Nevertheless, the profile continued, "Groucho is still a better field shot than any other ad-libber, and shows it by shooting from the hip at these clay pigeons." More flattering was its image of the comedian as intellectual: "One of his favorite occupations is sitting for long hours in his den strumming Gilbert & Sullivan (at which he is expert) on his guitar. He is also an expert on the novels of Henry James. Having had hardly any formal education, Groucho, by dint of greedy reading, has made himself a well-read man. His friends are endlessly amazed at his mastery of the contents of magazines which they regard as highbrow (*Atlantic, Harper's, Saturday Review of Literature,* etc.)." Groucho had indeed made Gilbert and Sullivan an obsession, but the notion of himself as an "expert" in James's fiction was too much even for his expanding ego. Complaints came in from people who really knew the

meaning of *The Golden Bowl,* and he fired off a comic disclaimer to James
Linen, *Time's* publisher:

> The picture of me on the cover of *Time* has changed my entire
> life. Where formerly my hours were spent playing golf and chas-
> ing girls, I now while away the days loitering around Beverly Hills's
> largest newsstand, selling copies of the December 31 issue of *Time*
> at premium prices.
>
> Admittedly the picture on the cover didn't do me justice (I doubt
> if any camera could capture my inner beauty), but nevertheless
> my following is so fanatical that they buy anything that even
> remotely resembles me. Yesterday, despite the fact that it was rain-
> ing, I made $13. This is all tax free, for I steal the copies of *Time*
> while the owner of the newsstand is out eating lunch.
>
> Please use my picture again soon and next time I promise to
> give you half of everything I get away with.
>
> Cordially, Groucho Marx.
>
> P.S. In addition to Henry James, I also read the *St. Louis Sporting
> News.*

Euphoric, rich, and recognized, Groucho now turned to his son. He
had not been kind about Arthur's novel about a tennis player, *The Ordeal
of Willie Brown.* Lately Arthur had been supplying continuity for Pete
Smith comedy shorts and selling an occasional nonfiction piece to magazines. These activities had failed to impress his father. To Groucho magazine writing would always be the road to oblivion. What Arthur needed
was a job—a real job. How about directing movies? To his son this
needling was worse than any rejection slip, and their relationship steadily
worsened.

Then, in 1952, things took an upward turn. *Collier's* editor in chief took
a liking to the work of Marx *fils* and asked if he would be interested in
doing a profile of Marx *père.* The freelancer hesitated. He was just emerging from his father's shadow; now the magazine was asking him to move
back. Arthur had just about decided to refuse when *Collier's* made an irresistible offer of $750. Upon reading the manuscript the editor was so
pleased he doubled the author's fee. Groucho, perhaps feeling a twinge
of guilt for all the things he had said in the past, voiced few demurs when
the issue hit the stands. An editor at Simon & Schuster read "Groucho Is
My Pop" and made Arthur a new offer: a $2,000 advance for a book about

that Pop. When Arthur told his father about the proposed biography, Groucho agreed to cooperate fully. Over the next year he invited Arthur and Irene to dinner once or twice a week, relating anecdotes and poring over old photographs.

During that interval Miriam's condition worsened. Her drinking binges had become so frequent and shattering that she sought help at the Menninger Clinic, a sanitarium specializing in addiction and other severe psychological problems. Arthur accompanied her to Topeka, Kansas; Groucho paid the bills. A letter from February 1953 survives. "I haven't written you," Padre informs Miriam, "because I wanted to give you a chance to adjust yourself to your new life and surroundings. Arthur was much impressed with the place and seems very optimistic about you and the institution." He tries to end on a humorous note, informing her, "I am leaving on Tuesday for Las Vegas. Eden has developed a system that she claims will break all the gambling houses. I am equipping her with $10 each night. She says this is all she needs. Well, if it wasn't for Eden Las Vegas would fold up and the whole state would become a giant dust bowl. Don't feel obliged to write. I would like to hear from you, but not if it's a chore. We all send our love—and don't worry about anything."

The Eden mentioned in the letter was Eden Hartford, his latest flame. The parade of vapid chorines and aggressive women had ended. Groucho, no longer in what he called his "mangy lover phase," was smitten. He had met the twenty-something beauty on the set of *A Girl in Every Port* when she and her sister Peggy had dropped by to see the third sister, Dee, soon to wed director Howard Hawks. Dee's part was considerably larger than Marilyn Monroe's but she had few illusions about the business. Her attitude appealed to Groucho, and the two had become friends. (That was something he could not say for her fiancé. Groucho and Hawks "were talking sports one day," he said, "and 'the great liberal' told me, 'Imagine allowing Negroes to play football.' ") Dee introduced her siblings to the comedian. "Give me a rundown on these two," he demanded. "Which one's married and which one isn't?" Informed that Eden was unattached, he took her aside. "I'll call you in six weeks when the picture is finished. I don't like to go out when I'm working." Dee advised her sister: "Forget it. Six weeks!"

"I forgot it," Eden said in fond recollection. "Well, almost. But sure enough, at the end of his work on the picture, he called." A dinner at Groucho's followed. Eden and Melinda got on, and Groucho and Eden started to see a lot of each other. The columnists made them a favorite item. Eden spoke about the evening he proposed: "One night Groucho finished off his favorite dinner of eggs and bacon and pumpernickel bread with lots of butter, and a glass of beer, and said to me, 'A man who runs a home has the same taxes as one who has a wife. So when I marry you, you'll know it's not just for the deduction.' " The couple kept their plans secret from his son if not from the columnists. Arthur read hints about Groucho's imminent wedding and confronted his father. Groucho assured him there would be no third wedding.

In early summer of 1954 Groucho took Eden and Melinda to Europe. There he mixed business with history, filming commercials for his sponsor, De Soto, and stopping off in Germany to look at the ancestral haunts of the Schoenbergs. In late July 1954 the three vacationed again, this time in Sun Valley, Idaho. From that address, Arthur received a wire: IF YOU'VE HEARD ABOUT THIS PLEASE REFUND THE PRICE OF THE TELEGRAM. LOVE FROM US BOTH. GROUCHO. The message to Miriam read: YOU NOW HAVE A MOTHER NAMED EDEN. LOVE FROM BOTH—PADRE.

Those words illuminated the relationship of father and daughter more clearly than any psychiatrist could point out. On one hand, Groucho was so emotionally remote from Miriam that he could not tell her in person about the marriage. On the other hand, he felt the need to say *something* to his daughter, and chose to do so not in his own voice, but in a flip Dr. Hackenbush tone that only made the notice more hurtful. Not that the information was new; Miriam had already read about Eden in the papers, and noted with some asperity that Eden was twenty-seven—just seven years her senior. Back home, the newlyweds were the honored guests at a party hosted by Harpo and Susan. Groucho and his new wife stood at the piano, singing a love ballad. Ben Hecht, who was in attendance, reminisced about the Brothers on that occasion. "Suddenly the tune changed. Groucho had taken over the piano. An ancient vaudeville ditty—*Is das nicht ein Schnitzelbank?*—came merrily out of him." All five of Minnie's sons harmonized their mother's favorite song. Their voices were "as fresh as they had been thirty years before. The wedding vanished out of the room. The saga of gay talent and family love that was the Marx Brothers turned us from a wedding party into a happy audience."

Arthur was not to experience much of that family warmth. While the father partied and celebrated, the son was hard at work rewriting the last chapters of his biography, describing Groucho's most recent bride. Eden Hartford, née Edna Higgins, had come from Mormon stock. Most of her life was spent in the tiny community of Bell, California, where as a teenager she married a local businessman. One day her big sister Dee, who had been out in the world, stopped by to see the folks. She observed that cities held great possibilities for girls with ambition and looks. Intrigued, Eden walked out on her bewildered spouse, obtained a divorce, and headed for L.A.

The last-minute rewrites were only the beginning of Arthur's difficulties. *The Saturday Evening Post* offered $45,000 for the serial rights to *Life with Groucho* on two conditions: Groucho had to help promote the book, and he had to contribute some humorous footnotes to accompany the text. The last presented no problem; Arthur would ghostwrite those. As for plugging the book, surely Groucho would give his son a hand up. For formality's sake the author dropped off a copy of the manuscript at his father's house, expecting a congratulatory note the next morning. An ominous silence followed. After several days, Arthur's nerve failed him and he called in. Groucho summoned his son to appear before him.

The interview took place in an upstairs study. Among other anecdotes about his parsimony, Groucho stated that he was made uncomfortable by the true story that he met Deborah Kerr at his show, escorted her to a party, and as the midnight hour approached, learned that she lived in Pacific Palisades. This was a full fifteen minutes out of his way—half an hour if he counted the round trip—and he had no intention of getting to bed late merely for a beautiful actress who had won an Academy Award. Climbing up on a chair, he had addressed the homeward bound partygoers: "Anyone for Pacific Palisades?"

Arthur tried to be conciliatory; he offered to make some cosmetic changes. His old man was not so easily appeased; he demanded wholesale alterations. Either the entire book would be rewritten, or Groucho would call his lawyer.

Arthur saw only two courses of action. He could consult his own lawyer, try to prevent Groucho from endangering the *Post* sale, and start a family feud in the process. Or he could wait out the situation and see how serious his father really was about killing the project. Before he could decide, Groucho telephoned.

His tone was a strange mix of reassurance and temptation. Arthur would not have to rewrite the entire book, merely the parts that Groucho found offensive. When the author demurred, Groucho went to plan B. He was, he reminded his son, a very rich man. Arthur could be a very rich beneficiary one day—if he played ball. What was $45,000 compared to monetary rewards that were probably just a few years away?

Arthur refused to succumb to the "old will bit," and their relationship remained remote and cold until he devised a scheme to mollify Groucho and keep the lawyers at bay. He asked the editors of the *Post* to send him two sets of galleys. One, he told them, would be for his own records. It went instead to Groucho, who was invited to make whatever deletions he pleased in all eight installments. Arthur picked up the galleys a few days later, casting his eye over the many deletions and emendations. He professed gratitude for all that editorial work.

"I hope this is the end of it," Groucho sighed. "I'm getting pretty sick of my life."

So was Arthur. So sick that he surreptitiously dumped Groucho's copy in a trash can on the way to the post office, where he mailed his own copy back to the *Post*. It was a strange declaration of independence, but very Marxian in its way. He was still his father's son.

In point of fact, *Life with Groucho* fulfilled Arthur's promise to his father. It offered sentiment without saccharinity, amusement without impertinence. Arthur wrote of Groucho's lifelong insomnia, his battles with Ruth, his difficulties with Miriam; he also described Groucho's hair-trigger wit and the old, merry times when the Marx Brothers were a four-star act. Grateful for this familial glimpse, reviewers gave the book a warm reception, with the *Herald Tribune* leading the way: "Many sons of distinguished men have written biographies of their fathers, but none has done so with a greater combination of affection and irreverence than the scion of Julius H. Marx." Groucho had read the installments in the *Post*; he knew very well that Arthur had betrayed him by ignoring the suggested changes (although he never learned that the manuscript had ended in the trash can). Yet for him money was the final arbiter, and when the book sold well he reconsidered the situation. Late in 1954 his old friend Fred Allen sent him a packet from New York. Groucho answered: "Thanks for the clippings on Arthur's book. Even *The New Yorker* praised it—that astonished and delighted me. As I said, it seems to me that I come off as quite a nut in this book, I don't mean a deliberate one. . . . I realize now I've been crazy all these years without being aware of it."

Father and son reconciled that winter, and in the spring of 1955 Arthur ghostwrote Groucho's "What's Wrong with the Giants?" for *Collier's*. "My lifetime batting average of .598 has never been equaled," boasted the piece, "and it would have been higher if I hadn't had to quit playing girls' softball at the height of my career. (I'd be playing with them yet if I hadn't tried dressing in the girls' locker room.)" Still, nobody ever forgets where he buried the hatchet, and Arthur sensed—wisely, as it turned out—that

Groucho with his second car, a Cord, in Great Neck, New York (1930)

Chico and Betty, Arthur, Marion and Zeppo, Miriam, Ruth, and Groucho on the ship to Europe (1931)

Chico, Harpo, Groucho, and Zeppo clowning on the set at Paramount Pictures (PGP19310) (1931)

(*MCA / Universal*)

Groucho and the writers of *Monkey Business*: Sol Violinsky, S. J. Perelman, Will Johnstone, and Arthur Sheekman (1932)

Groucho in *Monkey Business* (1932)
(*MCA/Universal*)

Chico, Zeppo, Groucho, and Harpo in *Duck Soup* (1934)
(*MCA/Universal*)

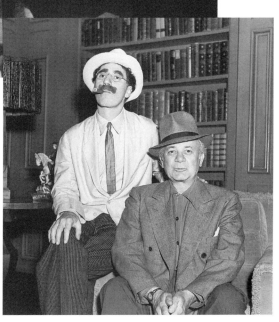

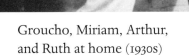

Groucho, Miriam, Arthur,
and Ruth at home (1930s)

Groucho and Al Shean on the set of
At the Circus (1099x35) (1939)
(*Turner Classics*)

Groucho and new wife Kay Gorcey (1945)
(*Wide World Photos*)

Groucho on the premiere of *You Bet Your Life* on ABC radio (1947)

Groucho on the TV version of *You Bet Your Life*, with grand-prize wheel (1950s)
(*NBC photo by Paul Bailey*)

Groucho and Eden Hartford (1956)

Groucho in *The Mikado* (1960)
(NBC photo)

Groucho receives an honorary Academy
Award from Jack Lemmon (1974)
(#544 © *Academy of Motion Picture Arts &*
Sciences by Sheedy & Long)

Groucho and Erin after the
Academy Awards (1974) (*AP newsphoto*)

Groucho celebrates his eighty-fifth birthday (1975) (*photo © by Frank Diernhammer*)

Prospectus for the private Groucho Club in London (1985)

1905   1933

1955   1974

Composite of Groucho that ran in the AP wire after his death (1977)
(© *AP wirephoto df72340fls*)

the good feelings were not to last. Groucho had nursed grievances all his life: to his way of thinking he had been let down by his mother, then betrayed by vaudeville compatriots, scheming managers, the stock market, Chico, women, his wives, his children. He was not a trusting soul, and lately he had been communicating this worldview to Melinda. He did it by wrapping it in a bedtime story, made especially for her:

> Tommy was a poor little boy. He got up one morning and his mother said, "There is no food in the house, so you better go out and get some money." Tommy went out and he was hungry. As he was walking along he saw a little girl run across the street just as a car was coming along. He dashed out on the street and saved the little girl's life. The little girl's nurse said, "Oh, you have saved the little girl's life. Her father is rich and he will reward you." So they went to the little girl's house and the nurse told the father that Tommy had saved the little girl's life. And the father said to Tommy, "You have saved my little girl's life and I will reward you. Here is $4,000." And Tommy said, "Oh good, now I can buy some food. I have not eaten anything all day." And the father said, "Wait a minute. Here are some cookies and a glass of milk." So Tommy drank the whole glass of milk and ate all the cookies. He was really hungry. When he finished, the father said, "You better go home now and here is your money: $3,500." He had reconsidered.

To appalled eavesdroppers Groucho would explain, "She's got to learn sometime." It was not an easy thing, being Groucho's kid.

All three of the children could testify to that. Melinda, the youngest, was now paying her dues. Groucho pushed her onto programs other than his own, and saw to it that she got a $2,500 fee for performing. A Sunday supplement writer watched her on the Perry Como show and wrote sourly: "Little Melinda is a born trouper in her doting pop's eyes and Groucho goes out of the way to promote her progress in show business. But his assessment of the cutie isn't generally shared by eagle-eyed talent scouts and booking agents. They are frequently embarrassed when Groucho tries to palm Melinda off on them, especially at his rates. They think it's a case of too little, too soon—too little talent, that is, for the time being, displayed far too soon. . . . She's a little ham, and she isn't getting any better by the curing she's getting at home."

Home was a different place these days. Although Arthur portrayed his latest stepmother as "extremely phlegmatic, almost torpid at times,"

Eden could sometimes display a flash of temperament. She felt discomfited in a house filled with Kay's touches, for example, and let Groucho know it. He understood, and contracted to build a $300,000 domicile in Trousdale Estates, complete with sunken tub and round bathroom ("I guess Eden figures it's harder for me to corner her in it," he told anyone who would listen). All the bills would be paid in cash; no loans or mortgages for Groucho Marx. As the days went on, Eden's low-key manner broke through Melinda's initial resistance. The closer the two became, the greater Melinda's emotional distance from her biological mother. Arce wrote of the time that the eight-year-old misbehaved and got called down for it. She sent an abject note to her father and Eden. It was more of a plea than an apology, saying how sorry she was for telling a lie. Melinda added contritely that if they sent her to live with Kay she would understand.

By now, through work and intensive therapy at Menninger, Groucho's other daughter slowly regained her physical and mental balance. Along the way she and another patient, Gordon Allen, became involved and told the authorities they planned to marry. Because Menninger specifically forbade inmates to wed, Miriam left the institution to work at a Topeka television station. Her father was ambivalent about this turn of events—relieved that he was no longer required to pay $20,000 a year in medical bills, but worried that Allen was not Mr. Right.

Groucho's ability to compartmentalize was never more obvious than in the kaleidoscopic mid and late 1950s. He dealt with Ruth and Kay and Miriam and Arthur, each in his or her own way, saving his truest energies and sentiments for Eden. The first two wives had rarely been able to budge their husband from his library, record collection, and guitar. Eden persuaded Groucho to attend parties and to stop avoiding photographers. Arthur, never the most dispassionate witness, was to write that the picture of the aging but still virile man and his sloe-eyed trophy wife seemed less than accurate. He offered an alternate portrait that concentrated more on the warts than on the man, with particular attention paid to the fact that Groucho looked the other way when Eden went out alone on selected evenings, supposedly to acting classes. These days the paterfamilias contented himself with material goods, making sure that he, Eden, and Melinda enjoyed a surfeit of them.

Meantime, NBC did what it could to keep him prosperous, vigorously promoting *You Bet Your Life*. The network's twenty-word trade ad had one of the most widely quoted copy lines of the 1950s. Around the silhouette of Groucho chomping on a cigar was the simple inscription, "One Man in a Chair Has Drawn More Viewers over the Last Six Years Than Any Other Attraction on Television." Nothing more needed to be said.

Groucho saw to it that the network stayed pleased and the sponsors unruffled, no matter what the cost. The show business blacklist was a case in point. Long before, the show's musical director, Jerry Fielding, had joined groups regarded as subversive by the Attorney General. He was served a subpoena backstage, and made it clear to the producers that he would not testify before the HUAC as a friendly witness, would not give names of others who had signed petitions or attended meetings with him. Originally, he said, "Groucho pooh-poohed the whole thing"— after all, how subversive were fanfares, or the music for "Hooray for Captain Spaulding"? Attitudes changed when Fielding took the Fifth Amendment during his testimony. There were rumblings from sponsors and from the network itself. The musician was dismissed without ado— or appeal. "I couldn't get Dwan on the phone," he remembered. "I couldn't get Groucho. I couldn't get my agent. I couldn't get NBC. . . . It was as if I'd turned to gas."

Fielding later expressed an ambivalence toward his old boss. "By putting me on that show, there's no question that Groucho did something for me. He made it possible for me to become enough of a household word to be able to get a lot of other work. But I did get angry, because I felt that he didn't make enough of an effort to stop this thing. I felt, being who he was, that he was strong enough to take a stand then and there. But he didn't do it. Somehow he got frightened off. I think the people with all the money in this talked him out of it. I took a burn at him, and I didn't want to talk to him." Groucho understood these feelings of revulsion only too well. "That I bowed to sponsors' demands is one of the greatest regrets of my life," he was to admit ruefully. But that was more than twenty years later. In the dark times of the 1950s he felt he could not afford to take a stand; there was too much to lose. Evidently the FBI thought so as well; the Bureau opened a Groucho Marx file dedicated to the comedian and his possibly suspect affiliations.

When Groucho was not operating in and around *You Bet Your Life,* he made a recording of songs by Bert Kalmar and Harry Ruby, the only composers to catch the surreal, antic qualities of Captain Spaulding. Intellectuals were back in the picture: poet Louis Untermeyer wrote the liner notes, lauding Groucho as "the world's fastest and funniest ad-libber; a matchless Master of Ceremonies and an unsurpassed comedian on every level in every medium." Among the album's highlights: "Show Me a Rose" ("and I'll show you a ship at sea, show me a rose, or leave me alone") and "There's a Place Called Omaha, Nebraska" ("in the foothills of Tennessee"). The unsurpassed comedian went on to new prominence, popping up on almost every TV show that would pay his fee. He was the subject on Edward R. Murrow's *Person to Person,* demonstrating his incompetence at the pool table, riding downstairs on the Inclinator he had hypochondriacally installed to save wear on his legs and heart—even though he had no trouble with either—and breaking up the interviewer. He received a salute on the *Look* magazine TV awards; parodied *You Bet Your Life* on Jack Benny's show; joked on programs hosted by Milton Berle, Martha Raye, Perry Como, Steve Allen; and made bookish remarks on *The Last Word,* a literate program hosted by Alistaire Cooke. He preferred to be the main attraction on these shows, but legal tender was the main object, as evidenced by a tart missive to Cooke: "I was a little disappointed on receiving your rather lengthy letter, to find no mention of money. I am of course, an artist, with my head in the clouds. And I was very happy to be invited to appear, gratis or thereabouts on *Meet the Press, The Last Word,* the City Center Theater in New York, two all-night telethons, etc. But my business manager, Mr. Gummo Marx, has a passion for money that is virtually a sickness. I am constantly being embarrassed by it. Still, he is my brother, and rather than upset him, I have to bow to his wishes."

As if to certify Groucho's prominence, *Confidential* went after him. In the days before supermarket scandal sheets and television gossip-mongering, this monthly magazine pulled in a large audience with calumnious tales of the famous, laying particular emphasis on their financial, chemical, and sexual misbehavior. It suggested that Groucho Marx ran a fixed quiz show, hinted that he spent his off-hours pursuing very young girls, and stated flatly that he was a most unpleasant star: "Groucho Marx is a 59-year-old crank with a snobbish air and a permanent case of indigestion and is considered far from a jolly old soul by the people who know him close up. Groucho has described himself as 'the brash, realistic type, equipped with a hair-trigger mind.' A friend with some psychological training sees Groucho somewhat differently: 'A defensive type with a permanent, built-in inferiority complex which he masks with arrogance.' " The family was naturally upset; only Groucho kept his head. Rather than expressing outrage, hiring a team of lawyers, and granting more publicity to his detractors, he sent an inimitable letter to the editor: "If you persist in publishing libelous articles about me, I will have to cancel my subscription." There were no more Groucho exposés from that periodical.

More to the comedian's liking was "I Call on Groucho Marx," an article that appeared in the spring of 1957. Pete Martin, *The Saturday Evening Post*'s celebrity interviewer, got Groucho to let down his guard for the first time in years. Asked if there were any occasions when his tongue failed him, Groucho replied: "Gabby as I am, there have been a couple of times when I've been at a loss for words. Not long ago there was a little 85-year-old lady on my show. She was alert and chirpy and sharp as a tack. I asked her a question and she gave me a long answer, and at the end of it she said, 'And I'd thank you to put out that very bad cigar, young man.' I put it out. I lit another one not long afterward, but first I did what she told me to do.

"The other time I was left speechless was one day when I was walking down Beverly and an elderly man came up to me and circled me as if I were a wagon train and he were a tribe of Indians. He called his wife over; they buttonholed me and they both said, 'Keep on living. Just don't die.'

"It really touched me, and I could think of no wisecrack comeback to that. I'm going to try to grant that couple's request."

•

ARTHUR COULD GO ONLY SO FAR in *Life with Groucho*. For all the paternal carping, the son had actually been discreet and circumspect. In the late 1950s he took up the subject again, and this time the gloves were off. Arthur's play *Everybody Loves Me* was written with Manny Mannheim, former head writer for the Milton Berle show. It concerned the life and hard times of a television comedian. Gordy Williams, a veteran of several marriages, has a volatile personality, a young and dissatisfied fiancée, a program with sponsor trouble, and a son anxious to break away from his father's control. In a rather odd turn of events, the producer of *Everybody Loves Me* was Max Gordon, once a close friend of Groucho's and now somewhat remote from his Hollywood connections. The show opened at the McCarter Theatre in Princeton, New Jersey. Gordon liked to try out his theatrical productions there, close to New York City, but distant enough to discourage the Broadway crowd from coming down and offering unwanted advice. He could not avoid *Variety*'s reviewer, who commended the star, comedian/actor Jack Carson, and noticed certain parallels with real people: "The authors carefully state that the characters are fictitious. Perhaps so, but they're alive enough to demand attention, if not respect." Princetonians had four chances to see *Everybody Loves Me* before it moved to the National Theatre in Washington, D.C. Attendance was poor, and word of mouth discouraging. Gordon, used to rocky pre-Broadway tryouts, pushed on to the Locust Theatre in Philadelphia. Here, too, attendance was off. The critical notices did not help. The *Philadelphia Daily News* praised Carson as "wonderfully cast as the aging network star, who can't bring himself to face competition from his own son," and admired the play's fast-paced beginning. "Throughout the first act, the gags fall thick and fast. Everybody in view has good lines to toss about and some of them are hilarious. Unfortunately, the writers are not able to sustain this high laugh quotient during the remaining two acts."

The *Philadelphia Evening Bulletin* characterized Gordy Williams as "a mean, arrogant, penny-pinching egocentric." It was, therefore, "to Carson's credit that he manages to squeeze just a little pathos out of the role, but it's hardly enough to get much sympathy from the audience."

The time for exposing the flaws of folk heroes and celebrities had not yet arrived. Few people wanted to know of Groucho's psychological manipulations or his tightness with a dollar. Again audiences failed to materialize, and now attention had to be paid. With great reluctance, Gordon took a loss of $75,000 and closed the show out of town. Groucho had protected himself from Arthur's latest invasion by refusing to see the show. Allegedly this was because of the same nervousness he felt in the old days, when his son competed in matches: "It's the worst thing for pop or mom to be up in the stands watching a would-be champ play tennis." So no rapprochement was necessary when Arthur came back to town, and Groucho could pretend that all was well between them.

At the end of the 1950s, *You Bet Your Life* suffered a battering because of much-ballyhooed quiz shows with big purses. By 1958, though, the public had grown somewhat sated with those programs, particularly when stories were leaked about a government investigation of *The $64,000 Question*, said to be rigged. In the resultant climate of rumor and scandal Groucho returned to his former prominence. His contestants were hardly the innocents they seemed, but the money they earned was too small to merit a federal probe. Even so, the demographics of *You Bet Your Life* were no longer what the De Soto people wanted. Theirs was a luxurious vehicle, and Groucho's audience seemed to be a mix of highbrow fans who preferred sensible cars, and lower-middle-class viewers who liked a good laugh at someone else's expense. The automobile dealers dropped out, to be replaced by Toni shampoo and other Lever Brothers products.

At sixty-seven, Groucho sensed that his long run might be approaching an end; Edgar Bergen, Fred Allen, Red Buttons, and even Milton Berle were already going or gone from TV. He was not pleased with the prospect of enforced leisure. A line in *Time for Elizabeth* had special meaning for him now. When Ed Davis's wife fears the retiree is so bored and frustrated he might commit suicide, he puts her off: "Kill myself? You know we're only insured for fire and theft." Suddenly, the thought of one-nighters, the bane of his early career, exerted a strange new appeal. He refused offers to perform in Las Vegas clubs—"I don't want to work for hoodlums and gangsters"—but beginning in the summer of 1957, and for the next three years, he and Eden toured in *Time for Elizabeth*. Almost everywhere they drew the kind of full houses he had dreamed about before the show bombed in New York. In Phoenix, the couple received a distinguished visitor. Thornton Wilder favored them with the requisite backstage compliments. The author made a modest suggestion to Groucho: "You should have ad-libbed more." The playwright/comedian took him at his word, embroidering the part and, on more than one occasion, giving a curtain speech of twenty minutes that prompted more laughs than the play itself. All along, he preferred to think of himself as a writer rather than as a performer. Krasna remembered that his collaborator sent him a letter boasting, " 'Our play is selling out.' He didn't say 'Groucho is selling out,' which was the actual truth."

In his late sixties, Groucho unbent so far as to spend money on a vacation condominium in Palm Springs. The desert was not new to him: Zeppo and Gummo already owned houses nearby. The purchase brought the brothers together—but only in the geographic sense. Gummo pointed out that the family had not been truly close since the vaudeville days. By the time of the movies, "Harpo had his group, Chico's friends were producers who gambled, actors who gambled, and women who screwed. A completely different class of people. Groucho went with a literary group. And Zeppo had his own group." Nowadays they rarely socialized. Yet the uncompetitive Gummo stayed on good terms with all of them, even though he, too, had his own crowd of business folk. What kept him in touch with the others was a unique willingness to take on the burden of responsibility. "If anyone was sick, or, God forbid, a funeral had to be arranged, I was the one who took care of these things. Not because I wanted to, but because I was expected to." The one activity that brought four of the brothers together on occasion was the rescuing of the fifth one. By this time Harpo had made profitable real estate investments, Zeppo's venture capitalism had assured his prosperity (his latest efforts concerned the development of a heart monitor), Groucho was at the top of his game, and Gummo continued to flourish as a talent agent. But whatever money they threw at the prodigal was not enough. In the face of declining health, Chico continued to work in the United States and overseas. "I guess I lost around $2,000,000 gambling," he told a British reporter. "I had money. I lost it—Las Vegas, the races, women. . . . The first crap game I played I lost $47,000 in one night. But I learned as I went along. In time I was able to lose more than that."

Groucho's own health suddenly began to fail at this time, and he needed the condominium more than he first thought. Hospitalized for exhaustion after *You Bet Your Life*'s ninth season, he recuperated in the Springs. His staff made some extraordinary calculations. In the process of hosting those 341 shows, he had appeared before a collective studio audience of 119,350 people. Contestants had spoken the secret word 256 times. The host had worn out three jackets and seven bow ties, and he had smoked 144 cigars. Little wonder that he was tired. And yet once the doctors established that there was nothing fundamentally wrong with him, he made ready to go back on stage and screen. At sixty-seven he had made a cameo appearance in *Will Success Spoil Rock Hunter?* and, for the strangest of all the Marx Brothers' valedictories, appeared in *The Story of Mankind*, adapted from Hendrik Willem Van Loon's history of civilization. The producer was Irwin Allen, who cast all three brothers so that he could advertise the film as the last Marx Brothers movie—and then used them as soloists. Hollywood's greatest comic trio never shared a single frame. In this humor-free production Groucho enacted the part of the seventeenth-century American settler Peter Minuit. As an in-joke, Harry Ruby and Eden played Manhattan Indians. In discrete episodes Harpo was a wordless Isaac Newton, and Chico a hooded monk.

The indifferent reception hardly mattered. Exposure was what counted to Groucho. As he saw it, the guest shots in film or on TV boosted the standing of *You Bet Your Life*, the engine of his career. Looking back was not his style; if this was autumn, he preferred to say, it felt like summer. He was unaware—or refused to acknowledge—that his biggest success was also his most impermanent. The New Groucho would always belong to the Eisenhower era of black-and-white TV and the nuclear jitters. The Old Groucho, the Groucho of the Paramount and MGM films, was timeless, disjoined from the man who created him, taken over by the kind of people who refused to have a television set in the house—if indeed they had a house. In Jack Kerouac's *On the Road,* selling widely in paperback during the late 1950s, Neal Cassady, the "holy goof," rushes "out of the car like Groucho Marx . . . that furious, ground-hugging walk with coattails flying." And Allen Ginsberg wrote to his fellow poet William Carlos Williams that he had recently created "a mad song to be sung by Groucho Marx to a Bop background." The Beat generation pored over the texts of these writers, elevating Groucho to a status he neither sought nor particularly liked, because they seemed to make him a traveler from an antique land. Columnist Leonard Lyons hoped to impress Groucho with news about another literary allusion, quoting a letter from Thornton Wilder:

"Re Groucho and *Finnegans Wake*—I have long thought he was in the book. Weren't the Marx Brothers once in a skit about Napoleon? I seem to remember them wearing tricornes, etc. Anyway, on pages 8 and 9 there is a visit to the Wellington Museum at Waterloo and I read . . . 'This is the three lipoleum Coyne Grouching down in the living detch.' "

Wilder, added Lyons, "once tried to explain to me the key to *Finnegans Wake*—involving his constant use of puns. The three lipoleum Coyne must be a reference to the Napoleon-type hats. And Grouching makes you a verb."

Laconically, Groucho wrote back: "There's no reason why I shouldn't appear in *Finnegans Wake.* I'm certainly as bewildered about life as Joyce was. Well, let Joyce be unconfined.

"Tracing this item down from the *Wake* could be a life project and I question whether I'm up to it. Is it possible that Joyce at one time was in the U.S.A. and saw *I'll Say She Is!*? [It was not.] Or did a New York policeman, on his way back to Ireland to see his dear old Mother Machree, encounter Joyce in some peat bog and patiently explain to him that, at the Casino Theater at Thirty-ninth and Broadway, there were three young Jewish fellows running around the stage shouting to an indifferent world that they were all Napoleon?"

With Irish and Beat literature taking him for their own, Groucho set out to reclaim his persona. The opening salvo, *Groucho and Me,* was published by Bernard Geis and composed without benefit of a ghostwriter. The memoir was a comic exercise in evasion. Groucho warned his readers that "one could write a factual, honest and truthful autobiography, but to play it safe it would have to be published posthumously. . . . what you're getting here is pure ersatz Groucho," and his statement was, as usual, truth covered with jest. (He was more candid with newspaper reporters. In several interviews, possibly out of guilt concerning Jerry Fielding, he addressed the political climate of the day. "There are no more Marx Brothers movies because we did satire, and satire is verboten today," he said in one interview. "The restrictions—political, religious, and every other kind—have killed satire. If Will Rogers were to come back today, he couldn't make a living. They'd throw him in the clink for being subversive. . . . Many people don't seem to realize that the first thing which disappears when men are turning a country into a totalitarian state is comedy and comics.")

Leniently reviewed, *Groucho and Me* landed on the *New York Times* best-seller list and gave Groucho the feeling that at long last he belonged in the company of his dedicatees, "Six Masters Without Whose Wise and Witty Words My Life Would Have Been Even Duller: Robert Benchley, George S. Kaufman, Ring Lardner, S. J. Perelman, James Thurber, E. B. White." Arthur and Miriam did not share the public's enthusiasm for their father's latest work, or for Groucho. Miriam's short-lived marriage had ended and she came back to California yet again. Treated with a drug to stop her from drinking, she started to suffer from neuropathy. The treatments stopped, and she resumed her old ways. Bewildered by Miriam's continuing alcoholism, Groucho allocated money for a trust fund but kept an emotional distance from his elder daughter. Miriam withdrew to a small house in Culver City, where she lived from time to time with a female companion. Irregular visits to hospitals became part of her routine. As for Arthur, he remained a solid and stable man, but not a happily married one. In keeping with the Marx Brothers' unspoken motto—Why have it simple when you can have it complicated?—he had fallen in love with his sister-in-law, Lois, and she with him. The resolution involved a great deal of shuttling between households, and some very unhappy in-laws, of whom Groucho was the most resentful. One evening he telephoned Lois and suggested that she was pursuing Arthur in order to get her hands on Groucho's estate. If he hoped to break up the romance, his efforts failed. The efforts only seemed to alienate Arthur for the year it took to obtain his divorce. "As a matter of fact," he remembered sadly, " I don't believe I ever quite trusted him again."

CHAPTER FIFTEEN

Groucho-off
and Groucho-on

IN 1959 the quiz show scandal broke wide open. *The $64,000 Question* was indeed fixed, as its most famous contestant, Charles Van Doren, publicly confessed. That program and its imitators vanished in disgrace. "Curiously enough," Groucho chortled, "the disappearance of all the big-money quiz shows has boosted my stock considerably. The last Nielsen rating had me on the top of the totem pole. Bob Hope remarked, 'I never thought the day would come when the only honest thing on TV would be the wrestling matches.' " From his perch Groucho received many offers and agreed to yet another Marx Brothers farewell, mostly to aid Chico. In 1959 the trio appeared in *GE Theater*'s half-hour production "The Incredible Jewel Robbery." Harpo and Chico acted in pantomime, stealing goods, running from the police, and assuming disguises, with Chico made up as a cop, and Harpo camouflaged as Groucho. At the last moment the real Groucho entered, articulating the show's only spoken line: "We won't talk until we see our lawyer." From above, a duck came down and the words "The End" were superimposed. The reuniting of the Marx Brothers was a gimmick from start to finish and fooled no one. Ratings for the frantic, unfunny show were abysmal, not least because Groucho, an NBC star, could not be advertised beforehand on a CBS show. Reviewers treated "The Incredible Jewel Robbery" with melancholy and disdain, best expressed by the *New York World–Telegram* reviewer: "The mocking hilarity of the old days was missing. Also missing was the mad, glad, bad brother, Groucho. True, he made a sudden, surprise appearance in the very last scene. But he was late by some 27 minutes."

A last-ditch attempt to resurrect the trio came a few months later. Phil Rapp, a British-born gagman, had written routines for the Brothers' contemporaries George Burns and Eddie Cantor; he seemed to know how to handle old vaudevillians on TV. Over the course of some meetings at the

Hillcrest Country Club he convinced the Marxes that they could make a go of *Deputy Seraph,* a situation comedy whose title evoked the words "sheriff" and "seraphim." The show was to feature Chico and Harpo as angels viewing earthly injustice from celestial heights, and making a weekly descent to set things right. Groucho would play the part of their boss, on camera every third week, an arrangement similar to his key but secondary role in *Love Happy.* Footage has survived and it shows everyone in a bad light. The jokes hark back to the 1930s, when they were done better: "You manipulate the uncle," says Groucho to Chico, "and I'll—ha, ha—I'll distract the girl." The remark is accompanied by a shameless waggling of eyebrows. Advised to put on a halo, Harpo extends his hand to Chico. "Hey," Chico corrects him, "not-a-hello, *halo!*" Disappearing and reappearing telephones and other props are never more than entry-level special effects. Yet the program might have survived these drawbacks had it not been for Chico's failing health. At the age of seventy-two he looked worn out, fighting gravity with face and body. The mind that once memorized twenty-digit numbers struggled with straight lines; scenes had to be reshot to accommodate his failings. Physicians diagnosed Chico's ailment as arteriosclerosis. After that, no insurance company would write a policy on his life. The pilot was never completed.

All the Brothers were feeling mortal chills as the 1960s began. Their great mentor, George S. Kaufman, died in 1961; the funeral was especially difficult for Groucho. In New York for the ceremony, he ran into comedian Dick Cavett. In later years, Cavett repeated their dialogue, spoken on a sweaty summer day: "Mr. Marx, I'm a big fan of yours." "Well, I could use a big fan long about now." Harpo went back to retirement in Palm Springs. Chico, having gambled away his last savings, went on the road with a "rag trade" comedy called *The Fifth Season.* In the play, a character explains that the garment industry has five yearly intervals—winter, spring, summer, fall, and slack—and it was the last that seemed to summarize the careers of all the Marxes. Groucho notified Norman Krasna, then living in Switzerland, "You won't receive any author's royalties this year from our mutual girlfriend, *Elizabeth.* In a way I regret not doing it again this summer. The audiences love the play and the laughs are loud and continuous, but the shabby accommodations were what did me in. I remember last year up in Sacandaga, it was 120 degrees during the day and 119 at night. I had a room about the size of an office desk with a window not much larger than the periscope lens of a submarine. This is hardly the way a rich man, or even a poor man, should spend his declining years. . . . P.S. I am starting my 14th season next Wednesday and this may be my swan song." Almost as a throwaway, Groucho mentioned that he would be "screwing up *The Mikado*" on television for the Bell Telephone Company. "This is my revenge for the lousy phone service they've given me over the years."

He was of course exhilarated by the opportunity to play Ko-Ko, the Lord High Executioner. Weeks were spent rehearsing the part, working on enunciation and nuance so that he would not dishonor his beloved William Schwenck Gilbert when he chanted the famous little list who never would be missed: "There's the pestilential nuisances who write for autographs / All people who have flabby hands and irritating laughs. . . ." The operetta received a first-class mounting. The producer was Robert Dwan, who had shepherded so many episodes of *You Bet Your Life,* and the adaptor was Martyn Green, Britain's preeminent Gilbert and Sullivan interpreter. Stanley Holloway took the part of Poo-Bah; the Mikado was Dennis King; and Katisha was played by the oversize Helen Traubel, the Metropolitan Opera's equivalent of Margaret Dumont. To please Groucho, Melinda was invited to play one of the Three Little Maids from School. "I plan on keeping a sharp eye on her," Groucho wrote a friend. "There'll be no 'Lolita' stuff if I can help it."

Try as he might, Groucho could not eliminate the Spaulding from the Savoyard; the bald wig and kimono never wholly masked the American clown. *Variety* called the evening *"Room Service* in a kimono." Groucho "failed to grasp the sense of the ludicrous, meddlesome, pain-in-the-neck characterization required of the role." Other papers made the same points, implying that the comedian was out of his element. In fact, Groucho knew more about Gilbert and Sullivan than most of his contemporaries and all three of his wives. At one time or another he had driven them to distraction by singing the patter songs over and over at home, backstage, and on movie sets. On this occasion, he decided to put his faith in the public and not the critics, especially when the ratings came in. *The Bell Telephone Hour*'s presentation of *The Mikado* had received the highest Nielsens of the season, and Groucho was pleased to point out: "We had a bigger rating the second half than we had the first. So apparently the audience stuck with it all the way." Immensely gratified, the sponsor asked Groucho to star in *The Pirates of Penzance* next season. He took the offer under consideration, but made no promises.

At three score and ten he thought long and hard about retirement. Chico was obviously in extremis, and Harpo suffered from heart trouble.

Groucho had taken care of himself all these years, bearing in mind the Marxes' genetic heritage: Minnie had died of a stroke at sixty-five, Frenchy at seventy-two, from a heart attack. Nobody knew exactly how old Opie was when he passed on, but his claims of longevity were surely exaggerated. After due consideration, Groucho turned down the request to star in *Pirates*. "Since we weren't speaking," Arthur later commented, "I never found out why, though I suspect he felt that having to memorize those rapid-fire tongue-twisting Gilbert lyrics was a little too arduous for a man of seventy." Intimations of mortality may have had something to do with the reconciliation between father and son. Late in 1960, after all the bitterness, Groucho abruptly invited Arthur and his new fiancée to dinner. The meal proceeded without incident. Old disputes went unmentioned; conversation became general and cheery. Afterward, Groucho invited Arthur into his study and presented a check for $5,000, as if the two had never exchanged a cross word. Several months later another change occurred. Groucho wrote Nunnally Johnson that he planned on "winding up a 14-year career as the world's most prominent quiz master. No tears will be shed by yours truly." Nevertheless, he observed, "It's rather odd not having anything facing me after this last show." Groucho would be asked to host some other television programs, but he saw no way to top what he had already accomplished. Offered a key part in the musical *A Funny Thing Happened on the Way to the Forum*, as well as a role in a Broadway comedy called *Young Enough to Know Better*, he returned both scripts on the grounds that he was "too old to be holed up in a second-rate hotel in New Haven, and at three in the morning, loaded with Seconal and Dexamil to be contributing my feeble best to rewriting the second act curtain and the entire third act." Yet he was unwilling to fully embrace retirement or to acknowledge any meaningful slippage. He was seventy and his wife twenty-six; as far as he was concerned, their mere appearance together was enough to certify him as an alpha male. When they were not on exhibit he played a little golf, a game that he had not taken seriously since the time he left the Immortals; went to parties and, as always, left early; wrote lively letters; and studied the mirror. Consoling an aging friend, he also assured himself that he had plenty of good years left: "It's certainly much tougher on a woman to wrinkle and crumble. A man, no matter how old he gets, can always wear an ascot tie and toupee and pretend he's Fred Astaire."

The pretending was still going on in May 1961, when he and Harpo were called to Cedars of Lebanon Hospital. In the cardiac ward a thin, diminished Chico recuperated from a severe heart attack. The healthy brothers cheered up the sick one, reminiscing and trading lines. After several days Chico felt well enough to go home to the modest Beverly Hills bungalow he shared with Mary, whom he had finally married the year before. His daughter Maxine came by. "I kissed him hello," she wrote in a memoir of her father. "He was quiet a moment. Then he said, 'I wish I were Groucho so I could help you out.' I looked into his eyes. 'I wouldn't exchange you for anybody.'" Particularly her intimidating, hypercritical uncle. Bearing in mind cousins Arthur and Miriam, Maxine went on to say that her uncle Groucho "succeeded in driving me away—just as he did most of those close to him."

Those siblings appeared with Chico one more time, a month after the final episode of *You Bet Your Life.* For years Groucho had speculated that Chico would die in bed—except that the bed would belong to someone else's wife, and that his demise would be caused not from angina pectoris but from a gun fired by the husband. But unlike the hectic, disordered life, the death in October was quiet and unobtrusive. Chico had been gone from the entertainment pages for years, and most newspaper obituaries were compiled from clippings. The *New York Times* proved an exception. Not only did the paper print a sizable notice, it ran a doleful editorial:

> When the news of Chico Marx's death was published millions of Americans had to accept another disturbing fact. The Marx Brothers as a band of slapstick clowns will never play again. . . . While Groucho, Harpo and Chico were all available, there was always an outside chance that they might vandalize the land of cuckoo once more. To theatergoers and moviegoers it seemed simple enough. All Groucho had to do was paint on that moustache, clamp a cigar in his mouth, and walk with a stoop. All Harpo had to do was slap on the wig, toot the rubber horn and leer at girls. Chico had only to put on the pointed hat and short jacket and shoot the piano keys. Nothing looked simpler. It can never be. The funniest team of 20th-century mountebanks is broken, beyond repair. . . . Alas, poor Chico. Alas, ourselves.

The funeral was stamped with Marx touches. On the way to Forest Lawn Cemetery, Groucho dealt with grief by assuring his fellow passengers, Gummo, Miriam, and Maxine, that there was not all that much to feel sad about. "Chico had more fun out of life than the rest of us combined," he assured them. Before they pulled up to their destination, he told a favorite death joke: In his last moments, a man makes a request. He inhales the aroma of coffee cake being baked in the kitchen. Could he have a piece? "Don't be silly, Sam," advises his wife. "That's for *after* the funeral." Jimmy Durante, George Burns, and Buster Keaton were on hand for the ceremony at Wee Kirk of the Heather Chapel, grieving as much for a vanished age of comedy as for Chico himself. Groucho's first wife, Ruth, stood uncomfortably at the edge of the crowd. A full-length mink coat enveloped her stout figure. She whispered, "Hello, Grouch." He returned her greeting with a wan smile and moved on. Counting the packed house of mourners and curious celebrity hounds, he muttered, "Well, at least it's SRO." The deceased had exhibited little interest in religion during his lifetime, but since a rabbi had been recruited for the occasion Maxine asked him to say that Chico Marx was the least *malicious* man that ever lived. The rabbi agreed. When it came his turn to speak he surveyed the crowd and intoned, "I have been asked by his daughter to say that her father was the least *mischievous* man in the world." Harpo leaned over and whispered to Groucho, "Listen, when I go, do me a favor and hire a mime."

That evening, Groucho took his son and daughter-in-law to dinner at Chasen's. For the first time, Arthur saw his father drink four straight whiskies. Groucho had always resented his older brother's cavalier attitude toward work and envied his success with women. But he needed to have Chico to criticize behind his back and to his face. The future looked bleak indeed.

Nineteen sixty-one was also the year that Harpo outshone Groucho in the literary field. *Harpo Speaks!* was precisely as advertised—the silent performer with his tongue untied at last, chatting with a journalist. Rowland Barber gave the material a chronological order and tidied up the anecdotes without losing Harpo's voice. It was a chatty, intimate autobiography, with many stories about the Algonquin crowd, Harpo's brothers, and his wife Susan and their adopted children. Unlike Groucho's evasive books, Harpo's held very little back. The man himself was presented on the pages, and *Library Journal* made a point that forced Groucho to wince: "Highly recommended. Harpo is the best writer of the Marx Brothers." Groucho could console himself with the fact that on television he was still the Marx of choice. NBC received so many letters of complaint when *You Bet Your Life* went off the air that the network offered to bring him back as the host of *Tell It to Groucho*. He allowed himself to be persuaded.

After all, he asked his friends, how many men are asked back in the spotlight at the age of seventy-one? The program debuted in January 1962 amid a flurry of publicity and personal appearances. "I am doing a new show," Groucho informed Goodman Ace, "which is precisely the same as the old show except that we have traded Mr. Fenneman for a spritely young doll with oversized knockers who leaps around the stage with all the abandon of a young doe being pursued by an elderly banker. Unfortunately, we have against us *Doctor Kildare, My Three Sons* and the public. If we are unable to woo any listeners away from the other networks, at the end of the season I will again be out of work." The courtship was futile. A victim of low ratings, Groucho's latest venture lasted twenty weeks.

The rest of the season was occupied with guest shots on other people's television programs, notably *The Tonight Show* in New York. The nation saw a new era in politics—the Kennedy administration was in full swing—and a new one in television. Jack Paar was on his way out, and for one week Groucho made a lively substitute, interviewing old friends Harry Ruby and Martyn Green, as well as the rising star Barbra Streisand. The nights passed rapidly and amusingly. NBC flirted with the idea of Groucho as the new host. Ultimately both parties acknowledged that a man in his seventies could not stand the pace and grind of nightly television. Groucho let it be known that an appearance once a month might be about right; network officials failed to respond, settling for Johnny Carson, full-time.

Before Groucho's spirits could flag, a new compliment came by mail. T. S. Eliot, of all people, wished to have an autographed picture of the comedian he so admired. Stunned, Groucho sent off a studio portrait. It was not what the poet had in mind. He requested the favor of another photograph—of the real Groucho, the one with moustache and cigar. This was forthcoming, and in a jocular mood Eliot wrote: "Your splendid new portrait is at the framers. I like them both very much and I cannot make up my mind which one to take home and which one to put on my office wall. The new one would impress visitors more, especially those I want to impress, as it is unmistakably Groucho. The only solution may be to carry them both with me every day."

Groucho had long expressed an ambivalence toward the British: he resented them for their treatment of the Marx Brothers back in the 1920s, yet he adored the quintessential Victorians Gilbert and Sullivan. He resented the BBC for failing to take a proper interest in an English version of *You Bet Your Life,* yet he cherished English novelists. Thus, when a query came from London, he was not sure how to respond. Would Mr. Marx be interested in doing something new for British TV? Without committing himself, he had Gummo check out the possibilities. As negotiations got under way, he turned his attention to local projects. Late in 1962 an unbilled Groucho Marx introduced the new host of *The Tonight Show,* and subsequently sat in the guest chair as Carson deferentially exchanged gags with him. Back in California Groucho worked on a new book, *Memoirs of a Mangy Lover.* The collage of old pieces, several written with the uncredited Arthur Sheekman, revealed more than a touch of Robert Benchley: "A man in my position (horizontal at the moment)." "I'm not going to tell you much about the Dark Ages because we historians know very little about that period. Frankly, it was so dark that no one could see what was going on, and those who did see were too polite, or embarrassed, to tell." "Love is not something you can learn from books, for love is an elusive sprite that leaps from nook to cranny and taps you with its magic wand, then flits away like the first hounds of spring. (It's not such a bad piece of writing, that last sentence. I've seen worse in books that sell for five dollars. In fact, that's where I saw this.)" Groucho had acquired some powerful friends by this time; Ogden Nash's encomium, "I read it with delight in one gulp," did more to sell the book than the indifferent and sometimes hostile reviews. The *New York Times Book Review* was particularly adverse, running a pan in the form of a letter: "Dear Groucho . . . Yours is the kind of humor that at its best hits fast, then scrambles on to the next one-liner. It doesn't bear re-reading, or even reading." The review suggested that the author had not composed his book alone. Groucho went into his never-apologize-never-explain mode, leaving the publisher, Bernard Geis, to defend him, falsely, as a man who never utilized a ghostwriter.

Norman Krasna, relaxing in his new home in Switzerland, received some jarring news from Groucho. Against Krasna's advice, his old collaborator had agreed to appear in a televised condensation of their play *Time for Elizabeth* for the Bob Hope *Chrysler Theater.* "The die is cast," said the letter, "and the deed is done. I just staggered out of Revue Studios which, in case you've forgotten, is at Universal. The script *Time for Elizabeth* was truncated to a rich 46 minutes, leaving 14 minutes for commercials. . . . I never worked so hard in my life. We shot 62 pages in five and a half days. I remember the lush days at MGM and Paramount when we all considered the day a triumph if we had one shot in the can by noon. Revue operates a good deal like a department store on 14th Street." The televised version, presented in the spring of 1964, made room for Eden in a small but significant part as a vamp on the loose, and played well enough for a sixteen-year-old vehicle. Bewigged and outfitted in a business suit, Groucho looked only slightly older than the part required. All the same, quite a few people complained that there seemed something odd about his appearance. It was not what he did—the waggling eyebrows at the end were out of character but expected. It was the broadcast itself: *Time for Elizabeth* was in color. True, Groucho had appeared in numerous TV variety shows in the full spectrum. But here, doing his own material, Groucho's style suggested a remote time and place, peopled with the likes of Charlie Chaplin, W. C. Fields, and the Marx Brothers, comedians who had established themselves in black-and-white.

Since no other invitations were being dangled in the States, Groucho did go to London during the time *Elizabeth* was being aired. It had been arranged for him to host a panel show called *The Celebrity Game.* He felt quite the important man seated alongside his fellow panelists, curmudgeon novelist Kingsley Amis, Beatles manager Brian Epstein, actress Susan Hampshire, and, as a concession to the American visitor, Eden. A flurry of interviews and a full-dress press conference stirred up interest and allowed Groucho to express his sexual theory of humor: "Women don't understand such crazy humor as that of Perelman or Benchley or even the early Marx Brothers." Whether this discouraged female viewers or not, the pilot show met with little enthusiasm. This setback was counterbalanced with a visit to the man Groucho referred to as "my celebrated pen pal," T. S. Eliot. The week before the dinner Groucho read *Murder in the Cathedral* twice and *The Waste Land* three times, and brushed up on *King Lear,* supposing that a literary reference or two might come in handy. Alas, the poet only wanted to discuss old Marx Brothers movies. Groucho memorialized the evening in a letter to Gummo: Eliot "asked if I remembered the courtroom scene in *Duck Soup.* Fortunately, I'd forgotten every word. It was obviously the end of the Literary Evening but very pleasant none the less. . . ." Only once did Eliot frown: "I told him that my daughter Melinda was studying his poetry at Beverly High; he said he regretted that, because he had no wish to become compulsory reading."

Back in the States, Groucho tried to revive the idea of a film based on the story of Minnie and her sons. Conversations with producer Frank McCarthy at Universal Studios led to a note: "If you're further interested I will let you read the Kyle Crichton book which is more about my mother who should be, it seems to me, the central figure in any story about the Marx Brothers." McCarthy did not follow up on the suggestion, and Groucho turned his attention to Broadway. He met with Fred Coe, hoping to interest him in a play about the Marxes. "If Mike Nichols could be snared for the project," he wrote the producer-director, "I would regard it as the coup of the season. However we must both realize that there are many successful shows surviving on Broadway sans Mr. Nichols." Coe did not respond with enough enthusiasm to satisfy Groucho, and he sent another letter: "I don't want to prod you, but other people are interested in various phases of the Marx Brothers. One chap named Harry Rasky wants to put together an hour on the Marx Brothers [as a TV special]. Then there is interest from Tony Curtis and perhaps Jack Lemmon and Jerry Lewis to do the Marx Brothers as a movie." Neither letter had the desired result. Resigned, Groucho moved on, visiting *The Tonight Show* and getting better acquainted with two idolatrous fans, comedian and host Dick Cavett, and the rising stand-up comic and writer Woody Allen. "The first time I met him," Allen said later, "he reminded me of an acerbic Jewish uncle, who you would meet at family gatherings, who makes biting and amusing remarks." Elkan Allan, an executive of British ITV, made the same comparison that year when he paid a call on Groucho in Los Angeles: "I found him personally very strongly reminiscent of all my Jewish uncles." Quite a different Groucho from the one Allan had been led to expect—was this a case of a man mellowing with age? Not so, as the Briton was shortly to learn.

With Allan guiding him, Groucho agreed to conquer Britain once more. Next year the American celebrity would be the host of a game show, provisionally entitled *Groucho in Britain*. For thirteen weeks' work, he would earn $40,000, a salary well below Groucho's customary price. Then again, no offers were coming in from American broadcasters. Groucho aimed to change all that. In the months before he was due to go overseas, he initiated talks with Sidney Sheldon, then the producer of a highly rated fantasy comedy, *I Dream of Jeannie,* hoping to generate ideas for a California-based TV show. These came to nothing. The turn of events eroded Groucho's morale a bit more. What brought him to the edge of a full-scale depression, however, was not a professional disappointment but a family tragedy.

The only brother to be truly content in retirement, Harpo had made his formal farewell to show business early in 1964 at the Pasadena Playhouse. Dressed in the customary raincoat, sneakers, and top hat, he broke his vow of silence: "Now, as I was about to say in 1907 . . ." It brought down the house. Nine months later, he suffered from unbearable angina. His doctors, bearing Chico in mind, advised him to consider surgery. Heart bypasses were at an early stage in those days, and as Harpo said, no one knew which way the cat would jump. The patient decided to take the risk. Groucho was apprehensive, but incapable of expressing emotion, no matter how deep, unless he came at it from an angle. And so on September 18, 1964, he fired off a letter to his brother, ostensibly warning him not to invest in banking stocks. "Dear Adolph," he began, "Not knowing how much money you are worth, and seeing no reason why I should, it is difficult for me to give you the benefit of my wisdom. I can only tell you that as far as I'm concerned, if I were to invest $100,000 in a project, it would have to be something like AT&T or Standard Oil of New Jersey. Take this for what it's worth, but remember, someday when you come creeping to my front door asking for alms for the love of Adolph, don't say I didn't warn you." He added lightly, "I'm glad you are in almost perfect physical condition, and not tossing that 100 grand into the crumbling sands somewhere east of Indio will surely help to keep you that way. Sincerely yours, Jeffrey T. Spaulding." Ten days later Harpo died at Mount Sunair Hospital in Los Angeles, with his wife Susan and two sons at his bedside. It took no great leap of the imagination for Groucho to see himself in that bed; Chico had been the first of the brothers to go, but he had almost asked for death with his risky behavior. Harpo had been serene and comfortable, and he had not been able to beat his genetic heritage. Groucho was the last of the big three, and who was to say how much time remained to him? A year? Two? Groucho cried when he heard the news, and surely some of those tears were for himself. Zeppo had joined the team late and left it early, and now there was no one to reminisce with. In addition, this older brother, unlike the other one, had achieved a status Groucho could never reach, that he could only admire from afar: Harpo was a loyal husband and an exemplary father. Groucho wished that he had spent more time with the man, and now it was too late to do anything but salute him in a letter to scenarist/lyricist Betty Comden. Having worked with the man "for 40 years, which is much longer than most marriages last, his death left quite a void in my life. He was worth all the wonderful adjectives that were used to describe him. He was a nice man in the fullest sense of the word. He loved life and loved it joyously and deeply and that's about as good an epitaph as anyone can have." Two months later, Harpo and Susan's daughter Minnie was married in Los Angeles, and Groucho gave the bride away. It was his last strong link with the brother whose family life he had envied but never truly understood. He also had trouble understanding family life a little closer to home. As he sat having lunch at the Hillcrest Club not long after Harpo's death, a youth approached him with a hearty, "Hello, Groucho."

"Who are you?" asked the comedian.

"I'm your grandson, Andy."

The two had been estranged for years because of the uncomfortable relationship of Groucho and Arthur. To his credit, an abashed Groucho then reached out to his grandchildren, inviting Andy and his brother Steven to join him on the Steve Allen show. But his effort came too late. The boys had their own interests, and to them Groucho was only a distant old man. "When I was growing up," Andy was to confess, "Groucho was not the superstar he later became. He was a TV star, but a lot of friends had relatives who were TV stars. He didn't become a legend until I was about twenty"—and it was only then that the relationship of grandfather and grandson resumed full-force.

In the spring of 1965, hoping to shake the blues, the seventy-five-year-old was back on television, hosting *The Hollywood Palace* just before flying to London. For years Groucho had tried to stage a reunion with Margaret Dumont, but she refused to appear on *You Bet Your Life* without a fee, and that was against the network rules. Now, at last, he could engage her to play Mrs. Rittenhouse in a reprise of "Here Comes Captain Spaulding." She came to lunch at Groucho's house, bringing along a book by columnist Russell Baker as a gift. It was a wise choice; Baker became one of Groucho's favorite writers. The television skit went off without a hitch. A few days after the taping, Dumont died of a heart attack. At the time Groucho was effusive in his praise: "She'd appeared in pictures with such great comedians as W. C. Fields, Jack Benny, Abbott and Costello, Laurel and Hardy, and Danny Kaye, and on television with Bob Hope and Dean Martin. But if the public chose to associate her solely with the Marx Bros., it was an association which had long been indelibly imprinted on our own hearts." Later, in a typically mixed memoir, he appended a note: "After the show she stood by the stage door with a bouquet of roses, which she probably sent herself. She was waiting to be picked up. A few minutes later some guy came along in a crummy car and took her away. She was always a lady, a wonderful person. Died without any money."

Just before he departed for foreign shores a saddened and somewhat bitter Groucho dropped a tongue-in-cheek fan letter to Russell Baker, adding biographically, "I am soon leaving for England where they appreciate a great artist. While there I shall toil for four months on British TV. Should we find it mutually agreeable, I may even continue for an indefinite period. As someone once said—or should have—a prophet is without honor in his own country." Upon arrival in London he adopted his familiar tone: "Our first program goes out June 17th. We may have to leave town June 18th." What was meant as comic self-deprecation contained a modicum of truth. In order to help organize the writers, Bernie Smith joined Groucho, and two weeks later Robert Dwan came over. Smith met him at the airport with a message: "We haven't got a prayer." One of the gagmen, Brad Ashton, remembered that Smith was put off by a new set of rules: "British viewers would take exception to Groucho bullying contestants in the same way he had done on *You Bet Your Life*. In Groucho's films he was the underdog and we sided with him, but on *YBYL* he was the bureaucrat and we tended to side with the contestants. When Groucho insulted them, he was insulting us." There were other differences and these were harder to overcome. *You Bet Your Life* had played with the house lights up. In England those lights were off; apparently British audiences preferred their laughter in the dark. And then there was the business of the indecently low budget. In America Dwan had used four cameras, leaving Groucho and his guests free to move just about anywhere they wished. In England the director was only permitted two camera positions. "So all I had to work with were two views," Dwan complained, "Groucho-off and Groucho-on."

From the opening shot *Groucho* looked cheap and the host discomfited. Reviewers were in no mood to cut anyone any slack. "One big yawn," said the *Daily Express*. "Dismal beyond belief," the *Observer* chimed in. The host seemed "ill at lease, almost unable to roll his eyes. It was downright cruelty to present him this way." *Groucho* never overcame these notices, and folded after thirteen weeks. In a postmortem, Ashton blamed the American comedian for bombing in Britain: "I would list as the main reason for Groucho's failure here the fact that he was just too lazy to learn his script. He read it off a big screen behind the backs of the contestants (and out of view of the audience). The screen was some twenty feet away from Groucho and I don't think his eyesight was that good anymore. Lots of really good lines had to be cut out of the recordings because he loused them up." It seems likely, though, that a farsighted Groucho would not have made the show a hit. Britons had been too long between Grouchos. They were intimately familiar with the monologists Captain Spaulding and Hugo Z. Hackenbush, and they knew the television celebrity of the 1960s, but nothing else. They expected the new Groucho to act like the old one, moving fluidly across the floor as he recited a cascade of non sequiturs and puns. That was no longer his style. Yet he was also incapable of delivering fresh material produced by his

British writers. Perhaps he had no style anymore, or perhaps, as he was to state upon his return home, "After sixty years in the business, I was tired. I was glad to get back to California."

•

GROUCHO'S ELDER DAUGHTER Miriam struggled with her habit, while his adolescent daughter Melinda fought her father on matters of authority and behavior. When Kay had expressed the desire to have a baby, Groucho had been in his mid-fifties. At the time, friends reminded him that if he became a father again the child would be reaching puberty when he was in his seventies. He ignored the warnings, determined to prove that in late middle age he was a still a man of vigor, like Chaplin. He was now paying the dues for that decision. The obedient little girl had grown into an assertive adolescent. These days she rejected Groucho's career advice, and sought singing and acting jobs on her own. Eden still enjoyed close relations with her stepdaughter; over the years she had become a confidante, going to the PTA meetings Groucho would never attend, driving the child to ballet lessons and play dates. It was too late for the nineteen-year-old and her father to reconcile their differences. She considered herself a rebellious woman of the sixties, just at the time when Groucho presented himself as a slippered pantaloon with neither the time nor the energy to argue with the young. "Like other friends," he wrote to scenarist Harry Kurnitz in the fall of 1965, "you seem concerned about my professional inactivity. You wonder how I make the days pass. Surely (you suggest) I must be bored. And I, in reply, can only say, How little you really know me!

"Let me give you a sample day. I hop out of bed at the crack of dawn. At 7 on the nose I have prune juice, whole wheat toast, a touch of marmalade and a pot of Sanka. After brushing my teeth I watch 'Woody Woodpecker' and 'Captain Kangaroo.' At 9 I take a nap until noon. Then comes lunch." In the evening "we play some old recordings of Lawrence Welk and his half-man, half-girl orchestra. At 8 we take two Seconals, three aspirin and a shot of LSD and fly to slumberland, eagerly looking forward to what thrills the next day has in store for us."

The caricature went down well with friends; it was not something Melinda wanted to confront. He had no way to reach her anymore. Unlike her mother and stepmother and cousins, Melinda showed no fear of Groucho. When he corrected her she gave as good as she got. "She was intolerant of her father's attitudes," commented Dorris Johnson. "She thought he was rigid . . . and wrong. I remember her saying, in defense of premarital sex, 'The arch evil is inflicting pain, not in sharing joy.' "

Of the three children, Arthur was the only one to find any real happiness that year. With a collaborator, Robert Fisher, he wrote a stage comedy based on the problems of his teenage stepdaughter (formerly his niece). The pre-Broadway tryouts of *The Impossible Years* broke box office records in Philadelphia, New Haven, and Boston—clearly, this was not going to be Arthur's *Time for Elizabeth*. The playwright could not wholly escape his lineage—in the *Boston Globe*, Elliot Norton wrote: "There are a number of very funny jokes in *The Impossible Years*. Possibly they were written by Arthur Marx, who is coauthor with Bob Fisher of this new comedy at the Wilbur, and most significantly, a son of Groucho. There are a great many other jokes in the same show which are not funny at all . . . the son of Groucho couldn't have written these." Still, the play was well received by most critics, and the star, Alan King, proved to be a huge draw. Arthur had written a bona fide Broadway smash, and he had done it without a word of encouragement from Padre.

Groucho failed to fly in for opening night, alleging nervousness, and omitted to send the customary telegram. Not until Arthur had returned to L.A. did he fabricate an excuse for coming into New York on business. He instructed his son that he wanted "good seats, and for nothing." Arthur phoned the box office, ordering house seats to be presented gratis. A week later Groucho flew back into town, with a rare compliment ("The most laughs I've had in a long time") and the inevitable gripe that he would hereafter be known as Arthur Marx's father.

Arthur's father could reclaim his own distinction later that year when he received a letter from a Dr. L. Quincy Mumford, director of the Library of Congress. Mumford had read an article in *The New Yorker* mentioning that Groucho and T. S. Eliot were correspondents. Assuming that the comedian had written to, and received replies from, other litterateurs, he asked him to consider donating his papers to the Library. The librarian added some additional bait: "In the Manuscript division may be found many of the national treasures, including the personal papers of most of the Presidents. These distinguished collections would be enhanced by the addition of your papers." Groucho found the suggestion irresistible. That the letters of a man with a seventh-grade education would be placed in the category of national treasure was tribute enough. That the request came from Dr. L. Quincy Mumford, a name worthy of Groucho himself, made the event even more delicious. He accepted during an appearance on *The Tonight Show*. Dressed in Captain Spaulding outfit of jodhpurs and clawhammer coat, with a loud plaid cap in place of the usual pith helmet, he extracted Mumford's letter from his pocket and demanded that Johnny Carson read it "with sincerity." When the host finished, Groucho, labeling himself a "part-time, on-the-fringe writer," agreed to donate the letters.

It would not be necessary for Grouchoites to visit the Library. Early in 1967 Simon & Schuster published *The Groucho Letters,* a compendium of the best missives Groucho had sent and received. These demonstrated that like Falstaff, the author was not only witty himself, he was the cause of wit in others. In fact, his correspondents were usually a lot funnier than Groucho. (Goodman Ace correctly advised the anthologist, "If you think that publishing a book of letters that people have written to you makes you a man of letters, you're mistaken.") The collector's broadsides at corporations were all too predictable, and his exercises in nostalgia, while amusing, were rarely personal, save for a brief commentary on his wives: "Like the Irish, the Jew, too, is being assimilated. I certainly did my share. I married a Mormon, a Swede and an Irish lass, all paupers." There was an astonishing lack of references to politics, social issues, or the Vietnam War. But there were the hilarious letters to the Warner Brothers, and when Groucho quoted his friends the letters evoked the great old days in 1930s New York, when cleverness was in the air. A note to Norman Krasna read: "[Harry] Ruby is now writing verses *about* verses. Explaining that 'Writing Poetry Is for Those / Who Can't Express Themselves in Prose,' he goes on to say:

> *When I consult Roget or March*
> *For words to weave upon my loom,*
> *My eyebrows testily I arch*
> *And order Junior from the room.*
>
> *I run my fingers through my hair,*
> *I pace the floor and curse my luck*
> *As I imagine Baudelaire*
> *And Shelley did when they were stuck."*

In a postscript Groucho informs Krasna that he had been "needlessly alarmed." He goes on: "Last night Ruby and I went to the ball game. When he yelled for the Dodgers, it was in 100 per cent prose."

Groucho flogged the book on occasional television appearances. Other than that he was quiescent, retreating to his home except for occasional lunches with old friends. He had lost his taste for the desert climate. Gummo and Zeppo were still there, but since Harpo's death something vital had gone from Palm Springs, and he seldom went back to the place. Because he appeared vigorous for a senior citizen, only a few people knew that he was fighting prostate trouble, followed by a chronic bladder problem, the result of a botched operation. The discomfort forced him to stay home, yet the things that once comforted him—the books, music, and guitar—only seemed to make him more restless and querulous. He badgered Eden, imagining that she had been carrying on with her piano teacher. "He keeps feeling your leg when you're on the piano stool with him," he complained. When that instructor died, he trained his sights on Jeff Corey, one of the most respected acting coaches in Hollywood. Eden had begun to take lessons with him, and Groucho suspected that *they* were having an affair. He issued a new order: "You have to decide whether you want to be married or be an actress." Eden chose to bend rather than break. She abandoned thoughts of the stage, and satisfied her artistic yearning by painting and sculpting.

Some relief to their distressed relationship came in the spring of 1967, when the Gallery of Modern Art in Manhattan staged a three-week tribute to the Marx Brothers. Groucho and Zeppo flew in for the occasion, accompanied by their wives. Zeppo, a believer in physical fitness since young manhood, looked trim and vigorous. Groucho seemed a bit frail but mentally agile, bandying wisecracks with newspaper reporters. *Time*'s cinema critic and several editors took him to lunch, hoping to extract some anecdotes about Paramount and MGM, but Groucho, running true to form, only wanted to talk about rereading Somerset Maugham. When the coffee came he pretended to drop his guard, mentioning that Marx Brothers festivals had taken place at a few revival houses. Had he attended? "One or two," he replied. And how were the audiences? He considered for a moment. "Hostile." Vestiges of the courtly old Groucho came out when he ran into the journalists and their spouses on opening night. "Why is it," he asked the crowd in the elevator, "that writers always have pretty wives?"

That night the Gallery showed a print of *Animal Crackers,* the one Marx Brothers film unavailable to viewers since the 1930s because of some copyright snarls. Groucho was greeted with a standing ovation. He invited Zeppo onstage, then brought on Eden, Zeppo's glamorous wife Barbara, and Chico's bright-eyed daughter Maxine. "I just want you to know," he told the audience, "that the Marx Brothers don't marry shleppers." As part of the program he sang a couple of songs with a lean, white-haired Harry Ruby at the keyboard. They had barely begun when Groucho held up his hand and assumed an expression of weary discontent. "Fine piano player. The least you can do is give me some support. I don't know where you learned to play the piano—maybe when you were sliding into second."

Ruby returned fire: "Ladies and gentlemen. I want to tell you something. Forty years ago when I first played for Groucho he insulted me. Success hasn't changed him a bit."

Forced laughter greeted their badinage. Never had the fault line been so wide between the dynamic wag on-screen and the belligerent old party onstage. Groucho tried a few more lines, but his listeners seemed to have their minds on other things and he could not bring them back to the matter at hand. For more than half a century, Groucho Marx had been able to turn any audience to his advantage, offering a leer, wiggling an eyebrow, waggling a cigar, creating merriment with the ease of a man jingling change in his pockets. Not now. Before his eyes the power had passed to the onlookers, and that evening they turned a comedian into an icon. No wonder Groucho seemed disoriented.

Having returned to California, he found his family almost as unmanageable as his image. Melinda had been a guest on a popular television show, *The Dating Game,* on which she had won a safari to Africa. From there she toured Israel and Europe—and thereupon disappeared from view. Groucho wrote Nunnally Johnson about his daughter, the runaway radical: "Melinda seems to be running out of countries. She's been in New York, Israel, Grecian Islands, Paris, Africa, London, and I'm predicting in two weeks she'll be in Viet Nam—in the northern section."

The tone of amused irritation vanished when after two weeks no word of Melinda had come, and it was not until Groucho hired private detectives in Europe that she was run to earth in an Israeli kibbutz. Shortly afterward, she announced her intention to marry a fellow kibbutznik, a French government worker. The engagement was called off several months later. A Parisian journalist, hoping to elicit a usable quote, placed a call to Beverly Hills and got what he was after. "If you want to worry about something, why don't you go after de Gaulle?" snapped Groucho. "He spent three days in Canada and tried to cut the country in two."

Having disposed of Melinda for the moment, Groucho turned his attention to the handful of invitations that came his way. He was briefly tempted by director Federico Fellini's offer to appear in his operatic new film *Satyricon,* until he learned that he would have to spend a whole winter in Rome. Another director, Otto Preminger, dangled a more acceptable proposal. Groucho would be paid $1,000 a day for five days' work on the new Paramount film *Skidoo.* Preminger did not add that Charlie Chaplin and Senator Everett Dirksen had already turned down the role of "God," a mobster who eventually becomes a drug-taking, peace-loving hippie. Groucho agreed to wear a long robe, and to wear a black toupee and heavily darkened moustache and eyebrows. Rather than give him a contemporary look, they smacked of the exhibits in Madame Tussaud's Wax Museum. Looking at the rushes, Groucho proclaimed himself "God-awful." Watching Preminger's antics behind the camera, Carol Channing, another cameo player, remarked, "Someone should shoot Otto directing this film." Realizing the full extent of the disaster, Groucho corrected her. "Someone should shoot Otto—period."

By the summer of 1967 he had just about decided to quit show business for good, confining himself to the organization of memory, putting his scrapbooks and photographs in order, and spending more time with cronies. Almost no offers came in nowadays, due in part to his advanced age, but also because there had been considerable talk about his eccentric behavior recently. On a visit to New York in early 1968, he attended a performance of Carl Reiner's screwball satire *Something Different.* The critics had not been sympathetic, and the orchestra was only half full. Groucho chose to lecture them at the end of act 2, rising from his seat to complain about humorless reviewers and an indifferent public. Word about the rant got around, and *Variety* called his hotel for further information. "Apparently the only thing audiences will go to see anymore," he grumped, "is complicated, obscure, non sequitur plays that make no sense. I think reviewing is in the wrong hands in New York, and most other places." Warming to the subject, he stated that the Broadway smashes in which he and his brothers starred—*I'll Say She Is!* and *Animal Crackers*—"would fail today. They were too funny." Groucho noted that the current cold spell and flu epidemic naturally hurt the show's box office receipts, and he tossed in a short opinion of New York City: "Of course, you can't get a cab. The only thing you can catch is leprosy." More bellows issued from Groucho when he got hold of a new novel, *The Cannibals,* by the actor Keefe Brasselle. The ironies were plentiful: Brasselle had played the title role in *The Eddie Cantor Story,* a screen biography of Groucho's old vaudeville colleague. The actor's roman à clef offered a derisive portrait of a Groucholike character called "Mr. Ad Lib." The narrator, Joey Bertelle, is entertaining a crowd at a Las Vegas casino when "a famous, rich, senile comedian" starts showing off at his table, talking throughout the performance. "It killed me to introduce him, but being show biz, I gave him the obligatory flowery introduction—whereupon he popped up and took his bows, but without looking at me once in the appropriate thank-you style. . . . At seventy-odd years, this hairpin was still walking around— with a beautiful wife and a couple of stale books he wrote." Bertelle wreaks his revenge by closing in on Eve, Mr. Ad Lib's wife: "Where's Moustache?" "Where else?" she replies. "Sleeping." From there it is only a quick step to the bedroom and a perfunctory seduction. Holding the book in his shaking hand, Groucho confronted Eden. She told him the book was not only vile in its writing but evil in its intent. No such seduction had ever happened. Groucho nodded and, to demonstrate his belief in her fidelity, pitched *The Cannibals* in the roaring fireplace. It was never mentioned again.

It did not have to be. There were other bones of contention between husband and wife, among them Groucho's unending criticism of the way Eden ran the house, how she conducted herself in company, the manner in which she sided with Melinda, and her recent retreats into heavy drinking. These could not simply be burned away, they could only be held in abeyance in the winter of 1968 when Melinda announced her intention to marry film producer Mack Gilbert. Melinda was starring in Gilbert's independent film *No Deposit, No Return,* and, having met the prospective groom, Groucho found him more than acceptable. The young man was not only rich, he was a Gilbert and Sullivan aficionado. On December 8, Groucho gave his daughter a $10,000 wedding at the Trousdale house. The process was not without its snarls. In one of his rare, quixotic gestures Groucho asked Melinda to involve Kay in the proceedings; Melinda was dead set against that, and got her way. In general, though, the ceremony was a lush, happy affair. The problem was that the marriage lasted only a little longer than the ceremony. Less than two weeks after the exchange of vows, Melinda ran off with the long-haired leading man of *No Deposit, No Return,* Sanh Berti. George Jessel, one of the wedding guests, quipped, "The marriage was so short, the bride got custody of the wedding cake." Looking back at that strange fortnight, Harpo's son Bill described Melinda's behavior as her one true rebellion in all the minor skirmishes against Groucho: "I believe Melinda resented her father's always making her a puppet. She probably felt it was better all these years not to test herself. All of a sudden she freaked. She decided to be herself. There was no turning back."

Understandably, Groucho was bitter, even though some part of him had to acknowledge that this was only the latest chapter in the why-have-it-simple-when-you-can-have-it-complicated history of the Marxes. A more severe and intimate blow came a few weeks later, and this one he could not dismiss with a crack and a shrug. On January 7, only a few weeks after Melinda's post-wedding rebellion, Arthur was summoned from the set of a situation comedy, *Mothers-in-Law*. A secretary, worried about Groucho's flaky voice, summoned Arthur to the phone. The old man could barely hold back the tears as he told his son the terrible news: Eden had walked out on him.

CHAPTER SIXTEEN

A Manager or a Keeper

THE YEAR BEFORE HER WALKOUT, Groucho and Eden had attended a crowded party. During the evening she took a long unhappy look at her husband. "I've waited this long," she was heard to philosophize. "I might as well stick it out all the way." But all the way turned out to be an unendurable length of time. In the months before she left him, Eden took to her room as soon as she heard the voices of Nunnally Johnson or Bert Granet or any of Groucho's other friends at the door. Rather than become the butt of her husband's jokes she had dinner sent to her room. "If only once he told me he loved me," she wailed to another confidante—a sentiment that cooled as soon as she left Groucho's bed and board. With the counsel of a high-powered attorney, Marvin Mitchelson, Eden Hartford Marx sued for divorce, charging that her husband possessed so vile a temper that he had once threatened to kill her. As compensation for pain and fear she asked for the Trousdale house, said to be worth $350,000; 50 percent of the couple's community property in excess of $3,000,000; and a monthly alimony of $5,500. Groucho countered that his third wife had been a heavy drinker, like the others, and that she had "no enthusiasm for running the house" because of her sloth. He added that he had not only given her all the money she ever requested for clothes and living expenses, he had also sent $100 every month to her mother. In fact, he pointed out, Eden had been given an allowance even before they got married. He could not stop wisecracking even in a deposition: "Since I'm a very bad lay, she was entitled to this." At the conclusion of his testimony Groucho implied that Eden had been running around on him. "I have a clear conscience," he told Mitchelson. "I haven't fucked anybody." In the end, he gave Eden close to $1,000,000, but as in his other marital splits, he retained ownership of the house. To Groucho, homes were never negotiable.

To everyone's surprise but Arthur's, the next romance was with . . . Eden Hartford Marx. Irwin Allen, producer of *The Story of Mankind,* asked a logical question: "What have you two got to talk about?" Groucho smiled benignly. "There's a wealth of material. We talk over our old fights," he answered.

While the lawyers worked out final terms of the settlement, Groucho's attention roved back to show business. The budding nostalgia industry was about to give him another chance at celebrity. Back east, Broadway producer Arthur Whitelaw had an idea for inaugurating the 1970s. He would bring the Marx Brothers back to Broadway as the subjects of a musical biography, *Minnie's Boys.* He signed Hal Hackaday and Larry Grossman to write the score, hired Groucho as "production consultant," and offered Broadway's hottest playwright, Neil Simon, first crack at the book. Simon turned it down cold. Next he went to comedian David Steinberg, whose bright standup act indicated that he might be right for the job. Steinberg's script was sent to Groucho for approval; he disliked it intensely. Whitelaw called in Arthur and his partner Bob Fisher with the reassuring words, "Frankly, we can't get anybody else to do it. At least nobody as qualified and who knows the Marx Brothers as well as you two." Arthur accepted the offer, a move he would learn to regret. By the summer of 1969, Groucho had suffered several minor strokes, was hard of hearing and forgetful, and often repeated himself.

Burdened by the pains and infirmities of age, Groucho still had to be included in some of the decisions—after all, it was his life that would be presented onstage. Whitelaw thought the pudgy comedienne Totie Fields, who could sing and dance, would be sensational as Minnie. Enraged when he found out the casting news, Groucho yelled at his son, "I won't have that Jew broad playing my mother."

"What are you talking about?" Arthur shouted back. "Aren't the Marx Brothers Jewish?"

"Yes," he replied with absolute seriousness. "But the world thinks we're Italian."

In a subsequent reminiscence Arthur recalled that line, then went on to identify his father as a confused figure but hardly a self-hating Jew. Groucho, he reminded the reader, continually spoke out against anti-Semitism and for the state of Israel. But the fact remained that Groucho's Jewish heritage was social rather than liturgical, ethnic rather than religious. His grandparents, Opie and Omie, were the last practicing Jews in the family. Frenchy and Minnie had only gone through the motions to satisfy the old folks, and of all the boys Groucho ran the farthest from his background, always seeking shiksas to carry on with or marry. Whatever Groucho's feelings about Jews in general, he would not be budged on the subject of Totie Fields, and Whitelaw capitulated, unwilling to create a public relations disaster. He hired Shelley Winters for the part. Groucho knew very well that Winters was also Jewish, but entered no objections because she was a serious Method actor, with none of the blatant ethnic mannerisms that marked a Fields performance. Furthermore, she was blond, with a vaguely Germanic aura, in keeping with his image of Minnie. With the business of casting out of the way, Whitelaw encouraged Groucho to stay on the West Coast, and out of the way of the writers. This he was content to do until just after New Year's Day, 1970. As soon as he learned that *Minnie's Boys* was in trouble, he booked a room at the Regency Hotel in New York and turned up at the Imperial Theatre on West Forty-fifth Street, eager to lend his unwanted expertise.

Groucho's idea of help was to sit around, reminiscing. His vaudeville stories enthralled the cast. The trouble was, while he related his favorite memories no one could rehearse. Whitelaw resolved the problem by paying one of his comely secretaries to take the consultant for long, halting walks through Times Square. These accomplished their purpose so well that Groucho offered to marry her, a proposal she politely refused. As the couple toured midtown, fresh material was inserted on a daily basis. Winters had been shaky enough with the old script; the added lines made her so insecure that she went onstage during previews holding the new pages. The star also battled with a persistent virus, and on several nights her understudy went on bearing the same papers. S. J. Perelman, who had managed to be in on the high and middle points of Groucho's career, turned up at the nadir. Whitelaw had summoned him to the Imperial, hoping the humorist might contribute some insights and gags. Perelman reported his findings to his friend Al Hirschfeld, theatrical caricaturist of the *New York Times:*

Night before last, I was sped by Rolls-Royce and uniformed chauffeur to the bedside of a sick musical called *Minnie's Boys*. Arthur Whitelaw—or Outlaw—its producer, thought that my genius could effectively save the patient.

Knowing me as a truthful reporter, you will not doubt me when I say that it was a scalding descent into a tub of such merde as hasn't been seen outside a Catskill Summer camp show. Shelley Winters wasn't appearing that night, doubtless taking refuge in a supposed laryngitis. Her replacement read the whole part off some onionskin pages that kept curling up in shame. The five hoodlums representing the Marxes as children kept crawling through each other's legs and armpits to evidence joie de vivre. Plot there was none, and laughter less. Groucho, whose son Arthur wrote this—with a collaborator yet—is listed on the house boards as technical consultant. As the patrons were handed their programs they found enclosed a mimeo'd message from Groucho, asking them to pretend that they were in Philadelphia watching a break-in of the show and to exercise compassion because admittedly there were some weak spots. (This was the official thirteenth preview.) In his postscript to the foregoing, Groucho said with elephantine humor that if anyone in the audience raised his hand, he'd be permitted to leave the room. He needn't have; the recipient was already in the toilet, and numbers of them left for it throughout the performance.

The musical continued to falter. Whitelaw brought in a new director and induced Joe Stein, who had written the book for *Fiddler on the Roof,* to punch up the dialogue. These strategies worked; laughs began to come in the right places. Winters's performance picked up, and the producer saw reason to hope. Groucho went so far as to praise his son openly when he learned that Stein was taking credit for the laughs. At a dinner at Luchow's he burst out, "What the fuck are you talking about, Joe—you wrote the show? My son and his partner wrote it. You just added a few jokes. And not very good ones, in my opinion." (Less openly, Groucho confided to friends that *Minnie's Boys* had the lineaments of a Broadway turkey.)

Notwithstanding, Groucho was in attendance on opening night, March 26, 1970. In the same row were Gummo and Zeppo, as well as Eden, flown in at his expense. The performance went better than expected. Shelley Winters knew her lines, and Lewis Stadlen, the actor playing the youthful Julius Marx, sang the one number that snared Groucho's spirit, "You Remind Me of You": "Cold sober or blind / Up front or behind / You'll always remind / Me of you." After most critics had gone up the aisle, the crowd stood to give a rousing ovation to all concerned. Groucho creakily stepped onstage, chomping on his familiar cigar. Privately he addressed Winters: "I never thought when I saw you at Saks buying sweaters for your big knockers that someday you'd wind up playing my mother." In a voice the ticket holders could hear, he complimented Stadlen: "You're better than I ever was—and younger." Continuing in a cloudy voice, he praised other cast members and then switched the subject to his current miseries with a catheter. The showfolk hustled him off to an opening night party to await the reviews.

Most were lenient, but the one that counted, Clive Barnes's critique in the *New York Times,* was composed of death sentences: "The idea of a musical on the Marx Brothers before they really became the Marx Brothers is splendid. Whatever happened to it? . . . The show at its best has you looking back fondly upon the old movies. You would be better at home watching the old movies." Barnes, who had stayed for the curtain calls, quoted Groucho on the excellence of Stadlen. "In a sense," remarked the critic, "he is probably right—but I wonder whether anyone is ever going to impersonate Mr. Stadlen, who is only a very fine actor. Mr. Marx is himself a way of life—and it is a way that *Minnie's Boys* can only reflect and hint at." On Sunday the *Times's* other drama critic, Walter Kerr, filed a more favorable opinion:

> Nobody ever just *liked* the Marx Brothers. The Marx Brothers didn't leave room in their toe-to-toe challenge on the edge of the handiest abyss for so tepid an emotion. It was one for all and all for nothing with them, an attitude that engendered as much passion, one way or another, in the beholder as there was in Groucho's swallow-tailed backward flips—he looked like a seagull doing entrechats—onstage. . . . As a result I have gone my long life never seeing an acceptable imitation of any Marx brother in full sail. Where *Minnie's Boys* was smart, unbelievably bright, really, was in starting them all out in birch-bark canoes, sans wigs, sans moustaches, sans tricks. This may seem obvious and even necessary if you're going to do a musical about the problems Mother Minnie had in figuring out a future for her five unemployable sons, but it's not, not at all. There must have been a strong temptation to underscore early, to plug for recognition instantly, to borrow their best bits in a hurry in order to get going, to *press.* That would have put us all off, right off. What they've done, instead, is to let the mannerisms grow casually, almost absent-mindedly, even to the point where for quite a while you may feel they may have forgotten a few.

Citing a favorite incident in the musical, Kerr concluded:

> *Minnie's Boys* is partly patchwork, here and there conscienceless, stuck with its gags-to-riches formula. I had a perfectly good time

because those four boys onstage honored the men they were not trying too hard to become, and because I still go all helpless when I see even two Marx Brothers toasting marshmallows over their hard-hearted wastebasket, to which they have set fire.

Kerr's bouquet arrived too late. In 1970 no Broadway show could work its way past a bad notice in the daily *Times*. Dwindling receipts forced Whitelaw to close the show on May 30, after sixty performances and a reported loss of $500,000. The Marxes returned to California, Arthur sadder but wiser, Groucho just sadder. Shuffling around Beverly Hills one day, he ran into Maurice Chevalier. The two old men exchanged memories of Hollywood. "Do you get invited out much?" Groucho inquired. "Not so much," answered the Frenchman wistfully. "The world has passed me by." Groucho knew what Chevalier meant. He, too, was a back number, forgotten or ignored by the new Hollywood of *Easy Rider, The Graduate,* and hallucinatory "head films" like *2001* and the Beatles' *Yellow Submarine.* Many days were whiled away with old friends in similar straits—Harry Ruby, Arthur Sheekman, Nunnally Johnson. They organized a Geezer Club, just as thousands of other golden agers did around the country. The difference was that these men had known fame. Groucho could be merry enough at the gatherings; once home, however, he descended into moodiness and random thoughts of suicide. He had but one trusted confidante at this time, his housekeeper Martha Brooks, a white-haired African American woman who had been at his side through two marriages. To buoy his spirits, she urged Groucho to renew his driver's license and show the world that he could still tool around Beverly Hills and whistle at pretty girls. She coached him on the questions until he felt secure enough to take the driving test. To ensure that he would pass, Groucho presented the examiner with an autographed picture and a box of cigars—"Not the cheap kind I usually give away," he pointed out. They did no good. Groucho's driving was uncertain and wobbly, and the examiner was forced to flunk him.

As was now customary with Groucho, whenever circumstances depressed or elevated him, a counterweight would manifest itself. At his lowest moment, when he was afflicted by precarious health, obscurity, and loneliness, several forces were working at restoration. The first was Woody Allen. The young comic had made an impression on Groucho from his earliest days. "He was an admirer of mine," Allen was to say. "I was a worshipper of his." In the film *Take the Money and Run,* released just as Groucho began his steepest descent, Allen shows the parents of his alter ego Virgil Starkwell. They analyze their wayward son, alternately cursing and blessing Virgil from behind two Groucho masks. Even young audiences had no trouble identifying the subject of Allen's homage. On the shelves of U.S. booksellers, there appeared a profusely illustrated volume entitled *The Marx Brothers at the Movies.* Written by *Newsweek's* film critic, Paul D. Zimmerman, the book went through the Brothers' cinema career feature by feature, applauding them for their intellect, their timing, and their humor, but mostly because "they transcend their time." For this tribute Groucho was not so grateful. He disliked works that took an uncritical fan magazine approach. "They're crap," he complained to the *New York Times.* "They do a new kind of writing. They rent our movies, tape-record them and write down all the good jokes in their books. Quite a writing feat!"

In 1970, the Marxes in general, and Groucho in particular, received a new imprimatur from the academy. Martin Gardner's 272-page Ph.D. dissertation, "The Marx Brothers: An Investigation of Their Films as Satirical Social Criticism," made powerful claims for their work, and enforced these with examples and commentary. Gardner's conclusions would have astonished the Brothers, who never claimed that they were anything more than entertainers. The thesis points out that Bertolt Brecht was influenced by *A Night at the Opera* when he wrote the wedding scene for *The Caucasian Chalk Circle.* Moreover, Eugène Ionesco "told the audience at the American premiere of *The Shepherd's Chameleon* that the three biggest influences on his work had been Groucho, Chico and Harpo Marx. And Philip Roth said that he would have liked to have seen a film made of Franz Kafka's *The Castle* with Groucho Marx as K. and Chico and Harpo as the two 'assistants.' " Breaking down the Brothers' satire into categories, Gardner examines their onslaughts against history, politics, and the economy; manners and customs; literature and popular entertainment. He finds that "although there are some elements of pure visual satire in the films, the greater emphasis of the Marx Brothers' satire is verbal, with Groucho acting as the major spokesman." This paper, in turn, was to be examined by another academic, Wes D. Gehring, in his monumental "bio-bibliography" of the Marx Brothers. Gardner, he stated, was to be complimented for showing the correlation between reality and satire, "best exemplified when he examined *Duck Soup* as a comic undercutting of paranoia in international diplomacy," expanding on the belief that World War I was a conspiracy between munitions manufacturers to gain profits. Gehring quotes from an early version of the film when it was known as *Cracked Ice* and cast Groucho as a munitions salesman. That script contained Groucho's unused spiel: "Gentlemen, do you realize that ammunition was never cheaper? Right now you can get two 16-inch shells for the price of one and shoot twice as far for half the money. With every $5,000 purchase we throw in a Big Bertha [a huge German cannon]. If you don't like her you can throw her right out again." Gardner's dissertation was the first of many to come. Soon enough, the study of popular culture would be an industry.

•

AT EIGHTY, AND IN PAIN, Groucho had no patience with scholars; it was difficult enough to get through the day without speaking about yesterday. Nothing his friends or family did could alleviate his physical suffering or mental anguish. His own doctor told him he was too old to gamble on a major urogenital operation, and this led to further despair. Arthur attempted to take matters into his own hands, consulting Dr. Joseph A. Kaufman, head of urology at UCLA. The doctor advocated the operation, and the next time father and son met Arthur relayed the information. Groucho refused to listen. Months went by, with Groucho alternately kvetching about his situation and voicing his prejudice against surgeons. One evening Lois could take no more: "But you said you don't want to go on living like this." Her father-in-law hesitated. "You're right," he admitted. "I'd just as soon die on the operating table as live this way. Maybe I'll go to see your friend Kaufman."

He was true to his word. Kaufman assured his new patient that if the bladder operation went according to plan, "There's no reason why you shouldn't have ten more good years ahead of you."

Groucho replied, "Just be sure to get me a pretty nurse."

Performed on the morning of September 23, 1970, the two-hour operation was a total success. Groucho was out of bed that evening, strolling the corridor and making passes at the nurses, just as he had planned. He returned home in better spirits, and threw himself a party to celebrate his eightieth birthday. Included in the gathering was Eden. Because of her presence, Melinda stayed away. Uncomfortable as she was with her father, the young woman had recently tried to make a separate peace with him. But since the divorce she had grown cold toward her stepmother, convinced that she was a gold digger. Eden's presence even infuriated Irwin Allen, who was at the dinner. He took her aside that night and inquired, "What are you doing—coming back for the other million?"

Once the festivities were over, the downhill course resumed. Arthur had familial and professional commitments that kept him away. Melinda married for the second time and moved to Mendocino in northern California. Miriam was out of work, still fighting her own demons. In 1971 Groucho suffered a minor stroke. It impaired his speech and made him less desirable as a luncheon companion, even among his oldest friends. He derived little pleasure from his family. "Children are rough going," he was to tell a reporter from the *New York Times*. "They have no respect for their elders. All daughters do is get married, and then get divorced. Either that or they drink. I think it's easier to raise the male than the female. Things happen to women at different times." As disappointments increased and faculties dimmed, however, his reputation as the movies' most prominent iconoclast began to rise. During a particularly low moment, reporters from *Take One*, an underground newspaper in the San Francisco Bay Area, sought an interview. Groucho mistook them for writers from *Esquire*, and warmed to his subjects—sex and politics. On the first matter, he stated, "As a rule a young fellow marries a girl to go to bed with her. This is normal procedure. I did that three times with very beautiful girls. When the beauty started fading, there wasn't any reason to stay married. The sex stimulant was gone."

Now, he only sought companionship. "For that you need a different kind of girl. You don't necessarily need a girl with big tits. You need a girl who normally you wouldn't marry, or you wouldn't try to lay. . . . You see, I don't believe there is such a thing as love. Love just means going to bed and fucking. You can get that anywhere, if you're young and partially attractive."

The journalists then solicited his opinion on the current president. "Do you think there's any hope for Nixon?" Groucho shot from the hip: "No, I think the only hope this country has is Nixon's assassination." An underground paper in London picked up that quote; so did the *Berkeley Barb*, another Bay Area journal. The next day it was on all the wire services. Before he could turn around, Groucho found himself under investigation by the FBI. He issued a typical denial: "I deny everything, because I never tell the truth. I lie about everything I do or say—about men, women or any other sex." The Nixon administration was not placated. The octogenarian was officially listed in File No. CO 1297009205 as a potential threat to the life of the Chief Executive. To agitated students, the contretemps made Groucho an elder statesman of the revolution. To Arthur it seemed a clear indication that his father needed more than a companion. "He needed a manager and/or keeper." Jerry Davis, producer of the TV comedy *The Odd Couple,* apparently had an answer, although not one that would meet with Arthur's approval. Davis invited Groucho to dinner to meet a visitor from New York. A former Canadian, the lady was slender, attractive, about thirty, and a Marx Brothers fan. Before Groucho committed himself, he wanted to know the name of the guest. Erin Fleming, Davis said. Susan Marx's maiden name was Fleming. A great believer in omens, Groucho agreed to attend. After all, what did he have to lose?

•

THE ACTRESS AND THE COMEDIAN hit it off immediately. Within days, Erin was on the job as Groucho's secretary, going through the clutter of unanswered fan letters piled up in Eden's abandoned studio. In conversation Groucho learned that his new employee had no permanent residence, so he offered her a room in his Trousdale house, where she could manage his business affairs and correspondence without bothering with time-wasting commutes. It had all happened too fast to please Arthur. He queried friends about Padre's newest companion and received a disconcerting vita. For the last two years Erin Fleming had made her home in an apartment on the East Side of Manhattan. A writer who lived in the same building recalled her as recklessly, not to say madly, ambitious. The building also housed composer Burt Bacharach and television writer Tony Webster, then working on *The Kraft Music Hall.* According to someone in a position to know, Erin came to Webster's apartment one morning and knocked on the door. A friend opened it and confronted Erin, stark naked, standing in the corridor. Apparently, it was her version of an audition. Webster, shocked but pretending to be unperturbable, went on typing.

Evidently she had gone through the same routine with Bacharach. One morning, recalled a friend, he answered the doorbell and found Erin standing there, nude, with an empty cup in her hand. "I'd like to borrow a cup of sugar," she said in a baby voice. These little adventures enlivened many dinner-table conversations that season.

More troubling incidents came to light when Arthur and Lois first met Erin. She and Groucho played host at the Hillcrest Country Club. Everything went well at first. Erin was well spoken and primly dressed; she even refused to join the others in a cocktail, as if separating herself from the Ruth-Kay-Eden history. But it soon came to light that Erin had sent a letter to Bob Evans on Groucho's letterhead, with Groucho's signature forged at the bottom. The missive complained that Erin had been passed up for a part in one of Evans's new movies. Groucho was clearly uncomfortable with what she had done.

To the chagrin of Groucho's relatives, however, Erin became an integral part of Groucho's life over the next several years. The disbeliever in love turned out to be the biggest romantic of them all, smitten, starry-eyed, and convinced that his latest companion was "stuck on me." At the start, Erin tried to prove her goodwill by refusing to take a salary for the work she did—room and board was enough. Her pay took the form of attention by association. Because she was always at Groucho's side she met Woody Allen, who obligingly cast her in his new film, *Everything You Wanted to Know about Sex but Were Afraid to Ask.* The fact that Erin was to appear in a comedy by his greatest acolyte excited Groucho. Then he read the script. He found it licentious—particularly the "Erection" sketch in which Erin would appear topless. Despite his fame for cinematic double entendres and suggestive bits with his TV guests, Groucho was a self-described "old-fashioned man" from the days of Albee's disciplined and sanitized vaudeville. Viewing such liberated comics as Lenny Bruce, he wrote: "Freedom of speech is one thing, but these gents are overdoing it. And when I say 'gents,' that is where most of them should be doing their act." When he heard about the rock musical *Hair,* he said: "I was kind of curious about six naked primates on stage. So I called up the box office and they said the tickets were eleven dollars apiece. That's an awful price to pay. I went into my bathroom at home and took off all my clothes and looked at the mirror for five minutes and I said this isn't worth eleven dollars. I don't think you have to show lovemaking on the screen any more than you have to show bowel movements." He complained to an *Esquire* reporter that Erin "does things in that film I've never been able to persuade her to do in the privacy of my own home." Yet Groucho could not help taking a certain pride in Erin as sex object; it implied a new lustiness in him. After the movie was released he referred to her as "My secretary, which is a euphemism for this girl over here." When Charlie Chaplin returned to Hollywood after years of banishment to accept an honorary Academy Award, he was pleased to see the spring in Groucho's step. He knew the reason why; Charlie had been down that road himself, many times. Holding on to the Oscar, Charlie advised, "Stay warm, Groucho. You're next."

With some effort, Erin talked the resurgent Groucho into giving a "concert" at Carnegie Hall. As the day of the concert grew closer, hostilities between Arthur and Erin intensified. Arthur advised Padre that he would need writers. "I just didn't want him to humiliate himself in front of his New York friends," the son was to recall. Furthermore, "I thought that Erin had a lot of nerve to push him into an appearance he really wasn't too keen to do in the first place, and then encourage him to go on unprepared." The argument was not meant as a solicitation; Arthur and his partner Bob Fisher were overcommitted as it was. Bowing to Erin's wishes, Groucho insisted that he could go on without any preparation. One evening, with this as Topic A, Arthur and Lois found themselves pitted against Groucho, Erin, and Erin's psychiatrist, Milton Wexler. Wexler suggested that perhaps the reason the younger Marx was concerned about Erin was that she might receive some of Groucho's money. Groucho had already bought her a new car, and there was talk of leaving her a minimum of $100,000 in his will. The evening ended with Groucho retiring to his bedroom and Wexler accusing Arthur and Lois of being selfish. The doctor protested that he was only trying to help his friends. "At how much an hour?" Arthur asked, just before he and Lois made for the door.

The following week Arthur received a letter from Groucho, typed by Erin. A check for $1,000 was included. "No matter what you think of Erin Fleming," it declared, "I intend to keep her in my life. She's been very good to me, and I am very fond of her. The enclosed check you can use to buy yourself a new car. Love, Padre." Notice had been served.

At eighty-two, Groucho had eyes only for Erin. His first wife, Ruth, died during this period, and he scarcely acknowledged her passing. The future was what consumed him now, and he was determined to show the world that he could still put on a first-class performance, using his companion as a foil and Marvin Hamlisch as his accompanist. The pre–New York tryout at Iowa State University ratified his claims. Antiwar sentiment was in the air there, as at virtually all campuses, and *Duck Soup,* the Brothers' send-up of diplomacy and conflict, found an exuberant new audience. Groucho entered the university wearing work shirt, red sweater vest, blue blazer, and, most significantly, faded blue jeans. The students took to the uniform right away, and his performance, filled with old jokes, reminiscences, and songs was greeted warmly. *Life* ran a picture of Groucho and

Erin strolling hand in hand through the campus, giving the impression that age had not withered, nor custom staled. The couple went on to Manhattan with high expectations; after the reception in the heart of the heart of the country, they were on a roll.

Promoted vigorously, the concert was sold out weeks before the epochal Saturday night of May 6, 1972. Celebrities filled the front rows: Mayor John V. Lindsay, Senator Jacob Javits, Woody Allen, Neil Simon, Mike Nichols. Ecstatic fans occupied every other seat. Dick Cavett introduced Groucho, who read the cue cards as best he could and got laughs every time he paused to look up. The thin voice quavered, especially during the songs. A movie camera, cued to show the stateroom scene from *A Night at the Opera,* failed to operate. None of these mishaps seemed to matter. When Groucho, unaware that he was on mike, made a series of disgusted remarks they drew as much laughter as the prepared material. The notices were kind, and an LP recording of the event, *An Evening with Groucho,* quickly released by A & M Records, became a best-seller. Now that he was on a roll, Groucho took Erin to Cannes, where he received a most unusual award: the French Commandeur dans l'Ordre des Arts et des Lettres medallion. Groucho ran true to form; as the president of the festival put the decoration around his neck, he cracked, "All the way from Beverly Hills for this! It's not even real gold." He maintained that tone when a representative of the British royal family asked if Mr. Marx would be kind enough to perform before Queen Elizabeth II. Groucho was tempted to accept—until someone informed him that proceeds from command performances were always given to charity. Back went a message to the Court of St. James's: "Tell the Queen that Groucho doesn't work for nothing." Some saw this as a fresh example of the comedian's matchless iconoclasm; to others it was a clear indication that the man was at the end of his tether, exhausted, cranky, and possibly at the edge of a breakdown. Erin chose to believe the former. As proof she showed off copies of the July *Vogue,* featuring her Q & A interview with the man whose home she shared. What it lacked in literary interest it made up for in vigor:

ERIN

You never use the word "lady."

GROUCHO

You're damn right. I hate that word. What is a "lady" supposed to be anyway? Some broad with white gloves on that you can't even approach? I like the word "woman," as in the sentence, "She is a great woman." God created woman. God didn't create *lady*. Some nut created lady and it wasn't me.

ERIN

Is there anything you like as much as a woman?

GROUCHO

Yes, a good cigar. Almost as much. But not quite.

ERIN

Who is the woman who has had the most effect on your life?

GROUCHO

My mother, Minnie. Next to her, the woman I'm currently in love with. Always the woman I am currently in love with.

ERIN

Who is that?

GROUCHO

I'm eighty-one years old, how do you expect me to remember? There must be somebody because I hear birds singing and bells clanging. I hear singing and there's no one there. Say. Maybe I'm crazy.

Before they went off to Europe, Erin arranged for two more concerts to be given in 1972, one in San Francisco as soon as they returned from Cannes, the other to take place in September at the Taper Forum in Los Angeles. Groucho thought he was up to them, and, indeed, the San Francisco performance went off without a hitch. He received four standing ovations, and those who had seen the concerts in Iowa and New York said this was by far the best of the three. The Los Angeles concert would have to wait; on September 13, less than two weeks after his latest triumph, Groucho was felled by a stroke. There seemed to be no permanent effects, no paralysis and only a slight and expected slurring of speech. The comic reflexes were still in full operation: asked whether he wanted an omelet for breakfast, Groucho reprised an old standby, "Omelet Christian Soldiers." Still, to be on the safe side, the doctors intended to keep him at Century City Hospital for a week of observation. During a visit, Arthur asked his father whether he was up to the Taper show, scheduled for the following month. "Definitely not," Groucho replied weakly. Nevertheless, Erin insisted that Groucho had to appear . . . otherwise, she stood to lose a lot of money. A week went by without any improvement in Groucho's condition. Erin postponed the September date to December 13. She confirmed the rumor that Groucho had been hospitalized, but used an international incident to cover for his indisposition. Rather than suffering a stroke or heart attack, she told the press, Groucho was suffering from exhaustion, attributed to "severe depression over the killings of the Israeli athletes at the Munich Olympic Games." This was not quite disinformation. Incapacitated as he was, Groucho made an effort to keep up with current events. When he learned of the assassinations he wondered aloud if they might signal the beginning of World War III.

On Columbus Day, 1972, the still-bedridden Groucho Marx signed a paper agreeing to employ Erin Fleming as his executive producer, coordinator, and secretary at a small weekly salary of $100. The fees spelled out in later paragraphs were not so modest. Erin would also receive 10 percent of his gross income from personal appearances, $5,000 of his $17,500 fee for endorsing Teacher's Scotch, and 50 percent of the net income from sales of the Carnegie Hall concert LP. Did Groucho know what he was signing? The family doubted it. For Arthur, worse news came three weeks later when Groucho signed another document making Erin his personal manager. As compensation she would be given 25 percent of all his earnings after agents' commissions and other deductions.

With all this in place, Erin booked Groucho into the Taper Forum for the long-delayed concert. The videotape of this event, never distributed, is heartbreaking. An infirm Groucho moves slowly and painfully. His voice quavers, his rheumy eyes have trouble making out the cue cards, and his anecdotes wander aimlessly. The *Los Angeles Times* covered the event and the coverage attempted to mask the worst of the evening. It simply suggested that the moment had come for "this Living Legend to retire."

In effect, that is what Groucho did. There were to be no more concerts, although he would stay in demand as a guest of TV talk shows and comedy specials. At the time Erin was grooming him for the next phase of his long career, David McKay Company issued Arthur's second book about his father, *Son of Groucho*. Essentially a retelling of the famous Marx Brothers' stories, along with some personal memories and insights, the dual biography could not resist a shot at Erin. Bowing to his father as an "extremely generous" man, Arthur added some details: "Every birthday and Christmas—even today, and no matter where I happen to be in the world—he never forgets to send me a good-sized check. Over the years, these checks have ranged from $500 to $3,000 on occasion, the variable depending on four things: (1) whether he's steadily employed, (2) the current state of the stock market, (3) how much alimony he's paying his last wife, and (4) what his girlfriend of the moment is euchring him out of in exchange for posing as his secretary." Arthur ended with a filial tribute: "If he was difficult, it's been worth it. If he inflicted pain (whatever the reason), it might have stung at the time, but it was never intentional. If it was hard to get out from under his shadow, it wasn't his fault. A giant's shadow often falls a great distance." Groucho was not as displeased as some of his friends expected. "In Groucho's conversations to me," wrote Hector Arce, he "paid his son the highest accolade: 'Arthur is a good writer.' " Most reviewers agreed with him. Not John Lahr. The son and skillful biographer of his own father, comedian Bert Lahr, could not resist a little preening at Arthur's expense. "To be born the son of a great man is an opportunity as well as an oppression, to live among the famous and talented, to experience the limitations and allure of America's golden payoff is something that should yield insight. But Arthur Marx, posing as an autobiographer, is really only interested in spinning some good stories about Pop. He never inquires with any depth into his father's art. He never sees the neurosis behind Groucho's insomnia and the maliciousness of his humor. He skirts the pain of the paternal bond and settles for puffery. . . . When he read Arthur's first literary effort, Groucho threw it aside, exclaiming, 'Amateur Night.' Thirty years later, Dad's verdict would be apt for *Son of Groucho.*"

The book sold well anyway; the Groucho industry rolled on. Erin gave Arthur more reason for resentment during the redecoration of Groucho's house. Lois Marx, who had begun to compile serious credentials as an interior decorator, was elbowed out of the way in order to make room for a bigger name, Peter Shore, who had worked for James Stewart, Paul Newman, and Henry Fonda. Shore was inventive and bright: Groucho's headboard was made of doors from an old circus wagon, a tribute to the itinerant entertainers Opie and Omie Schoenberg. The name Lydia was painted in the center, honoring the Tattooed Lady. "I want to show you my headpiece," Groucho liked to tell his visitors. "It's the only piece I get these days." Stopping by her uncle Groucho's one day, Maxine Marx professed herself "amazed by what Erin Fleming had accomplished. She had turned a skinflint into a spendthrift. He had round-the-clock nurses, cooks and housekeepers, a secretary, and a gardener . . . and the lavish food was a far cry from the skimpy fare served in the past. This wasn't the man I knew."

The profligate felt flush enough to buy his companion a small house on Vista Grande Drive, also exquisitely furnished by Shore. Much as Erin prided herself on the decor, she spent little time admiring it. Almost every day and most evenings were spent with Groucho. Between their rendezvous she pursued an acting career with indifferent success. The best she could manage was a part in a small avant-garde play, and Arthur and Lois drove Groucho to see it. Erin had not prepared the family for what they were about to witness—the bit actress strolling onto the stage naked to the waist. "I don't know what's happening to show business," Groucho mused on the way back. "What became of good clean family comedy?" That question was still nagging at him several weeks later. Arthur had called, and learned that Groucho would be dining alone that night. Erin would be attending an acting class. "I figure if she learns to be a better actress," Groucho explained, "someone will give her a part sometime where she can keep her clothes on." Arthur invited him to join the family at Matteo's, a popular Westwood restaurant, but his father begged off; he was not up to going out. That evening, Arthur and Lois saw Erin enter with a handsome escort. Led to a booth, they began to exchange intimacies. It was too much for Lois. Lois took matters into her own hands. As she and Arthur left Matteo's, she made a detour, picked up a glass of ice water and poured it over Erin's head, and silently walked away.

News of the incident did not stay private for long. The tormented old man hardly knew which way to turn. Arthur was blood of his blood; Erin was his last chance at life. In the end he lashed out at his son with an ultimatum. Either Lois would apologize to Erin or Arthur would be cut out of Groucho's will. Lois did not express regret, and Arthur and Groucho returned to their old estrangement.

During the decline Groucho allowed a new person into his life: Richard J. Anobile, a freelance writer who had done his own paste-up job of *Why a Duck,* reprinting dialogue under the appropriate pictures. For reasons known only to him, Groucho wrote the introduction. Anobile then persuaded him that it was time to set down his memories and reflections. What could be easier, he argued, than to talk into a tape recorder? The comedian's words could be transcribed for all time. There was no risk; Groucho would be guaranteed the ultimate say about what went in and what was to be excised. An agreement was worked out, and for months the veteran performer spoke of his early days, his brothers, his friends, his enemies. Anobile dutifully recorded the words, and included them in The Marx Bros. Scrapbook. Along with some rare photographs and the testimonies of Jack Benny, Morrie Ryskind, Susan Marx, Zeppo, and other relevant personalities, the book also included outbursts by Groucho himself. These were often scatological and cranky—the declining comedian with his guard down, unprotected by the interviewer he trusted. In a review of several books about the Watergate scandal, Wilfrid Sheed took a sideswipe at Anobile as one more exemplar of "sleazy breaches of trust . . . wherein the great Groucho is revealed to have grown a dirty mouth in his old age—to whose benefit revealed I know not." Anobile answered Sheed a month later. During the months of tête-à-têtes, he pointed out, "Groucho was told that he should not say anything in the taped interviews that he did not want published. Furthermore, he signed the author's copy, 'This is a wonderful book, Richard, thanks to you.' After he received bound copies of the book, a month later, he indicated to me in a telephone conversation, 'I like the book; it's the best one on the Marx Brothers,' and volunteered to go on talk shows to promote it."

Anobile's reply was disingenuous. His book brimmed with errors that a fully aware Groucho would have caught. Max Gordon's real name, Salpeter, for example, was listed as "Saul Peter." The vaudeville circuit known as Pantages became "Fantasia." A photograph of Maurice Chevalier was misidentified as director Robert Florey. These and other slipups indicated that Anobile had taken advantage of his distracted and weakened subject. When Groucho realized what had happened he took legal action against Darien House, the publisher; W. W. Norton, the distributor of the Scrapbook; and Penthouse Publications, which planned to run excerpts. In the legal brief, he asked that the book be taken out of circulation because it contained "defamatory, scandalous, obscene and inflammatory matter." Microscopically, the lawsuit enumerated error after error: " 'Schwartzeh' Objection: It is a slang expression not my choice of a word in a book purported to be authored by me. 'Fooling around' Objection: Not contained in transcript. Not what I said. Also, the way Mr. Anobile constructs this sentence it sounds like we were fooling around [with] my mother, which implies a different meaning entirely. I object to this meaning. Objection to exclamation mark after the word 'rodent.' This is not the punctuation I, as an author, would choose." The judge did not see it his way. Regardless of Arthur's belief that the interviews were not "how my father would speak if he had been in complete control of his mental faculties," injunctions were lifted on the magazine, and then on the publisher and distributor, because Groucho had signed a binding contract with Anobile allowing those interviews to be printed in toto.

The suit was ruinous to Groucho, not so much because of legal fees but because it drained him of the little energy he had left. In the summer of 1973, and then again in early fall, he was hospitalized with heart and circulation problems, as well as a chronic urinary tract infection. In mid-October he went into the hospital for a third time, emerging testier than ever. He and Arthur had reconciled, only to collide over *Minnie's Boys* yet again. Irwin Allen had an idea that the premise of the show might make a television sitcom, and naturally asked Arthur and his partner Bob Fisher to write the pilot. Meanwhile, Arthur Whitelaw, who had produced the Broadway show, also expressed interest in a TV version. If he obtained the rights, Whitelaw intended to use Larry Gelbart, creator of the sitcom *M*A*S*H,* to do the adaptation. The producer cannily offered Erin the title of associate producer. In response, Groucho called his son, asking him to get out of the way. "If you don't," he warned, "I won't approve the deal." What followed would have been unseemly for a teenager and his inflexible parent. For a man in his fifties and another in his eighties to engage in such quarreling had to be degrading for all concerned. Arthur reminded him that Fisher and Marx actually owned the show they had written. Groucho pointed out that it was *his* life they were writing about and accused his son of being as egotistical as a movie star. Two days went by before Groucho blinked, calling Arthur and requesting a visit. When his son dropped by Groucho handed him a check for $100,000. Arthur refused the money.

"Take it," Groucho ordered, "or we're through."

"Is this a bribe so that I'll let Erin get the job?"

"No, you can have the pilot deal too."

"But why do you feel you have to give all this to me?"

"Because I don't want you to think your father's a son of a bitch! Now put the check in your wallet before you lose it."

•

THE YEAR 1974 was marred by a continuing deterioration in Groucho's health—and a cluster of heartening events. Whatever Erin's liabilities, and there were many, she continued to be an energetic lobbyist on her companion's behalf. For some months she had worked tirelessly to get Groucho an honorary Academy Award. Nunnally Johnson was enlisted to write a letter to the American Academy of Motion Picture Arts and Sciences. Some months before, Arthur had sent a similar note, but Johnson apparently made the more persuasive argument. After due deliberation the Academy announced that it would present Groucho Marx a special Oscar for "the brilliant activity and unequalled achievement of the Marx Brothers in the art of motion picture comedy." While preparations went on, episodes of *You Bet Your Life* were being prepared for syndication. (The old tapes had been in a jumble, neglected and forgotten; Andy Marx, Arthur's twenty-two-year-old grandson, fresh out of UCLA, was hired to put them in order.) And *Animal Crackers,* the one Marx Brothers film that had been out of circulation, due to copyright tangles, was about to be released for general viewing after an absence of twenty-four years. Universal Pictures had originally resisted the idea, assuming that the print had outlived its time. Steven Stoliar, a history major at UCLA, thought otherwise, and so did Erin. She and Groucho went before television cameras on the university campus, hoping to embarrass studio executives into changing their minds. Their strategy worked. Universal agreed to limited engagements of *Animal Crackers* at the United Artists Theater in Westwood and the Sutton in Manhattan. The showings, aided by Groucho's personal appearances, would break attendance records at both houses. Fan mail flowed in great quantities for the first time in years. Groucho was too infirm and Erin too busy to attend to it. She hired Stoliar to keep the Grouchophiles happy.

One of Groucho's lowest moments came just before he was given the Academy Award. Harry Ruby, old friend, composer of the best Groucho songs, mainstay of the Geezers Club, died at the age of seventy-nine. Groucho grumbled about organized religion again, but attended the funeral. "I went to the synagogue for Harry," he told Hector Arce. Groucho's melancholy lifted for the evening of April 2. In what amounted to a love-in he shuffled onto the stage of the Music Center in downtown Los Angeles, to be greeted with a long, loud standing ovation. Jack Lemmon presented the statuette. Groucho grasped it firmly and told the affectionate crowd, "I only wish Harpo and Chico could have been here— and Margaret Dumont. . . . And then, I'd like to thank my mother, without whom I would have been a failure. And last, I'd like to thank Erin Fleming, who makes my life worth living and who understands all my jokes."

Most of viewing audience, as well as the one in the theater, responded warmly. There were a few exceptions, however. One of them was Arthur, whose relations with Erin were minimal and growing smaller. He distrusted her, and he had reasons. Several months after the Awards ceremony, one of Groucho's accountants notified Arthur that for the first time his father was spending more money than he was earning. He needed a conservator, before the assets drained away. Unhappily, it was impossible for father and son to negotiate any financial arrangement. They argued about small things and large ones—anything but the main topic. On one occasion Arthur was summoned to the house, only to be accused of writing an uncomplimentary article about Erin in a Canadian publication. He had done no such thing, but he had been in Toronto, trying out a new play. The drama had not gone well, as the trade papers said, and Groucho was only too eager to repeat that information. Arthur countered by reminding his father that the only play Groucho had ever written bombed on Broadway. Arthur walked out of the house, determined never to return. He did not see his father again until September of 1976. In the interim, Arthur was tormented by worse news. Erin knew that Groucho would never marry again; he had called himself a three-time loser too often. So she decided to seek another avenue: Groucho would adopt her. She had quietly converted to Judaism some time back. Why not take this last step? Martha Brooks, Groucho's housekeeper, was sure that her boss was against the move. Out of Erin's hearing he had said rather plaintively, "I already have two daughters. What do I want with another one?" Willing or unwilling, Groucho ordered his attorneys to file adoption papers early in 1975. Physicians were asked to determine if the old man was compos mentis. One found Groucho "terrified that Erin would leave and abandon him," and also found that Mr. Marx's "I.Q. was at such a diminished level that his ability to respond to all but the most routine kind of things was essentially gone." Another thought that Groucho seemed competent enough, but physically debilitated. There was no more talk of adoption. Just the same, Arthur's troubles with Erin and his ailing father were only beginning. As Groucho's light dimmed, his shadow extended.

CHAPTER SEVENTEEN

Everybody Has a Temperature

GROUCHO VOICED LITTLE SATISFACTION at having outlived so many relatives, friends, and colleagues, from Harpo and Chico to Harry Ruby, Jack Benny, and T. S. Eliot. Of the Marx Brothers' contemporaries, only Bob Hope and George Burns still regularly worked at their trade. Nunnally Johnson lay stricken with emphysema. Arthur Sheekman, who had tinkered with Groucho's prose in the days when the Marx byline made the magazines, was bedridden with arteriosclerosis. Groucho stopped by the nursing home when he could, always bringing a token box of cookies and bottle of whiskey. Yet a lack of fellow Geezers did not confine him to meals à deux with Erin. Groucho's popularity rode a new wave thanks to the Oscar, to the resuscitation of *Animal Crackers,* and to the second life of *You Bet Your Life,* viewable five nights a week in eighteen cities. Young viewers sent some seventy-five fan letters a week. They liked to think of him as the Don Quixote of comedians, a battered, honorable figure in perpetual opposition to the Establishment. QUESTION AUTHORITY read the bumper sticker of choice for seventies youth—and who had sassed the powerful more insistently than Groucho? In the academy, scholars fell all over themselves following Martin A. Gardner's lead, parsing and dissecting the Brothers' routines. *New Yorker* cartoonist William Hamilton skewered their pretensions, much as Groucho would have in the 1930s; his cartoon showed a professor lecturing on semiotic cinema: "The tautology of their symbolism thus begins to achieve mythic proportions in *A Day at the Races, Duck Soup* and *A Night at the Opera.*"

To certify her companion's iconic status, Erin encouraged prominent showfolk to drop in. Mike Nichols took advantage of the invitation; so did Jack Nicholson, Barbra Streisand, Betty Comden, Adolph Green, George Jessel, Woody Allen, and Bill Cosby. Streisand paid him a compliment on film by wearing Groucho disguise in *The Way We Were*, recalling Hollywood in the 1930s. She stopped by to flatter him in person. Fellow octogenarian Mae West sashayed in, serenading Groucho to the piano accompaniment of Harpo's son Bill; Jack Lemmon also played piano; Fred MacMurray, once a bandsman, entertained on the saxophone; Carroll O'Connor, star of the hit sitcom *All in the Family*, warbled a few numbers; Sammy Davis Jr. tap-danced on a coffee table. Several bystanders watched their host and his friends at these events, making notes. In due time Stoliar would write an evocative book, *Raised Eyebrows*, about the last years chez Groucho, and several others would publish their own versions of that period. Freelancer Hector Arce had in mind a light history of *You Bet Your Life*. He spoke with Groucho and various personnel associated with the show, and produced *The Secret Word Is Groucho* (not to be confused with a privately printed book bearing the same title, written by Groucho's flamboyant cook, John Ballow). Lyn Erhard, another writer in search of a subject, was on hand to tape-record Groucho in situ. Under the pen name Charlotte Chandler she published a one-on-one interview in *Playboy* and, later, *Hello, I Must Be Going*, a grab bag of celebrity chatter:

GROUCHO

(*To ERHARD*) We were playing a small town in Ohio, and a man came to the box office and said, "Before I buy the ticket, I want to know one thing: is it sad or high kickin'." That's the best line I ever heard about show business. That's all of show business. (*To GEORGE JESSEL*) Tell 'em about Norma Talmadge.

GEORGE JESSEL

She was a wonderful woman. Until the third drink, she had the manners of a princess. Courted, she was like a queen. Third drink, she'd pee on the floor.

GROUCHO

You had a fight, and you gave her the ring, and she threw it back at you. She said, "I don't want anything at all to do with you." (*To ERHARD*) So she threw him out, and slammed the door. He rang the bell, and she opened the door. He said, "I'm sorry I can't make up with you, but is it all right if I use the swimming pool?"

. . .

GROUCHO

(*To his grandson*) Remember when you used to come here, Steve?

ANDY

I'm Andy, Groucho. He always calls me that, "Steve." Steve's my older brother.

GROUCHO

His older brother is Amos.

. . .

BILL COSBY

You know who I recommend to have dinner with you, Grouch? You know Bobby Short?

GROUCHO

No, but I knew him when he was long.

COSBY

Well, he's short now.

GROUCHO

He was short about fifty dollars when I saw him.

. . .

MIKE NICHOLS

Do you remember how you couldn't get on the elevator with Walter Winchell? . . . Anytime he got on the elevator, nobody else could get on.

GROUCHO

I was in the elevator at the Plaza, and a priest came in and said, "You're Groucho Marx, aren't you? My mother's crazy about you." And I said, "I didn't know you guys had mothers. I thought it was done by immaculate conception."

. . .

WOODY ALLEN

Are you planning to do any more movies?

Erin's busy putting together a documentary about me. In the meantime I plan on dying.

The continuing houseful of guests and adulators came at a price. Dorris Johnson's unhappy memories of the procession included a Groucho who "seemed so helpless in the face of all that whirled around his life. He had reached the age and diminished health that needed *some* area of serenity. He needed calm, and his alliance was with a young girl who needed the excitement and stimulation of celebrities, of the big names of Hollywood. Oh, my, what allure! You can't put down a longing like that when you have only one access to it . . . and the access was through Groucho."

Stoliar wrote of the exhausting social schedule, and of some revelatory conversations. During one lunch, Nat Perrin joined Red Buttons and Groucho. Buttons had a long face; he had just come from a visit with Joe Smith, of Smith and Dale, a headline team in vaudeville. "He didn't know me," Buttons told his listeners. "He kept playing this game from his childhood where he'd reach over and try to flip my zipper up and down. He was acting just like a little kid. I kept saying 'Joe! It's me! Red Buttons, the comedian!' but he didn't recognize me. It's like he isn't there anymore."

Awkward silence greeted Buttons's account. Then Groucho looked up from his soup and said, "It's sad when that happens." Stoliar noted, "Red and I turned to look in Groucho's direction as he returned to the soup and I knew, at that moment, that we all had the same thought."

Yet through the long decline, vestiges of the old Groucho would appear, sometimes to his regret. Invited to the Dick Cavett show, he entered wearing a knitted tam with three spherical tassels dangling down. His fellow guest was Truman Capote, who took up most of the conversation with complaints about the income tax. Groucho broke in: "If you were married, Truman, your taxes would be smaller. Why don't you get married?" Replied Capote, "Nobody has asked me." Groucho tossed his cap flirtatiously. "I'm available. Why don't you marry me?" Capote shook his head. "Because, Groucho, you have three balls." Groucho had nothing to add. Against slower minds he could still be exasperating. In May of 1975, just four months before his eighty-fifth birthday, he was asked to join Lucille Ball as presenter on the Emmy Awards show. A producer dropped by the house to go over the script.

GROUCHO

I didn't know you could read.

PRODUCER

(*Paying no attention*) O.K. Lucy says, "And now we present—"

GROUCHO

I don't like it.

PRODUCER

—a man who needs no introduction.

GROUCHO

That's what *you* think.

PRODUCER

(*Indulgently*) If you want to add a little something, that's fine, but we're going to have to keep it reasonably tight.

GROUCHO

I know *she* will be.

PRODUCER

Anyway, at six o'clock, we go live.

GROUCHO

Live?

PRODUCER

That's right.

GROUCHO

Well, then, you'd better get someone else.

The only person who seemed impervious to these onslaughts was Erin. On the credit side, her strength and drive kept Groucho on the qui vive; she flatly refused to let him sink into degenerative old age, prodding and goading him into performances, even when he hated the result—as was the case on the Emmy broadcast. On the debit side, she manifested little respect for his family or for his associates unless they were famous. Slowly she eliminated or replaced all rivals until no one remained to countermand her orders. Arce was present when Erin learned that Groucho's accountant had sent Kay a $200 check to take care of a dentist's bill. Erin loudly declared that she was going to fire the man on the spot. Groucho tried to defend the CPA. Erin continued her harangue. Groucho explained to the writer, "She has no compassion," and he meant it. Not that her tirades made him want to part company. When things became unpleasant, he simply used his technique of turning misery into a joke. Out of the blue one morning he asked after Erin's health. How could she be well if she hadn't fired anyone that day?

Martha Brooks watched Erin's takeover until she could endure no more. Groucho's longtime housekeeper preferred to quit rather than work for a woman she had come to loathe. According to the latest revision of his will, Groucho intended to leave Martha $25,000 provided that she was in his employ at the time of death. She valued her dignity more than the money. Selwyn Shufro, who had steered Groucho through the Depression and helped him accumulate a sizable portfolio, was given the gate along with Groucho's lawyer and business manager. Lyn Erhard was banished without cause. These days, Arthur, Miriam, and Melinda were already somewhat estranged; Erin took care to see that they were not invited back into the fold.

To some extent the Marx children had strengthened her hand. Arthur's complicated and often rivalrous relations with his father continued to keep them apart, and Miriam struggled with her self-destructive habits. Melinda, having searched for an identity in and out of show business, with men and without them, at home and in foreign countries, had married again and become the mother of two small children. The young family relocated to northern California, far from the sad or high-kickin' life she had never truly wanted. Wyatt Cooper, the romantic lead in the touring company of *Time for Elizabeth*, recalled the relationship of father and daughter in those days: "He really adored her. Anything she did was funny, divine. A few years ago, I met Groucho, and I asked about Melinda, and he just mumbled something. To his dismay, Melinda grew up. To adore someone doesn't mean you have any idea about her." Given this background, Erin found it easy to stigmatize the trio as an ungrateful brood. The ultimate weapon was the notion, utterly untrue, that Arthur planned to put Groucho in a home for the aged.

It was no surprise, when Groucho's eighty-fifth birthday party approached, that Erin made no plans to include his children. Her guest list of some two hundred people did include several of Erin's favorites, like actors Elliott Gould, Sally Kellerman, and Bud Cort. (For a time Cort became an uninvited house guest, taking over Melinda's old room and giving a party for some fifty of his friends without asking Groucho's permission. Groucho demanded, "Do you know the meaning of *chutzpah?*" But he already knew the answer was no.) Erin's friends were joined by Zeppo and Gummo, and Hollywood's respected old guard of Bob Hope, Jack Lemmon, Morrie Ryskind, Nat Perrin, Milton Berle. Woody Allen sent a telegram: HAPPY 85TH BIRTHDAY. NOW YOU OWE ME A WIRE ON MINE. Peter Sellers quietly joined the group, content "just to sit there and realize you are in the same room with Groucho Marx." Tom Bradley, the mayor of Los Angeles, had given the festivities an official status by proclaiming Groucho's eighty-fifth "Groucho Marx Day," and for a moment Groucho seemed to make that day very much his own. He kidded with Hope and Berle, allaying any fears about his fitness: "I'm still in perfect health, except mentally," and sang some old favorites, including "Peasie Weasie," and, with unconscious irony, the Harry Ruby number "Father's Day."

> Today, Father, is Father's Day
> And we're giving you a tie.
> It's not much, we know,
> It's just our way of showing you
> We think you're a regular guy.
> You say that it was nice of us to bother,
> But it really was a pleasure to fuss,
> For according to our mother, you're our father,
> And that's good enough for us.
> Yes, that's good enough for us.

The performance took a great deal out of Groucho and he ostentatiously retired to his room, put on his pajamas, and bade the well-wishers say their good-byes at his bedside. Carroll O'Connor and Sally Struthers got under the covers with him, clowning for the camera. The picture made the next issue of *People,* and suddenly Groucho was back in demand, his presence requested at all sorts of fetes in his honor.

A week after the big party, S. J. Perelman came to dinner for the last time. The writer had been shabbily treated in the *Scrapbook.* (Anobile: "Did you work with Perelman at all on the script of *Monkey Business?*" Groucho: "Very little, very little. In the first place I hated the son of a bitch and he had a head as big as my desk.") But there seemed no point in reproaching his disabled host, and the two men merely engaged in repartee, rather like the edgy comics of Neil Simon's *The Sunshine Boys.* "Do you mind if I smoke?" Perelman asked solicitously. Riposted Groucho, "I don't care if you burn." Perelman ignited his cigarette and took on the tone of a film director. "That was good. Now let's try it for time." The men parted in a friendly manner that night; Groucho remained ignorant of Sid's enduring resentment, ranging back to the days at Paramount. Late in his life Perelman told a friend that he had "never gotten over the reading of the script of *Monkey Business* and Groucho's utter silence after the reading ended. 'Imagine that—not saying a word!' He described Groucho as 'One of the most detestable people [he had] ever met.' " Having been tyrannized and insulted in the Paramount days, the writer had reasons for his unabated dislike. But there may have been other reasons as well. Perelman had also been married for decades to an alcoholic, and he, too, had trouble relating to his own children. In a sense, contemplating Groucho in closeup was like looking at himself in a distorting mirror. He was not pleased with the image.

But Groucho's list of denigrators was short. Ordinary fans and cineastes continued to write letters of appreciation. Viewers of Bob Hope's television special *Joys,* a send-up of Steven Spielberg's film *Jaws,* were pleased to see that Groucho could still remember lines, even if they were ghastly. (The deservedly forgotten parody featured major comedians being consumed by a giant "land shark.") Marx Brothers film festivals took place on campuses throughout the country, and on Groucho's home turf the University of Southern California scheduled a literary luncheon in his honor. The event would take place on Columbus Day, "right around your birthday," his grandson Andy reminded him. Groucho was in no rush to celebrate. "I can wait. They're coming fast now." And what did he want for his birthday? "Last year." Yet he again tapped reserves of strength for the occasion, resurrecting his old routines with the moderator, George Fenneman. Jack Lemmon gave the honoree a long, involved introduction mentioning Groucho's contributions to the Marx Brothers films and ending with the question, "Why is it you declined to take writing credit for these most famous of your works?" Without missing a beat Groucho replied, "I'm nuts about your wife." Lemmon, straight man for the night, stood in wonder as "the place fell in. . . . The longer the question was, the funnier that idiot answer was because it was totally obtuse, as he often was. He seemed to make no sense very often and yet it's funny." Joined by Lynn Redgrave and Roddy McDowall, Lemmon then read selections from Groucho's six books. By way of thank-you, Groucho went to the piano, where he sang selected favorites accompanied by Bill Marx. He made a point of thanking his nephew afterward. With more wonder than rancor Bill remarked, "That's the first time in all my life that he ever said anything gracious to me."

The operative word for the lunch was "literary"; the shelf of books by or concerning Groucho was about to be lengthened by several volumes. First would come a paperback reissue of Groucho's first book, *Beds,* originally published in 1930 and now illuminated by photographs of the author entertaining an assortment of visitors in his bed, among them Valerie Perrine, Phyllis Diller, and a Great Dane. This would be followed by *The Secret Word Is Groucho,* written with Arce. The two would then collaborate on *The Groucho Phile,* a large-format, profusely illustrated book meant to celebrate the life and art of Groucho—and, incidentally, to erase memories of Richard Anobile's displeasing *Scrapbook.* Satisfied with his new collaborator, Groucho gave permission for Arce to begin work on an official biography.

A very different sort of volume was published early in 1976. Sidney Sheldon, a scenarist and a friend for many years, knew what was going on at Groucho's house. It cannot have been coincidence that his novel *A Stranger in the Mirror* concerned an aging comedian, Toby Temple, and a failed young actress, Jill Castle, who beguiles and uses him to advance her own career. At first Jill's youth and beauty bring the funnyman back from a stroke. ("Dr. Kaplan could not conceal his astonishment. 'It's unbelievable,' he told Jill. 'It's—it's like a miracle.' 'It is a miracle,' Jill said. *Only in this life you made your own miracles, because God was busy elsewhere.*") Later, she takes over Toby's identity ("The Friars Club gave a Roast with Toby Temple as the guest of honor. . . . Jill was asked to stand up and take a bow. It became a standing ovation. *They're cheering me,* Jill thought. *Not Toby. Me!*") The comedian suffers a second, more debilitating stroke; Jill becomes involved with a former lover; and the incubus-succubus relationship results in Toby's death when Jill allows him to drown in a swimming pool. (In fact, Groucho had nearly gone under for the third time when Erin pulled him out of his own swimming pool in March 1974. The notion that Sheldon had twisted actual events for his own purposes should have caused a squall. But Erin would not be provoked; she told curious friends that Sheldon's speculations were, after all, "just a novel.") Stoliar, well acquainted with all participants, offered his own interpretation of *A Stranger in the Mirror.* "Obviously the book doesn't purport to be any sort of accurate depiction of Erin and Groucho—and Sheldon denied that it had been based on them—but the inspiration is readily apparent." However, "if Sheldon's book with its unmistakable dedication [to Groucho] was meant to be a wake-up call it fell on deaf eyes: Groucho never read it." Another 1976 book he overlooked was *Goldwyn,* a new biography by Arthur. Also neglected were Groucho's daughters, who had been keeping their distance. Someone should have stopped the old man from alienating those who loved him, and vice versa. But there was no one to stay their hands.

•

IN 1976 Groucho's television appearances dwindled down to a precious few. His eighty-sixth birthday loomed. The occasion seemed to come too soon, just as he had predicted, and once again the reporters were on the phone and at his doorstep, pleading for quotes. Increasingly feeble, he could only manage an occasional wisecrack, usually from one of his old films. Sometimes even these were elusive. At dinner, Erin asked about *A Night at the Opera,* cuing Groucho for anecdotes about Al Boasberg. He was unable to recall one. His companion erupted, "You stupid, senile old bastard!" Stoliar wrote: "Everyone at the table was embarrassed for him. But above all, we just wished she'd stop doing things like that to the poor man." On another occasion Groucho coughed loudly and continuously at the dinner table. It was not an uncommon occurrence; he had been experiencing difficulty swallowing ever since his second stroke. Erin displayed no sympathy. "Oh, stop that, Methuselah!" she ordered. "You know I can't stand it when you do that!" Groucho continued to overlook these humiliations, ceding all decisions to her—including the roster of personal appearances. At a time when he appeared wan and brittle, he surprised everyone by putting on formal clothes and attending a banquet in downtown Los Angeles in honor of Zubin Mehta. The conductor beamed as Groucho sang a vaudeville song by Gus and Grace Kahn, "Oh, How That Woman Could Cook." Grace Kahn accompanied him at the piano. Because the evening went so well, Erin arranged to have Groucho perform at a fund-raiser for Ralph Nader's consumer advocacy organization in Washington. A three-thousand-mile plane ride seemed risky for a man in Groucho's condition, but Erin insisted that he was up to it. Press releases were sent out, booming the magic Marx name and promising laughter for dollars. Then, only a few days before departure, she abruptly expressed doubts about the function. She told Stoliar and Arce, "I just can't get up and perform in front of people anymore." Looks were exchanged; she was not the headliner, Groucho was. Had there been a transfer of personality? No one dared to express anything short of a sigh of relief when she canceled the appearance, ostensibly because of Groucho's chronic bladder trouble. A month later, Arce happened to be in New York doing research for the biography. Erin was also in town and the two met for dinner. For reasons only she knew, Erin announced that this was the time for the father to reconcile with his children—the three she had so sharply criticized for the last several years. To Groucho's nineteen-year-old assistant and custodian of films, Henry Golas, she gave instructions in the form of an ultimatum. She would not return to Los Angeles until all the Marxes made peace. Golas gently transformed her instruction into a question. Would Groucho like to see Arthur and Lois? He would. Golas sent a telegram to the son and daughter-in-law: PLEASE CALL ME. WANT TO SEE YOU. LOVE, FATHER. Arthur's suspicions were aroused by the signature. He reasoned that if Groucho had dictated the wire he would have used the name Padre. Strangely enough, Golas had taken down Groucho's message word for word; the familiar sign-off had slipped the old man's mind.

The couple showed up the next night, to be greeted with unaccustomed warmth. Father kissed son, hugged Lois, and indicated the bar: "Name your poison, but you'll have to fix it yourself. I don't drink anymore. In fact, I don't do anything that's fun." Certainly making conversation was not fun for anyone. Members of the household staff stayed within sight and hearing throughout dinner; Groucho and Arthur were never allowed a moment alone. Golas broke in to offer Arthur a look at Groucho's financial books. Arthur declined—what could this teenager possibly know of Erin's wheeling and dealing? As the meal progressed, Groucho defensively spoke of Erin's plans to generate new revenue. For example, "she set up this company for me—Groucho Productions. We both own fifty percent of the stock." He detailed the company's plans for licensing wristwatches, dolls, greeting cards, clothing, all bearing the trademark glasses, eyebrows, moustache, and cigar. Arthur pointed out that the arrangement benefited Erin more than Groucho: "She's going to get fifty percent of *You Bet Your Life*, which she had nothing to do with, plus a management fee from all your income." Groucho found nothing untoward about the plan; Arthur felt uncomfortable pressing his point;

and the evening ended inconclusively at 9 p.m. when the host presented his son with an autographed copy of *The Secret Word Is Groucho* and toddled off to bed.

Apprised of this meeting, Erin came back to California and began working on plans for Groucho's eighty-sixth birthday party. This time Arthur and his wife made the A list. Lois had not forgiven her father-in-law for past offenses and begged off; Arthur attended, fearing that this could well be his father's last such celebration. The house was filled with well-wishers, and Groucho amused them by offering a thin echo of the Three Nightingales:

> My mother called Sister downstairs the other day.
> "I'm taking a bath," my sister did say.
> "Well, slip on something quick, here comes Mr. Brown."
> She slipped on the top step and then came down.

From the sidelines Erin called on him to encore with "Oh, How That Woman Could Cook." The entertainment concluded with a soft-shoe routine performed by Jack Lemmon, George Burns, Elliott Gould, and Groucho. Halfway through, Groucho slumped to the floor. The other three resolutely danced on, while Arthur and a nurse carried the fourth member of their quartet off to the bedroom.

From this and other instances of weakness, Groucho watchers expected to see an obituary notice in the *Los Angeles Times* by the weekend. He surprised them all, bouncing back, taking short walks, turning up at business lunches, and even planning some more personal appearances. He also attempted a reconciliation with Miriam, the most difficult of his children. For over a year she had been in the care of a couple in Culver City, hired to look after her during the debilitating alcoholic phases. During that time the father-daughter relationship was confined to brief and sometimes incoherent telephone calls. Then came a call that was not from Miriam but about her. Cedars-Sinai Hospital notified Groucho that his daughter was confined to a bed with deep bruises and contusions. Like most battered women, she claimed to have taken a bad fall. Investigation showed that she had been beaten severely and frequently. When she came to her senses, she told doctors that the caretaking couple would sometimes lock her in a room for days at a time, with a chamber pot as her only furniture. In a strange way, this horrific episode was to effect the relief Miriam had been seeking for more than thirty years. From here she stumbled toward a complete recovery and a way of dealing with her demons. Melinda remained a question mark. Recently, Groucho had stopped sending her a monthly stipend. "Melinda can have her allowance back," Erin told Arce. "All she has to do is pay some attention and respect to her father." Early in 1977 the young woman showed up at the front door, but the drop-in was not what Erin intended. At Melinda's side was a lawyer, brought in to investigate a rumor that Erin had been physically abusing Groucho. However uneasy the relationship of parent and child, Melinda would not countenance such intimidation. She and the lawyer questioned members of the household; the answers were, at best, ambiguous. Golas, for example, seemed ready to be a witness for the prosecution, confessing that he had indeed witnessed unpleasant scenes between Groucho and Erin. However, when Melinda told him she had not received financial aid from her father, he became less forthcoming: Golas had seen the canceled checks. Groucho himself gave nothing away, and Melinda and the lawyer left unsatisfied. Erin was livid when she learned of the visit. How dare this ungrateful child accuse her of anything? "She's been to see you five times in seven years," she reminded Groucho. "Is *she* going to take care of you?" He gave the response Erin sought. "That little bitch! She'll never set foot in this house again!" He started to cry. Tears came easily these days.

Again Groucho seemed decrepit and totally vulnerable; again he rallied and accompanied Erin to George Burns's eighty-first birthday party. The smile congealed on his face when someone told him he would not be asked to sing a song or tell any jokes. His mood darkened, and when he ran across Milton Berle, Groucho asserted, "I don't think you're funny." Berle smiled at what he thought was insult humor. "Everything I know I stole from you," he said mildly. Groucho would not be placated: "Then you weren't listening." Erin chose this occasion to make her own scene. Two of Groucho's former lawyers were in attendance and she confronted them, raising her voice before the assembled crowd. She and Groucho were asked to leave. It happened that Norman Krasna was in town, and he ran interference. Peace was restored, but at a price. The old man and his companion were not invited to any more private Hollywood festivities. Still, Groucho could not be ignored. The town was well aware that he had recently been inducted into the Hollywood Hall of Fame, and that a poll of New York University freshmen had found that their three most admired men were Jesus Christ, Albert Schweitzer, and Groucho Marx. He was still a force to be reckoned with.

So much so that early in 1977 Erin convinced a production company to back her latest idea: a TV special starring Groucho at home and featuring major entertainers trading lines with the host. Groucho's nurses noticed that he began to sleep badly, arising early and shuffling to the piano in his bathrobe. "I've got to rehearse!" he explained. "I'm doing a show!" When Erin joined him he went through some creaky arm and leg gestures, which she mimicked. These practice sessions formed, Stoliar observed, a grotesque tableau. One morning they grew more grotesque: Groucho could not find his way around the house. He had suffered another minor stroke, one that affected his peripheral vision. A feeling of malaise settled over the house; staffers were convinced that the end was only a matter of days. On a sunny afternoon, several of them witnessed a discomfiting incident. Groucho was steered into Erin's office, seated, and asked to sign some legal documents. No attorney was present, and he was not told what he was signing. After he had scrawled his name in the designated places, a nurse guided him back to his room.

Yet even now Groucho could not be counted out. He rallied once more, and when Olivia de Havilland came to town made plans to receive her. He wanted to reminisce about the war bond tours of the mid-1940s, and to tell the actress that in those days he had a "terrible crush" on her. But sometime before she entered the house, he injured himself while dressing. He had to remain seated when his guest entered, and their conversation, pleasant enough at the beginning, was marked by his distress. "You're not getting any younger," he said crankily at one point; de Havilland responded with a mechanical laugh. It was obvious that the interview had been a mistake. Groucho laboriously inscribed a copy of *The Groucho Phile* and she went on her way. The pain did not diminish that night. He was driven to Cedars-Sinai the next day, where doctors determined that he had suffered a fracture of the right hip. With his permission, surgeons went in.

During the difficult recuperation there came a series of misunderstandings, hostilities, and finally an all-out war. Arthur, Miriam, and Melinda were informed about their father's indisposition by a lawyer assigned by Erin. Arthur was made unwelcome when he went to see his father at the hospital, told that his visits raised Groucho's blood pressure, and effectively banished from the room. He wasted no time giving Krasna his interpretation of the Groucho-Erin relationship. Krasna, who had seen Erin in action at the Burns birthday party, fell in with the anti-Erin cause. He went to Arce and pleaded: "If Groucho were in his right mind, he'd have never let this happen. You have to help Arthur." Arce was hesitant: "Groucho's so dependent on Erin that I'm afraid he'd die if Arthur took Erin away from him." As things turned out, Erin took Groucho away from Arthur, spiriting the patient away from the hospital without doctors' permission. An outraged Arthur now felt certain that he had enough evidence to prove what he had suspected for years—Erin was exerting "undue influence" on a helpless and rich old man. His lawyer, J. Brin Schulman, filed a petition to that effect with the Superior Court in Santa Monica, and notified the Bank of America's trust department, custodians of Groucho's financial resources. The court ruled against Arthur, holding that a paper signed by Groucho in 1974 remained legal and binding. Erin would remain as Groucho's legal conservator. On the other hand, the three children could not be barred from the house, and the bank would oversee all transactions. During all this, Nunnally Johnson suddenly passed away. The news was kept from Groucho on the grounds that any shock might finish him. Erin went to the service in his stead, and while there got into an argument with Krasna over the conservator issue. Voices were raised; battle lines were firmly drawn. Convinced that Arthur and his allies would stop at nothing to wrest control from her, Erin hired two private detectives to comb the house for listening devices. The investigators discovered no bugs, but they did come across a stash of drugs and syringes in the storm drain. One of the detectives, Fred Wolfson, asked Erin what should be done with the material. She told him to bury it in the backyard. Wolfson wanted no part of her plan. When Erin made threats, he and his partner, Norman Perle, turned their backs and took the material in question to the Beverly Hills police. An investigation got under way. This was the kind of lurid celebrity tale that tabloid journalists dream about, and the *National Enquirer* headlines played up every angle: MARX MANAGER THREATENED TO KILL 2, COURT TOLD. THREAT TO GROUCHO MARX'S LIFE CLAIMED. SAW MANAGER GIVE MARX TRANQUILIZER, NURSE SAYS. While the sniping went on, Krasna said to Arce: "You have to understand something. This isn't just a fight for Groucho. It's a fight for money."

Back in 1939 W. H. Auden had scribbled a note about comedians. Far ahead of its time, the aphorism was published during the conservator fight. It might have been written for the occasion. "The anarchist hidden in the heart of everyone," observed the poet, "even the administrator, has made every society tolerate and even demand the existence of the Fool, the licensed buffoon-critic. Witness the popularity of Charlie Chaplin and the Marx Brothers. But it only tolerates a very few, and furthermore, this enviable position is precarious. At any moment the Fool may go too far and be whipped." For Chaplin, that moment came in the 1950s when he was marked as subversive and effectively exiled. Now the bell seemed to be tolling for the remaining buffoon-critic.

•

BECAUSE THE THEATER OF WAR was a Santa Monica courtroom, newspapers referred to scenes from *Duck Soup*. In fact, with both sides presenting their versions of the Groucho Marx story and summoning witnesses to bolster their claims, the movie most relevant to the proceedings was *Rashomon*. On Erin's side was Morely Kert, Groucho's physician for twenty years. According to the doctor, Erin could "stimulate and cajole" Groucho into a state of well-being that was beyond his own capacity to heal.

Zeppo, called to the stand, had only praise for Erin, calling her "the greatest gal in the world" and saying, "she's done a fine job of caring for him." He agreed with Arce; were she to be taken from Groucho, he predicted, "It would kill him." Those who knew Groucho's history had to acknowledge that there was more than a grain of truth in Zeppo's remarks. At the terminals of Groucho's life were two women who had given him a place and a purpose, and they had done so on their own terms—Minnie and now Erin. The duo had more than Groucho in common. They were domineering, single-minded, ruthless, fiercely protective to the point of madness. Who was to deny that without that madness Erin might well have shared the fate of Ruth and Kay and Eden? Or, for that matter, Miriam and Melinda? For many bystanders Zeppo's seemed the final words; surely Groucho's brother would know what was the right thing to do. Insiders had their doubts: Groucho had been sending Zeppo $1,000 a month, bearing in mind that his younger brother had retired, had no source of income, and had become, like Chico, a man with large gambling debts.

On the other side of the battlefield, Arthur's lawyer tried to establish Erin's conduct as a "clear and present danger" to her companion. To that end J. Brin Schulman cross-examined the two detectives. They told the court that Erin had told them to conceal evidence, an order they had refused. She had then threatened to kill them. Her violent temper was directed not only at the operatives she had hired, but at the man she was supposed to be protecting. According to Wolfson, when the aged comedian had difficulty endorsing a payment to the detectives an exasperated Erin shouted: "Sign the fucking check! What's the matter with you? Can't you write your own name?"

Over the next several days a file of employees and ex-employees made their way to the stand. *Saturday Night Live* picked up on the proceedings; Jane Curtin updated the news with a satirical bulletin: "In addition to asking the court to appoint her conservator of the ailing Marx," Erin Fleming "has also requested that her name be legally changed to Flemmo." But there was no humor in the testimonies. Martha Brooks described a domineering Erin urging Groucho to perform when he was fatigued and defenseless. She went on to speak of the day Erin convinced Groucho that Melinda was only after his money, then watched approvingly while he tearfully ripped up photographs of his daughter and Miles and Jade, the grandchildren he had so rarely seen. A nurse, Jean Funari, described Erin's physically "abusive treatment of a little old man," including a threat to "slap him all the way to Pittsburgh" if he did not take a nap. On one occasion when Groucho proved particularly difficult, Erin moaned, "I wish he'd die." Another nurse, Terrie McCord, told the court that Erin had shaken and slapped Groucho, and that she had given him meprobamate, a prescription tranquilizer, "on many occasions." McCord provided tabloid writers with a new and salacious incident. One of the other nurses had been smoking marijuana, and McCord reported it. Erin blew up—but not at the smoker. She took her aggressions out on the messenger, accusing her of a power play. She was acting like a man, Erin implied, jettisoning her pantsuit and stripping to her panties. Running her fingers through her pubic hair, according to McCord, Erin yelled: "Why don't you fuck me? You want to wear the pants around here? You think you're a man? Fuck me!" That day the nurse walked out for good.

Then it was Erin's turn. In a deposition that ran more than nine hundred pages, she categorically denied any physical or psychological abuse and iterated her undying love for Groucho. Her best moments came when she spoke of finances. "Are you aware," she asked Schulman, "that it was my idea to syndicate *The Best of Groucho*? Are you aware that at any time within the last seven years Groucho Marx would have married me or given me any amount of money that I would have asked for, and that I insisted, 'No, I would like to be paid and earn what I am paid, thank you, Groucho Marx'?"

Burdened with contradictory testimony and evidence, the court found great difficulty in determining the right course of action. Straining to be fair, Judge Edward Rafeedie asked both sides to nominate their candidates for conservator. Erin's lawyers offered Zeppo. Bert Granet, Groucho's neighbor and friend, was the first choice of Arthur's team; when he turned down the job, they floated the name of Nat Perrin, Groucho's friend from the radio days of *Flywheel, Shyster, and Flywheel*. Rafeedie determined that Zeppo lived too far from his brother, and that in any case Arthur found his uncle unacceptable. Perrin, the last man standing, was named conservator until a more permanent arrangement could be made by the deadline of July 18. "Be fiercely independent," the judge instructed him. "You're under no obligation to anybody in this case. You may change the locks at the house and determine who has the keys. You have the power to dismiss any employee, although you should maintain the status quo in respect to those who are performing satisfactorily."

Perrin followed instructions, further infuriating Erin. No longer the martinet, she watched the staff moving about the house freely and unafraid. "Fucking servants are running this place!" she wailed to a friend. "They're treating me like a cockroach!" Perrin tried to consider her feelings along with those of the individuals who disliked Erin, making Groucho the ultimate arbiter. Unhappily, Groucho was not sure of what or who he wanted around him. Asked about his companion, he sometimes replied, "I love her." On other occasions he would murmur bitterly, "That woman is stealing my money." In general he showed great affection to Erin when she was around, and seemed to forget her the moment she left. Yet the haze could suddenly disperse, revealing glimpses of classic Groucho. Admiring the house pet, a nurse asked, "How long have you had cats?" Her charge snapped back: "I've always had cats. And before that I had measles." George Fenneman made a social call, lifting Groucho from a wheelchair and carrying him to bed. With his arm around the announcer's neck Groucho exclaimed, "Fenneman, you always were a lousy dancer." George Burns also dropped by to reminisce, and Steve Allen to play the piano and kid around. More significant and poignant was a visit from Melinda, Miles, and Jade. Without Erin around, his daughter lowered her guard, became affectionate with Groucho, and tried to explain her past behavior to Perrin: "I was being pushed into an area for which I had no talent. It was torture. I had to run away from that and from general lifestyles that really did not appeal to me. I got off into a totally opposite kind of life, and I've never been happier. I still love my father as deeply as any child could love her father." Watching them kiss and embrace, no one could doubt her words. Each time Melinda prepared to leave, Groucho pleaded with her to stay, and when she finally departed he beamed, saying, "She's coming back!" Groucho was equally affectionate with Lois, whom he had never taken to, and seemed to enjoy his conversations with Arthur. Miriam was not in evidence, but the news about her was positive. She later wrote about herself: "From 1967 to 1977 I was in and out of various hospitals and clinics being treated for alcoholism. I got sober in June of 1977; I was fifty years old."

Through this period Groucho seemed as frail as a porcelain teacup. Perrin considered it unwise to inform him of Gummo's fatal heart attack on April 21, or of Goddard Lieberson's death from cancer on May 29. Fading rapidly that summer, Groucho composed his last letter. Norman Krasna had returned to Switzerland, where he took his time going through the text and photographs of *The Groucho Phile*. "I am obligated to you for a relationship which influenced my life," he wrote to Groucho. "I wouldn't say you were a surrogate father to me but certainly an older brother. You gave me the ambiance of *Dear Ruth* and endorsement by your companionship that undoubtedly boosted me many rungs up the Hollywood pecking order. . . . You have been one of the great influences in my life and I love you very much." Groucho laboriously dictated an answer to Stoliar: "Dear Norman, I miss not seeing you. We had a lot of great times together until you moved to Switzerland. Come back. We need you." Stoliar presented the typed version for signature. Groucho examined his own words, pronounced them good, and took pen in hand. He began to make two vertical lines instead of a G. Was Erin right? Was Groucho unable to sign his own name anymore? Stoliar recalled the moment: "While I was wondering how I was ever going to fix it, Groucho made a horizontal mark between the two vertical lines, like a goalpost, creating a capital H. This was followed ever so slowly by a-c-k-e-n-b-u-s-h. Hackenbush." Groucho had not misspelled his name at all; he simply picked up an old comic routine and a long tradition with an old friend. A few days later, Groucho returned to the hospital with a dislocated hip. The slow, unpromising recuperation had only one blessing: he knew nothing of the next skirmish for control. Perrin had hoped for a permanent conservator to be named by June; July rolled around and still no one had been put forth. The *Los Angeles Times* elbowed its way into the drama two days after Groucho's admission to Cedars-Sinai, printing excerpts from the testimony of John Ballow. Groucho's onetime cook had given a detailed and damning account of Erin boasting that she "had enough drugs of her own in her purse to kill a bear!" Ballow had testified: "I used

to say, 'Where do you get all these drugs?' and she'd say 'I have ways.' "
Fruitless negotiations went on through the early summer. Then, to
the surprise of the press, lawyers hammered out an agreement. The
permanent conservator, agreeable to both sides, was to be Andy Marx.
Groucho's twenty-seven-year-old grandson was granted the title after a
twenty-minute court session in the hospital room, where Groucho nodded his approval. The war was over and everyone could see that Erin was
the loser. But no one could determine who had won.

Groucho was rarely lucid in these final days. Yet every now and then
he rose to the surface and spoke as if he were still on the sound stage.
Shaking down a thermometer, a nurse explained, "We have to see if
you have a temperature." He muttered: "Don't be silly. *Everybody* has a
temperature."

That was his last rejoinder. Soon after, Groucho lapsed into a coma
and word went out that death would be a matter of days if not hours. In
newspapers all over the world obituaries were ready to go; editors had
foreseen the end months before. What they had not foreseen was the end
of another entertainer who had not even been born when *A Night at the
Opera* was released. On Tuesday afternoon, August 16, the most popular
white singer of his time died of heart failure and years of overindulgence.
Elvis Presley was forty-two. The shocking news came three days before
Groucho's death and consumed most of the ink reserved for appraisals of
pop icons.

On August 19, 1977, in the company of Arthur, Lois, and Andy,
Groucho Marx died of respiratory problems—or as Andy was to put it,
"too many birthdays."

Reporters found Erin weeping in the hospital corridor. Miriam joined
the group of mourners too late to see her father alive, but with a sober
and forthright demeanor from which she would never depart. There
was no official word from the family, save for Erin's eerie statement:
"Groucho's just having a nice little dream now. He's just going to have a
nap and rest his eyes for the next several centuries. But he's never going to
die. He told me."

Arthur and Andy recited prayers in a family service at Temple Beth El
in Hollywood. Zeppo was not invited for reasons that seemed obvious to
him, and he said as much in an angry press conference: he had backed
Arthur's enemy in court. He did show up at a memorial service staged by
Erin at Temple Emanuel in Beverly Hills. There were no crossover guests.
Groucho's body was cremated and his remains were taken to Eden

Memorial Park in the San Fernando Valley, far from Chico's, Harpo's, and Gummo's gravesites in the overstated Forest Lawn Cemetery. An unadorned six-inch bronze plaque marking his niche read only GROUCHO MARX 1890–1977. A handful of friends, among them George Burns, Steve Allen, Red Skelton, and Bob Hope, eulogized him, vying with one another for the best Grouchoism. They settled for his answer to a journalist's inevitable question, "How would you like to be remembered?" "Alive," he replied. "If not that way, then dead."

Television news displayed many clips from Marx Brothers films, *You Bet Your Life,* and guest shots on the Dick Cavett show. The *Los Angeles Times* ran a cartoon showing the deceased beating a hasty retreat from the Pearly Gates, even though a sign reads WELCOME GROUCHO. Cigar in hand, he declares, "I would never join a club that would accept me as a member." But, in general, newspaper and magazine obituaries were smaller than they might have been had Groucho died three days before Presley instead of three days after. Editors reasoned that the old man's best work had been done decades before, and so a truncated notice would suffice, whereas Presley was a comparative youngster with a vast following between the ages of eighteen and thirty-five—the age cohort avidly pursued by advertisers. *Time's* coverage was typical: a large article about Groucho was hammered into a thirty-one-line "Milestone," while the Elvis piece stretched out over three and a half pages. "Is it my imagination," Woody Allen wrote sardonically, "or were you guys a little skimpy with the Groucho Marx obituary?" Dick Cavett continued that tone in his letter: "I can only assume that the Groucho Marx I knew is not the same one whose passing was noted briefly in your Milestones column. I hope the excuse is not that he chose to die on a weekend. I doubt that *Time* would want to suggest that, of all people, Groucho's timing was off." Alden Whitman, the dean of American obituary writers, commented on the general news coverage of Groucho's passing:

By the middle of the '70s, his brothers had died, his friends were gone and Groucho was a sad and lonely man pretending sometimes to be a youth, turning on his leer again occasionally, reciting a worn-out gag. His overwhelming sorrow was that he hadn't quit when he was ahead. None of the obits I read touched on this aspect of his humanity. Groucho Marx was an illusion in death. He was not what he seemed on the surface. Underneath was a human being vastly more complicated and engaging than the cardboard cutout that got into print. He hinted at his inner turmoils when he replied to a fan who remarked how pleased he was to meet the famous Groucho. "I've known him for years," Marx said, "and I can tell you it's no pleasure."

In those last seven words lay the key to the man and his persona. All these many years, Julius Henry Marx had been buried deep within Groucho Marx. Unlike the thin man who is supposed to writhe inside his fat host, Julius never struggled to be released. From the beginning he let circumstances control him: Minnie's manipulations; early celebrity; late wealth; the attention of critics, audiences, beautiful women. But Julius never left the premises. Through the years he was to remind Groucho of the idealistic youth he once was, and the flawed character he became. The sleepless nights, the unpleasant relations with family members outside of the Brotherhood (and even within it, when it came to Chico), the complicated business affairs, unwise liaisons, and doomed marriages—all testified to the conflict between Julius and Groucho. In the end the persona unhappily agreed with the man: living with Groucho Marx had been no pleasure, for his wives, his children—or himself.

More controversy followed Groucho's demise. In October Erin Fleming was sued by the Bank of America, charged with illegally and improperly siphoning $400,000 from an estate valued at some $2,000,000. The suit asked for punitive damages and the return of gifts such as two houses, a Mercedes 450 SEL, and half of the two thousand shares of Groucho Marx Productions, for these had been obtained through "connivance, control, direction, wheedling, intimidation, extortion, tormenting, threats, inveiglement, deceit, duress, menace and manipulation." Erin's attorneys countered with a creditor's claim against the estate. It asserted that she was owed monies for legal fees and for her work as Groucho's personal manager. In addition, Erin demanded royalties on the two books written with Arce and her manager's share of royalties from the album of the 1972 Carnegie Hall concert. Both sides were still dueling when Arce's biography, *Groucho*, was published in 1979 to generally favorable reviews—except from Arthur. In the *Hollywood Reporter* he took exception to the biographer's charge that "his children deserted him in his dotage," and that "he was sexually maladjusted all his life." Arthur reminded readers that he and Lois were the ones who talked Groucho into having the bladder operation that extended his life by seven years.

"Regarding Groucho's sex life," he went on, "all I know is Groucho used to tell me that sex was one of the world's two greatest inventions (the other was 'sitting down')."

Arce took the criticism in good grace and joked about seeing a settlement of Groucho's will within his lifetime. That was not to be; the following year the writer died suddenly at the age of forty-two during a routine hernia operation. Zeppo had gone by then, the victim of lung cancer. The last surviving brother never wavered from his view that Erin had kept Groucho secure and content in his final years. The complicated, foggy, Dickensian lawsuits carried on and on and on. Erin, the Marx family, their attorneys, and the world were not through with Groucho. Nor was he through with them. His influence was to outlive him, reaching well beyond the columbarium in the memorial park.

CHAPTER EIGHTEEN

O Splendid
and Disreputable Father!

CUSTOMARILY, THE DEATH OF A GREAT JESTER signals a dip in his reputation, followed in time by revival and reappraisal. Such was the case with Chaplin, Keaton, Laurel and Hardy, W. C. Fields, and many other pantheon figures. It was not so with Groucho. His exit occurred in the summer of 1977. In autumn he was back as the animating force of *Madder Music,* Peter De Vries's iridescent comic novel. The central character, Robert Swirling, suffers from the delusion that he is Groucho Marx. As evidence, he speaks in staccato phrases reminiscent of the Master. To a comely woman: "Perhaps I might tuck you in, if I may end a sentence with a proposition." To a rival: "I'll bet the ladies just adore that great big Kirk Douglas dimple in your chin. I thought at first it might be your navel, everything is so high these days." To the world at large: "I was hauled down to the police station and told that anything I said might be held against me. So I said, 'Elizabeth Taylor.' " Obviously *Madder Music* was composed before Groucho's demise, but in addition to being witty, De Vries was prescient. Faced with death, Groucho/Swirling invokes the name of God: "I'm dying to meet Him." As Paul Theroux observed in a *New York Times* review, "It is entirely logical that T. S. Eliot was a fan of Groucho's: De Vries pays homage to both men, and in this book Groucho is by far the darker figure and Eliot the wiseacre."

Beyond the bookshelves, Groucho illuminated television schedules, newspapers, and magazines. A year after his passing, a young Marxophile, Paul Wesolowski, founded the *Freedonia Gazette,* a semiannual journal devoted to the Brothers in general and Groucho in particular. That year also saw the publication of Lyn Erhard's book as Charlotte Chandler, *Hello, I Must Be Going,* interviews with and about Groucho in decline. The *Gazette* went on the attack with a passion only another Marx student could display: "All things considered, one truly begins to appreciate the suitability of the author's last name. It seems only fitting that the imposter in *Animal Crackers,* Roscoe W. Chandler (a.k.a. Abie the fish peddler), coincidentally carried the same surname as she.

"On the whole a most appropriate appraisal of Chandler's book is something Groucho once said in reference to his father's tailoring ability to size up customers without the benefit of a tape measure. In short, they were both 'about as accurate as Chamberlain's predictions about Hitler.' "

In 1979, *A Day in Hollywood, A Night in the Ukraine* opened in London. Subtitled *A Thirties Double Feature,* the two-act comedy was loosely based on Anton Chekhov's *The Bear* and featured four costumed farceurs. Though they bore Slavic names, their efforts caught the enterprising spirits of Harpo, Chico, Zeppo, and Groucho. The latter's opening line appraises the talent of his colleagues: "That music goes straight to my heart. It doesn't do my stomach much good either." The author, Dick Vosburgh, did not forget a Margaret Dumont character to play against. Told that her husband owes money to the Groucho character, she asks, "Why didn't you say so in the first place?" He responds: "I got thrown out of the first place. This is the second place." The show became an overnight smash, and did well on its trip to the United States.

Editorial cartoons used Groucho as a symbol of mismanagement. Following the seizure of the American embassy in Iran in 1979, the *Los Angeles Times* ran a drawing of a heavily moustached Iranian spokesman. He stands behind a lectern, gesturing with a cigar. "Say the secret word," he instructs contestant Jimmy Carter, "and the hostages go free." Above the president hovers a duck holding that word: "Apology." When U.S. Army helicopters failed during the abortive "mission in the desert," the *Washington Star* added its own Marxian comment. A cartoon showed Groucho attempting his own rescue of the U.S. hostages in Iran. He heads the two-man chopper crew: a dizzied Harpo, and a studious Chico perusing a pamphlet labeled "Helicopter Maintenance."

The early 1980s were the peak years of M*A*S*H, a long-lived television situation comedy starring Alan Alda as battlefield surgeon Hawkeye Pierce. The doctor's womanizing and leering delivery were clearly based on Groucho's persona. Early in 1980 Chuck Jones, Warner Brothers' preeminent animation director, tipped his hat to Groucho, whose work had influenced him forty years before: "In the 30's, Bugs Bunny was just a wild, funny but unmotivated character. I wanted to keep Bugs outrageous, but make him someone to root for. Groucho became one of the models I thought about, because he managed to be a wiseguy and a sympathetic antihero at the same time. He was also as interesting visually as he was verbally."

Jones referred to a memorable lunch in postwar L.A. that had started his thought processes: "It was a hot day and there wasn't a lot of air conditioning. I was sitting in my shirtsleeves and Groucho came in with a couple of his writers. The writers took off their jackets and put them on the back of their chairs. Groucho took off his *pants* and put them on the back of his chair. No one said a word—it was just Groucho being Groucho. That was the kind of understood lunacy we wanted for Bugs."

Also in the 1980s, Lewis Stadlen, the Julius Henry Marx of *Minnie's Boys,* created a solo turn he called *An Evening with Groucho Marx.* Adding fresh material and biographical detail, he allowed the character to grow up and get old. The solo performance was a great success in New York and on tour. Over the years many other actors impersonated Groucho, including the Englishmen Ron Moody, John Romney, and Michael Roberts and the Americans Gabe Kaplan and Frank Ferrante. The latter toured for fifteen years in *Groucho, A Life in Revue,* written by Groucho's son Arthur. And then without warning, images of the antic, freewheeling Groucho vanished into melodrama. It was January 1983, time for the second campaign in the war for the estate.

•

No one seemed to know the exact value of Groucho's holdings; unofficial estimates put it at about $2.6 million. The bulk of the money and property had been willed to Arthur, Miriam, and Melinda; Erin had been granted just $150,000. But what of the salaries, percentages, houses, automobiles, and other valuables she had received before Groucho's death? Were they obtained legitimately, or were they wheedled out of a feeble and irresponsible old man? Certainly not, protested Erin. She was outraged by the question, the children by her answer.

One thing was assured. This time around, the fight would be far more explicit and vicious; neither side was in any mood to take prisoners. Two years before, the California State Labor Commissioner had awarded the Bank of America, executors of Groucho's estate, an $80,000 judgment against Erin Fleming. The ruling stated that she had acted as an unlicensed artist's agent. This was not the only grievance against her. The bank still awaited the return of some $250,000 in salary, bonuses, gifts, and business and travel expenses Groucho had allegedly given his long-time companion. When Erin appealed the most recent judgment, the bank decided to settle things for once and for all, combining both actions in a single lawsuit. Again, J. Brin Schulman was chief attorney.

Erin's legal team filed a countersuit against the bank. Her lawyer, David Sabih, partner of the flamboyant Melvin Belli, charged the institution with harassment, and with illegally tying up his client's inheritance and royalties. These measures, he maintained, had pauperized her (she still had not paid lawyers from the conservatorship hearing six years before). The suit asked for $101 million in punitive damages and $1.1 *billion* in general damages—the supposed value of Erin Fleming's wrecked life.

In January 1983, after nearly two years of delays, *The Bank of America vs. Erin Fleming* came before Santa Monica Superior Court Judge Jacqueline L. Weiss. The trial took place in courtroom K, a chamber normally assigned to divorce and child-custody cases. It had seats for only thirty-five onlookers, and nine of those chairs were reserved for reporters. On the day of jury selection one of the wags guessed that no Marx had played in a room that small since the turn of the century. Another made a pregnant observation. A clause in Groucho's will specified that anyone who challenged it would receive only one dollar. Arthur, Miriam, and Melinda were mentioned in that document; it would be impossible for them to go to court without losing everything. But suppose the bank were to be their surrogate? Suppose they wanted to strike back at Erin—and in a sense at Groucho—without endangering their inheritance?

Four days later the actual trial began, without the presence of Erin. She had been temporarily hospitalized for "emotional problems." Acting as the plaintiff, the bank opened with its most damaging witness. Martha Brooks, Groucho's cook and confidante from 1965 to 1975, maintained that Erin had "forced herself" into her employer's life, encouraging him to host parties attended by "strange people." (Under cross-examination, she conceded that the guest list for these parties included Steve Allen, George Burns, Bill Cosby, and Bob Hope.) Brooks also claimed that Erin had given Groucho tranquilizers to make him more manageable, and had once struck Groucho on the leg so severely he needed stitches to close the wound. Brutalized as he was, Brooks went on, Mr. Marx grew pathetically dependent on Erin, performing in concerts whenever she demanded. In 1975 the cook had been "retired" from the Marx household, and went to work for Sidney Sheldon. While she was on the job Groucho paid frequent visits to the house, where he repeatedly expressed a fear of Erin. In cross-examination, Brooks denied that her testimony was the result of bitterness about Groucho's will—had she stayed on the job until his death she would have received $25,000. But Sabih had planted a doubt in the jurors' minds.

On the third day Schulman introduced a surprise witness. Brought in from Palm Springs, John Ballow testified that he had been a cook and house servant from 1975 to 1977, when he was dismissed. According to Ballow, Erin gave Groucho sedatives, took drugs herself, slapped the old man more than once, and forced him to sign checks. He had overheard Groucho say "I can't get rid of Miss Fleming because, quite frankly, I think she would kill me," and he added a quote from Erin: "Black people are supposed to be subservient." Three African Americans sat on the jury; the words had a visible impact.

Day four brought Dr. Mary Schindler to the stand. The psychologist had been called to Groucho's home in 1975 to determine if he was mentally capable of adopting Erin. Referring to notes, she remembered asking him what he would do if he were lost in a forest. The answer: "I would find a phone and call my parents." This was thought to be a juvenile reply; nonetheless Dr. Schindler added that Erin seemed an "organizer" and the proper person to care for Groucho. She came to this conclusion when Groucho pointed to his head and exclaimed, "Erin's got it up here. She would never leave me. She loves me. She's been with me for six years and I haven't made a decision without her." Up to this point Dr. Schindler had been credible. But she ended her testimony with a surprising lack of humor and an ignorance of Groucho's comic style. She said she decided that it was pointless to continue her test when she asked Marx, "What direction is Panama?" and he replied, "You get in your car and drive down Sunset Boulevard." This did not agree with the doctor's map of the Americas.

Melinda came to court on January 28. Groucho's thirty-six-year-old daughter stated that she felt very close to her father, and that she could notice the difference once Erin became a part of his life. Remembering Groucho's "drugged" appearance, Melinda broke down on the stand, prompting Judge Weiss to call a short recess. Upon her return, the witness alleged that Erin screamed at Groucho and forced him to go onstage against his will. Melinda made the mistake of talking about Groucho as a meticulous dresser who delighted in shopping in expensive stores—a habit that stopped, she said, when Erin put him on a minuscule clothing allowance. Groucho's friends knew that he had always been notorious for spending as little as possible, that in fact it was he who restricted his wives to very tight budgets.

On cross-examination Sabih implied that Melinda was testifying solely because she had a financial interest in the outcome. This was emphatically denied. Well then, if she was so concerned about Erin's mistreatment, why did she wait several years before consulting a lawyer? The witness stated that it "took a while to make sure" of the abuse. Pressed, she admitted to missing Groucho's funeral; the absence was deliberate, she maintained, in order to avoid confronting Erin.

On January 31, the forty-two-year-old Erin appeared in court for the first time. Dressed in a mink coat over a beige-and-rust knit dress, she hardly seemed the impoverished waif described by Sabih. After establishing herself as Groucho's "helper," she described his successful fight against depression, isolation, and age. Until the very last days, she said, he was in full possession of his faculties; the only reason he had round-the-clock nurses was that he had insurance policies with three different companies, each one covering eight hours of work. As the day drew to a close, the overwrought witness turned on her interrogator, attacking Schulman for taking $200,000 in legal fees which "rightfully belonged to Groucho's children."

Over the next few days, Erin walked a thin line between rage and instability. Asked how she had managed to buy a house in Los Angeles in the 1970s, she told Schulman, "None of your goddamn business." The judge admonished her: "You'll have to control yourself. You can't use profanity in the courtroom." Erin expressed contrition and made no further outbursts. The next day, however, she claimed that Groucho "was tortured and murdered: . . . Mr. Brin Schulman is an assassin and he murdered Groucho Marx." Again Judge Weiss stepped in: "This isn't a forum for you to remonstrate." Again Erin apologized and struggled for self-control.

On February 2 she was unprepared when a sheriff's deputy attempted to frisk her and search her handbag. "This is a civil case," Erin exclaimed. "If you want to charge me with criminal charges, then do. But until then, I'm not going to let anyone search my pocketbook or my body." The protest was duly noted—and disregarded for the rest of the trial, for Schulman, claiming that the defendant was hostile enough to make an attempt on his life, had persuaded the court to make her submit to a daily body search for weapons. After the scuffle, the witness returned to the stand. Judge Weiss asked her whether she had any problems. "There is nothing wrong with me," came the angry reply. "*You* may have a few problems." It was a pivotal moment. Judge Weiss ordered a psychiatric examination of the witness. Dr. Ronald Marman, a psychiatrist often consulted by the court, found Erin Fleming was "very incoherent, very angry, and very mentally ill." If her outbursts were part of an act, he maintained, then "she is one of the greatest actresses of all time." Nevertheless, because she understood the proceedings of the trial and what was at stake, she was ruled competent to continue.

The attorneys pressed on. Harpo's son Bill Marx stepped to the stand, speaking of projects and parties at which Groucho appeared. "I always felt I had just been to a Fellini movie," he said. "There was something unreal about them." Sabih won a point when he got Bill to admit that Erin did "a wonderful thing" by lobbying for his uncle Groucho's Academy Award.

Erin returned to court on February 12. The court ruled that she was not to be photographed during testimony, and this seemed to ease the pressure. For several days she defended herself capably against Schulman. Insisting that she was no manipulator of a doddering star, she swore that only "Groucho was in control of Groucho's money." The comedian was generous with her because he wanted to shower the beloved with expensive presents. "He wanted to give me everything, including the Empire State Building." Schulman reminded her, "He didn't own that." Well, she returned, "if he could have bought it he would have given it to me."

What Groucho did give her at Christmas, 1973, was the green Mercedes-Benz, with a ribbon tied around it and a card inscribed, "To Erin, I Love You." She notified the court that in the past five years she had financed that vehicle twice, to borrow $22,000 for living expenses. Erin added that Groucho had wanted to buy her a $125,000 home in Beverly Hills. "I turned him down like a fool. It's now worth $5.5 million." Bearing in mind the exploding real estate values in L.A., onlookers burst into appreciative laughter. Their spontaneous reaction seemed to indicate a change in public sentiment. Assessing the situation, the *Los Angeles Times* reported that even Fleming's bizarre outbursts "may have turned courtroom opinion sympathetic to the Defendant. The sympathy seems to have shown up in various ways in recent days. For instance, an elderly Santa Monica court observer had this comment at the end of one session this week: 'If that woman is found guilty, it will be a miscarriage of justice.' Other court observers have been chatting with Fleming either before court or during recesses."

Taking advantage of the shift, Sabih called Arthur Marx to the stand. Groucho's son testified that he and his father had once been close, but that when Erin entered the picture she "drove a wedge" between them. One day in March 1977, he visited Groucho in the hospital. Emerging from anesthesia, the old man mumbled something about "money downhill and to the left." These directions described the relation of Erin's place to Groucho's, and Arthur took the six words to mean only one thing: Groucho was worried that the young lady was stealing his money. It was pointed out that most of L.A. lived down the hill and to the left from Groucho. Sabih went on to subject the witness to close questioning, referring to the time Arthur allowed his father to make manuscript changes in *Life with Groucho*—and then secretly threw the alterations in a waste basket. The encounter between lawyer and witness was, at best, a draw.

Over the next weeks Sabih marshaled his defenses, calling witness after witness to praise Erin's dedication—and denigrate Groucho's children. Dee Hartford Cramer, whose sister Eden was Groucho's third wife, told the jury that she had heard her former brother-in-law quarreling with Arthur (" 'My son finally wrote a book to destroy me' ") and with Melinda (" 'I hope the next time I see you, you'll be in your grave,' she said"). Cramer concluded, "The fact that he left them anything at all is a miracle." Bud Cort related the story of Erin rescuing Groucho from drowning. Asked if he had seen any beatings at Groucho's house, the actor stated that he had indeed. One evening Groucho chased Erin around the dining room table, striking her with his bedroom slipper because she said he was too tired to go out.

A major celebrity made his way to the stand. The eighty-seven-year-old George Burns stated that he had known Groucho for more than four decades, and that Groucho loved the parties he hosted and attended in old age. Schulman, who had asked the judge to prohibit public laughter only a few days before, began his examination of Burns by playing to the gallery. Alluding to the film *Oh, God,* in which Burns had played the title role, the attorney stated coyly, "I've never cross-examined God before, so I'm going to do it very carefully." Without cracking a smile, Burns informed him, "I'm only God when I get paid." Schulman then attempted to discredit the comedian's testimony, asking him if he was sure Groucho really sang. Burns replied, "Certainly. He wouldn't let *me* sing." But didn't Groucho retire early, in the middle of the parties? Burns said that he never noticed that Groucho had gone to bed, even when the parties lasted until midnight: "He never stopped singing." Before he departed in a large black limousine, the witness took questions from reporters. When one solicited his private opinion of Marx and Fleming, Burns responded diplomatically, "I think she was a charming lady, and he was a great comedian."

The defense summoned more witnesses to the stand. Sally Kellerman remembered that Groucho "was always putting his arm around Erin, giving her a kiss." Dena Brown, a legal secretary for Groucho Marx Productions, said that when Erin walked into the room "Groucho's eyes would light up . . . he'd sparkle. She was the light of his life. She made him realize that he was a living legend." She quoted Groucho verbatim: "Without Erin, I wouldn't be alive," and confirmed that it was Groucho's idea to adopt Erin and not the other way around.

A more telling defense witness followed. Christina Finlayson, who had served a term as Groucho's executive housekeeper, described her employer's despondency after the conservatorship battle. She said Erin's visits were curtailed, and Mr. Marx was "like a dead man" when she wasn't around. During her visits, Groucho perked up. He became "like a sixteen-year-old . . . the happiest person God ever created." Sabih elicited an odd piece of information. Groucho used to stare at a bedside photo of Miss Fleming, awaiting her visit. A day or two after his death the picture was torn into pieces. Schulman broke in at this point, and the judge sustained his objections. The destroyer remained unidentified.

Sabih moved in his heavy ordnance. Dr. L. James Grold, identified as Groucho Marx's personal psychiatrist, had no doubt that Groucho "felt very alienated from his children," and worried that "they would try to take his money away from him and put him in a nursing home." Erin, on the other hand, "encouraged him, stimulated him, motivated him," the psychiatrist said, and continued: "On the several occasions I saw Groucho after the enforced separation, he really appeared to wither away, and I feel he basically gave up. His greatest fear, of losing Erin, was realized."

Another doctor, Joseph A. Kaufman, head of urology at UCLA, agreed that Erin "had an extremely salutary effect on Groucho. She resurrected his life." This was too much for Schulman, who badgered the witness repeatedly, asking for intimate details of Groucho's sexual capacity. The judge put a stop to that. "It's most unfortunate," she scolded Schulman, "that when a person is dead, they shouldn't have any privacy as to any of their bodily functions." She kept on: "To drag out his sexual prowess or lack of it, and his urinary problems, goes beyond the bounds of any need in this lawsuit."

Celebrities passed in review. Speaking of Erin and Groucho, George Fenneman remembered that "prior to their being together, he was really despondent," and that "he didn't want to see anybody and felt nobody wanted to see him." A phenomenal change began with Erin's entrance onto the scene; Groucho "felt involved, he felt wanted. He felt people cared." Carroll O'Connor agreed: "If not for Miss Fleming, he would have lost contact with many of his friends. . . . The parties she arranged were keeping him in touch, keeping him, in his words, alive." Democratic Assemblyman Tom Hayden said that he first met Groucho in 1975, at the seventieth-birthday party of his father-in-law, Henry Fonda. In the spring of 1976 Groucho helped the politician campaign, speaking to senior citizens from a flatbed truck. Far from being senile, insisted Hayden, "he was particularly shrewd. He was lucid, intelligent, and funny."

Sabih edged close to the finale, calling yet another medical man to the stand. Dr. Milton Wexler was a psychologist who had treated Erin, and who occasionally saw her in the company of Groucho. He was a witness to the signing of Groucho's will in 1974, at which time he concluded that Groucho was "not demented in any way" and showed no signs of senility. During cross-examination, Schulman asked for Wexler's evaluation of Erin. The doctor stated candidly that she possessed an infantile personality, which accounted for her temper tantrums and her belief that she was a great actress. Furthermore, she suffered from the condition of paranoia, aggravated by the two lawsuits against her. But before Schulman could move this testimony to the win column, Wexler continued. Had there been no Erin Fleming in Groucho's life, "no stimulation such as she provided," her companion might have degenerated much faster than he did. "While I do not find Erin to be a very appealing person," he went on, "obviously Groucho Marx did. I also think Groucho Marx was a very astute person, very direct, very clear-headed. He was very fond of Erin Fleming, and very unthreatened by her." Wexler finished by characterizing Arthur as hostile to his own father, exhibiting "contempt, anger, rage."

On the twenty-seventh and twenty-eighth days of the trial Erin returned to the witness stand. She spoke resentfully of her financial predicament. The Bank of America had prevented her from selling or refinancing her house, and in recent months she'd had to borrow cash from Sabih for food and medical bills. Again, Erin firmly denied that she had ever demanded money from Groucho; in fact, she said, she had "asked Groucho to please not include me in his will." He followed her instructions, she reminded the jury. To be sure, she owned 50 percent of Groucho Marx Productions, but the company had yet to show a profit.

Finally she broke into tears as she related Groucho's dying words. "I was there when he died. I said he was my baby, and he said he'd come back to me."

The crowd was audibly moved by all this, but no one could be certain what the jury thought as the plaintiff's rebuttal began. John Guedel, producer of *You Bet Your Life*, was asked if he alone was responsible for rescuing tapes of that show and syndicating it as *The Best of Groucho*. "Well, yes, I guess so," he responded, and stated that Erin had nothing to do with bringing the show back. Miriam Marx Allen, fifty-six, spoke wistfully of a "wonderful childhood" with Groucho. The years afterward, she conceded, were not so happy. She stopped seeing her father in the 1970s in part because she did not want him to see her in an alcoholic state. Indeed, Miriam was too drunk to see him accept his Oscar—but she watched a videotape later and was "horrified" because Groucho resembled a puppet who could scarcely walk or talk coherently. Kay Gorcey Marx stated that she did not stop loving Groucho, but divorced him because she had been "so sick." In her time, she recalled, Groucho hated parties and all Hollywood actors except Ruth Gordon and Spencer Tracy. After Erin came into Groucho's life, Kay said sadly, "He would hang up whenever I telephoned." Lois Marx, Arthur's wife, cheerfully summoned up memories of "one of the highlights of my life": the evening she spotted Erin with a date and poured a glass of water over her head. Lois claimed she had no interest in Groucho's money and denied that Erin was present the moment that her companion breathed his last. Erin had left the room, Arthur and Lois had entered, and then Groucho died. This was confirmed by the attending physician, Dr. Richard Gold.

Sabih rebutted by summoning Eden Hartford Marx, Groucho's third wife. She testified that she saw Erin at Groucho's side in the hospital, "holding his hand and staring at him. She was staring so intently she didn't notice me." Eden had attended a party shortly after the Oscar presentation, at which Groucho offered a toast: "To Erin, who makes my life worth living. I love her a lot." To Eden, her ex-husband sounded "perfectly natural."

A vignette now occurred that all the Brothers would have appreciated, if only as impromptu vaudeville. J. Brin Schulman was speaking to reporters just before the closing arguments. Suddenly one of the defense witnesses, a nurse, whacked him with her umbrella, pursuing the lawyer down a hallway and reviling him as an "evil, evil man." The astonished spectators cheered her on. Later, fully composed, Schulman summarized his case by telling the court that Erin had threatened to kill Groucho, that she dominated, terrorized, and programmed him to do her will. "She was loud, she was abusive, she was disrespectful. She made the place shake and quake." Of course, "she didn't do it when George Burns was around, she didn't do it when Mr. Fenneman was around, she didn't do it at parties when a lot of people were around," but there were many private times when she abused him. The attorney stated firmly that he was not arguing the case as anyone's surrogate, but because the Bank of America was "duty bound to be here." The jury was cautioned not to think of the departed "as some myth or legend, not some person in history known as Groucho Marx," but as a senile old man. Schulman listed Groucho's illnesses and infirmities and summed him up as "someone who couldn't even find his way to the bathroom." How could there have been any genuine love between the pair, he asked, when "Groucho really didn't know what was going on?"

Sabih summed up his case by reminding the jurors: "The issue is not whether I or you like Erin Fleming. The question is whether Groucho loved her." The assault here, he emphasized, "is on each one of us. . . . What the Bank of America is trying to say is that we do not have the right to do as we please with our money." Should Sabih's own children desert him in old age, he hoped that he would have "someone like Erin Fleming, even with all her craziness, to take care of me." Charging that Arthur, Miriam, and Melinda "didn't bring one beautiful moment in Groucho's life," he posed a rhetorical question: "Don't you think Groucho is turning in his grave right now, [when] he sees she has to come in and defend herself for the money he gave her out of love?" The sorriest part of all, in his opinion, was that if the jurors found in Erin's favor, they were powerless to award her a cent even in legal fees. They could only decide how much, if anything, she had to give back. He concluded by playing videotapes of Groucho and Erin smiling and embracing. Schulman objected; the tapes, he said, offered no insight into Groucho's real life. He was overruled. On the thirty-seventh day Judge Weiss handed over the case for deliberation. Both lawyers confidently predicted that they would be vindicated within a day. That was on March 16. The verdict did not come in for two weeks.

•

AT LAST, on March 30, the judgment was read: the jury had found in favor of the plaintiff. Erin was to pay $221,842.09 in actual damages and

$250,000 in punitive damages. Stunned, Melvin Belli pronounced the verdict "the damnedest thing I've ever seen in fifty years of law." He said: "It's the last episode in a wonderful life—*A Day in Court* by Groucho Marx. They'd have to get Groucho and Harpo and Chico and maybe Zeppo too because only they could understand it. Groucho, where are you now when we need your help?"

The defendant was caught completely off guard. Appearing on ABC's *Nightline,* Erin was asked how she planned to pay. "I was going to ask you if you'd lend it to me," she told Ted Koppel. Upon reconsidering, she wondered "if I could put it on my Master Charge." In another exchange, CNN correspondent Sandy Kenyon posed a tasteless question. Given the unfavorable judgment, had Erin thought of killing herself? The interviewee vowed to keep on living: "I'm afraid the world is going to be punished with my presence. You'll see me scrubbing the floors at the Bank of America."

Journalists were no less puzzled by the events in Santa Monica. In the *Los Angeles Herald Examiner,* Jean Vallely wondered "how the jury decided to disregard the testimony of Groucho's friends, his psychiatrist and of Groucho himself in favor of the bank." Syndicated columnist Carole Hemingway called the verdict "not only strange, it's sick." She wrote: "Groucho made written agreements as far back as 1972 with Erin—the woman, he told his psychiatrist privately, was his 'reason for living.' And now, six years after his death, other people are deciding for him what he really wanted. Horsefeathers. The live schemers don't care what he wanted. They care about his money. What arrogance and disrespect to fight for it through a post-mortem examination of his feelings for her." Joe Morgenstern, also of the *Examiner,* allowed that Erin "may have been mean to the old coot from time to time, but she earned her keep, and then some. Groucho was a difficult old man. He was a difficult young man." The columnist concluded with a question to his readers: "What about the pleasure of having a younger woman in the house, even if it was mixed with pain, like most pleasures in life? Hasn't Schulman ever seen or read *A Christmas Carol?* Does he really think the good life when you're old is staying home and stroking your passbook?"

To some extent, Judge Weiss may have agreed with these post-mortems. She let stand the judgment of actual damages, but concluded that "after weighing all of the evidence I am convinced the jury should not have awarded punitive damages." The preponderance of evidence "demonstrates a caring relationship between Defendant Fleming and

Groucho Marx." Given an opportunity to contest the court's ruling, Schulman elected to drop the whole matter. Fleming and her attorneys took their case to the California Court of Appeals, hoping to have the judgment on actual damages overturned. They were unsuccessful; the court confirmed Judge Weiss's decision on February 6, 1987. After all the hearings and trials and appeals, Arthur saw no reason to gloat in this instance. Everyone had lost. The various legal fees had depleted most of Groucho's estate by the time it was distributed to the family, in 1988, *eleven years* after his death.

To the women of *A Day in Court*, many things would occur in the next few years. Some were auspicious, some heartbreaking. In midlife, Miriam began an altruistic career, dedicating herself to the aid and counsel of substance abusers. Melinda went back to a housewife role in northern California; she rarely saw her siblings after the trial. Eden died of cancer in December 1983, only a few months after she testified. Kay continued the unending struggle with her precarious health. Erin's route was, to put it in the kindest light, bizarre. She dropped completely out of sight after the final, failed appeal. Sporadically, someone answering to her description was spotted at a store or walking on the street talking to Groucho's ghost. In 1990 she walked into a West Hollywood sheriff's station. As Miss Fleming spoke with deputies, said an official, "she placed the handbag on the counter. Visible within it was a .357 Magnum revolver which, after inspection, was found to be loaded." She was arrested and released on her own recognizance; a computer check showed that the handgun had been legally registered to her. After that incident she dropped out of sight until 1995. Shortly after his ninetieth birthday, Nat Perrin ran into Steven Stoliar and informed him: "Erin's a bag lady on Santa Monica Boulevard now. A celebrity bag lady, I guess you could say." Stoliar asked if this was an attempt at humor. "No. I'm serious," Perrin assured him. "She's had a lot of problems over the years. My wife gave her money once and some of the restaurants give her food from time to time."

Could this be true? Stoliar wrote in his memoir. Could the same woman "who had ruled Groucho's house with an iron fist now be reduced to poverty and homelessness? What a curious irony that the woman whom many had said bore a slight resemblance to Vivien Leigh should now, like Blanche DuBois, be dependent on the kindness of strangers."

Curious, too, that nothing had worked out as Groucho intended. In the final days a doctor had teased him: "Don't you feel uncomfortable in the company of a woman fifty years your junior?" Groucho saw nothing funny about the alliance. "This is someone very dear to me. This is someone I love. I don't want to have her joked about," he said. Yet that was the way people spoke of Erin, now that she had vanished into the squalid world of mental hospitals and outpatient wandering on the streets of Los Angeles. Perhaps there was no other way the arrangement could have ended. As Groucho admitted years before, counting three wives and two daughters and numerous liaisons, he had rarely had any luck with females—or they with him. No wonder that so many moviegoers believed that he and Margaret Dumont were married; their male-female relationship was the one that worked because it was pure farce. Of all the women, only Minnie had known how to handle Julius Henry Marx, and the son's feelings about his mother had never been truly resolved. "Minnie loved children," was the way he handled such thoughts. "She'd have given anything if I had been one." As always, truth resided in the offhand crack.

Julius Henry Marx never did have much of a childhood, and as a consequence his adult life was marked with immaturity and contradiction. He was a socially ambitious scamp, a loving and insensitive father, a faithful and contemptuous husband, a scripted ad-libber, an infantile grownup, a fearful iconoclast, and, above and below all, a depressive clown. The last category is one of the bromides of show business, and one that Groucho particularly loathed—but that does not make it false. The man who said he hated "Pagliacci gangrene" nonetheless crammed the "Grock" anecdote into his autobiography for a reason:

> I'm sure most of you have heard the story of the man who tells an analyst he has lost the will to live. The doctor advises the melancholy figure to go to the circus that night and spend the evening laughing at Grock, the world's funniest clown. "After you have seen Grock, I am sure you will be much happier." The patient rises to his feet and looks sadly at the doctor. As he starts to leave the doctor says, "By the way, what is your name?" The man turns and regards the analyst with sorrowful eyes.
> "I am Grock."

•

"WHY SHOULD I CARE about posterity?" Groucho liked to ask. "What's posterity ever done for me?" Everything, as it developed. In

England, the very serious poet Martin Bell offered a posthumous "Ode to Groucho":

> *What you had was a voice*
> *To double-talk faster,*
> *Twanging hypnotic*
> *In an age of nagging voices—*
> *And bold eyes to dart around*
> *As you shambled supremely*
> *Muscular moth-eaten panther!*
>
> *Black eyebrows, black cigar,*
> *Black painted moustache—*
> *A dark code of elegance*
> *In an age of nagging moustaches—*
> *To discomfit the coarse mayor,*
> *Un-poise the suave headmaster*
> *Reduce all the old boys to muttering fury.*
>
> *A hero for the young,*
> *Blame if you wish the human situation—*
> *Subversivest of con-men*
> *In an age of ersatz heroes:*
> *Be talkative and shabby and*
> *Witty; bully the bourgeois;*
> *Act the obvious phoney. . . .*
>
> *O splendid and disreputable father!*

The splendid and disreputable father of modern comedy is recognized as such by a group of disparate comedians. Acknowledging an ancestor, Jerry Seinfeld reminisces about Groucho: "He was a very silly, full-grown man. 'What a good idea,' I thought. If you see one grown man acting silly, the next one does it more easily." Paul Reiser remembers starting out and seeing in Groucho "this comedy father-figure acting adolescent and producing irreverent, hip comedy that was so wonderfully incongruous." To Richard Belzer, "Groucho was the ultimate bad boy; he gave anarchy a good name." As a teenager, Belzer realized, "I was getting punished for the kind of wisecracks Groucho was getting paid for—maybe someday I could be like Groucho." Robert Wuhl is analytical:

"Like all great comics, Groucho was also a musician with a great sense of rhythm. You can hear his influence in the delivery of every standup line spoken today."

That influence extends beyond straight comedy. When the U.S.S.R. broke apart, editorial cartoonists revived the superannuated joke of substituting Groucho for Karl. The *New Haven Register* showed a Polish leader declaiming, "I'd never belong to a government that would have me as a member." His assistant corrects him: "Comrade Jaruszelski, you're quoting the wrong Marx." *New York Newsday* used the occasion for a double pun that would occur to many artists and writers. Over the caption "Gorbachev's going too fast!" were the faces of Russia's most famous leaders—except that Marx and Lenin were now Marx (Groucho) and Lennon (John). In that spirit, the so-called government of Abkhazia (actually the invention of some sharp American entrepreneurs) issued stamps with faces of the late comedian and the Beatle side by side. Another Marxist connection was made by Jon Weiner, professor of history at the University of California, Irvine, when he acquired Groucho's FBI files through the Freedom of Information Act. The investigators could find no connection between the comedian and Communism. However, with bureaucratic propriety they quoted informants saying that Groucho had once referred to the "United Snakes" on his quiz show, and that he had contributed to an antifascist rally in the 1930s. The story ran in all major newspapers in 1998, with predictable references to a man who wouldn't want to join any Party that would have him as a member.

Back in those prewar days, Groucho entered the American vocabulary and put down roots. They are still firmly in place. "Groucho glasses," those plastic spectacles overhung with black eyebrows and attached to a nose and moustache, remain as ubiquitous now as they were in the 1940s. They decorate the faces of children at birthday parties and adults on odd occasions. Supreme Court Justice Sandra Day O'Connor wore a pair to a Court conference one Halloween evening. (In a scene out of *Horse Feathers*, her lofty colleagues greeted her with total silence.)

The name of the comedian surfaces in surprising contexts. *New York Times* columnist A. M. Rosenthal sarcastically described the fumbling attempts to impeach President Bill Clinton: "Ah, what a pity, what a pity— the Senate performance is ending when we are still enjoying the artistry of turning a national drama into comedy. That was difficult to achieve, turning Hamlet's soliloquy into a Grouchoian shtick, but they did it." No further explanation was necessary. Obituaries of scientist Thomas McMahon noted that he was the inventor of a "low-impact, high-energy form of exercise called Groucho Running." No illustrations were necessary here, either.

In London, the private Groucho Club boasts a large membership and an outstanding kitchen. The name derives from the overused paradox about not joining any club that would accept one as a member. Groucho would no doubt have appreciated another paradox: some 75 percent of those who apply for membership are turned away. "The criterion employed by the committee," says its manager, "is that you have to be pretty far ahead in your line of work. It isn't done by age: if you are twenty-five and have a column in a newspaper, fine. If you are forty-five and going nowhere—no. The feeling of belonging and continuing to belong to something that is a success is important."

Two documentaries on Groucho and his siblings, *The Unknown Marx Brothers* and *The Marx Brothers in a Nutshell,* circulated in the 1990s; both have been shown on television, awakening a new generation to the origins of modern humor. There are more than twenty Web sites devoted to Groucho. Some are just excerpts from the quotable Marx: "Outside of a dog, a book is man's best friend. Inside of a dog, it's too dark to read"; "If you want to see a comic strip, you should see me in the shower." Others suggest an intimacy that seems as unlikely as it is possible, as in Paul Krassner's recycled memoir, "My Acid Trip with Groucho," originally published in the February 1981 issue of *High Times* magazine. " 'Everybody has their own Laurel and Hardy,' he mused, 'A miniature Laurel and Hardy, one on each shoulder. Your little Oliver Hardy bawls you out—he says, 'Well, this is a fine mess you got us into.' And your little Stan Laurel gets all weepy—'Oh, Ollie, I couldn't help it. I did the best I could. . . .' "

Still others examine the career in knowledgeable detail. On-line stores sell thirty-two different videotapes starring the comedian, ranging from *The Cocoanuts* to highlights from TV specials starring Lucille Ball and Jimmy Durante. In the last year of the century, a stage version of *Duck Soup* was performed at the Yale Cabaret in New Haven. The director-adaptor Will Frears, a first-year student at the School of Drama, remembered seeing the film for the first time in England, before his thirteenth birthday: "I fell in love with the movie instantly—with Groucho as Rufus T. Firefly, the leader of the mythical country of Freedonia. . . . By the time I came here to go to college I knew every pun, every gag, every bit of business." Frears added an element whose absurdity might have intrigued or appalled the original Firefly: "Our Groucho is a girl. . . . At first, she wasn't doing the walk right. I didn't say anything to her, because I wanted to give her time to figure it out. Like the rest of the cast, she watched the movie every night before going to bed. Then, suddenly, she got the walk!" *The New Yorker* rarely covers out-of-town student productions, but it sent Lillian Ross to cover the opening of this one. "The lights dimmed," she reported. "Frears looked numb as the play began. Onstage the Newsboy was crossing, shouting, 'Extra! Extra! Firefly appointed new leader of Freedonia!' The audience started giggling expectantly, and they never stopped hooting and applauding and whistling and groaning with enjoyment all the way through to the end."

Of all devotees, the one who most consistently and creatively salutes Groucho is Woody Allen, the filmmaker Groucho called "so bright he could have been the sixth Marx brother." In physical presentation and verbal style, Allen owes much to the comedian who went before him. The debt has been freely acknowledged, particularly in two highly polished features. The title of Allen's musical, *Everyone Says I Love You,* is taken from the theme song of *Horse Feathers,* and features a party where everyone is dressed as Groucho. *Hannah and Her Sisters* stars Allen as Mickey, a terminally depressed writer. Convinced that he exists in a godless and meaningless universe, Mickey points a rifle at his head. It misfires, and he wanders the West Side of Manhattan, alternately hysterical and despondent. Without quite realizing it, he enters a movie house specializing in revivals. On the screen is *Duck Soup,* with Firefly leading his brothers in a musical number, urging the citizens of Freedonia to go to war with the citizens of Sylvania. The merry black-and-white of the film contrasts sharply with the muted colors of *Hannah.* Mickey experiences the closest thing to an epiphany ever seen in a Woody Allen movie. On the basis of a 1933 comedy he asks himself, "How can you think of killing yourself?" and decides to take an existential gamble. Mickey lives. So does Groucho.

Tributes like these are Julius Henry Marx's Graceland. No U.S. commemorative stamp bears his portrait. His resting place is surprisingly modest and out-of-the-way; it receives few visitors. He lives through his influence, and if you would see his monument, look around—at comedy channels, videos, animated cartoons, journalism, humorous novels, and at the common mistrust of the haughty and powerful.

In an essay, "The Simple Art of Murder," Raymond Chandler discusses the centerpieces of the modern detective story. About the most durable of them he observes, "Sherlock Holmes after all is mostly an attitude and a few dozen lines of unforgettable dialogue." Chandler might have been describing Groucho. Like Sherlock, he endures because of an attitude, and because of lines that keep popping up in anthologies, dictionaries, and the national consciousness. And like Sherlock, he is one of a handful of characters who are instantly recognizable worldwide, even in silhouette. (Don Quixote and Chaplin's tramp are two others; Groucho is in rare and good company.) Since his heyday other comic artists have enjoyed a vogue, made films and records, became adored objects of popular culture, and moved on. They are forgotten now; the appetite for the new has rendered them obsolete. Yet Groucho remains. For more than any other comedian he represents the history of twentieth-century entertainment: vaudeville, theater, film, radio, TV, and even CD-ROMs. Many an entertainer, if the truth were told, has tumbled from his clawhammer coat. A new century has begun, with fresh faces and new routines. Let them come; above the general tumult will continue to float the whiff of a large cigar and the reverberating echo of the last laugh.

Suggested Reading

WORKS WRITTEN BY AND WITH GROUCHO MARX

The author Groucho Marx is responsible for a small shelf of works, most of them semiau-
tobiographical, all of them accenting humor above accuracy. In chronological
order:

Beds. New York: Farrar & Rinehart, 1930. A light essay on sex and sleep. Groucho was an
uncertain writer in the late 1920s and early '30s, and he needed the assistance of his
friend Arthur Sheekman.

Many Happy Returns: An Unofficial Guide to Your Income Tax Problems. New York: Simon &
Schuster, 1942. A wry, mistimed attack on the Internal Revenue Service, published
in the first year of World War II and never reprinted.

Time for Elizabeth. Norman Krasna with Groucho Marx. New York: Dramatist's Play Service,
1949. Groucho's one and only Broadway play, now very dated, written in collaboration with a colleague whose solo work for the stage enjoyed far greater success.

Groucho and Me. New York: Bernard Geis, 1959. This is as close as the author ever came to
autobiography, carefully omitting anything that might reveal the man behind the
cigar and greasepaint moustache, but sympathetically recalling the Marxes in the
heyday of vaudeville, Broadway, and Hollywood.

Memoirs of a Mangy Lover. New York: Bernard Geis, 1963. A series of alternately amusing and
strained anecdotes about the comedian-author and his misadventures with the
opposite sex.

The Groucho Letters: Letters to and from Groucho Marx. New York: Simon & Schuster, 1967.
With this book, Groucho picks up velocity. Not all the correspondence is of value,
but his cranky missives to Warner Brothers and his exchanges with T. S. Eliot, E. B.
White, Fred Allen, and other notables show a sly wit and an intelligence often kept
from public view.

The Secret Word Is Groucho. With Hector Arce. New York: Putnam, 1976. The backstage story
of *You Bet Your Life,* the radio and TV quiz show that solidified Groucho's reputation as the master of spontaneity by setting up his ad-libs beforehand.

The Groucho Phile: An Illustrated Life. Indianapolis: Bobbs-Merrill, 1977. A compendium of old
routines and dialogue, unusual photographs, and anecdotes from six decades,
arranged in chronological order but with no other organizing principle, and with
an indifference to such niceties as page numbers.

*Groucho Marx and Other Short Stories and Tall Tales. Edited by Robert S. Bader. Boston: Faber & Faber, 1993. A scrupulously assembled and annotated collection of fugitive writings by Groucho, ranging from an article in *Judge* in the winter of 1925 to an ad in *Playboy* in the fall of 1973.

Love, Groucho: Letters from Groucho Marx to His Daughter Miriam. Edited by Miriam Marx Allen. Boston: Faber & Faber, 1993. Idiosyncratic, increasingly melancholy letters to a gifted daughter through her much-troubled childhood, adolescence, college career, and maturity. By her own account, Miriam's battle with alcohol was not won until Groucho's last year of life.

KEY SECONDARY SOURCES

The Marx Brothers. Kyle Crichton. Garden City, N.Y.: Doubleday, 1950. A collective biography controlled by the Brothers, who glamorized their mother, Minnie, and made sure that their own flaws were minimized or left unmentioned. Of interest as entertainment rather than history.

A Child of the Century. Ben Hecht. New York: Simon & Schuster, 1954. One of Hollywood's most successful scenarists offers knowing glimpses of the Marx Brothers off-camera.

I'll Cry Tomorrow. Lillian Roth with Mike Connolly and Gerold Frank. New York: Frederick Fell, 1954. This story of a Jewish girl's rise and fall in Hollywood includes an account of the time that Paramount Studios, upset at her offscreen behavior, decided to punish the actress by assigning her to appear with the Marx Brothers in *Animal Crackers.*

Life with Groucho. Arthur Marx. New York: Simon & Schuster, 1954. A disenchanted, complicated profile of the comedian as father. The author's *Son of Groucho* (New York: David McKay, 1972) presents more of the same, with alternate notes of forbearance and acrimony.

The Funny Men. Steve Allen. New York: Simon & Schuster, 1956. Contains an amusing essay about Groucho by Allen, another comedian who was never quite on the elder's wavelength. Allen followed this with another piece, twenty-five years later, in his *Funny People* (New York: Stein & Day, 1981).

Harpo Speaks! Harpo Marx with Rowland Barber. New York: Bernard Geis, 1961. A beguiling account of the Brothers' early days, of the Algonquin set (Alexander Woollcott, Robert Benchley, Dorothy Parker, et al.), and of Harpo's bachelor shenanigans and his later life, when he astonished everyone by becoming a happily married man and adopting four children. Groucho often looked upon this branch of the Marx family with envy; Harpo had the gift of happiness, a blessing generally denied to his younger brother.

The Marx Brothers at the Movies. Paul D. Zimmerman and Burt Goldblatt. New York: Putnam, 1968. A nostalgic rerun of the Brothers' thirteen films, accompanied by pictures and rapt commentary.

*Note: Space does not permit the listing of articles about or by Groucho Marx—over two thousand in all—to be found in the catalogs and stacks of libraries in New York; Washington, D.C.; Los Angeles; and places between. The two starred books have listings of relevant sources and sites.

The Marx Brothers: Their World of Comedy. Allen Eyles. New York: Barnes, 1969. A British critic examines the Marxes, often with insight, but sometimes missing the point of the jokes. See also Eyles's *The Complete Films of the Marx Brothers* (Secaucus, N.J.: Citadel Press, 1992).

"The Marx Brothers: An Investigation of Their Films as Satirical Social Criticism." Martin Gardner. Ph.D. diss., New York University, 1970. A highly original dissertation, examining the team's work feature by feature and making a case for the Marx Brothers as important American gadflies and social parodists.

George S. Kaufman: An Intimate Portrait. Howard Teichman. New York: Atheneum, 1972. A biography of the Broadway director and writer who had the strongest influence on Groucho's verbal and physical style. Also see Scott Meredith, *George S. Kaufman and His Friends* (Garden City, N.Y.: Doubleday, 1974).

Groucho, Harpo, Chico, and Sometimes Zeppo: A History of the Marx Brothers and a Satire on the Rest of the World. Joe Adamson. New York: Simon & Schuster, 1973. A jaunty account of the quartet's career, emphasizing their film work. Distinguished by pioneering research and an iconoclastic tone very much in the spirit of Groucho.

The Marx Bros. Scrapbook. Compiled by Richard J. Anobile. New York: Darien House, 1973. Contains interviews with Groucho as well as his friends and relatives. The book became the subject of a lawsuit when the aging Groucho got around to reading it. Despite what he thought was a prior agreement to excise his indiscreet comments and explicit language, the monologues were printed verbatim. Transcription errors abound. Anobile was also responsible for two other books about the Marxes: *Why a Duck?* (New York: Darien House, 1971) and *Hooray for Captain Spaulding* (New York: Darien House, 1974). The first oversize book bills itself as a compilation of "visual and verbal gems" printed verbatim from various Marx Brothers films; the second confines the gems to *Animal Crackers.*

Cavett. Dick Cavett and Christopher Porterfield. New York: Harcourt Brace Jovanovich, 1974. Recollections by the younger comedian who became a friend of the older one, entertained Groucho (and a large audience) on various late-night shows, and served as master of ceremonies for Groucho's Carnegie Hall farewell.

The Marx Brothers. William Wolf. New York: Pyramid Communications, 1975. An uncritical, pleasant salute to the team by a New York film reviewer.

Hello, I Must Be Going: Groucho and His Friends. Charlotte Chandler. Garden City, N.Y.: Doubleday, 1978. An ominum-gatherum of interviews with the aging Groucho and such rising young friends as Woody Allen and Jack Nicholson. Indispensable, but offered without any sense of order or overview.

Groucho. Hector Arce. New York: Putnam, 1979. Written by an admirer and friend, this was the first full-length biography of Groucho Marx. Arce was a little too close to his subject, and he died before the last battles over the Marx estate. Nevertheless his is an essential work, unaccountably out of print for years.

The Original Dead End Kid Presents. Leo Gorcey. New York: Vantage Press, 1979. The former husband of Groucho's second wife, Kay, offers his side of the divorce settlement in a vanity publication. Even so, he cannot entirely mask his abusiveness, or the reasons why she sought Groucho's protection.

Growing Up with Chico. Maxine Marx. Englewood Cliffs, N.J.: Prentice-Hall, 1980. A fond, discerning reminiscence of the wildest Marx by his only child. En route she has a good deal to say about Uncle Groucho and his conflicted relationships with women of all ages.

S. J. Perelman: A Life. Dorothy Herrmann. New York: Putnam, 1986. A journeyman biography of the humorist and Marx Brothers scenarist (*Monkey Business, Horse Feathers*), whose love-hate relationship with Groucho is chronicled in some detail. Other aspects of their association can be found in *Don't Tread on Me: The Selected Letters of S. J. Perelman,* edited by Prudence Crowther (New York: Viking, 1986); Eric Lister, *Don't Mention the Marx Brothers: Reminiscences of S. J. Perelman* (Sussex: The Book Guild Ltd., 1985); and in two compilations of Perelman essays, *The Road to Miltown* (New York: Simon & Schuster, 1957) and *The Last Laugh* (New York: Simon & Schuster, 1981).

*The Marx Brothers: A Bio-Bibliography. Wes D. Gehring. New York: Greenwood Press, 1987. A vital reference work crammed with biographical details of the quartet, filmography, and a highly detailed bibliography of periodicals in which the Brothers are mentioned. Of greater use to the researcher than the common reader. Gehring's provocative *Groucho and W. C. Fields: Huckster Comedians* (Jackson: University Press of Mississippi, 1994) considers the two personalities as classic American archetypes.

Flywheel, Shyster, and Flywheel: The Marx Brothers' Lost Radio Show. Edited by Michael Barson. New York: Pantheon, 1988. A collection of the Marx Brothers' long-forgotten radio shows from the 1930s, developed by Nat Perrin and Arthur Sheekman. All twenty-six shows feature Groucho as a detective and Chico as his bumbling assistant.

The Marx Brothers. Kate Stables. Secaucus, N.J.: Chartwell Books, 1992. A pop biography for the uncritical fan, with a lively, superficial text and many illustrations. The same must be said of Peter Tyson's *Groucho Marx* (New York: Chelsea House, 1995).

I Shot an Elephant in My Pajamas. Morrie Ryskind with John H. M. Roberts. Lafayette, La.: Huntington House, 1994. One of the Marx Brothers' greatest gagmen looks back in benignity, emphasizing the epochal period when he and George S. Kaufman wrote *The Cocoanuts* and *Animal Crackers.*

Language-Based Humor in the Marx Brothers Films. Peter Meijes Tiersma. Bloomington: Indiana University Press, 1996. An analysis of Chico's stage-Italian dialect and Groucho's torrent of puns and wisecracks as more than mere word-play.

The Marx Brothers Encyclopedia. Glenn Mitchell. London: B. T. Batsford, 1996. Anyone who had anything to do with the quartet no matter how peripherally (Robert Grieg, a butler in *Animal Crackers;* Dan Seymour, a heavy in *A Night in Casablanca*) seems to be profiled in this large-format British publication, written for aficionados rather than scholars.

Raised Eyebrows. Steve Stoliar. Los Angeles: General Publishing Group, 1996. The author, a member of Groucho's household staff, provides a convincing and well-written narrative of the comedian's final years, when he was alternately cosseted, prodded, and tyrannized by the last woman in his life.

The Freedonia Gazette. Published and edited by Paul Wesolowski in New Hope, Pennsylvania, since November 1978. A unique periodical, devoted entirely to the lives and accomplishments of the Marx Brothers. Invaluable to the enthusiast and the academic alike.

HISTORICAL AND PERSONAL BACKGROUND

The Spirit of the Ghetto: Studies of the Jewish Quarter in New York. Hutchins Hapgood. New York: Funk & Wagnalls, 1902; 1965.

The Conning Tower Book. Edited by Franklin P. Adams. New York: Macy-Masius, 1926.

The Second Conning Tower Book. Edited by Franklin P. Adams. New York: Macy-Masius, 1927.

Since Yesterday: The 1930's in America, September 3, 1929–September 3, 1939. Frederick Lewis Allen. New York: Harper & Brothers, 1940; Bantam, 1965.

Delight. J. B. Priestley. New York: Harper & Brothers, 1949.

The Great Crash of 1929. John Kenneth Galbraith. Boston: Houghton Mifflin, 1955; 50th anniversary ed., 1979.

Robert Benchley: A Biography. Nathaniel Benchley. New York: McGraw-Hill, 1955.

Our Crowd: The Great Jewish Families of New York. Stephen Birmingham. New York: Harper & Row, 1967.

The Greatest Jewish City in the World. Harry Golden. Garden City, N.Y.: Doubleday, 1972.

Gangsters: From Little Caesar to the Godfather. John Gabree. New York: Galahad Books, 1973.

The Good Old Days—They Were Terrible! Otto Bettmann. New York: Random House, 1974.

The Land That I Show You: Three Centuries of Jewish Life in America. Stanley Feldstein. Garden City, N.Y.: Anchor/Doubleday, 1978.

The Thirties: From Notebooks and Diaries of the Period. Edmund Wilson. New York: Farrar, Straus & Giroux, 1980.

The Rise and Fall of the Jewish Gangster in America. Albert Fried. New York: Holt, Rinehart & Winston, 1980.

The Prolific and the Devourer. W. H. Auden. Hopewell, N.Y.: Ecco Press, 1981.

America in the Twenties: A History. Geoffrey Perrett. New York: Simon & Schuster, 1982.

Jewish Life in Twentieth-Century America. Milton Plesur. Chicago: Nelson-Hall, 1982.

Modern Times: The World from the Twenties to the Eighties. Paul Johnson. New York: Harper & Row, 1983.

The Rest of Us: The Rise of America's Eastern European Jews. Boston: Little, Brown, 1984.

Just around the Corner: A Highly Selective History of the Thirties. Robert Bendiner. New York: Dutton, 1987.

1929: The Year of the Great Crash. William K. Klingaman. New York: Harper & Row, 1989.

Wills of the Rich and Famous. Herbert E. Nass. New York: Warner Books, 1991.

VAUDEVILLE

American Vaudeville: Its Life and Times. Gilbert Douglas. London: Whittlesey House, 1940.

Vaudeville from the Honky Tonks to the Palace. Joe Laurie Jr. New York: Holt, 1953.

A Pictorial History of Vaudeville. Bernard Sobel. New York: Citadel Press, 1961.

American Vaudeville as Seen by Its Contemporaries. Edited by Charles W. Stein. New York: Knopf, 1984.

The Voice of the City. Robert W. Snyder. New York: Oxford University Press, 1989.

BROADWAY AND HOLLYWOOD

Thirty Years with G.B.S. Blanche Patche. London: Gollancz, 1951.

The Vicious Circle: The Story of the Algonquin Round Table. Margaret Case Harriman. New York: Rinehart, 1951.

The Fifty-Year Decline and Fall of Hollywood. Ezra Goodman. New York: Simon & Schuster, 1961.

Max Gordon Presents. Max Gordon with Lewis Funke. New York: Bernard Geis, 1963.

The Memoirs of an Amnesiac. Oscar Levant. New York: Putnam, 1965.

Notes on a Cowardly Lion: The Biography of Bert Lahr. John Lahr. New York: Knopf, 1969.

Thalberg: Life and Legend. Bob Thomas. Garden City, N.Y.: Doubleday, 1969.

Toms, Coons, Mulattoes, Mammies & Blacks: An Interpretive History of Blacks in American Films. Donald Bogle. New York: Viking, 1973.

Cavett. Dick Cavett and Christopher Porterfield. New York: Harcourt Brace Jovanovich, 1974.

Hollywood. Garson Kanin. New York: Viking Press, 1974.

Heywood Broun: A Biography. Richard O'Connor. New York: Putnam, 1975.

Mayer and Thalberg: The Make-Believe Saints. Samuel Marx. New York: Random House, 1975.

On Being Funny: Woody Allen and Comedy. Eric Lax. New York: Charterhouse, 1975.

Smart Aleck: The Wit, World, and Life of Alexander Woollcott. Howard Teichmann. New York: Morrow, 1976.

Wit's End: Days and Nights of the Algonquin Round Table. James R. Gaines. New York: Harcourt Brace Jovanovich, 1977.

Unspeakable Images: Ethnicity and the American Cinema. Edited by Lester D. Friedman. Urbana: University of Illinois, 1991.

Woody Allen: A Biography. Eric Lax. New York: Knopf, 1991.

Winchell: Gossip, Power, and the Culture of Celebrity. Neil Gabler. New York: Knopf, 1994; Vintage, 1995.

Buster Keaton. Marion Meade. New York: HarperCollins, 1995.

RADIO AND TELEVISION

Show Biz, from Vaude to Video. Abel Green and Joe Laurie Jr. New York: Holt, 1951; Port Washington, N.Y.: Kennikat Press, 1972.

A Pictorial History of Radio. Irving Settel. New York: Citadel, 1960; Grosset & Dunlap, 1967.

About Television. Martin Mayer. New York: Harper & Row, 1972.

Tube of Plenty: The Evolution of American Television. Eric Barnouw. New York: Oxford University Press, 1975.

The Golden Age of Television: Notes from the Survivors. Max Wilk. New York: Delacorte Press, 1976.

The Golden Years of Broadcasting: A Celebration of the First Fifty Years of Radio and TV on NBC. Robert Campbell. New York: Scribner's, 1976.

Television: The Critical View. Edited by Horace Newcomb. New York: Oxford University Press, 1979.

The Great American Broadcast: A Celebration of Radio's Golden Age. Leonard Maltin. New York: Dutton, 1997.

Raised on Radio: In Quest of the Lone Ranger, Jack Benny . . . Gerald Nachman. New York: Pantheon, 1998.

THEORIES OF COMEDY

The Seven Lively Arts. Gilbert Seldes. New York: Harper & Bros., 1924; Sagamore Press, 1957.

Tynan Right and Left: Plays, Films, People, Places, and Events. Kenneth Tynan. New York: Atheneum, 1967.

The Great Funnies: A History of Film Comedy. David Robinson. London: Studio Vista / Dutton, 1969.

The Crazy Mirror: Hollywood Comedy and the American Image. Ramond Durgnat. New York: Horizon Press, 1970.

We're in the Money: Depression America and Its Films. Andrew Bergman. New York: New York University Press, 1971.

The Comic Mind: Comedy and the Movies. Gerald Mast. Indianapolis: Bobbs-Merrill, 1973; 2d ed. Chicago: University of Chicago Press, 1979.

Yesterday's Clowns: The Rise of Film Comedy. Frank Manchel. New York: Franklin Watts, 1973.

Word Play: What Happens When People Talk. Peter Fard. New York: Knopf, 1974.

America's Humor: From Poor Richard to Doonesbury. Walter Blair and Hamlin Hill. New York: Oxford University Press, 1978.

Comedian Comedy: A Tradition in Hollywood Film. Steve Seidman. Ann Arbor, Mich.: UMI Research Press, 1981.

Canned Goods as Caviar: American Film of the 1930s. Gerald Weales. Chicago: University of Chicago Press, 1985.

The Lively Audience: A Social History of the Visual and Performing Arts in America, 1890–1950. Russell Lynes. New York: Harper & Row, 1985.

American Film Comedy. Scott Siegel and Barbara Siegel. New York: Prentice Hall, 1994.

Classical Hollywood Comedy. Edited by Kristine Brunovska Karnick and Henry Jenkins. New York: Routledge, 1995.

American Laughter: Immigrants, Ethnicity, and 1930s Hollywood Film Comedy. Mark Winocur. New York: St. Martin's Press, 1996.

The Laugh Crafters: Comedy Writing in Radio and TV's Golden Age. Jordan R. Young. Anaheim, California: Past Times Publishing, 1998.

FILM CRITICISM

Agee on Film. James Agee. New York: McDowell, Obolensky, 1958.

The American Cinema: Directors and Directions. Andrew Sarris. New York: Dutton, 1968; Da Capo Press, 1996.

Film Criticism of Otis Ferguson. Temple University Press, 1971.

American Film Criticism, from the Beginning to Citizen Kane. Edited by Stanley Kaufmann with Bruce Henstell. New York: Liveright, 1972.

The National Society of Film Critics on Movie Comedy. Edited by Stuart Byron and Elisabeth Weis. New York: Penguin Books, 1977.

RELATED FICTION AND VERSE

The Cannibals: A Novel about Television's Savage Chieftains. Keefe Brasselle. New York: Bartholomew House, 1968.

A Stranger in the Mirror. Sidney Sheldon. New York: Morrow, 1976; Warner Books, 1981.

The Faber Book of Movie Verse. Edited by Philip French and Ken Wlaschin. Boston: Faber & Faber, 1993.

Groucho Marx, Master Detective. Ron Goulart. New York: St. Martin's Press, 1998.

Index